THE BOSTON GLOBE
HISTORIC WALKS IN CAMBRIDGE
by JOHN HARRIS

Photographs by Janet Knott

The Globe Pequot Press

OLD CHESTER ROAD, CHESTER, CONNECTICUT 06412

Cover photo by Phil Rizzo/Anthro Photo File

Copyright © 1986 by John Harris

Library of Congress Cataloging-in-Publication Data

Harris, John (date)
    The Boston globe's historic walks in Cambridge.

    Companion vol. to: The Boston globe historic walks in
old Boston. c1982.
    Includes index.
    1. Cambridge (Mass.)—Description—Tours. 2. Walking
—Massachusetts—Cambridge—Guide-books. I. Harris,
John (date).   Boston globe historic walks in old
Boston. II. Boston globe. III. Title. IV. Title:
Historic walks in Cambridge.
F74.C1H28   1986   917.4'44   86-7640
ISBN 0-87106-899-0 (pbk.)

Manufactured in the United States of America

First Edition/First Printing

TO MY WIFE, PEG

CONTENTS

HARVARD SQUARE   I

   HARVARD SQUARE OVER THE YEARS   3

   MAKING HISTORY IN HARVARD SQUARE   10

   FIRST LAW SCHOOL TO KIOSK   15

CAMBRIDGE COMMON   21

   GREAT MOMENTS ON THE COMMON   23

   HEROES TO HILARITY ON THE ANCIENT PATH   29

THE OLD YARD   35

   ENTRY TO HARVARD YARD   37

   FROM FLAMES TO FAME   42

   HOLLIS AND THE HOLDEN QUADRANGLE   48

   THE OLD YARD: NORTH   53

   UNIVERSITY HALL—V.I.P.S, PRANKS, AND RIOTS   61

   THE OLD HARVARD YARD: SOUTH   69

MID-HARVARD   75

   TERCENTENARY THEATER   77

   SEVER QUAD, WIDENER, AND ITS NEIGHBORS   84

OLD CAMBRIDGE   93

   STROLLING KENNEDY STREET   95

   WINTHROP SQUARE AND SOUTH STREET   100

   NEWE TOWNE'S "MAIN STREET"   106

   TO WADSWORTH HOUSE AND ITS OLD NEIGHBORS   113

   PORCELLIAN, PUDDING, AND ALONG HOLYOKE STREET   121

   LOWELL, *LAMPOON*, OLD GOLD COAST   129

   APTHORP, *CRIMSON*, ARROW STREET   135

CAMPUS BY THE CHARLES   143
    DEWOLFE ROUTE TO RIVER HOUSES   145
    WINTHROP, KIRKLAND, AND ELIOT VIA GRIFFIN GATE   152
    SOLDIERS FIELD TO "BAKER BEACH"   159

TO AND ALONG TORY ROW   171
    JFK-LAND, ELIOT, AND BRATTLE SQUARE   173
    FAMOUS DOINGS ON BRATTLE'S ACRES   180
    APPIAN WAY TO CREATIVE MR. GILMAN'S GATE   188
    RADCLIFFE YARD AND OLD ASH STREET   194
    E.D.S., VASSALL, AND LONGFELLOW-LAND   202
    SPARKS STREET TO ELMWOOD   213
    FRESH POND, MT. AUBURN, AND GERRY'S LANDING   223

BEYOND THE COMMON   233
    GOD'S ACRE TO WASHINGTON ELM   235
    ALONG GARDEN STREET TO RADCLIFFE YARD   245
    HEADING NORTH TO O'NEILL-LAND   256
    NORTH OF THE OLD YARD   267
    TO NORTON'S WOODS, MEMORIAL HALL, QUINCY STREET   277

NEAR AND BY THE CHARLES   293
    THROUGH CAMBRIDGEPORT TO THE OLD CAUSEWAY   295
    TO M.I.T. WEST CAMPUS: SPORTS AND DORMS   309
    ROAMING THE EAST CAMPUS, M.I.T.   323
    EAST CAMPUS: EASTMAN TO EASTGATE   337
    KENDALL SQUARE TO EAST CAMBRIDGE   353

BIBLIOGRAPHY   368

INDEX   371

KEY MAP

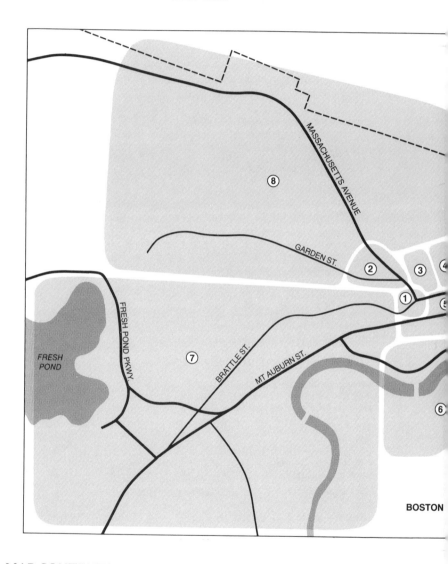

MAP CONTENTS

1	Harvard Common 2	4	Mid-Harvard 76
2	Cambridge Common 22	5	Old Cambridge 94
3	The Old Yard 36	6	Campus by the Charles 144

Numbers on map refer to map contents below

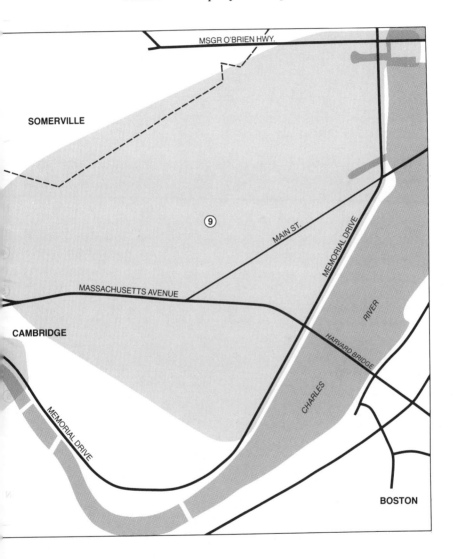

7 To and Along Tory Row .. 172
8 Beyond the Common 234
9 Near and by the Charles ... 294

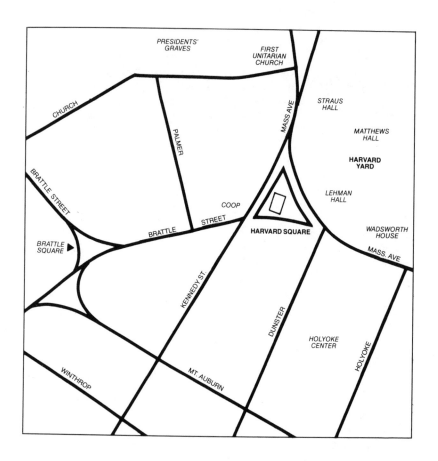

HARVARD SQUARE OVER THE YEARS

"**I** wonder more and more just where I might have come out if I had never seen Harvard Square. . . ." The poet Edwin Arlington Robinson was reflecting, in a letter to a student friend at Bowdoin College, on the time he spent in 1891–93 as a special student at Harvard. Here he became "quite a fiend" for the bowling courts in the gym and a fan of "beer, oysters, pipes, cigars and literary conversations," ate at the commons in Memorial Hall, and wrote poems. The prospect of adventure in education seemed unlimited. Most of all, though, he found that delightful memories came flooding vividly back to life.

Nearly a century has passed since Robinson's day; still, for an ever greater tide of Harvard–Radcliffe students from every continent, Nobel laureates and Rhodes scholars, congested Harvard Square's greatest fascination is that it has been a crossroads for centuries. Truly prominent people have come here, people all the way from the era of America's first poetess, Anne Bradstreet, whose house in 1631 looked out upon the Square; to teenage Joan Baez, daughter of a Harvard–M.I.T. teacher, guitar in her hand and en route to stardom, making her way to espresso shops hereabouts to sing her folk songs; to hearty House Speaker Thomas P. "Tip" O'Neill on rounds in his district, popping in to local shops for a chat, a cup of coffee, or a meal.

The earlier reaction of Ralph Waldo Emerson, after attending the events of Harvard's 200th jubilee in 1836, was quite like Robinson's: Cambridge was "at any time" just full of delightful memories and eminent ghosts.

A few over the years:

Young Charles Dickens, on the first of his visits to Cambridge, alighting here in 1842 from Morse's stage with his genial companion Cornelius Felton, a future Harvard president, and heading on foot along Brattle Street—past the smithy's still spreading chestnut tree—to breakfast with the then unbearded young professor Henry Wadsworth Longfellow, lodging in Craigie House, which, about a year later, he would receive as a wedding present from his new father-in-law. . . .

Eight-year-old future author John P. Marquand registering surges of astonishment and envy upon entering a shop here and first encountering two dudes from Harvard's old Gold Coast. Marquand's grandmother had given him a nickel for a sarsaparilla, and he had come three blocks from her Hilliard Street dwelling to get it—only to marvel at the free-spending wealth exhibited by the students who in 1901 would, without hesitation, pay a staggering 15 cents for a banana split. . . .

Gertrude Stein, special student at Radcliffe, heading in the early 1890s for her favorite classrooms, experiments, and lectures by William James, an experience that would pave her way into print . . . or the first president of Radcliffe and one of its founders, Mrs. Louis Agassiz, putting into effect the educational program for women that, until Harvard–Radcliffe freshmen were commingled, long had Harvard professors hurrying through Harvard Square to Radcliffe Yard to repeat their lectures. . . .

Nineteen-year-old, mostly self-taught Winslow Homer, ever a dandy in his attire, waiting to catch the omnibus to downtown Boston to his picture-copying job that he saw as a treadmill and hated—and from which on his twenty-first birthday in 1857 he would escape to a life of creative freedom as a freelancer. . . .

Another artist, Daniel Chester French (who in 1884 in his early thirties would make the long-famous statue of John Harvard seated in bronze), coming through the Square as a child with his grammar-school pals to roam the nearby river marshes and woodlands to hunt birds or birds' eggs, snare partridge, or do some "chestnutting". . . .

George Washington, the day before he took formal command of the Revolutionary Army centered on Cambridge Common, heading on horseback through the Square to nearby, still-standing Wadsworth House, his first headquarters in Cambridge, which we will be seeing on our walks. . . .

Charles W. Eliot, who began his career as an M.I.T. chemistry professor and became probably Harvard's greatest president, a devotee of rowing and daily exercise, cycling in later life through Harvard Square to do his marketing . . . Richard Henry Dana, the author, hurrying in pre–Civil War days with his green bag to catch the horsecar to his law office in Boston . . . the young poet Robert Frost, in 1897, in the second of his two years at Harvard already married with one child and another on the way, pacing the nearby streets and Square anxiously pondering whether he should stick with teaching (which he was doing nights in North Cambridge) or try writing for a livelihood. . . .

Harvard Square, this sophisticated, international center before us, began an edge-of-the-wilderness existence quite simply with very little bustle and far, far less traffic, no street musicians, no fast or gourmet food, indeed not a single café nor a banking staff fluent in six tongues to service depositors dropping in from all over the world.

The Square was just an open space on the northern edge of newly settled Newe Towne when Deputy Governor Thomas Dudley and his small band of followers began building dwellings by the Charles River in early 1631, expecting their community to replace Boston (which it did for a while) as the seat of government of the Massachusetts colony. In a few years Newe Towne became the home of the nation's first college. But the university of today, with some 400 buildings utilizing 450 Cambridge acres, had very modest beginnings—a single small dwelling on one-and-one-eighth acres just a few steps east of the Square.

The space we now know as the Square connected Newe Towne (renamed Cambridge in 1638) with a path on its north side— later called the King's Highway—which roughly followed the present Kirkland to Mason to Brattle Streets. The path went east to west across the present Cambridge Common and connected neighboring Watertown and Charlestown. It is the oldest pathway in Cambridge, even a few months older than the town itself.

Harvard Square's early growth, just like the town's, was quite slow. The Square had very little development until trade in the open marketplace, a block to the south, started shifting into shops here. There was a boost when the original meeting house a block down Dunster Street, which had the entire town for its parish, was replaced by a new one atop Watch House Hill, a hillock, later leveled, then on the east side of the Square where we now see Lehman Hall. Another boost came in 1677 when the College moved a few yards northward in the present Yard and completed, on the same site as the current one, its first Harvard Hall.

For years a stream, which originated in the Yard, ran through Harvard Square. It flowed past where John Harvard's statue now stands; bent and emerged from the Yard at mid–Strauss Hall; ran under a stone bridge on the present Massachusetts Avenue, then southward past the present Coop site and around the curve of Brattle Street to Eliot Street (then called Creek Lane); and slanted eastward and on to the Charles River.

Such was the Square on the eve of the Revolution, with buildings still few and the town with barely 1,500 residents. It was, of course, familiar ground to recent Harvard graduates in the forefront of the resolute Sons of Liberty—Samuel Adams, John Adams, John Hancock. Here in the Square, as we shall presently see, open warfare nearly erupted just prior to the outbreak of the Revolutionary War on Lexington Green.

Shortly before Paul Revere mounted his horse, William Dawes, also dispatched that fateful night, galloped through Harvard Square, dashing across the stone bridge on his mission to spread the alarm that the Red-coats were coming. Cambridge Minutemen rushed to arms, and, in the battle that April 19th, 1775, Cambridge (then including the present Ar-lington) suffered the greatest loss of lives. This is a tale told by the memo-rials we will see in the old burying ground just north of the Square.

A few hours after Dawes—and after crossing, as Dawes had, the an-cient wooden bridge that then spanned the Charles River near the present Harvard Stadium—Lord Percy, with 1,000 Redcoats and two artillery pieces, came through the Square on his way to Lexington to cover the King's troops. The King's troops, recoiling from defeat in Concord and Lexington, faced a running battle all the way back through Cambridge.

It was in command posts that are still standing today just east and west of the Square that George Washington pursued his plan that scored his first victory of the Revolution, forcing the Redcoats to take to their ships in Boston and flee. And Harvard Square witnessed a dramatic aftermath in the victorious turning point of the Revolution a year and a half later at Saratoga when defeated, dejected General "Gentleman Johnny" Bur-goyne arrived with his tattered army and officers as prisoners in Cam-bridge, some to be housed in and near Harvard Square.

A momentous increase in the population growth of Cambridge, one that led in a few decades to its becoming a city in 1846, came with the construction of toll bridges across the Charles River two-and-a-quarter miles east of the Square—the West Boston Bridge of 1793 (site of the present Longfellow Bridge) and Craigie Bridge of 1809, where we now have the Charles River Dam.

These bridges transformed Cambridge into a fast, direct highway link between the interior communities of Middlesex County and the downtown port of Boston. What are still today some of the principal Cambridge thoroughfares were originally turnpikes for traffic to move quickly across Cambridge to these bridges—Concord Avenue, Broadway, Cambridge Street, parts of Mt. Auburn Street, and all of present Main Street. Two rival centers to the old Cambridge village around Harvard Square developed along the approaches to the bridges—dwellings, shops, taverns that with newcomers and settlers steadily grew into the separate villages of Cambridgeport and East Cambridge.

In mid–Harvard Square there used to stand a stone slab that was set up in 1734 to inform wayfarers that it was an eight-mile route to Boston. We will see the stone presently in God's Acre, the old burying ground by the Common. The stone also has, added on the back when the 1793 bridge was built, the new Cambridge–Boston distance of two-and-one-quarter miles. But the original 1734 message of the milestone carried only word of the eight-mile route to Boston via Brighton (called "Little Cambridge" in its early years), Brookline, Roxbury, and Boston Neck. This was the roundabout land route used by Dawes and Lord Percy.

The present eight-minute trip from Harvard Square to Boston on the "T" is the tale in capsule of the wondrous, indeed sensational, change over the centuries from when most Cantabrigians walked, if they went at all, to the days of current rapid transit. Even after the old West Boston bridge was completed in 1793, the woodland and meadow route had so few houses and was so lonely that students, lured by Boston attractions, preferred to go protectively in groups.

Transition from shanks' mare and horseback and chaise was slow but moved faster in the nineteenth century—from two-horse stagecoaches to four-horse omnibuses and horsecars. By the 1860s, the novelist Anthony Trollope described Harvard Square after his arrival as "20 minutes by horsecar from Boston." A decade later, even delay from the drawbridge's

7

being open on the old West Boston bridge did not bother homeward-bound William Dean Howells, editor of the *Atlantic Monthly*, for he felt the river vista of Boston and Cambridge from the bridge was "stuff that dreams are made on."

Change in the final decades of the nineteenth century was much faster—horsecars became horsecars on tracks, and then came electric cars (at first rebuilt horsecars) with street widenings for poles and traffic thrusting some sidewalks in Harvard Square to the very doorsteps of the buildings.

By 1912 there came completion of the subway tunnel, and with it rapid transit and soon trackless trolleys, trolley buses, and diesel buses. And in the early 1980s came the remining of Harvard Square for subway enlargement along with extending rapid-transit service to Porter Square and North Cambridge.

Nostalgically, the most charming era of Harvard Square—for Cambridge folks and fans—was from the early decades of the 1800s until just after Cambridge, on reaching 13,000 citizens in its villages, assumed city-hood in 1846. Back then Harvard Square was most often endearingly called "The Village." Here in the earliest years were just about all the essentials of community life: church and meeting halls, courts for a while, post offices, a marketplace and shops.

In the Square's center beside the big arching elm stood the town's hay scales, the town pump, and a trough for quenching the thirst of horses unharnessed, at route's end, from the waiting omnibus or horsecar. "The Village" over the years was mighty familiar to well-known literary figures of those days—Longfellow, Lowell, Holmes, and Margaret Fuller, all of them frequent users of the Square.

With just about everyone in old Cambridge acquainted, life was as friendly as it was leisurely. Howells tells of riding in the Cambridge horse-cars; it was like enjoying "small invited parties of friends" as they left Harvard Square.

Still, the peaceful village had moments of commotion hard to imagine nowadays as happening in ever lively and thronged Harvard Square. On market days, cattle in herds and flocks of sheep moved through the village from Porter Square en route to abattoirs across the river in Brighton.

8

President Eliot told more than once of seeing sheep entangled in trying to jump the granite-post and square-rail fence that before the splendor of the present gates, railings, and brick walls enclosed the college yard we will shortly visit.

First, though, we start our walks on the south side of the Square.

MAKING HISTORY IN HARVARD SQUARE

K ennedy Street, which leads southward from the Square to the river, was just recently renamed for the deeply admired chief executive, creator of the nation's happy Camelot years, whose life was cut short by assassination. He knew the street well; often in his student years he ate in its lunchrooms or cafés and shopped in its stores.

Cambridge's earliest settlers used the present Kennedy Street as the way to their "Little Common," the original Newe Towne Marketplace, now Winthrop Square. And when the town's first bridge was built across the Charles River, it was from here in Harvard Square that they set out on foot or by horse for the long eight miles to Boston. This is the way President Eliot also saw cattle headed across the river to slaughter.

Most Cantabrigians and College folks, however, most fondly recall the joyful, cheering, banner- and balloon-carrying throngs moving this way to press across the Anderson bridge to the football games in the Stadium, most of all for the annual Thanksgiving-time encounter between the Harvards and the sons of Eli Yale.

The triangular shape of the Abbot Building on our right (west) on the corner of Kennedy and Brattle confirms that we are at the northern edge of the small grid of streets along which the first Cambridge settlers built their dwellings. That grid has, as does the Abbot Building, a slant and curve on the west end. This turn was to adapt to the stream that then did a semicircular flow through Brattle and Eliot Streets and then turned eastward to the river and the town's first wharf and first ferry.

Among the earliest homesteads on the Abbot lot, quite naturally for its era, was the home and forge of a blacksmith. As many a Cambridge youth did in the town's early decades, the blacksmith's son went across Harvard Square to college and became a clergyman. Later a post office located here long served the community, and many a noted Cambridge son and daughter frequently dropped by.

The Abbot Building was built in 1909 by a Harvard graduate, Edwin H. Abbot, who made a fortune in the frenzied post–Civil War era of railroad building; but he is probably better known locally for the stone mansion on Follen Street (which residents call "The Castle" and which we will presently visit)—a landmark that Abbot built on the former first state arsenal acres that he had purchased.

The opposite lot on the Massachusetts Avenue corner of Kennedy Street, indeed the entire block facing the Square, is among the most historic in Cambridge. When the founder of Cambridge, zealous churchman and Deputy Governor Thomas Dudley, started building his mansion two blocks away on the south side of the street grid, his son-in-law, Simon Bradstreet, built on this lot. Like Dudley, Bradstreet would later serve the Massachusetts colony for many years as its governor. He was highly popular and indeed was the colony's foremost citizen during the bitter years under King James II, winning the accolade of "The Nestor of New England."

Bradstreet was an orphan fourteen years of age when he came into the household of Dudley, who was steward to the Earl of Lincoln. He succeeded Dudley as steward when twenty-five and married Anne, then sixteen, eldest of Dudley's four daughters. All came two years later to the New World on the *Arbella* with Governor John Winthrop and the Bay State Charter. Anne's first child (she would have eight) was born here, and here also Anne began writing poems that would make her America's first woman of literature. She did her writing between her household tasks. Her admirers came to call her "The Tenth Muse"—the title of her poems, America's first. Bradstreet's extensive land holdings included the land across the stream on the west side of Harvard Square up to God's Acre.

This Bradstreet homestead and land, along with Dudley's, on that family's moving to Ipswich, came into possession of an Englishman of noble family: Herbert Pelham, grandson of Lord Delaware, who filled a number of public offices, local and colonial, before returning to England and serving in Parliament. While living in Cambridge, he began serving in 1643 as the first treasurer of Harvard College in its formative years.

This intersection at Kennedy Street was for decades called Farwell's Corner—for the same man commemorated by the well-known Farwell Place, a short distance from here along Brattle Street. The man, Levi

Farwell, was very civic minded and also served as treasurer of Harvard College. Although Farwell, deacon of the first Baptist Church in Cambridgeport, served in many capacities, from selectman to state senator, his grip on local regard came from the pleasure he brought folks in "The Village" with his country store with its dry goods and chinaware from faraway places. His was succeeded here in later years by other stores—but the name Farwell's Corner lived on for decades.

In midblock, facing the Square, long stood from the early 1800s to the 1900s Willard's Hotel, its bar (the Cambridge Tavern), and, most remembered, the main Cambridge waiting room for public transportation. From here departed the hourly stage to Boston. Morse, he of the four-horse coach, was a big, strong fellow who loved his two trips daily, announcing imminent departures with blasts on his tin horn. This terminus has seen all the changes from horse power to electricity. Cambridge lads, recalled Ernest Longfellow, artist son of the poet, were great admirers not so much of the coachman as of the bus boys in the 1840s who collected omnibus fares en route. To be a bus boy, he declared, was the ambition of every wide-eyed lad he knew. By the mid-1800s, with three coachlines consolidated, departures for Boston were running at a four-an-hour clip.

A lifelong devotee of Cambridge lore, John Holmes, brother of the poet Oliver Wendell Holmes, recalled that the Cambridge Tavern was a sort of crowded senate for village politicians: "Great questions from embargo downward have been settled and resettled," Holmes reported. Commencement time, with old grads swarming back for reunions, saw conviviality at peak heights. In what seemed like bucket brigades, Willard's punch and Porter's flip from a famous tavern around the corner from the present Kennedy Street used to flow to parties and gatherings throughout Harvard Yard.

The first printing in all the worldwide British colonies was done in 1638 by forty-four-year-old Stephen Daye, whose dwelling was on the Dunster Street corner lot of this block. Although Daye came from a long line of London printers, he was himself a locksmith and not an accomplished printer. Still, his printing included the Freeman's Oath, his pioneer project; the Bay Psalm Book, British America's first book; and papers for

Harvard College, especially for the early commencements. The actual printing in the first few years was done a block from here, as we shall see when we visit Holyoke Street, but Daye's homestead is of great interest beyond printing.

His son, Matthew, a very able printer, carried on the actual printing when Harvard's first president, Henry Dunster, for whom Dunster Street was named, apparently wanted the printing improved. Dunster had become owner of the first press through his marriage. No feathers were ruffled, for Matthew, a bachelor, was quite friendly with Dunster and gave the College most of the Fellow's Orchard on which Harvard would one day build now-vanished Gore Library and present-day Widener Library. Matthew served also as Harvard's first steward—a post long virtually second only to the president's.

The entire block was for generations associated with one of Cambridge's oldest and most eminent families, the Bordmans. Stephen Daye, while in England, had married a Bordman widow, and, along with their children, he brought over William Bordman, a stepson who became a tailor, then a cook, and then another steward to Harvard College in its earliest days.

William Boardman built a house on the east corner lot of Dunster Street that was mighty handy for cooks and stewards of the young College just across the street. He inherited the Daye homestead, and his son acquired the old Bradstreet lot at Farwell's Corner. William's family, which became one of Cambridge's largest land owners, furnished Harvard with a line of stewards and the town's top officers for more than a century before the homestead became College property.

Just across Massachusetts Avenue, Lehman Hall, with its Grecian pediment and fluted white pilasters dominating Harvard Square, is on the old Watch Hill site, where stood in succession the town's gradually enlarged second, third, and fourth meeting houses from 1652 to 1833, when the fourth—the most famous—was demolished and the College acquired the land.

The meeting houses, as the town's largest auditorium, were for nearly two centuries the setting for the peak events of College life: annual commencements and inaugurations of presidents. Even into the 1800s the College presidents were all clergy. Sometimes they were simultaneously ministers of the meeting house and always the key figure at commencement gatherings, handing out honors and, in later years, diplomas. During these years the president, faculty, and students held Sunday worship in these meeting houses at the tolling of the bell that summoned parishioners. The College shared in the building costs and gave some of the president's orchard so that churchgoers could use it to secure their horses, chairs, chaises, and so on. Most elegant assemblages of provincial times met here, and, following ancient tradition, there was a resplendent turnout—with music and military escort—when our last royal governor, Thomas Hutchinson, was welcomed on his accession in 1771.

In defiance of General Thomas Gage and his Redcoats, John Hancock presided at the first Provincial Congress session here in late 1774 at which the patriots organized their own civil government and their militia "to march at the shortest notice." This was the birth of the "Minutemen" who would, in a few months, flock to Cambridge and form George Washington's army. General Washington, when here, joined his men in attending service in the meeting house.

The Massachusetts state constitution, soon used as a model for our federal Constitution, came from the 1779–80 convention here, over which patriot and future Governor James Bowdoin presided. Future United States President John Adams did almost all the actual writing of it. Hancock, who was elected the first Bay State governor under that new state constitution, presided here in 1783 when medical professors were inducted into Harvard College's first graduate school.

A triumphant occasion in the final years of the meeting house was the outpouring of dignitaries and state and College officials to welcome the Marquis de Lafayette, early in his 1824–25 tour, as a guest of the nation. The applause—men cheering, the women waving their handkerchiefs— was so prolonged when the heroic Lafayette entered the meeting house that it stretched the ceremonies into late hours. The next day, Lafayette came from Boston again to join the Phi Beta Kappa Society session, also in the meeting house.

FIRST LAW SCHOOL TO KIOSK

Harvard Law School, the College's second graduate school, also had its birth in Harvard Square, on the west side. The school's first building, however, was on the Square's east side, in a Greek temple-like structure called Dane Hall that would in part be on the site of the demolished meeting house. Built in 1832 north of the meeting house, it had to be shifted some seventy feet southward in 1870 to provide room for the great size of the present Matthews Hall.

Dane Hall, in its day, with pediment and four big Ionic columns facing the Square, dominated "the Village." It was named for its donor, Nathan Dane, an Essex County lawyer who in 1787 drafted the Northwest Ordinance, which banned slavery there. Linked with his gift was Dane's wish to have the young law school come under a great leader—and he got his wish when United States Supreme Court Justice Joseph Story took the helm.

Young Charles Sumner, friend and student of Story's, acted as librarian while studying law. Sumner had a room on the school's second (top) floor that looked out on the Square, and he enthusiastically pronounced the view from beneath the pediment the best in the world. A visitor might wonder if this would still be Sumner's judgment were he to survey the bustling, modern Square from his seated statue just to our north.

After fifty years in Dane Hall, the Law School had so flourished under still another great administrator, Professor C. C. Langdell, that he was able in 1883 to transfer it to a new building north of the Yard that we will be visiting. Portraits of many great law teachers and graduates may be seen there, but one who became president of the United States should be mentioned here. Rutherford B. Hayes, a law student in Dane Hall from 1843 to 1845, went on to become a country lawyer and a three-time governor of Ohio before arriving at the White House.

In its later period, Dane Hall had a variety of uses, among them as a famous psychological lab associated with William James, a philosophy lecture center, and the earliest location of the ever-expanding Harvard Coop, now across the Square. Dane Hall ended up in flames in 1918.

A current view of Harvard Square, from the early vantage Sumner enjoyed, is available from Lehman Hall. Built in 1924, Lehman is one of the barrier buildings—along the Massachusetts Avenue side of the yard—built by President A. Lawrence Lowell to spare the Yard, which all the barrier buildings face, from the din of traffic. And that came some fifty years after Professor Langdell was impatient to leave Dane Hall behind because of Harvard Square's "great increase of traffic." Lehman Hall long served as the domain of the Harvard bursar, shifted there from Dane Hall. Currently it is part of the scattered buildings of Dudley House, devoted to providing a gathering place, lounge, food, some social life, and other amenities to commuting students.

Most of the west side of Harvard Square was for decades occupied by College House, gradually developed in the mid-1800s, 1832 to 1870. It comprised the still-to-be-seen central five-story mansard portion at 1430 Massachusetts Avenue, a four-story section on its north side up to Church Street, and a similar one to its south side of the mansard, replaced in the 1920s by the bank building. During World War I Harvard College exchanged College House for one of the big private dormitories on the Mt. Auburn Street "Gold Coast," Randolph Hall. Once there were trees giving 'shade and beauty at the sidewalks' edge, but they disappeared when the avenue was widened for electric streetcars in the 1890s.

The name "College House" was first designated back in 1772 by the President and Fellows a month after they made Harvard's first venture into student housing outside the Yard. The room rent affords current collegians a comparison with some costs in those days. The rent set for the front chambers and studies was the same per quarter as in Hollis Hall in the Yard, 10 shillings; the back rooms the same as upper rooms in Massachusetts Hall: "*viz.* eight shillings a quarter." College House #1, a three-story, twelve-room white clapboard with brick ends, was popularly known as Wiswall's Den after its prior owner, Daniel Wiswall. Wiswall's Den stood at the south corner of the present Church Street.

The birthplace of Harvard Law School was in a two-story wooden, gambrel-roofed house acquired in 1790 by the College and called College House #2. It was fifty feet south of College House #1, set back somewhat from a wooden fence at the angle of the present block at 1430 Massachusetts Avenue. In the intervening fifty feet was a one-story shed sheltering a primitive College fire engine. College House #2 provided shelter to resident graduates who could not get rooms in the Yard, some uncertain of their future profession or, as university preacher Dr. Andrew P. Peabody put it, "waterlogged on their life voyage."

The Law School, the first continuous one in the nation, got going in 1817 with six students. There were two rooms, "the lower north room to be a lecture room and library." A regular school had been recommended in 1816 by Bay State Chief Justice Isaac Parker, who had given a series of law lectures during the prior College year.

The Law School's first professor, Asahel Stearns, was part-time, for he was also Middlesex district attorney. By 1829 the school was down to one law student. But a great Harvard College president, Josiah Quincy, had been encouraging the benevolence of Nathan Dane, and in that year persuaded Justice Joseph Story, a man close to the great legal figures of the age, to become the first Dane professor of law. Three years later, Justice Story was able to move a revived and growing Law School into new Dane Hall.

Among the Square's most historic buildings was the yellow-painted old Court House, with its big red door and impressive cupola, on the site of the present Harvard Coop. It was here that open warfare of the Revolution came close to eruption in 1774. The courthouse, built from 1757 to 1758, replaced an earlier 1707 courthouse directly out in mid-Square on the east side of the vanished stream that was crossed, at this place, by two small foot ramps to the courthouse.

Here, on September 2, 1774—just months after the Boston Tea Party and with the First Continental Congress assembling in Philadelphia—fully 4,000 patriots poured into the Square to express outrage at General Thomas Gage and his Redcoats for seizing two fieldpieces and Middlesex County's supply of gun powder. In front of the courthouse steps, the patriots demanded and got two elderly Cambridge judges to confirm their resignations from the all-Tory Mandamus Council, named in London as a tool for Gage to put the Bay Province under George III's thumb.

At least every fourth man in the throng was armed. Observing this and their intense anger, Lieutenant Governor Thomas Oliver—also picked in

London—rushed to Gage's Boston headquarters to appeal to him not to send in his troops. Gage agreed, but wild rumors further aroused the throng, and before nightfall the patriots had massed outside of Oliver's house on Tory Row—which we will soon see—and forced Oliver, too, to resign his office and soon flee.

When Middlesex Court proceedings were shifted to East Cambridge in 1816, the courthouse was used as a Town House (city hall). By 1832 Cambridge got a new Town House in Cambridgeport and the old building saw a variety of community activities that increased when Lyceum Hall, predecessor of the present Harvard Coop building, replaced the old courthouse. Local memories are legion:

Noted Cantabrigian Thomas W. Higginson, as a boy, stayed in the Lyceum to hear Ralph Waldo Emerson lecture after Higginson's chums had dashed out to play baseball in "the place that is now Harvard Square." When Higginson rejoined his friends, they asked him what Emerson had said. Higginson told them he had not understood, but added "I kind of liked to hear that man!"

The Harvard Glee Club, organized in 1857–58, a couple of years before Harvard became America's first college to have a music department, held its first concert in Lyceum Hall in 1858. It was joined by the Pierian Sodality, founded in 1808, a band of Harvard students who enjoyed playing musical instruments together, a group that helped inspire creation of the Boston Symphony Orchestra.

In the bitterly divided decade leading up to the Civil War, the poet Longfellow went to hear his friend Charles Sumner, who brought to the U.S. Senate a new voice demanding abolition of slavery. The Lyceum Hall audience was sharply split. Longfellow said that Sumner's powerful oratory was like a Beethoven symphony played in a saw mill. Sumner's fiery delivery brought many shouts and hisses amid the applause.

Beside being mid–nineteenth-century Cambridge's top place for festivities and grand occasions, Lyceum Hall had for dance enthusiasts something of Papanti's great dance hall in Boston, where a gala dinner with America's top authors hailed young "Boz," Charles Dickens, on his first visit. Here in the Lyceum, Papanti's son gave dancing lessons and young, bewigged Lorenzo Papanti played his violin for the dancers, often the Cambridge elite.

High prices sought from students by coal merchants hereabouts led a group of students to form the Harvard Cooperative Society in 1882. It has grown like dandelions in springtime to cover nearly every conceivable student need. In the mid-1920s it built the present Coop. Currently it has part of the bank building, and, via a skybridge in back, over Palmer Street, links with its mostly new four-story building that occupies all of the west side of Palmer Street.

There are acres of student wares on the Coop's many floors; overall, there is fascinating browsing, especially on the three Palmer Street floors, which are stacked with all sorts of books (art, fiction, nonfiction, professional tomes), records, tapes—all composing the largest bookstore in the vicinity of Harvard Square. And from the skybridge is a delightful glimpse northward of earlier Cambridge times: the red-brick, two-story, pitched-roof old Cambridge police station and jail house (the bars can still be seen on the upper windows) on Church Street, built during the Civil War at the southwest corner of the old burying ground.

One nostalgic tale of Harvard Square has become a classic:

At the east end of the Brattle Building at the corner of Brattle Street, there was in James Russell Lowell's day Ramsay's Pharmacy, run by a popular Harvard Square character. Lowell, who wrote some of the most delightful prose showing his affection for the Square, lived all his life in Cambridge save 1877–85, abroad as ambassador in Madrid and London. He had a homesick response when asked about highly popular travel along the Nile, declaring he would "rather see Ramsay's in Harvard Square than Ramses the Great in Egypt."

A modern landmark in mid-Square is the kiosk on its red brick with gray stone trim pedestrian plaza. The kiosk was refurbished in 1985, after Harvard Square denizens endured for six years a cavernous pit as the subway was rebuilt and extended north to Alewife Brook. This more utilitarian kiosk is a successor to the circular wedding cake–like structure, with pillars and finials, put there when the rapid transit tunnel terminus was originally completed in 1912. The twenty-one-foot granite post and cross-pieces, near the kiosk, a modern sculpture by the Harvard instructor Dmitri Hadzi, was added in 1985. Hadzi, some of whose work is in M.I.T.'s art collection, entitled it *Omphalos*, navel in Greek, which in the tradition of the ancient Delphic oracle signified the center of the universe. Harvard Square over the years has possessed other mid-Square landmarks beyond its long-remembered towering elms. The county's first courthouse—which, like later Dane Hall, went up in flames—stood here until 1671. It was by the side of its successor that the town placed the 1734 milestone, and it still stood there with its helpful message—"Boston 8 miles"—when a larger courthouse replacement, the famous one with the big red door, was erected nearby on the present site of the Coop.

The most surprising mid-Square structure was a one-story covered stall erected beside the town pump and milestone in the first year of the War of 1812. It was soon a centerpiece amid commotion, horses, carriages, carts, and oxen drawing wood and hay. For a time the Square was known as "the Marketplace." There was an oyster bar in a cellar dug under the market-structure level, though "gambling, tippling, or riotous behavior" were officially banned. With traffic on the increase, protests arose that the marketplace structure was an encroachment on public land—and so it was torn down in 1830 to leave the Square open to the public.

The blameless milestone became a casualty of the various demolitions and diggings for horse troughs and hay scales. For a time the milestone was lost, but it was rescued by an admirer from among the stones to be broken and used for fixing Cambridge streets. It was set up again forward of old Dane Hall but was soon moved again to the burying ground, where we will, on our next walk, see what burial and neglect and time have done to this ancient Cambridge landmark.

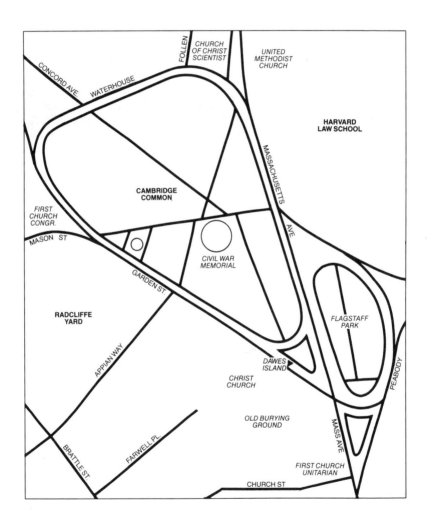

GREAT MOMENTS ON THE COMMON

On our way to Cambridge Common, one of the nation's most historic grounds—just north of Harvard Square—we see on our left a successor church to the Old Meeting House and get a closer view of Charles Sumner's statue.

The statue stands on a triangular segment of land severed by a traffic curve from Flagstaff Park, once a part of the Common. Sumner is most remembered for his fight against slavery, "the lords of the lash." He was a Free Soiler, a pioneer in seeking emancipation—even urging President Lincoln to advance its timing to help end the Civil War. During the long antislavery struggle, Sumner, at his seat in the nearly empty Senate, was beaten and left senseless by a South Carolina congressman wielding a heavy gutta percha cane. Three and half years passed before he could fully resume his fight to free slaves.

The location of the statue underscores Sumner's many links both with the Square and with the College. In addition to his perch in old Dane Hall, attendance at law classes there, and speeches in the old Lyceum Hall, Sumner often strolled the Square with his lifelong friend Longfellow. While at college he roomed in the old Yard's Hollis and Stoughton Halls and boarded a half block to the west in the Howe dwelling at 2 Garden Street. He was a lecturer in the Law School, throughout his life was a generous donor to the College library—especially thousands of tracts and pamphlets relating to the growth of slavery—and in his will bequeathed to Harvard all the thousands of volumes in his extraordinary personal library.

Sumner's statue is also a monument to the campaign of women for equal rights. The sculptor of this colossal bronze, Anne Whitney of neighboring Watertown, had created many successful likenesses of fighters for human rights: those of Samuel Adams in the national Capitol's Statuary Hall and its copy in front of Boston's Faneuil Hall, Harriet Martineau, Toussaint L'Ouverture, and William Lloyd Garrison.

But when in 1875 a woman, namely Anne Whitney, was found to have won an anonymous competition for the rendering of a statue of Sumner, the committee awarded it instead to a man. Although the man was her close friend and a great sculptor, too, the injustice was not eased for her until 1902, when the eighty-year-old Whitney converted her 1875 model into this statue and it was unveiled in front of Dane Hall with her in attendance.

The 1833 church on our left was built by the Unitarian members of the old meeting house. This construction followed a division among the parishioners that led the Congregational members, under Reverend Abiel Holmes, father of Oliver Wendell Holmes, to build their new church on Mt. Auburn Street, a block south of Harvard Square.

Harvard, which acquired the old meeting house and replaced it with Dane Hall, joined in building this Unitarian Church because of its desire to use it for College commencements and other major events. Outwardly, the main church looks much as it did in 1833, save that the fierce 1938 hurricane tore away part of the steeple. A Gothic stone parish house was added in the rear of the church in 1902. The well-known Cambridge Forum is currently conducted here.

Harvard held its annual commencements in the church from 1834 to 1873, many of them exceptionally famous assemblies. Celebration of Harvard's 200th anniversary got under way here before a distinguished audience that heard "Fair Harvard" being sung for the first time by a choir. President Josiah Quincy for two hours fascinated the audience with an oration that he later expanded into his renowned history of the College.

Ralph Waldo Emerson, early in his public career, drew another distinguished audience when he delivered his sensational 1837 Phi Beta Kappa address, calling upon American scholars to shed deference to European scholarship and fearlessly embrace cultural self-reliance. The address drew instant praise from Emerson's audience. James Russell Lowell called it a classic, and Oliver Wendell Holmes proclaimed it "our intellectual Declaration of Independence."

All Harvard presidents, from Edward Everett, orator-statesman, to Charles W. Eliot, who masterminded Harvard's growth from a College to a University, were inaugurated in this church. At Eliot's inauguration in 1869, Emerson sat in the front pew nodding assent as the youthful Eliot advocated a new era of education on all subjects, an elective system of study, greater standards for graduate study, and higher education for women as well as men.

As we go now past God's Acre, the ancient cemetery on our left that we will visit on a later walk, notice—just inside the northeast corner railing of the cemetery at Garden Street—the old milestone, "Boston 8 miles." The initials "A.I." are those of the stone cutter, Abraham Ireland, buried nearby. Although the stone has been broken through neglect and its own burial, the message is still distinct. So, too, is the 1794 carving on the back telling the shorter distance by the then new West Boston Bridge, which began to speed up the growth of Cambridge from town to city.

Ahead of us lies Cambridge Common—once an area for the town's cows with a pasture stretching five blocks north to Linnaean Street until 1724 when the pasture north of Waterhouse Street was cut into house lots. The present area was not enclosed until 1830.

In the Common's most glorious years—at the beginning of the American Revolution—it was criss-crossed by the Charlestown–Watertown King's Highway and the turnpike northward from Harvard Square. Christ Church on our left, an old Tory house on the northwest Waterhouse Street side, and four old red brick buildings, among the oldest in the Harvard Yard, still stand as in 1775 with the Common as their front yard.

The high flagpole on our right in Flagstaff Park, topped by a gilded eagle with wings uplifted, is a memorial to the "suffering and fortitude of the men and women of Cambridge during the Revolution." The beginning of their ordeal is marked by the small traffic island just ahead of us. It is dedicated to the patriot William Dawes. The hoofprints of Dawes's horse, at a gallop, are simulated in the brass of the pavement.

Dispatched late on April 18, 1775, by the patriot leader Joseph Warren, who would soon give his life at Bunker Hill, Dawes was sent first by the longer old eight-mile route before Paul Revere set off on the shorter but cross-water route through Charlestown. To avoid a Redcoat mounted patrol on the Charlestown–Cambridge highway, Revere went roundabout through Medford to Lexington, where he was met a half hour later by Dawes.

At Dawes's alarm, Cambridge Minutemen responded in the still-dark early hours of April 19th. Many would give their lives that day, and many more would be wounded. The Minutemen assembled on the Common, where local militiamen had trained since the founding of Cambridge, before heading toward Lexington to fight the Redcoats.

By midday, Lord Percy, on a white horse with two cannons and a thousand soldiers and marine enforcements, arrived in Cambridge seeking to rescue the Redcoats caught in a running battle on their way back from Concord and Lexington.

Percy's troops marched through Harvard Square and past the Common. The ringing of alarms, the drumbeats, the musket fire, the columns of Redcoats, and the fact that their own men had gone off to fight combined to terrorize the women and children, and they fled from their dwellings along the path of war—at times crossing the bloody route "strewed with mangled bodies," as told in the distressing eyewitness account of Mrs. John Winthrop, wife of the famed Harvard professor and scientist.

The memorial gateway to the Common was erected in 1906 by the Daughters of the American Revolution in commemoration, as the bronze tablets inform us, of George Washington's taking command of the American army on July 3, 1775—a little more than two weeks after the Battle of Bunker Hill. American soldiers wounded in that fight were still dying in makeshift army hospitals along Brattle Street's Tory Row and being buried in God's Acre.

Cambridge Common was the center of George Washington's army. He would spend many sleepless nights of worry trying to deal with the army's lack of gun powder, munitions, and supplies. Right in the face of the well-equipped enemy he would accomplish the amazing task of reorganizing and enlarging his army and with it would score the first major victory of the Revolution, forcing the beseiged Redcoats of the world's top military power to take to their ships and flee Boston.

We now go westward along the Garden Street side to see where Washington took command and where arrived the cannon that made possible his great victory. First, though, notice how beautifully the Washington

Memorial Gateway frames our view of the Civil War Monument near the midpoint of the Common. The black asphalt path takes us past the seats and shelters for folks waiting for buses—and also past Christ Church, across Garden Street.

Continuing along the asphalt, we come to the flagpole and the three old captured cannons (sent in 1875 from the state arsenal) placed about a circle of cobblestones—roughly opposite the midway point of the red brick wall enclosing Radcliffe Yard, which we see across Garden Street.

The scene of General Washington on horseback with sword extended, taking command under the Washington Elm, can be seen in bronze. Close by is a scion of the Washington Elm. The site of the original elm, where tradition locates the July 3, 1775, event, is farther along the asphalt. It was in mid–Garden Street between the Common and the First Church in Cambridge, Congregational, on the corner of Mason Street.

Some folks still recall when streetcars—and the rails, of course—ran along either side of the elm, which managed, though sickly from traffic, to survive until 1923. The granite marker we now see on the Common, which was the parade area of the citizen army, long stood at the foot of the old elm.

General Washington's taking formal command came the day after he arrived in Cambridge, much fatigued from his nine-day journey from Philadelphia—a journey on which he learned (while in New York) of the heavy losses at Bunker Hill. Unlike the rainy day of General Washington's arrival, July 3 was a clear day. A Minuteman writing to his wife said that "a great deal of grandeur" would attend the event, and he added, "There is at this time one and twenty drummers and as many fifers beating and playing round the parade."

Notice another granite marker, with its message in bronze, facing Garden Street near the curbing a few feet from the home-plate high-wire backstop of the baseball diamond. This is the final marker on the long route that twenty-five-year-old Colonel Henry Knox followed in midwinter 1775–76 down the Hudson Valley and across the Berkshire hills to deliver to General Washington fifty-nine heavy iron and brass cannons and mortars and barrels of flints and boxes of lead captured at Fort Ticonderoga by Ethan Allen—"a noble train of artillery," as Knox called it. Knox had left camp November 16th with Washington's orders to spare no trouble or expense for "the want of them is so great." Knox was back January 18th, delayed by sudden thaws, for his vehicles were snow sleds drawn by eighty yoke of oxen and, at time, horses.

Our red brick walk across the Common, leading past the left side of the tall Civil War Monument, marks the ancient path of the Charlestown–Watertown King's Highway.

At either end of the path, near the west and east borders of the Common, are lectern-like granite pedestals with bronze markers showing maps of early Cambridge. On the left side (the west end marker), the 1718 Abraham Hill house is shown on the site of the present First Church in Cambridge, Congregational. On the right-side marker, notice the small grid of streets that formed early Cambridge when the settlers envisioned moving the capital inland from Boston; and also notice the extensive salt marshes, coves, and expanse of water before landfill and embankments narrowed the Charles River Basin.

A fascinating aspect in America's development is that the Bay Colony's surveyors in 1636 did not think they would ever have to lay out roads west of the Charlestown–Watertown Path. They considered it far enough from tide water for any settlement. Yet is was in that same year that the Reverend Thomas Hooker, first pastor of the ancestor church of the first Congregational Church just across Mason Street, and 100 of his parishioners with 160 head of cattle, took off on this path to Watertown and on through the wilderness to found Hartford, Connecticut.

Notice, as we head eastward on the old Charlestown Path, the playground within the circular wire fence on the northwest (Waterhouse Street) side. The Concord–Cambridge turnpike of 1807 (the present Concord Avenue–Broadway route) crossed the Common to the left of this playground. Along this northwest side, more than covering the playground area, were some of the barracks that General Washington ordered built for the winter when he found a decisive strike against the Redcoats in Boston impractical until he could obtain heavy cannon and powder. In the meantime, he strengthened discipline, emphasized training, and sought more enlistments to increase his force from 16,000 men on his arrival to 22,000 in 26 uniform regiments.

The people of Cambridge shared with General Washington the sacrifice and strain that became part of life in the small community when thousands of Minutemen, from all over New England, converged on Cambridge

Common in response to the Lexington–Concord alarm. Here, makeshift, was the first campground of the Revolution. Reverend William Emerson (heroic grandfather of Ralph Waldo Emerson), who would give his life in the struggle for freedom, came and prayed with soldiers sunrise and evening when Washington arrived. Cambridge, said Emerson, was "covered over with the American camps, and cut up into forts and entrenchments, and all their land, fields and orchards laid common."

Many women and children who had fled stayed away with friends. The soldiers occupied abandoned Tory dwellings. Harvard shifted to Concord, and all its buildings were used by the soldiers for quarters, along with Christ Church. Fences and trees were cut down for firewood. Lead from roofs of Harvard structures as well as lead memorials in God's Acre were used for bullets. But then, that is the improvised course of life in wartime. In World War I the Common was wholly covered with long two-story barracks for Navy trainees.

There was a jubilant scene on the campgrounds in late November 1775 when a ship in "our little squadron," named and commissioned by General Washington (our first American Navy) captured a British transport bound for Boston and on it a thirteen-inch brass mortar. When the cannon was dragged here to the Common, one of Washington's greatest fighting men, Major General Israel "Old Put" Putnam, swung astride the cannon with a bottle of rum at this military godsend, amid great cheering, and christened it "The Congress." It was then mounted to guard the river approach to the camp.

The Soldiers' Monument, near mid-Common, was dedicated in 1870 to the "valor and patriotism" of Cambridge soldiers and sailors who gave their lives in the Civil War. The soldier figure atop was modeled after a Cambridge police officer severely wounded in the battle. He was Samuel E. Chamberlain, a member of Cambridge's Company C, the first company in the United States to respond to President Lincoln's call for volunteers when Fort Sumter was fired upon.

Twenty-one of these men, about a quarter of the company, gave their lives, and their names are among the 340 on the monument panels. The commanding officer of the company, gravely wounded in battle, was a great-grandson of a Minuteman killed on April 19, 1775, and buried nearby in God's Acre. We will see later in Cambridgeport where he worked and lived and recruited his famous company.

Lincoln's statue, facing toward Harvard Square, was added some years later. It is a copy of a sculpture by Augustus St. Gaudens, 1887, but without the bronze chair in back as originally conceived and displayed in Chicago.

The granite pedestal with bronze marker—on our left, near the east end of the brick path—tells of heroic colonel William Prescott, on the eve of the June 17th Battle of Bunker Hill, heading his 800-man detachment off along the old Charlestown path. Before leaving, the men, led by two men with hooded lanterns and followed by wagons with entrenching tools, gathered ahead of us across Massachusetts Avenue and to the right and diagonally east of the 1838 Gannett House. This is the Harvard Law School building with a white, temple-like portico of four pillars on its east side; we will see it on a later walk. There, led by Harvard President Reverend Samuel Langdon, they prayed for the Lord to bless their "secret" mission to fortify Bunker Hill.

To our left, about seventy-five feet northward along the Massachusetts Avenue side of the Common, a stone slab marks the site of the Election Oak, by which the pioneer freemen chose their magistrates. In spring 1637, with the colony split by the bitter Anne Hutchinson controversy, John Winthrop regained the governorship, defeating twenty-five-year-old Governor Henry Vane, a supporter of Anne and religious freedom, when a champion of orthodoxy, Reverend John Wilson, Winthrop's ally, climbed on a limb of the oak and harangued the voters. A few months later, Vane returned to England, where he would be knighted and later beheaded by King Charles II as a regicide.

A few steps farther northward, we can see the statue of John Bridge and how some Cambridge men at the time of the Winthrop–Vane election were attired. "A Puritan," Bible in hand, the work of Boston sculptor Thomas Gould, depicts a man who came to Cambridge with Reverend Hooker but remained in Cambridge, served as deacon and local and colonial official, but most of all supervised creation of Cambridge's public grammar school in 1635. The statue was a gift to Cambridge by a sixth-generation descendant who also persuaded Daniel Chester French to create the likeness of John Harvard that we will see—on our next walk—in Harvard Yard.

As we head back toward the main gate to Harvard, the gate opposite Sumner's statue, we are reminded that the Common as the College's front yard has been used over the years for College athletics and other activities.

Harvard's first student militia, inspired by the 1759 capture of Québec, drilled here when they found the College's "play place"—then the northwest corner of the Yard, now occupied by the Phillips Brooks House—too small for their drills. Their uniforms were mighty showy, consisting of three-cornered hats, white stockings, and buff and blue coats.

Their successors, the College's Washington Corps, were even showier, with white pantaloons and white gaiters. "Old Quin," no-nonsense President Josiah Quincy, put an end to the Corps for the students' "Great Rebellion" of 1834 when they tosssed their muskets from their armory room in the Old Yard. Their successors, the Harvard Cadets, saw many serve in the Civil War, and seventy-three of them gave their lives.

During the Civil War, some College freshmen brought baseball—called the "New York game"—to Cambridge, formed the baseball Club of 1862, and did their early practice on the Common. Six years later, Harvard played its first baseball game with Yale—and won. In winter the baseball field was used for hockey. Early science students used the Common—as well as the Yard—to practice surveying and map making. The young artist Winslow Homer, who, as we will see, lived right by the Common, made sketches of his older brother playing football here with his Harvard classmates. Early college football, a fierce form of rugby, was so rough that the Harvard faculty twice banned it.

For becoming really rough, however, Harvard commencement doings on the Common finally took top billing. "Old Quin," as sternly as when, as Boston's mayor, he had cleaned up the wild nightlife on Beacon Hill's north slope, cracked down again. Back in the beginning of this Puritan colony, with public holidays few, commencement had become a festival day on the calendar. There did come times in the College's first century when the faculty banned "plumb cake" or "distilled *lyquors*" from College rooms and the Middlesex sheriff was asked to keep booths and tents off the Common.

But in years just prior to the Revolution, the faculty did permit punch so long as "it was not intoxicating." During the Revolution, commencement was not held while the College was in Concord or the year General Burgoyne's defeated army occupied many Cambridge houses and all of College House #1, old Wiswall's Den.

After the Revolution, doings on and about the Common started downhill to the "gambling, rioting and dissipation of all kinds" against which "Old Quin" objected and acted. For years the approaches to the Common and the area surrounding it had been increasingly lined with booths and tents as attractions to crowds coming from all over the Commonwealth. The Common itself became little different from the approaches. A student at the time and later a distinguished College preacher, Reverend Andrew P. Peabody, pictured the Common just prior to President Quincy's clampdown. It was covered, said Reverend Peabody, with "drinking stands, dancing booths, mountebank shows and gambling tables; and I have never heard such a horrid din, tumult and jargon of oath, shout, scream, fiddle, quarrelling and drunkenness as on those two nights"—the night before and commencement night.

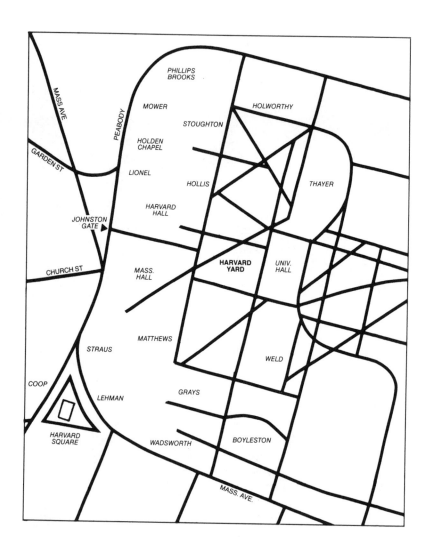

ENTRY TO HARVARD YARD

A prosperous midwestern alumnus back to watch Harvard celebrate its 250th anniversary in 1886 got to feeling that the nation's first college deserved a main entrance more in harmony with elegant events like academic processions or the official arrival of Bay State governors escorted by lancers on horseback than just a plain carriage-wide passage.

The red-brick-and-wrought-iron gateway erected in 1890 began a process, affectionately supported mostly by class gifts at their 25th reunions, which in a few years completed the brick-and-gates enclosure of the entire Yard. This main gate was named Johnston Gate for its donor, Samuel Johnston, Harvard 1855, of Chicago. It replaced the old-style granite-post-and-wood-rail fencing, such as we see around Sumner's statue and around the Common and some neighboring areas of the Yard.

Plaques on either side of the gateway tell of the beginnings of the College. The rivals in the 1637 election on the Common beneath the Election Oak played vital roles in the birth of Harvard. Henry Vane, then only twenty-three, was governor in 1636 when the Bay Colony voted to give those 400 pounds mentioned on the plaque—a huge sum in that day. College historian Samuel Eliot Morison said that in 1636 it was a quarter of the colony's annual taxes. John Winthrop again held the governorship in those years, 1637 to 1638, when the Bay ordered the College built here; the town's name, Newe Towne, changed to Cambridge; and the College named after young Reverend John Harvard, who had bequeathed to the College all his library and half his 1,700-pound estate—about double the initial gift of the Bay Colony.

As we enter the Yard, notice the seated statue ahead midway between the white fluted pilaster entries of University Hall. The statue depicts Reverend Harvard, who seems to keep a eye on everyone coming through the gateway. Here, between Massachusetts Hall on our right and Harvard Hall on our left and with three other buildings from the 1700s nearby, we are amid the oldest extant structures of the College—a sort of entry area or court to the old Yard.

The oldest of these venerable buildings is Massachusetts Hall, currently in the second half of its third century. Built in 1720, Massachusetts Hall is on the site where Henry Dunster, Harvard's first president, after the death of his first wife, used his own and friends' funds in 1644 to build a president's house to which he brought his second wife.

Their five children, born here, contributed to Dunster's forced resignation after he publicly declared—in the nearby meeting house—that he no longer believed in infant baptism. The Bay's General Court thereupon voted that no man "unsound in faith" could teach. Thus came to an end the service of one of the College's greatest leaders. He had saved its very existence when it was nearly ruined by its shameful first master, a man we will encounter later.

Dunster, in 1643, was responsible for Harvard's seal, *Veritas* (truth), which he would not betray under any circumstances; and it was Dunster who in 1650 won from the General Court the charter under which the College is still governed. Dunster, too, in 1644 moved into a lean-to chamber off his new hall "a great presse," the nation's first printing press, which he bequeathed along with his library, to the College to which he remained devoted.

Massachusetts Hall, save that the clock high on the west gable is painted instead of being the original, looks very much on the exterior as it did when it was completed. Credit—for tremendous foresight was involved—goes to another great Harvard president, John Leverett, who had to fight the inflexible orthodoxy of the Mathers, the foremost clerical family, to implant in the College a tradition of liberalism.

It may seem incredible with Harvard's current huge enrollment, but Leverett was doubted in those early decades of the 1700s when he believed that the student body (then a little more than one hundred) would continue to grow. Those who opposed him in the General Court twice cut the size of the proposed Massachusetts Hall appropriation in half—but Leverett, who had once been Speaker in the General Court, finally won. The demoliton and resultant loss of his old Dunster presidential house, though, put him personally in debt.

Future United States President John Adams lived in Massachusetts Hall, as did several other Sons of Liberty: James Bowdoin, James Otis, and a classmate of John Hancock's, Benjamin Church, who would stray from the path of patriotism, shock General Washington, and face prison and death at sea. For young John Adams and his cousin Samuel Adams, future "Father of the American Revolution," the path ahead would be one of glory. But their college days were much like those of their classmates.

The "court," as John Adams knew it, was the modest center then of College life. He was not yet sixteen years old when, on a small borrowed mare named "Polly," he came to old Harvard Hall, directly opposite us, to seek admission, submitting himself to questioning by the College president and the tutors.

On learning of his son's acceptance, Deacon Adams hitched up the farm cart and delivered young John, along with clothes and bedding, to his Massachusetts Hall lodging. John was planning to be a clergyman but would, like many other students, change his goals more than once.

College life followed clangs of the College bell atop Harvard Hall, from first bell at 5 A.M., with prayer at 6 A.M., followed by breakfast, a morning bever of bread and beer. The day was a long, rugged one of classes, just a couple of hours for ball or cricket in the afternoon, then more classes, 6 P.M. supper, and study by candlelight until curfew bell at 9 P.M.

Adams had different roommates as he progressed through upper classes and joined the declaiming and debating of his Discussion Club in the library of old Harvard Hall. With classmates he climbed on the roof of old Harvard to gaze through a telescope at Jupiter and its satellites, and they would return singing across the court to their quarters.

Massachusetts Hall was designed strictly as a dormitory, but, through recurrent remodelings—especially in 1939, when the entry on the yard side was added and President James B. Conant moved his staff and office to the first floor and the overseers' meeting rooms to the second—the building has served the College in many ways, even in part as a gallery for the marvelous portraits of great College figures by John Smibert, John Singleton Copley, and Gilbert Stuart.

Nowadays—since 1971, when Radcliffe and Harvard launched co-resident dorms—the upper floors of Massachusetts Hall furnish lodging for both Radcliffe and Harvard freshmen. Moreover, Harvard–Radcliffe freshmen now occupy all the dorms we shall see in Harvard Yard. Entry keys are issued to the students, and the dorms, of course, are strictly private. Through redesign, the two entries on our right to Massachusetts Hall lead just to the dorms on the upper floors. In prior years they also gave access to the lower floors and some quite-famous student activities.

The west entrance, Entry B, was to Professor George P. Baker's 47 Workshop, a famed course in playwriting and acting in the World War I era. Tall Tom Wolfe, the novelist, when a graduate student in the Workshop, used to pause outside the window beside the entry, lean in through the pulled-down upper sash, and converse with Baker's secretary at her desk. So too did President A. Lawrence Lowell on his well-known strolls through the Yard with his red cocker spaniel, Phantom.

Wolfe, who wanted to write plays, acted here in a play he wrote and used Baker as a character in his novel *Of Time and the River.* Eugene O'Neill, turning from poet to playwright, studied under Baker, and later the Nobel Prize–winning playwright praised Baker as "one of the truest friends my work has ever known."

America's oldest collge building nearly went up in flames on a January morning in 1924, burning on the west side of the Hall from the roof downward. President Lowell, Professor Baker, and students rushed to help the firefighters. Baker's scenery and show properties on the second floor were damaged, but equipment, desks, and a piano were carried out from the first floor to the lawn. Luckily, most of Baker's equipment had already been set up in Radcliffe's Agassiz Hall for one of the 47 Workshop plays.

Ironically, Harvard's princely donor of its multimillion-dollar House Plan, Edward S. Harkness, contributed to Harvard's losing Professor Baker to Yale. Harvard, busy funding other buildings, could not build a theatre, and when Harkness in that year of the fire gave Yale $1,000,000 for a theatre, Yale got Baker, too.

Entry A led formerly to a large chamber on the ground floor that the author-naturalist Henry David Thoreau and some of his 1837 classmates used for the Natural History Society they formed, filling the chamber with examples of flowers, plants, and minerals. Other naturalist members included Alexander Agassiz (who would immensely benefit from the zoological contributions of his father, Louis Agassiz) and the historian Francis Parkman, who lived during his junior and senior years in Massachusetts Hall.

Before we walk across the court to Harvard Hall, we may recall what College life was like for a Brahmin in the 1840s, the pre-war period when Harvard was changing from a college to a university but was still described as being "little more than a boys' boarding school"—even though total enrollment had reached five times what it had been in President Leverett's day when Massachusetts Hall was built.

Parkman belonged to just about all the College clubs, was president of Hasty Pudding student theatrical club, and had wine parties in his dorm. He loved going to plays, dancing, attending stag dinners, hunting fowl on the Charles River marshes, and rowing on Fresh Pond. In his senior year, exhausted by too much workout in the gym, he went for months on a grand tour of Europe, returning in time to complete earning his diploma. Friends said he had "Injuns on the brain," and he went, on their advice, to explore the Oregon Trail, which brought him early fame.

The guardhouse just inside the gate, although it seems old, is a prefab added to its historic surroundings in 1983—after lively and lengthy debate about its design.

FROM FLAMES TO FAME

Harvard Hall has distinctions that place it among the University's most historic buildings. Erected between 1764 and 1766, the present Harvard Hall is on the same site as old Harvard Hall, built between 1674 and 1677 (with delays due to King Phillip's War) to replace the then-deteriorating first large College building, whose location we will presently see on the south side of the Old Yard.

In 1764, at midnight in January during a snowstorm with intense winds, a fire that started under the library hearth burned Old Harvard to the ground. Seventy-five-year-old President Edward Holyoke, in his nightclothes, set an example for President Lowell in fighting the flames. It was winter vacation time, and there were few students and neither College pump was working. But Holyoke had the help of Royal Governor Francis Bernard and all the General Court, who, fleeing a smallpox epidemic in Boston, had been using Harvard Hall.

The firefighters did save nearby buildings that caught fire several times—Hollis Hall, old Stoughton Hall, and Massachusetts Hall. Hollis was then less than two weeks old. Old Stoughton, on land now an open part of the Old Yard, then stood at right angles to Harvard Hall and Massachusetts Hall, forming the third side of the grassy court. The roof of Massachusetts was showered with wind-driven embers.

Lost in the fire were early College treasures—all 5,000 books save those out on loan; all but one of the 400 books given by John Harvard; portraits; and scientific apparatus assembled as teaching materials in his Philosophy Chamber by one of the nation's foremost scientists, Professor John Winthrop, namesake and great-great-grandson of the Puritan governor. Winthrop had begun expanding the collection—which he had made with the help of his friend and fellow scientist Benjamin Franklin—back in Massachusetts Hall before moving across the court to old Harvard Hall.

Governor Bernard saw to it that the General Court made amends, providing funds for a new building and giving the College a fire engine. Bernard himself designed Harvard Hall's replacement and laid the cornerstone. Unlike old Harvard Hall, which had an additional third floor with a dozen gables and chambers for students, the present Harvard Hall became the first College building for all functions other than those it served as a dormitory.

Completed in 1766, it had a new chapel to the left of the entry and the College library above it on the second floor. At the right of the entry was the College Hall or Commons, and above it on the second floor the Philosophy Chamber of Professor Winthrop. College Hall, center of College life for half a century, has been the setting for many historic events.

The Bay's last royal governor, Thomas Hutchinson—a direct descendant of the fearless Anne Hutchinson, who had been exiled by the Puritans—arrived in 1771 at the steps of Harvard Hall with all the magnificent panoply of office after his commission came from George III. Here, following processions to and from the meeting house for oratory, Hutchinson was wined and dined. Originally, the east wall of College Hall had no windows, just a great fireplace and niches displaying huge portraits of George III and Queen Charlotte. Largess from John Hancock had helped furnish the chamber with rich wallpaper and carpets.

The royal portraits did not last long in the stormy years just before and directly after the Boston Tea Party of December 1773, trigger of the American Revolution. There were times when the General Court assembled here, and here the leaders of the Sons of Liberty, James Otis and Samuel Adams, an officer of the General Court, defied Hutchinson's taking direction from London instead of from his fellow citizens.

Other royal adornments of College Hall met with irate rejection. Someone cut the heart from Governor Bernard's portrait. Bernard had felt relieved on giving up his office and no longer being an on-site target of Samuel Adams. Three decades earlier, in his student days, Samuel Adams had argued here in his thesis that it was lawful to resist a supreme magistrate if that was the sole way open to preserve the commonwealth.

George Washington knew this building well. College Hall, the commons, was the largest eatery in all of New England, with storage rooms for barrels of salt beef and great kitchen facilities in the basement and the buttery. Here was the dining place for General Washington's Revolutionary soldiers housed in the neighboring College buildings.

The crowding—with resultant damage besides precious lead stripped from the roofs—was extreme. Massachusetts Hall had been built to shelter 72 students. Massachusetts—and Hollis, however, built for the same number—were each barracks for 640 men. Old Stoughton held 240, and 160 were billeted in fairly small Holden Chapel, which we shall see on our next walk.

After General Washington's victory, he was too occupied shifting his soldiers off to New York to confront the British, to come for the honorary degree voted by the College. He returned to Cambridge in 1789 during his grand tour of all the original states after his election as president. Bell ringing, cannonading, banqueting, and jubilant throngs all the way greeted the beloved hero. En route to Boston he reviewed three battalions of Middlesex militia as he passed through the town where he had taken command.

The morning after he left Boston, via the Charlestown ferry, he came here to Harvard Hall. There was a late breakfast in the College Hall, then President Washington, seated in an old chair in the library, greeted guests and former comrades-in-arms. His wish to College President Joseph Willard was that "the muses may long enjoy a tranquil residence within the walls of your university." To an old Cambridge friend who had visited him at Valley Forge, Congressman, diplomat, and Bay State Chief Justice Francis Dana, President Washington recalled that visit, saying, "We have seen worse times."

Marquis de Lafayette made an earlier visit to Cambridge than his 1824 tour. The year after the end of the war, 1784, General Washington's heroic young aide, who had been severely wounded at Brandywine and suffered through Valley Forge, came to Harvard Hall and was given both an honorary degree and a banquet.

The occasion is often recalled also because of the reaction of a great American hero, John Hancock, first signer of the Declaration of Independence. Lafayette sat to the right of President Willard, facing the audience, while Governor Hancock sat facing Willard.

Willard, in need of powerful arguments because of Hancock's still-pending offer to build a fence around the Harvard Yard, wrote letters to soothe Hancock, who felt that he should have sat at Willard's right hand.

Willard explained that Hancock, under custom since medieval days, really had the seat of honor. Willard was right—but Hancock was still angry and shifted from Harvard to Yale two boys for whose education he was paying.

Satisfying students' hunger throughout the early decades, when arriving freshmen included many not yet in their early teens, brought the faculty more than headaches in College Hall. Commons here was the center of the 1766 "Butter Rebellion" (it was springtime, and stored butter had become rancid) with the first student militia, the Marti-Mercurian Band, strutting in protest in the Yard.

But College Hall did not rid itself of hellions and rebellions in that year. In 1805 there came a "Bread and Butter Rebellion," and in 1807 there came the "Cabbage Rebellion," with students parading a soup tureen across the court to the president's house to exhibit maggots in the broth.

As for rowdy happenings in the mealtime commotions, most remembered is the misfortune of sixteen-year-old junior William Prescott, the future historian, who while leaving some frolic in commons here for his dorm in Hollis Hall, heard a loud noise, turned to see the cause, and was struck in his left eye by a large, hard crust of bread. He fell unconscious at the door of the Hall. Sight in his left eye was destroyed, and the effect on his right eye left him blind for much of his life.

Harvard Hall abounds with long-remembered scenes and sidelights. Here we find the early roots of both Harvard's medical and law schools.

While a junior in College, John Warren, younger brother of Dr. Joseph Warren, killed at Bunker Hill, organized with other undergraduates an Anatomical Society for dissecting animals and studying human skeletons. He went on to teach in a military hospital that he helped set up in Boston during the Revolution and proposed that medical instruction be given at Harvard.

When the President and Fellows agreed, Dr. Warren late in 1782 began anatomy lessons in the basement of Harvard Hall. The Law School, as we have seen, started in College House #2 in Harvard Square. Its creation, however, was suggested by Massachusetts Chief Justice Isaac Parker on completion of a dozen law lectures he started in spring 1816 in Harvard Hall's Philosophy Chamber.

Generations of students, alumnae and alumni, especially as the latter grow older, enjoy the mixture of sidelights afforded by Harvard Hall from the bell site in the cupola, with its tales of College pranks, to the basement.

In the attic, when not in use or stashed in the library, was long kept the curious three-cornered sixteenth-century chair—a gift some trace to the Mathers, others to President Holyoke—an heirloom with triangular cushion used for centuries by the president in awarding degrees on Commencement Day. A small room off the second landing, once called the Hebrew Room, where the language had been taught, was for years an armory for the muskets and arms of the Marti-Mercurian Band, still later of the Washington Corps.

For years tip-top scholars of the venerable Phi Beta Kappa held their annual literary exercises in the chapel and their spreads in College Hall—also long the scene of academic processions arriving for academic dinners. It was on the board in the ancient buttery wall in the basement that students once had to post their names, when in attendance, to have even a chance of getting their then-meager meals.

The entry to the old buttery, down the stone steps on the east side of Harvard Hall, now leads to the basement quarters of the Harvard Athletics ticket office. Here, fans can purchase seating at hockey, basketball, and football games and can get up-to-the-minute information on all other Harvard–Radcliffe athletic activities.

Above all, old grads recall the professors performing in the lecture rooms of Harvard Hall.

Edward Everett's lectures here were so brilliant as to bring Emerson to say that the effect of Everett—orator, future College president, senator, and speaker with Abraham Lincoln at Gettysburg—was like living in the age "of Pericles in Athens."

Often mentioned in later years is the revered Shakespearean authority George Lyman Kittredge, a pupil of the equally renowned Chaucer expert Francis J. "Stubby" Child. Kittredge used to leave his lectern and move toward the door as he was completing his final sentence so that he would be the first out of the lecture room; he wanted to get quickly to the court so that he could have more time to light his cigar and stroll about before his next lecture. Amused students called it the bearded Kittredge's "George Bernard Shaw act"—and they loved it.

Old Stoughton Hall, which stood on a line with Hollis Hall until, dilapidated, it was demolished in 1788, is known mostly for its having, on orders of the Committee of Safety, provided quarters for a printing office during its occupation by the Continental soldiers. The Hall brothers from Salem, Samuel and Ebenezer, did printing both for the army and the Provincial Congress in addition to getting out their *New England Chronicle: Or, the Essex Gazette*. The *Chronicle* was shifted to Boston when General Washington's army left, and Cambridge, although home to many editors and writers, did not have a local newspaper again until it became a city seventy years later, in 1846.

Old Stoughton was the first outright gift to the College of a dormitory by an individual, Lieutenant Governor—and for several years acting Governor—William Stoughton, whose coat of arms in stone were displayed on the building's brick façade. Governor Stoughton is best known for his acting as chief justice during the witchcraft frenzy in Salem and sentencing victims to die on Gallows Hill. Still, there were few so generous as Stoughton to the poor, to needy students, to churches, and to his College. Stoughton simply believed the witch-madness testimony and was trying to clear the land of witches.

The powerful influence of Stoughton in his era may help explain an occurrence in the court here that is still a surprise to many people—a book-burning in Harvard Yard. The book, Robert Calef's *More Wonders of the Invisible World*, satirized the witchcraft proceedings in which Stoughton and other Bay leaders participated. Harvard's part-time President Increase Mather ordered the bonfire. The year was 1700—the year in which old Stoughton Hall was completed. President Mather would one day regret the witchcraft delusion, but in 1700 he strongly felt that Stoughton honestly believed that he was acting in the public interest.

HOLLIS AND THE HOLDEN QUADRANGLE

Hollis Hall, on our left (north) in the Old Yard, was dedicated by Royal Governor Bernard just eleven days before the 1764 fire that destroyed old Harvard Hall. If book-burning mars Harvard President Mather's record, Hollis certainly embellished it. On a mission to London for the province—from which Mather brought back a new Bay charter and a commission for one of his Boston parishioners as the new royal governor—Mather made the generous-hearted Hollis family acquainted with the weak finances of the young college.

As the bronze plaque on Hollis attests, three generations of the family, Thomas Hollis after Thomas Hollis, responded. Harvard's first endowed professorship, created in 1721, bears the Hollis name. They were Baptists, yet made the professorship open to all beliefs, though it was decades before a Baptist could be appointed in this still rigidly Puritan early New England. Indeed, Harvard's first president had been ousted for his dissident views on baptism.

Above all, Thomas Hollis of Lincoln's Inn in our pre-Revolutionary era sent over books to encourage young people "to prize freedom." On the books he had his binder put the Hollis family symbol, an owl, positioned head up or head down, books still to be seen in Harvard's magnificent Houghton Library. Owl's head up on books signified good "republican" thinking. These, by the great political philosophers, made avid reading for the young students who were destined to become the founders of our republic.

Hollis has provided lodgings for many famous students. At age eighteen, future U.S. President John Quincy Adams, believing "an American education best for an American career," left London, where his father was U.S. Ambassador, won admission to the junior class, and was graduated in fifteen months. He had rooms with a cousin on the third floor of Hollis, and in his last terms, his two younger student brothers, Tom and Charles, also had quarters in Hollis.

John Quincy was no drinker, ever eager to set a good example for his brothers. But there was a big spread in the Adam's chamber for John Quincy's graduation in 1787, with loads of food brought by wagon from

Braintree, with cakes and wine, too. Among the guests participating was the first governor of the Commonwealth, John Hancock.

Ralph Waldo Emerson, on entering college, was fourteen years old, served as freshman orderly to the president, and lived in the president's house, but then had lodgings for three years in Hollis in three different rooms. To help his widowed mother meet costs he, still in his teens, taught school during vacations. In his sophomore year, 1819, he lived in the room that would become the most celebrated in the dormitory, Hollis 15.

Future Harvard President Charles W. Eliot, at eighteen years of age, would occupy number 15 in his senior year and legendary "Copey," Professor Charles Townsend Copeland, would in his era make it a mecca for world-famous writers and performers. Eliot's folks lived on Boston's Beacon Hill and on weekends he often walked from Hollis to home, carrying his laundry.

After interrupting classes for two years before the mast, Richard Henry Dana, just turned twenty-one, was admitted to the senior class in 1836 and lived on the southwest corner of Hollis on "the upper floor." It was a life of "luxury," he said, "after the one I had been leading." He promptly was invited to join club life, both Hasty Pudding and Porcellian.

When Thoreau came to College as a sixteen-year-old, President Quincy informed him, "You barely got in." Thoreau lived two floors above Dana on the top, fourth floor, and from the rear window of Hollis had a fine view of the Common and the western sky. Historian William Prescott, at the graduation of his son in 1844, observed that he, his father, and his son had all occupied as students the same room in Hollis Hall. Despite Prescott's eye episode his parents back in 1814 had celebrated his graduation with 500 guests in a huge tent.

George Santayana, like Emerson and Thoreau far from affluent, lived for his four years to graduation on the ground floor in the northeast-corner room he called in his autobiography "one of the cheapest to be had in Cambridge." Still, he made several clubs, among them Hasty Pudding, and a cartoon he drew got him on the *Lampoon*. He has left a vivid picture of what life was like in the Yard in the 1880s.

Santayana slept on a sofa bed that he made up, though the "goody" or servant who went with the $44-a-year rent, put it up. For economy he blacked his own boots. He carried coal and water from the cellar of Hollis Hall, or "water in summer from the college pump that stood directly in front of my door." He ate with friends at commons in Memorial Hall. After paying tuition and board he had $1 a day left over for clothes, books, and pocket money.

"Copey," a short man with a black derby, pacing across the Yard from his lecture room to his domicile, developed quite a reputation as a spell-binder and dispenser of wit and wisdom during roughly a decade as he lived in the Yard before moving to Hollis 15 on the top floor. Three flights of stairs never bothered him, a devotee of strolling in the country-side, nor did they deter the students devoted to him and the growing num-ber of eminent visitors who shared his hospitable evening sessions in number 15, sometimes on Monday, sometimes Wednesday, from 1904 until he retired in 1932.

On hand at Copey's were madeira wine, chartreuse, and other potables; the gaslights and candlelights he loved; fire blazing in the fireplace; spar-kling conversation; and above all Copey's reading—for Copey, at heart, was a dedicated actor. He was dedicated, too, to his students. Future pun-dit Walter Lippmann said that the attention Copey gave his pupils made him "an incomparable teacher." The poet David McCord described the evening as sheer enchantment.

These were the sentiments, too, of some of his other famous pupils: T. S. Eliot, John Dos Passos, Robert Benchley, and John Reed. Reed, who won fame covering Pancho Villa's revolt in Mexico and the Bolshevik Revolution, was a profound admirer of definitely non-Communist Copey; he still sent letters and gifts and, when he visited Cambridge stayed over-nights in Copey's extra chamber, a floor below, number 11. Famous visi-tors, of course, delighted Copey's students: Ernest Hemingway, Archibald MacLeish, Alexander Woollcott, Stephen Benét, and stage stars Mrs. Fiske and John Barrymore when performing in Boston.

The pump replica outside Hollis locates the one installed when Hollis was constructed, the one used by Santayana. Nearer the south entrance once stood an elm dubbed "Liberty Tree" and "Rebellion Tree" by students of pre-Revolutionary days, who included seven future signers of the Declaration of Independence. Rebellion at times was more against the alleged tyranny of the tutors than any tyrants abroad.

But secret clubs were formed, marching and patriotic oratory practiced, and a senior class voted to shun despised tea. Just a few weeks before warfare started in Lexington, the faculty put a ban on tea being brought (by a Tory few) into commons in Harvard Hall. The most rebellious scenes at the elm, however, as we will see when we visit University Hall, came long after the Revolutionary War.

The passage north of Hollis on our left, between Hollis and Stoughton Hall, leads to the Holden Quadrangle and one of Harvard's oldest buildings, the Holden Chapel of 1744. Back in 1741 future Royal Governor Thomas Hutchinson, while in London, met Jane Holden, widow of the governor of the Bank of England, Samuel Holden, and persuaded her to give the college its first chapel. The Holden coat of arms on the pediment is a copy of those on the chapel's west pediment, facing the Common, above what was once the original entrance to Holden.

Holden, with pulpit on the east end, was used for daily prayer (Sunday service was still in the meeting house) for only two decades, until the new chapel was ready in new Harvard Hall. Over the years, through many restructurings of its interior, Holden has had a great variety of uses: to store the college fire engine, sessions of the General Court rusticated to Cambridge by Governors Bernard and Hutchinson, barracks for our Revolutionary soldiers, Revolutionary Army courts-martial, even for lumber fetched from Maine on the college sloop and cut up to feed college fireplaces. And much more.

Harvard's Medical School, shifted in 1783 from its earliest days in the cellar of Harvard Hall, spent nearly three decades in Holden before moving to Boston for access to more clinical patients. Those years here witnessed a forum for some of the Medical School's more famous instructors besides Dr. John Warren, the first Harvard professor of anatomy and surgery.

Dr. Benjamin Waterhouse, who became professor just a month after

Dr. Warren, introduced vaccination to the United States. Dr. John Warren's son, Dr. John Collins Warren, and Dr. James Jackson, both early graduates, would found Harvard's medical teaching hospital, Massachusetts General Hospital, and Dr. John Collins Warren would perform the world's first operation with ether.

To provide lecture rooms and labs for these professors a second floor was built (removed decades later), and here Dr. Waterhouse cautioned his students about the "ruinous effects of smoking tobacco." He also gave recurrent warnings, heard over the years, that students shun liquor and drink cider, for he felt students were drinking "six times as much ardent spirits as in the days of our fathers."

Holden has seen lighter-hearted moments. In December 1872, Harvard University's pioneer Football Club, which would lead to the first football match on Jarvis Field, north of the Yard, was formed here; and that was in the rough-and-tumble days of football when each side had fifteen members, and a couple of years before rules were adopted to eliminate the early savagery.

Crimson as the college color began its reign in Holden on May 6, 1875, when all departments selected it above all the varieties that had come into use. The *Harvard Crimson,* which had started life as the *Magenta* in January 1873, promptly changed its name to *Crimson* in its next issue.

Interestingly, the color selection traced to a choice made by future Harvard President Charles W. Eliot, back in the 1850s when he was an assistant chemistry professor involved in a boat race and trying to catch the attention of his bride-to-be. Song and music currently provide enjoyment in Holden, headquarters for the Radcliffe Choral Society and the Harvard Glee Club.

On the north side of Holden Quadrangle stands Phillips Brooks House, the three-story 1900 brick building with Palladian window over the entry, which was built by his admirers in memory of this beloved preacher to the university. He was most influential in making morning prayer voluntary, ending centuries of mandatory attendance. He still drew many students to old Appleton Chapel in mid-Yard. He was rector of Boston's great Trinity Church, Episcopal bishop, a man of ever-sunny disposition and easy-flowing eloquence made more impressive by his towering build, for he stood six foot four.

The building is the center of about two dozen undergraduate groups doing community work in noncollege hours to help the disabled, homeless, and needy of all ages and engaging in social action. Brooks, among other deeds, wrote the words of the Christmas hymn "O Little Town of Bethlehem." When he died the undergrads asked that the funeral procession go through the Yard. It did, passing Gothic Gore Hall, the old library, through Johnston Gate to Mount Auburn, where the Harvard crew carried the coffin.

The two dormitories, Lionel and Mower Halls, on the west side of the Holden Quadrangle, were built in the mid-1920s as part of President Lowell's effort to keep traffic noise from the Yard. Both halls were gifts in memory of Harvard men. Notice the sundial midway between them, a gift, like the now-closed gate in the yard wall, of the class of 1870.

The memorial on the north wall of Lionel, just beside the sundial, tells that this young man, killed in World War I, was the only kin of John Harvard ever to attend Harvard College. Not mentioned is the name of the donor of the building, President A. Lawrence Lowell. On our walks we shall find that although President Lowell was Harvard's greatest builder of buildings, he was himself—though always anonymously—among the most steadfast contributors.

Notice the tree on the south side of Holden a few feet from the westernmost of Holden's tall arched windows. Here, a few feet farther out from Holden, stood the Class Day Tree from the later 1700s until it was axed in 1911. Still, annual Tree Spreads continue in Holden Quadrangle, with returning alumni at commencement time dining under tents or on the lawn, enjoying reunions and tipping glasses in the temporary class-by-class bars improvised in the lower-floor rooms of the nearby ancient dorms. The merrymaking is far, far tamer than in the early 1800s.

Back in those days seniors pulled out all the stops: after-class poems, odes, and oratory were done to mark the end of their undergraduate years. Buckets of punch came from Willards's and Porter's nearby Harvard Square taverns. Bands and Glee Clubs made music. There was dancing and lanterns were hung in the trees. But hilarity got out of hand and "Old Quin" tamed it.

Bishop William Lawrence, telling of post–Civil War days, described seniors dancing around the Tree as "the great social event of college years." Families and friends stood or were on tiers of seats near the building and the public watched by the two-bar open fence, then the only separation between Holden and the Common. A broad band of flowers was strung around the Tree about nine feet from the ground. The seniors would march in, cheer, sing and dance around, and at a signal leap and struggle for the flowers—"tokens of victory," he called them—which they presented to their favored ladies.

THE OLD YARD: NORTH

On leaving Holden Quadrangle by the path where we entered we have on our left Stoughton Hall, which, in 1805, led Harvard building into the early nineteenth century. Stoughton, following Hollis, is the only other early dorm with the chamber-study setup of the Middle Ages. That had little attraction for a renowned student resident of Hollis, Henry Adams, though he would specialize in medieval history before writing his *Education of Henry Adams.*

Adams found his quarters in Hollis "the coldest, dirtiest and gloomiest in Cambridge." Yet residence in Hollis of another noted student, future architect Charles Bulfinch, was happily quite different. Bulfinch designed Stoughton, and made it appear like a Hollis twin, even to the identical number of rooms.

Some of the best-known student activities and clubs had their beginnings in these oldest Old Yard dormitories. It was here in Stoughton that students obtained from the faculty their first regular quarters for the Porcellian Club and the Hasty Pudding Club and that the *Harvard Crimson*, though born with a different name, got under way.

The Porcellian, a secret society in those times, had club roots going back to 1789, with members gathering in one another's rooms. Specific records trace it, however, only to 1791 and founder Joseph McKean, who would become a clergyman and Harvard professor. McKean had a head full of lively ideas and pranks.

The reader certainly has noticed the short gap between Harvard Hall and Hollis. There's a Harvard tradition that McKean, bent on silencing the Harvard bell, found himself about to be caught from inside by a tutor, ran down the roof of Harvard Hall and escaped by jumping across to the roof of Hollis. McKean thought up the menu of a whole roast pig. First regular club quarters was a room in Stoughton, but more of its tale when we see the present clubhouse with its gracious Palladian window.

Hasty Pudding Club began in 1795 "to cherish friendship and patriotism" by celebrating George Washington's birthday with a poem and an oration, and holding gatherings—also in various members' rooms—at the sound of the evening commons bell. Instead of dining on routine bread and milk from the cellar buttery at Harvard Hall, members dined on tasty hasty pudding delivered hot in a pot by two members "in alphabetical order."

As the club developed into a debating society, and from holding mock trials to staging theatricals, it had temporary room in neighboring Hollis and Holworthy, but its first real home was Stoughton 29, an upper north-west-corner room, where, when allowed to remove partitions and add three more chambers, the club erected a stage and found ways to produce even *Romeo and Juliet*. Again, more about the club, and how it can claim to be Harvard's oldest, when we reach the clubhouse on Holyoke Street.

The *Crimson* might have been a stillbirth if a group of juniors, class of 1874, had been less enterprising. College journals had been exceedingly short-lived since the first one, *The Telltale* of 1721, even when they had outstanding student writers such as Edward Everett, Oliver Wendell Holmes, or James Russell Lowell. They simply lacked customers.

And so when Henry A. Clark, class of 1874, went to tell the dean of his fellow juniors' plan to publish a new journal, the dean expressed "strong disapproval." Clark's sole question was whether the dean was forbidding publication. The dean said he was not, but "thought the project very ill-advised." It followed that late on the night of January 23, 1873 the juniors were waiting in Stoughton 22, with Clark, to receive the first printing of the *Magenta*, a biweekly, soon to be renamed the *Crimson*.

Ever on the lookout for better quarters, some students got to live in a number of the old dorms. Orator James Otis, then known as "Jemmy," lived here with a classmate from his Cape Cod hometown. Thoreau, whose ill health made him appear withdrawn to classmates, spent his senior year here. Genial Oliver Wendell Holmes, whose family dwelling was only a short walk away on the east side of the Common, lived only one of his undergraduate years in the College, his senior one in Stoughton.

It was merry. Wine, said Holmes, "was freely drunk in those days." Holmes recalled that on an exhibition day, with his parents' permission, "I laid in a considerable stock and my room was for several days the scene of continuous revelry." Future Reverend Phillips Brooks left more than a memory in Stoughton. He carved his initial and class in the floor near the fireplace.

Before he shifted to Hollis, Copey lived six years here on the second floor during his early years, lecturing on literary figures, and here he started his remarkable Wednesday night gatherings. Finances can make quite a difference living even in nearly identical quarters.

On invitation by William James, Santayana, now equipped with a degree in philosophy, became an instructor and, at last, had the means to choose lodgings. He picked the ground floor southeast, directly across from his undergraduate lodgings. Now a janitor brought him coal and water. He had a round bathtub under his bed for a daily sponge bath. He shopped at the grocers, often cooked his own breakfast, made afternoon tea, loved his fireplace, the leaping flames, the simmering kettle.

Holworthy Hall, at the north end of the old Yard, was built in 1812, seven years after Stoughton. By locating Holworthy at right angles to Stoughton the college began forming the quadrangle that is now the Old Yard. In that era the Commonwealth, still the main source of college financing, utilized lotteries in part to build both buildings, though they were named for two of the college's more munificent seventeenth-century benefactors, Acting Governor William Stoughton and Sir Matthew Holworthy, a merchant in Bristol, England.

In its early decades Holworthy was for seniors only and Santayana, a first-hand critic of these old dorms, said Holworthy was considered the "Seniors' Paradise." Each suite had two single bedrooms in back with a large study in front and a view of the Yard. Author of "rags-to-riches" tales Horatio Alger and the great abolitionist orator Wendell Phillips lived here as seniors.

To Alger, Holworthy was a choice lodging. He lived here as a sixteen-year-old freshman—he was the smallest in the class, only five feet two inches—and came back as a senior after his middle years in Stoughton and Hollis. Size was no handicap. Alger won many prizes, gave the Class Ode, and became Phi Beta Kappa. Holworthy has had great professors, too: art professor Charles Eliot Norton and his first cousin, future president Charles W. Eliot, at twenty-eight years of age, beginning his career as a math tutor.

Eliot, living second-floor middle entry, believed that he was the only one ever to eat with a picturesque, ascetic professor of Greek and Greek literature, his neighbor living second-floor west entry, Professor Evangelinus Apostolides Sophocles, a short, stout, longhaired man who strode across the yard in a black cloak he had brought from Greece. In those times of no telephones the kind woman "goody" had found Professor Sophocles lying sick on his floor and fetched young Eliot to come and help.

Eliot was later invited to a meal. Sophocles lived the frugal life of the folks with whom he corresponded, the monks on Mt. Sinai who had reared him. He cooked his own food and fed Eliot a simple stew and French bread. Kindly Maria Fay, his friend, let him keep hens in her cellar and yard of future Radcliffe's Fay House. Walks to feed the hens provided his exercise and his hobby was giving friends the eggs with the hens' names written on the shells.

Even in his tutor days Eliot was busy modernizing Harvard. He got college permission and in 1855 introduced gaslight (from the new Cambridge Gas Company) into his own room, Holworthy 11. Within a couple of years it spread to all the college dorms and also to the Yard, where previously, said Eliot, there had been "no light at all."

There were other great moments at Holworthy. In 1860 Prince Albert Edward of Wales made a summer visit in royal style, with the governor, mounted lancers, a reception at old Gore Library, and banquet in Harvard Hall. Eleven years later came Grand Duke Alexis. On each occasion Holworthy 12, second-floor middle entry, was chosen as the suite to be shown. Prince Albert (the future King Edward VII), then nineteen, later sent his portrait in uniform and it was displayed on the wall of number 12.

Theodore Roosevelt, twenty-one and a few days before graduation, entered the middle door of Holworthy and went up the three flights to a classmate's quarters for a meeting of one of his numerous clubs, Alpha Delta Phi, of which he was president. Presently, perched on window-seat cushions, T.R. and friend talked of coming careers.

Ever an outdoor enthusiast, T.R. had planned to enter a scientific field. But now he disclosed to his friend that he had decided to study law to seek an idealistic goal, not knowing, of course, that it would lead to the White

House. Said T.R., "I am going to help the cause of better government in New York City. I don't know exactly how."

Thayer Hall, on the northeast side of the Old Yard, is one of the four large dormitories promptly built under young President Charles W. Eliot—three of them completing the old quadrangle—with students arriving in ever-increasing numbers as Harvard expanded from a college into a university. Big Thayer Hall, finished in 1870, has more student quarters than both Hollis and Stoughton, which face it across the Yard.

Like the others in the south part of the Yard, Thayer was a gift of Bay State business leaders, none a Harvard graduate but all with close ties to the University. The donor, Nathaniel Thayer, Jr., left college early to seek his fortune. By age twenty-one he was a partner in a Boston firm trading in the West Indies, went on to join his older brother in banking, and built one of New England's biggest fortunes in railroads and manufacturing.

This building Thayer gave in memory of his father, a Harvard graduate and clergyman, and of his brother John, the banker. His gifts to Harvard, as we will see, went far beyond Thayer Hall. And brother John in 1857 expanded by several times the number of scholarships then available for meritorious, needy scholars.

E. E. Cummings, who for some time had been writing his avant-garde poetry, lived so near the Yard that he did not become a resident student until his senior year here in Thayer. He quickly developed friendship—which would be lifelong—with John Dos Passos, already contributing articles to the Harvard undergraduate magazine.

In 1915, along with College mate Robert Hillyer, Cummings and Dos Passos formed the Harvard Poetry Society, before they would read their own poetry or listen to great stars like Amy Lowell and Robert Frost. At the 1915 commencement, Cummings, as the class orator, spoke on "The New Art," quoting and praising writings of Gertrude Stein and works of Henri Matisse—for Cummings was also an artist.

In that year, 1915, Dos Passos lived in Thayer 29, one of Thayer Hall's most renowned quarters.

Young Louis D. Brandeis, who would become a famous U. S. Supreme

Court justice following appointment by President Woodrow Wilson, lived in Thayer 29, 1877–78 while serving as a proctor and doing graduate work. Brandeis was considered "the most brilliant student" in that era of the Law School. He had entered before his nineteenth birthday and was so remarkable that his professors were soon listening to him. Little wonder Brandeis felt that "for me the world's center was Cambridge." Law School rules had to be suspended for his graduation because he was still under twenty-one years of age.

And Thayer 29 became lodgings in 1889 for twenty-five-year-old George Santayana, who as an instructor in philosophy had a course transferred to him by William James. He stayed only a year before shifting to Stoughton. Curiously, he considered Thayer "graceless quarters," though in Thayer he had spent some of the happiest time in his undergraduate life.

Santayana, as a freshman, had been invited to join the *Lampoon* after he submitted a cartoon. He and his southern friends, also "pooners," ate at the same table in Memorial Hall commons and used Thayer 1 as a *Lampoon* sanctuary, exchanging ideas, making drawings, and thinking up puns for a *Lampoon* column they concocted. They preferred it to the fine sanctum William Randolph Hearst, *Lampoon* business manager, had provided on Brattle Street. But then, Santayana, while agreeing that Hearst was "invaluable to the *Lampoon*," did not like—probably envied—Hearst's show of wealth in those big cigars Hearst smoked as he crossed the Yard.

In its almost two centuries as the center of student and faculty life, University Hall has amassed a treasure trove of college lore.

This first Harvard College building of stone, white Chelmsford granite, was designed by the same renowned architect who planned Stoughton Hall, Charles Bulfinch. Despite alterations—particularly the first-floor portico erected between the two main entries and removed in 1842—University Hall has kept much the same external appearance it had on completion in 1815.

The Hall was constructed under the guidance of a great college president, Reverend John T. Kirkland, a charming man in the liberal, common-sense tradition of President Leverett. Kirkland sought to accommodate the steadily increasing number of students, to attain here a commons larger than the old one in Harvard Hall, and also to have a larger chapel in which to hold both daily and Sunday services. It was under President Kirkland that Harvard at long last established both law and divinity (theological) schools.

To improve the long-neglected Yard area, Kirkland removed the scattered privies from along the ancient stream that flowed through the Yard and located them in a discreet pine grove in back of and northeast of new University Hall, and went on to give the Yard scenic beauty by disposing of the last of the Yard breweries, planting lawn and trees, and creating neat paths.

John Harvard's statue has been here since 1924 on some of the site of the vanished portico. An imaginary likeness—for none exists—it was first unveiled in autumn 1884 on the old Delta playground beside Memorial Hall. Sculptor Daniel Chester French and the donor, Samuel Bridge, merchant, donor of his Cambridge ancestor's statue, *The Puritan,* which we saw on Cambridge Common, were present to hear President Eliot accept it for the College.

President Eliot genially went along with Mr. Bridge's description of John Harvard (on the base of the statue) as the college's founder in 1638. It was back in October 1636, under ill-fated Governor Henry Vane, that the General Court (the legislative body) voted £400 to establish "a schoale or colledge." But John Harvard, who did not arrive in the New

World until 1637, had a big role, for his deathbed will gave the College about twice the colony's £400, and half a year later the General Court voted that it would be called "Harvard Colledge."

President Kirkland had the honor of greeting two very distinguished visitors when they arrived at the old portico: newly elected President James Monroe in the Era of Good Feeling that followed the War of 1812, a mighty unpopular war in the Bay State; and Lafayette on his 1824 visit. Monroe, like Lafayette, had been wounded in battle during the Revolution.

Lafayette remarked in later years that Kirkland's reception of him and his entourage, with the students assembled by class on the lawn, had "transcended all similar ceremonies" in his honor. After the long program in the meeting house Lafayette came back to the commons in University Hall for a formal dinner. Lafayette told Kirkland that the great improvements he saw since he had been here in 1784 were striking evidence of the institution's promoting "the progress of civilization and learning."

President Andrew Jackson, when he arrived in the portico in 1833 with Vice President Martin Van Buren, who would succeed him, was unaware of the discomfort his visit brought to one of his predecessors, John Quincy Adams, then Harvard's best-known overseer. Adams would not attend. He thought Harvard would disgrace itself if it gave an honorary degree to "a barbarian who could not write a sentence of grammar and hardly spell his own name."

But Harvard President Josiah Quincy as strongly believed the College should honor Jackson because the "people have twice decided that this man knows enough law to be their ruler." The charisma and dignity of the Hero of New Orleans won about everyone present as he accepted a law degree—as had Monroe—in the crowded chapel then occupying most of University Hall's second and third floors, greeted students, visited Harvard Hall, and attended a levée at President Quincy's residence in the Yard, Wadsworth House.

Every floor in University Hall has tales with memorable names. The basement, as in Harvard Hall, was originally for the storage and preparation of food to be consumed in commons upstairs on the first floor. The basement was divided for a variety of uses, however, for students ate increasingly in boarding houses, and the commons was closed down in 1849.

A year later, Harvard named its first professor of chemistry, Josiah Cooke, who was permitted, at his own expense, to set up a laboratory in a basement room. Here, two years later, Charles W. Eliot, a seventeen-year-old junior, launched his career in chemistry, which in a couple of decades would see him move from the cellar to the presidential office on the second floor. In that year, 1869, Reverend Phillips Brooks, newly appointed rector of Boston's Trinity Church, was asked by some Harvard students to address them in a basement room, where they installed a piano and sang hymns. Thus began Reverend Brooks's career that led to his becoming college preacher and helping to end compulsory prayer.

On going from the old Yard into the south-entry hallway, the most noticeable embellishments are ornate six-foot-diameter circles in the walls. They are now used for notices or directories or, on the interiors, for shelves, but once they were big, circular apertures to give dining unity to the partitioned class-eating areas.

It did not take fun-prone youngsters long to discover that these made marvelous openings through which to lob buns or even crockery—with what sometimes shocking results we will presently recount. For many students, like sixteen-year-old Ralph Waldo Emerson, always eager to help cover costs, commons was a place both to eat and to earn a bit as a waiter.

This entry was the way poet Longfellow took, then up the stone staircase, to the elegant Corporation Room, near the presidential office, where he and his pupils sat around a long table. Future Colonel Thomas W. Higginson, who would lead the first regiment of freed slaves into battle in the Civil War, was a pupil and said that he thought this kindly, friendly Longfellow "was the first Harvard professor who addressed his pupils as Mister."

Short, stocky, curly-haired Professor Francis J. "Stubby" Child, always sunshiny cheerful, gave his lecture on Chaucer and old ballads in an upstairs room, and so too did poet James Russell Lowell, and on the third floor future President A. Lawrence Lowell lectured on political systems at the start (he had given up law) of a new career that would lead to the second-floor presidential office. En route to that office both Eliot and Lowell would also teach at Massachusetts Institute of Technology, at that time in Boston.

The Faculty Room, up the stone staircase, on the second floor, is regarded as among the most beautiful and historical of Harvard's treasures. Basically it is the original chapel, as restored in 1896 without the third-floor-level north and south balconies, the pulpit that once stood on the east side, and an organ opposite on the west side. And so the lecture rooms that had occupied the space in the two floors here, from 1858 when religious services were moved to new Appleton Chapel until 1896, disappeared. Many of the noted lecturers may be seen still in the collection of portraits and busts by distinguished artists around the spacious room.

Overhead, on the wall, on entering the Faculty Room from the south, can be seen a portrait of William Stoughton made additionally interesting by its depiction of the original Stoughton Hall. Just to the right on entering is the bust of Benjamin Franklin, who left Boston Latin School at age ten to work in his father's tallow shop, making soap and candles. Franklin was voted an honorary degree in 1753 for his great scientific work, "particularly with respect to electricity."

Franklin, both in England and France, obtained scientific apparatus and books for the College, and kept corresponding for years with his friend, Professor John Winthrop, who would unintentionally disturb some clergy by showing that nature, not God's wrath, caused earthquakes.

Franklin, he of the penny-saved, penny-earned philosophy, left this tickled observation in his famed autobiography about this and other honorary awards he received: "thus without studying in any college I came to partake of their honours." The big round table on the right is where the College president presides at these gatherings.

The Harvard Graduate School of Business Administration (the "B School"), and its gracious cluster of buildings that we will see on the south bank of the Charles River, had its beginnings in University Hall in 1908, a decade after President Eliot began thinking about experimenting on another new graduate school. The first dean he selected was Professor Edwin F. Gay, who had been giving a course in economic history. Gay arranged his office just off the north entry, number 17, and started organizing courses for graduates of approved colleges or scientific schools seeking professional training for M.B.A. (Master of Business Administration) degrees.

The beginnings were far from lavish. Lectures in new courses were in any available space, even in basements, or as part of other courses in scattered lecture halls. On opening day, October 1, 1908, the school began with twenty-four full-time students and thirty-five special students taking only courses of their own choice—in contrast to the school's current annual first-year enrollment of about 800 women and men, from about every state and some forty nations, seeking M.B.A.s.

The commons in University Hall has been the setting for some of the College's wildest scenes, and at times even the chapel, both the original and the restored one, has been close behind.

Thrifty diets, with early stewards trying to hold down costs despite ravenous young appetites, proved to be most often the cause of the recurrent riots. As for the food, at times the young scholars felt they were merely sharing their diet with the dozen or so pigs in the sties behind University Hall, then without entries on the east side, at that time the most eastern reach of the Yard.

As students from more prosperous families, many from the South, succeeded a student body once heavily composed of sons of poor clergy, students won permission in 1825 to eat away from commons in clubs and boarding houses. In the last year of commons in University Hall, shrunk to just some basement rooms and leased out, many of the few student patrons before the shutdown in 1849 called it "Starvation Hollow." Prices, though, were quite low—just $2 a week.

Over the years, pranks in the Yard, traditionally part of school life, have sometimes been so ingenious as to make deviltry admirable. These are not mere exploits such as marauding in local hen-roosts, tumbling cannon balls down dormitory stairways at midnight, surprise drenching of freshmen, simple hazing, or more modern swallowing of goldfish. Harvard annals are jam-full of such doings. There are, though, hearty chuckles in oft-supressed Med Fac, a group of students in upper Hollis who joined in

1818 to mimic College greats by conferring bogus medical and honorary degrees that even took in the Russian Czar when one was dispatched to Moscow.

Or the young devils who, on a winter's night, snitched the signboard from Porter's Tavern near Harvard Square. On learning that a tutor was on their trail, they started feeding it piecemeal to their dorm's fireplace while one student stood praying loudly near the closed door. Figuring a prayer meeting was in session, the tutor waited patiently—and on his finally entering, the fireplace provided not the least sign of the sign.

In the chapel, unlike the commons, we hear mostly of pranks until evening prayers were no longer mandatory—the young lads, after all, preferred afternoon games. Imps among them would manage to cut ropes to the bell that announced services, mislay the preacher's Bible, hide a firecracker in the lid of the Bible, or even ship the Bible by express to Yale.

Like his father and his uncle punished for earlier "rebellions," author Richard Henry Dana, a sixteen-year-old freshman, was rusticated to Andover for six months for refusing to name a classmate who, as the preacher opened the Bible, got the other classmates to "set up a hissing, groaning and scraping which completely drowned his voice." Dana knew the name, but believed telling would violate "good faith between young men."

At evening prayer on the day he was chosen class poet, nineteen-year-old senior James Russell Lowell, just as the preacher began service, popped up and, smirking, bowed his thanks left and right. He did not get to read his poem, was rusticated instead to Concord until after Class Day.

In commons at times, pranksters turned into hellions. A mock epic of an 1818 outburst among juniors on a Sunday evening, "The Rebelliad," tells the start of this transformation:

> When Nathan threw a piece of bread
> And hit Abijah in the head
> The wrathful freshman, in a trice,
> Sent back another, bigger slice . . .

And thus arose a fearful battle.
The coffee cups and saucers rattle;
The bread bowls fly at awful rate
And break many a learned pate.

Bonfires were built at the pump that night and there was dancing around Rebellion Tree. All but a few of the sophomore class were expelled. The class of 1823 topped 1818's antics, was so rowdy it was even called the Rebellion Class. After adding gunpowder explosions to many bonfires and dancing around Rebellion Tree, more than half the graduating class was expelled.

The rebellion of 1834 had even more embellishments in hell-raising, smashing University Hall windows and the furnishings of an unpopular tutor, undraping a black flag of rebellion from Holworthy's roof, hanging President Quincy in effigy on Rebellion Tree because he sought grand jury indictments. But "Old Quin" did clamp down. Save for the bedlam-makers of 1823, expulsions cut the class of 1836 to the smallest number in almost three decades.

Violence in this century reached still higher peaks during nationwide campus revolt against the Vietnam War, leading to capture of University Hall, eviction of the dean and the staff, and rifling of College record files. The S.D.S. (Students for a Democratic Society) grew through the 1960s, denouncing the war, the draft, the R.O.T.C., and even mobbing the Secretary of Defense during a 1966 visit to the College. The climax came at noon on April 9, 1969, when S.D.S. activists staged their takeover, renamed University Hall "Che Guevara Hall," and flew the S.D.S. banner from the third-floor window.

The elegant faculty room was turned by the S.D.S. into a disorderly lounge. Bullhorns blared. Outside was a mob of students, some passing out leaflets, some yelling "R.O.T.C. must go!" and others shouting "S.D.S. get out!" At nightfall floodlights were focused on the Hall. As daybreak neared next day, state police, helmeted, clubs handy, arrived to aid the Yard police. President Pusey, in the style of "Old Quin," had called for outside help, but, just as back in "Old Quin's" day, some students reacted by yelling for the stoning of Pusey's house!

Just after 5:00 A.M. the police moved in. Fearing tear gas, the activists passed around soaked rags. They were met mainly by swinging clubs. There was a bloody scene, activists climbing out of windows, police rushing them into waiting vans, later booking nearly 200 men and women. Students called it "the Bust."

The S.D.S., however, did not fall into a decline until a year later. Then, after marching from an antiwar rally on Boston's Common there came "the trashing of Harvard Square," as rowdies joined in, smashing windows and setting fires, with many injured, and this time helmeted police swung clubs and fired off tear gas canisters.

THE OLD HARVARD YARD: SOUTH

To our left as we leave University Hall is Weld Hall, one of two big dormitories—the other is Matthews Hall directly opposite Weld—which President Eliot built by 1872, just after he took office, to complete the southern end of the Old Yard Quadrangle. Weld, with its distinctive staircase towers—plus, originally, a lift to get coal to student fireplaces—was a gift by his brother, a Boston businessman, in memory of Stephen Minot Weld, teacher and overseer, one of the first to promote creation of Memorial Hall.

Future United States President John F. Kennedy, who had gone with a Choate School buddy to start college at Princeton, but shifted after becoming ill, came in 1936 to live as a freshman in Weld Hall. Then nineteen, J.F.K. had decided to follow in the footsteps of his father and his older brother, Joseph, Jr. The latter would talk of how he would one day win election to the White House, but young J.F.K. was more interested in Joe's football achievements.

Football practice would bring injury to J.F.K.'s back, which would affect him all his life—but, never a quitter, he still played. Here in Weld he became roommate of another football aspirant, Torbert H. Macdonald, future captain of Harvard's football team and All-American star. By personally campaigning, J.F.K. would one day help elect "Torby" Macdonald, lifelong friend, to join him in Washington in the Congress.

Grays Hall, on the south end of the Old Yard, was built in 1863 from college funds mainly to provide for students who had been living in poorer quarters. It was named for three generous benefactors of the College, sons and grandsons of William Gray, of Salem and Boston, Revolutionary Army veteran, ratifier of the U.S. Constitution, Bay State lieutenant governor; Gray built up his fleet to sixty square-rigged ships in trade to East India, China, and Russia. His son, Francis Calley Gray, 1809 graduate, followed his father into public life and is most remembered for his gift of 3,000 rare prints, a cornerstone of the Fogg Art Collection, and other princely gifts to the Harvard library and museums.

The Signet Club, of which both Roosevelts, T.R. and F.D.R., were members, was founded upstairs in Grays Hall in 1870 by a group of juniors as an alternative, as they put it, to the "illiberal policy" of the Hasty

Pudding. Moreover, for sixteen years they barred Pudding members from their club, which sought to keep alive a tradition of "literary culture and social intercourse" through recognition of merit. The club membership over the years is filled most impressively with distinguished and famous names.

Matthews Hall was also the gift of a Boston businessman, Nathan Matthews, at the time that his son, a future Boston mayor, was an undergraduate. This was the large building that made it necessary to move old Dane Hall. Matthews Hall at once became highly desirable lodging for, as President Eliot recalled, it ws the first in the Yard to have bathtubs—though they were in the basement. This alteration boosted donor Matthew's plans, for he had arranged that half the income from rents would go for scholarships for students studying to be Episcopal ministers.

President Eliot recalled that when he took office in 1869 the Cambridge Water Company was new and nineteen-twentieths of the students carried their own pails from the two pumps in the Yard. (The other pump was southeast of Massachusetts Hall.) The water supply was soon extended to all the Yard's dorms. Eliot was equally overjoyed when sewer pipes were installed across the Yard; he could end the privies in the pine grove back of University Hall, and students no longer had to bring pails of dirty water from their rooms to the cesspools.

Matthews Room M17 was the birthplace of the *Harvard Lampoon*, and the lodgings of the Sherwood brothers: Samuel, a senior of the class of 1876, and Arthur, a sophomore. Samuel played host to a handful of '76 classmates whose wit gave birth to the humor magazine that was, a few years later, as we will presently see, rescued by a later resident of Mattthews Hall.

Just a decade after Matthews's completion, one of its best-known freshmen took up residence, nineteen-year-old William Randolph Hearst, only son of a fabulously rich California miner and land owner soon to become a U.S. Senator. Hearst's youthful mother, Phoebe, was eagerly on hand to see that her only child would enjoy the very best. She hired a decorator, added a library, installed lavish furnishings that astonished even sons from very rich mansions.

Some say Hearst majored in pranks, practical jokes, and mischief. He certainly enjoyed himself. He kept "Champagne Charlie," a pet alligator on a string; played a banjo; joined just about all the clubs; gave midnight parties—even helped prepare potatoes and Welsh rabbit; loved the theatre; and took his pals in a carriage to the Boston shows. He always had an ample stock of spirits, though he drank only beer and little of that. He deeply missed the lofty California mountains he loved and his courses, save for Professor Charles Eliot Norton's "Fine Arts," held his attention but slightly.

Behind all the merrymaking and horseplay, Hearst did develop a purpose. A few years earlier his father had acquired, for political use, the bankrupt *San Francisco Examiner*. Increasingly, it aroused young Hearst's interest. When the existence of the *Lampoon* was endangered by lack of readers, Hearst stepped in as business manager, opened a drive for circulation that quickly put it so comfortably in the black that the editors could resume their carefree staff parties. Hearst's father did not want him to waste his time on the *Examiner*. Through his mother, young Hearst emphasized that he had saved the *Lampoon* and could do the same for the *Examiner*. Father still said, "No."

Came the 1884 election, young Hearst cast his first vote for Grover Cleveland, and when Cleveland won Hearst staged a celebration with fireworks, a brass band, beer, marching, an all-night victory party with crowing roosters at dawn in the Yard. He was rusticated. Undaunted, Hearst went happily off to Washington, D.C., where his father, now a Senator, took him to the White House to meet his hero, President Cleveland.

When Hearst was allowed back to Matthews Hall in the spring he thought up another headline scheme. He dispatched unusual gifts to his instructors: chamber pots with the name of each beautifully painted on the bottom inside. Expulsion from Harvard promptly followed, and soon he did take over the *Examiner,* made it prosper and become the foundation of his newspaper empire.

While excavating for Matthew Hall, workmen uncovered an old brick wall not far from the present southern end of Matthews, thus locating the college's first brick building, the two-story Indian College built in 1655 with funds from a society in England hoping to spread Christianity among Indians. No more than five Indians ever came, and of those one was killed by Indians on Nantucket when cast ashore on a visit home just before his graduation. The only graduate, Caleb Cheeshahteaumuch, also from Martha's Vineyard, died a year after he got his degree.

With hopes faded the building, before its demolition in 1698, was used by other students but chiefly as a printing shop. Here was installed, when moved from Dunster's new presidential house, the colony's first printing press and, in 1660, another press and type sent over by English friends for printing in the Indian language. The presence here of Reverend John Eliot, "The Indian Apostle" and translator of the King James version into Algonquin, helped its printing here (1661–63) in the Indian College by an eminent printer, Samuel Green, who at sixteen had arrived with Governor John Winthrop.

Notice, on the path leading south past Matthews to Massachusetts Avenue, the ocher building with white trim on the left just before the gate. This is Wadsworth House, a 1726 structure, for decades the presidential residence, which we will further describe on our walk along Massachusetts Avenue. For now, Wadsworth was the site where ill-fated Nathaniel Eaton, a man of defective, deceitful character, in 1637 commenced teaching Harvard College's first student class.

Just forward of Grays Hall was once the first structure built exclusively for the College. Though still incomplete it was used by President Dunster for the first commencement on September 23, 1642 with the governor, the clergy, and all the dignitaries of the colony present to see Dunster confer degrees on the nine graduates. Eventually called the Old College, the building, of lumber and cedar clapboards, stood three stories high. On the south side of the ground floor was a spacious hall that Governor Winthrop called "the scholars commons," used for prayer, lectures, and public events, for it was the showiest assembly place in the colony.

John Harvard's books were shelved in the large library on the second floor with a lengthy chamber for the students. The gabled third floor provided student quarters and studies. In the building's center in back was a staircase turret leading to the upper floors and the college bell. At either end of the building in back were wings containing kitchen facilities and more student chambers.

The building, possibly from the misdoings of Master Eaton under whom it was started—for he seems to have pocketed some of John Harvard's legacy—became prematurely decayed and by 1677 the College had moved to newly completed Old Harvard Hall.

The name Anne Radcliffe appears first in College records in connection with President Dunster's efforts to raise funds for construction of the Old College. Wife of an English knight, Lady Anne responded from overseas by sending the College's first scholarship endowment, a gift that led 250 years later to Radcliffe College's being named in her memory.

We now head by the path south of University Hall to the Tercentenary Theatre.

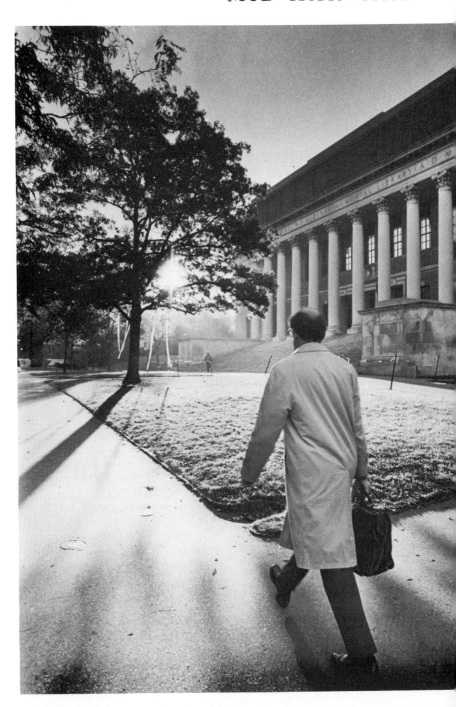

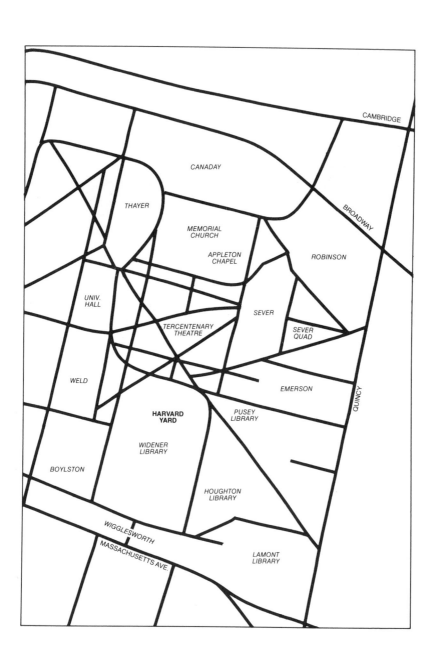

TERCENTENARY THEATRE

S ome of the greatest events in the three and a half centuries of Harvard—with some of the world's greatest individuals present—have taken place here in the center and still largest open area of the Yard's twenty-two acres, once part cowyard and part ox pasture, in recent years called the Tercentenary Theatre.

A key role in three such events became the good fortune of a recent Harvard president, the late James B. Conant, who welcomed President Franklin D. Roosevelt to the seat of honor at Harvard's 300th-anniversary celebration, handed an honorary degree to Winston Churchill midway through World War II, and two years after that war did the same for General George Marshall, then Secretary of State, when Marshall proposed a plan that Conant called "epoch making" to resurrect the war-shattered economy of Europe.

Conant, who had gone to England in 1941 to coordinate Allied research that would lead to development of the atomic bomb, had met Churchill in his underground shelter while bombs whistled down from Nazi planes during the blitz of London. Churchill had taken charge of an ill-prepared wartime Great Britain and had appealed to the United States: "give us the tools and we shall finish the job."

Harvard had voted the honorary degree in the spring but it was not until September 1943, on one of his cross-Atlantic missions to confer with F.D.R., that Churchill managed time to come to Cambridge for a few hours, all his itinerary safeguarded by strict wartime secrecy. The degree was presented in Sanders Theatre, just north of the Yard, before a distinguished audience at "an academic meeting" without advance knowledge of what was afoot. Directly afterward Churchill came to the Yard.

The chubby, confidently smiling Prime Minister, during a pause in Memorial Church, had changed from the medieval black velvet cap and scarlet gown of a doctor of civil laws from Oxford that he wore in Sanders back to his gray trousers, black jacket, and black homburg. Presently he came from the War Memorial vestibule to the church's south portico before 6,000 uniformed Army and Navy trainees and a company of Waves from Radcliffe. In his brief remarks, with his cane at times pounding the granite steps for emphasis, he praised those serving their country, warned of battlefields ahead, but drew loud cheers when he raised his right hand in the V-for-victory salute.

The area here between Memorial Church and Widener Library on the south, and between University Hall and Sever Hall on the east, has in recent decades been the setting for the joyful climax of all college life, the commencement. Since the first nine graduates got their degrees in the Old College of Governor Winthrop's era, commencement exercises have progressed from the successive meeting houses and the Unitarian Church—with spreads in Harvard and University Halls—to Sanders Theatre with spreads in adjoining Memorial Hall.

When that arrangement was outgrown, in 1911, commencement moved into a big tent in Sever Quadrangle, on the east side of Sever Hall, with 3,000 attending. As Harvard's 300th anniversary approached, President Conant, anticipating that 10,000 would be present, moved commencement here to mid-Yard. Well he did, for it drew 15,000 from many lands. Colleagues, bringing congratulations and gifts, came from hundreds of colleges just about everywhere, and the setting acquired a new name, Tercentenary Theatre.

A century earlier, three elaborate arches were erected between Harvard and Massachusetts Halls, and the 1,500 attending, after exercises in the then new 1833 Unitarian Meeting House we have seen, gathered in a huge pavilion erected in the Yard, flying high on a pole overhead the *Veritas* banner. "Old Quin" presided. Toasts followed toasts. There were songs, music, and orating. Oliver Wendell Holmes sang a funny song he had written. Edward Everett spoke. Daniel Webster spoke. All continued exuberantly deep into the evening.

President Eliot, during his record long presidency of four decades, introduced several United States presidents, whose presence was the high point in the banqueting and festivities, graduating classes entertaining families and friends, music and dancing, alumni back for class reunions, and always the academic processions in colorful attire denoting all sorts of rungs on the ladder of degrees and scholarship.

In 1877, a few months after President Hayes entered the White House, he came as a "son of Harvard" and received an honorary degree from Eliot. President Cleveland came to the 250th celebration in 1886 to the delight of 2,500 guests. Cleveland, though he had been elected to the White House and later would win a second term, had informed Eliot that he would not accept the proffered honorary LL.D., for he did not feel eminent in law.

Still, over the years more than a dozen presidents, some before reaching the White House, have accepted honorary Harvard degrees, including all six Harvard graduates elected United States president. Future President John F. Kennedy received this honor in 1956—"Brave officer, able Senator, son of Harvard"—after the voters advanced him from the House of Representatives to the Senate.

The most remembered photograph of the 300th celebration—with pictures of the fireworks display on the Charles River certainly runners-up—was the patient, lonely looking F.D.R. seated conspicuously isolated on the sheltered platform forward of Memorial Church and rain pouring down on the audience that wall-to-wall packed, even overpacked, the Tercentenary Theatre.

President Conant had been told that there was a little hurricane off shore, but, true to Harvard's traditional commencement-time luck, there would still be fine weather. But the hurricane made an unexpected shift. Rain began to fall, lightly at first, then heavily, as the classes lined up for the academic procession.

Folks without umbrellas (and they were many) were drenched. Plans were changed. The procession was abandoned. Dignitaries and scholars gathered hurriedly in Widener Library for the break before lunch, were grateful for nips of scotch or other whiskey. Yale's president is said to have remarked that he heard an alumnus say, "This is Conant's way of soaking the rich."

Commencement has been more delightful since 1970. Until then the participants were in tune with the line in the Harvard ode "thy sons to thy jubilee throng." It was in 1970 that the long relationship of Harvard and Radcliffe blossomed into combining their commencements.

These academic celebrations suggest through the centuries the surprises of both change and continuity. A recent Harvard commencement was addressed by a descendant Spanish King of the Bourbon dynasty speaking eloquently on behalf of democracy, urging that the democracies on both sides of the Atlantic Ocean join in 1992 to celebrate the 500th anniversary of Christopher Columbus's discovery of America.

On the platform was William Saltonstall, Harvard official, son of Governor Leverett Saltonstall. William, devoted like his father to public service, is of the tenth successive generation, father to son, from the son of Sir Richard Saltonstall, one of those nine young first graduates in 1642.

Memorial Church was a gift from Harvard alumni in memory of College mates killed in World War I. Like Widener Library directly opposite, the church was built during the presidency of A. Lawrence Lowell, the greatest builder in Harvard's long history. It was Lowell who built all seven of the Yard's barrier buildings, donating one of them himself, and also, as another gift, building the president's house east of Widener on Quincy Street. These buildings alone about doubled the floor space in the Yard and are still only a fraction, as we shall see, of all Lowell constructed north of the Yard, along Quincy Street, and the many other buildings of the House Plan and the Harvard Business School on either side of the Charles River.

Memorial Church, completed in 1932, has two porticoes. The one on the south side was planned to complement the grand staircase and portico of Widener, completed in 1914. With its soaring white tower and gilded vane it makes an ideal background for staging commencements. In the tower is a bell also donated anonymously by Lowell, both to the memory of Harvard men who gave their lives in war and "to summon the young to classes, the faithful to daily prayer and Sunday worship."

Let us enter Memorial Church by the main portico on the west side. The interior, with arched windows, the arched ceiling supported by white pillars, provides a strikingly beautiful setting for Sunday worship. Daily service is held in the smaller chancel back of the pulpit, amid the graceful screen woodwork and iron grilles. This area is equally attractive with its medieval-style, facing carved oak stalls for the choir that are used by those attending morning prayer. This chancel is called Appleton Chapel, the name of the prior church that stood on this site from 1858 to 1931, a gift of a Boston merchant, an uncle of Mrs. Henry Wadsworth Longfellow's.

President Eliot, with the help of his new College preacher, Reverend Francis G. Peabody, and Phillips Brooks, was able in 1886 to end compulsory prayer, which, from the days of the Mathers, as Bishop Lawrence described it, used to force "Young men to leap from a deep sleep into their clothes and make their hurried way along the muddy paths and around the puddles of the Yard to the chapel." Several of the College community continued to be regular in attendance. President Lowell came every morning to the Old Chapel, sat in the same side pew, then was off across the Yard to his desk in University Hall. President Eliot did likewise but sat in his third-row pew.

The war memorials extend now over several wars. On the north wall, on our left as we entered, are three plaques. The nearest, just under the gallery, is in Latin and commemorates four Harvard men who "under opposite flags gave life for their country" in World War I. The two large memorials are for sons of Harvard who gave their lives in the Korean War and the Vietnam War.

On the opposite wall are listed in marble faculty, students, and alumni, classes 1904 to 1948, killed in World War II, among them a chaplain with the German forces. On the walls of the World War I Memorial Room are inscribed the names of 375 men, classes 1880 to 1918, who gave their lives in that war. Around the top of walls in the room, a vestibule to the south portico, is a message that applies to the heroic dead of all these wars, "that we might learn from them courage in peace to spend our lives making a better world for others." The youth of these men adds to the poignancy of the sculpture, *The Sacrifice,* a mother mourning her crusader son.

Go right on leaving Memorial Church and along its north side, across from us, north of the church, is Canaday Hall, built in 1974, newest of the Yard's dormitories with many modern—even solar—conveniences. Near the doorway to Canaday Common Room a plaque to the right of the entry tells of the donor, Ward Murphy Canaday, class of 1907, and his belief that "true success is to labour." His career certainly gave a Horatio Alger example of success. After being graduated with honor he had told how he went to New York with only $10 in his pocket "determined to lean no longer on the generous, devoted kindness of my parents with three more sons to educate."

Soon he was engaged in advertising and selling based on ideas he learned from economics Professor Frank W. Taussig, a founder of Harvard's Graduate School of Business Administration. Those ideas, said Canaday, laid the foundation for the half century of his business life. Canaday became an international financier, founded America's first automobile credit company, and headed the corporation that produced the world-famous, low-cost, four-cylinder Jeep. Canaday Hall is on the original site of Fogg Art Museum, in which the displays, unlike now, were more plaster casts than originals. That 1895 building, renamed Hunt Hall, later housed the Graduate School of Design before its demolition for Canaday Hall.

Turn right at the east end of Memorial Church and notice the big bronze plaque depicting the original Appleton Chapel. Professor Copeland—"Copey"—told a tale about the day the poet Longfellow was buried after services in the Chapel. Prior to the services, friends had gone for a last view of Longfellow at his mansion on Brattle Street. Among them was seventy-eight-year-old Ralph W. Emerson, who had for years suffered from loss of memory and would himself die five weeks later. "Copey" said that Emerson had looked intently at Longfellow's corpse and then remarked to a companion that the man in the coffin was "a most lovely soul but I have entirely forgotten his name."

As we approach the front of Sever Hall there is an amusing yarn about "Copey." He gave his lectures in a little amphitheatre in Sever. In 1925, when he was named to the prestigious Boylston professorship going way back to John Quincy Adams, "Copey's" admiring students discovered that the Boylston professor was still entitled to keep a cow in the Yard, a privilege stemming from the Yard's origin as part of cowyard row. And so the pupils fetched a cow from the Brighton abattoir and tethered it to a tree ouside the main (west) entry to Sever—until the Yard police ended the prank. That tale brings back old times like the turn-of-the-century rounds of John the Orangeman, a Harvard Square fruit peddler, hawking from the basket on his right arm.

Sever Hall, gift of the widow of an 1817 graduate, Colonel James W. Sever, is one of two outstanding buildings designed for his Alma Mater by Henry H. Richardson. It was completed in 1880 just after his Romanesque style Trinity Church in Boston made him famous.

Fame can often be mighty slow in coming. Poet E. E. Cummings would one day draw an overflow of admirers to Sanders Theatre, but earlier in his life, though it was a quarter century after his graduation, the scene was quite different when he was offered a $25 fee by an assistant professor friend to give a reading in the lecture auditorium, Sever 11. The bohemian Cummings came in sweater and sneakers, feeling wretched and "nervous during the ordeal"—for fans were few in the hall.

The lecture rooms of Sever have been most often associated with classes in English and literature, but these lecture rooms were extensively used by celebrated philosophy teachers before they got their own building, which we will presently see.

A student of William James has described James's teaching a class of graduate students while seated at the window end of this tower room in Sever. James was a patient, pleasant man seeking to pass on his thinking to his pupils. He was tolerant even to one of his greatest pupils, George Santayana, with whose views James had little rapport. Santayana, in turn, met his renowned pupils, among them Justice Felix Frankfurter, and later in Emerson Hall, Walter Lippmann and poet Robert Frost.

Among great events in Sever came the announcement in June 1890 by President Eliot that he had just received a letter from Major Henry L. Higginson giving the college "Soldiers Field," a lion's share of all Harvard's land on the south side of the Charles River, in memory of six college mates killed in the Civil War.

On coming out of the east entry of Sever we are in the Sever Quadrangle, where commencement exercises were held for a quarter of a century before being shifted to Tercentenary Theatre. They were moved here in 1911.

Sanders Theatre could no longer accommodate those eager to attend and graduates not twenty-five years out had been excluded from the drawing for tickets. Sever Quad could provide for 3,000 young and old, a turnout three times larger. A platform for the president and the dignitaries was built at Sever's east entry and wooden stands were erected on the street side.

To our left, as the names of great architects and exterior embellishments indicate, is Nelson Robinson, Jr. Hall, built in 1901 for the new School of Architecture and Landscape Architecture. His family built and endowed it in memory of student Robinson, who died in his junior year. Instruction specifically in architecture was then quite a recent discipline, going back only to courses in Greek and Roman architecture in 1893. It expanded rapidly with President Eliot's backing and the sudden death of young Robinson, who had been devoted to architecture, provided adequate facilities. In 1972 when larger Gund Hall became available farther north of the Yard, Robinson Hall at last gave an attractive, separate home to the history department.

Though Harvard is the oldest school in the nation teaching American history, strangely, as in teaching architecture, continuous instruction in history has had but a comparatively recent beginning, despite the many famed historians associated with the college over the years. True, back in 1838 Jared Sparks became the first American professor of civil (in contrast to ecclesiastical) history. But he gave it up to be Harvard's president.

In 1870 President Eliot asked the freelance writer Henry Adams to accept a new assistant professorship in medieval history. When Adams, who in the future would write *Mont-Saint Michel and Chartres,* said he knew nothing about medieval history, Eliot remarked, "If you will point out to me anyone who knows more, Mr. Adams, I will appoint him."

Adams taught for only seven years, during which he developed techniques for teaching history. His pupils carried on. Those were the days of

Albert Bushnell Hart and Edward Channing. In 1891 came a department of History and Government and in 1910 they split, and history went on with renowned teachers: wake-'em-up lecturer Roger B. Merriman, Samuel Eliot Morison, and Arthur M. Schlesinger, Sr.

Emerson Hall, on the south side of Sever Quad, was completed in 1905 with donations from friends of Ralph Waldo Emerson. It was the first college building in America just for a philosophy department and was dedicated on the 100th anniversary of Emerson's birth. Just inside the entry we can see, in bronze, a statue of Emerson, seated, relaxed, by Frank Duveneck in 1905.

Here in Emerson Hall were the lecture rooms in Harvard's Golden Age of Philosophers: always-charming, kindly William James, who even made time to visit pupils when they were ill; equally gentle George Palmer, husband of Wellesley College's first president, Alice Freeman Palmer; picturesque Josiah Royce; big, brilliant Hugo Munsterberg, always with strong German accent, embroiled along with Harvard in criticism as America was becoming involved in World War I; and unique, aloof George Santayana, poet, novelist, walking elegantly to and from class with his cane and gloves. All these philosophers—and their successors, among them Alfred North Whitehead—have contributed pamphlets, books, in some instances entire collections—to the philosophy library that began life in 1905 along with the building.

In the department's faculty room, Bechtel Room, immediately on our right from Emerson's statue, are individual portraits of all these philosophers. But, of even greater interest, possibly, is a group portrait hanging in the large lecture room at the east end of the main first-floor corridor—with two of the great philosophers represented only by gaps. "Too many philosophers!" was the comment as told by her daughter, of the skillful portraitist Winifred Rieber.

In her temporary studio arranged for her here in Emerson Hall she had her sketch all ready when all five came to inspect it. Santayana, who was to be shown seated in the now empty chair in front, after listening to the comments of his colleagues, walked out. Big Munsterberg, who was to occupy the gap in back but wanted the seat in front, did not come back, either. Palmer, described by Royce as the "center of gravity" among these diverse thinkers, insisted they were warm friends, had differing viewpoints, "wished our students to cultivate the critical habit," but the goal of all was to find truth, "a friendly, not a hostile, process."

We head now toward Widener Library. Besides the president's house we will see when we walk Quincy Street, there are three libraries: Lamont Library in the yard's southeast corner, Houghton Library connected in back by overhead passage to Widener, and underground Pusey Library. All three stem from an identical College problem going back to the first library in old Harvard Hall: the recurrent need of a growing college to expand its library space.

On taking office in 1933, President Conant found that even big Widener Library would soon be outgrown. The three new structures were devised to avoid building another huge edifice or a high-rise in the Yard. Houghton and Lamont were named for two generous graduates who responded with funds to Conant's "cry for help." Houghton Library, finished in 1942, holds Harvard's fabulous collection of manuscripts and rare books, among them the only book of John Harvard that escaped the fire. Some great treasures of the collection are exhibited in displays or bookcases in and near the lobby.

Thomas W. Lamont, New York banker and donor of other major gifts, enjoyed the idea of providing for this undergraduate library, completed in 1949 just after his death, where students would have its comfortable arrangements for reading and study and right-off-the-shelves access to books. Indeed, one of Widener's greatest charms, beautiful cozy Farnsworth Room for recreational reading, named for a 1912 graduate killed three years later serving with the French Foreign Legion, was shifted to the top floor in Lamont.

That the visitor has to go downstairs to enter Pusey Library suggests immediately that it is entirely underground, linking its great capacity with other underground stacks of both Widener and Lamont.

Pusey Library houses three great collections shifted from Widener: a map room dedicated to a great Harvard librarian, Justin Winsor, with one of the nation's largest map collections; a theatrical collection based on the world's largest and most important one given by Robert Gould Shaw in 1915; and Harvard's archives with over-the-centuries annals of graduates, teachers, activities—and birth records and priceless souvenirs of the College, including the original charter of 1650, and the keys, seal, and records transmitted at inaugurals to each new president. This library, completed in 1976, was named for then president-emeritus Nathan M. Pusey, gratefully remembered for his accomplishments beyond the distress of student riots.

Pusey was Harvard's first non–New Englander president. Coming to Harvard in 1953 from a college presidency in Wisconsin, Pusey defended Harvard and its faculty from Commie-hunting Senator Joseph McCarthy's attack upon it as "The Kremlin on the Charles." He was a gigantic fund raiser and, to save the Cambridge terrain, for the first time gave Harvard skyscraper buildings that we shall see.

Pusey added many women professors, advanced coeducation by experimenting in 1970–71 with fifty students from Radcliffe and fifty from Harvard integrated in six dorms, in suites at Harvard, by floor at Radcliffe. For a classical scholar he started something sensationally new in 1961, something that had the students protesting "Latin, si, Pusey, no!" He abolished diplomas in Latin and distributed them in the American tongue, English.

The magnificent entrance to Widener with its dozen Corinthian columns and broad stone steps proclaim the bountiful gifts in the spirit of John Harvard's original gift to the University library that has become, with its more than 11,000,000 volumes, the world's largest university library.

Two other great donors call for recognition. The site was mainly a gift from Matthew, the college steward, son and successor of America's first printer, Stephen Daye, and long known as the Fellows Orchard. The first building here, Gore Hall, an earlier library completed in 1841, was named after a 1776 Harvard graduate, Governor Christopher Gore, up to then the most generous of donors to the college.

Gore Hall, built of Quincy granite, was inspired by one of the glories of King's College in Cambridge, England, its chapel built in Gothic style with towers and numerous pinnacles. Indeed, two of these were saved from the demolition in 1913 and can be seen on either side of the back (south) entrance to Widener. Cambridge, on becoming a city five years after Gore Hall's completion, expressed widespread admiration by depicting Gore Hall on the city's official seal.

For scholars, libraries have always been the center of college. Gore, like its successor, was both treasure house and showplace, attracting many celebrities. It had been open only a few months when twenty-nine-year-old Charles Dickens, beloved "Boz," arrived in America for his first visit and came to see the poet Longfellow, then a young, unbearded Harvard professor.

Students lionized Dickens when, after breakfast at Longfellow's house, they walked here to visit the Yard and see Gore Hall, then, too, America's largest library. Prominent Cambridge folks were on hand and there was much excitement around "Boz" in Gore Hall, along with handshaking, before he headed back to Harvard Square and took Morse's hourly stage back to Boston.

President Lowell responded lightning-fast to Mrs. George D. Widener's offer to build a library. Despite at least two additions to Gore, including the nation's first space-saving steel stacks, Gore became increasingly inadequate. The college had been hoping for years for a donor, with Gore crammed top to bottom with books, thousands of needed volumes kept in cellars of dorms, Appleton Chapel, and as far off as Divinity Hall. In 1915 Mrs. Widener, at the new library's happy dedication, handed the key to President Lowell and the long-dispersed books were eagerly reassembed in Widener.

The collection still grew steadily and in 1928 Mrs. Widener, now married to Harvard Professor A. Hamilton Rice, again came to the rescue, funding space for 500,000 more books in the two lowest stories of the stacks.

Widener Library itself houses about a third of the university's entire collection. The other books and publications are in some 100 separate or departmental, special, or house libraries of the University. On the library's first floor, at the top of the broad stone steps, are facilities of the Union

Catalog, a researcher's dream, which identifies and brings together all the tremendous University-wide resources.

The marble staircase leads to murals by John Singer Sargent and, at the landing partway to the second floor, leads to the jewel for which the entire building is a setting: the extraordinary private collection of books, particularly rare first editions and manuscripts, made by young Harry Elkins Widener, Mrs. Widener's son, in whose memory she gave the library.

Harry Widener, 1907 graduate, had been in Europe acquiring more rarities for his collection and was returning on the "unsinkable" *Titanic* in 1912 when it struck an iceberg and sank. The rotunda off the landing leads to his private library of 3,300 volumes, a magnificent room with fireplace, lovely bookcases presenting bindings almost as remarkable as their contents, and, in display cases, exhibits that include an original Gutenberg Bible, first ever printed with movable type, which Gutenberg invented, and the 1623 First Folio edition of William Shakespeare's plays.

The library's main reading room is on the second floor. Here, too, are rows of card catalogues, the delivery desk, and entry (open only to scholars) to the literally miles of stacks on thirteen levels, five of them underground, including three underground levels of Pusey Library. Within the stack areas are alcoves, nooks, or carrels for students to study in, and for the faculty there are private study rooms both here, such as the plain one used by official Harvard historian Samuel Eliot Morison in the southeast corner of the stacks, Room 417, and on the building's top (third) floor. Little wonder that researchers and scholars come by the thousands every year from all over the world.

Tom Wolfe, the novelist, has given us a sort of snapshot of scholars who for many decades have headed for the Widener stacks. Wolfe was describing his own feelings as a student in portraying his fictional character Eugene Gant, who would "prowl the stacks . . . pulling books out of a thousand shelves and reading in them like a madman. He simply wanted to know about everything on earth. . . ."

Or we have Thornton Wilder, in Cambridge to give a series of Harvard lectures, hustling into the stacks to keep his performance on a steady factual basis. He was even seen hobbling back in after his recovery from a breakdown induced by overwork.

Before leaving the library, take time to look at three dioramas on the main floor, at either side of the staircase leading to Harry Widener's private library. They depict Cambridge in three centuries, 1677, 1775, and 1936 during the Tercentenary.

Especially notice two aspects: all the marshes and creeks that once lined the Cambridge (also the Boston) banks of the Charles River, and particularly in the 1677 diorama, the small grid of early lanes rounded on the west by the stream that once flowed out of the Yard and across Harvard Square. Our next walk will be in that grid of lanes, now streets pretty much in the original pattern devised by the founders of Cambridge.

Turn left on leaving Widener and notice, near the northwest corner of the library, a bronze plaque presenting a view of old Gore Hall.

On turning left, come to a 25-foot-high marble dragon that a provincial Chinese governor gave nearly two centuries ago to the Emperor. Harvard received the dragon as a Tercentenary gift from the Harvard alumni of China. It was erected here to be near the Harvard–Yenching Institute, now in a separate building we will see on Divinity Avenue, north of the Yard; the institute was then in Boylston Hall, the 1858 Rockport-granite structure south of Weld Hall.

Boylston Hall is a landmark in the teaching of science at Harvard. Originally, it was only two stories high. One had lecture rooms and laboratory for Harvard's first chemistry professor, Josiah Cooke, whose initial lab was the one he himself paid for in the cellar of University Hall, without gas or running water. The other floor provided lab and lecture facilities for a great anatomist, Dr. Jeffries Wyman, who trained leading medical and scientific scholars. Tourists flocked to see his anatomical collection, especially the skeleton of a prehistoric mammoth that he took to the present Peabody Museum, of which he was director.

The growing chemistry department took over all of Boylston Hall, plus recurrent additions—some underground—and a third, mansard floor added by President Eliot, former chemistry student of Professor Cooke.

Another future Harvard president, James B. Conant, a brilliant organic chemist, studied and taught in the labs of Boylston Hall, which became a world center for chemical research. By 1928, chemistry, which had been expanding into some new labs north of the Yard, was able to move into the big Mallinckrodt Laboratory we will see on Oxford Street. A remodeled, modernized Boylston Hall has become a center for modern languages and literature, German, Slavic, and Romance.

We head now along the path in front of Grays, past Matthews and Straus, to Harvard Square. The gate, a gift of the class of 1875, had to be moved 50 feet south in 1926 to provide space for Straus Hall, which, like Widener, was a gift of three sons in memory of their parents, who lost their lives in the sinking of the Titanic.

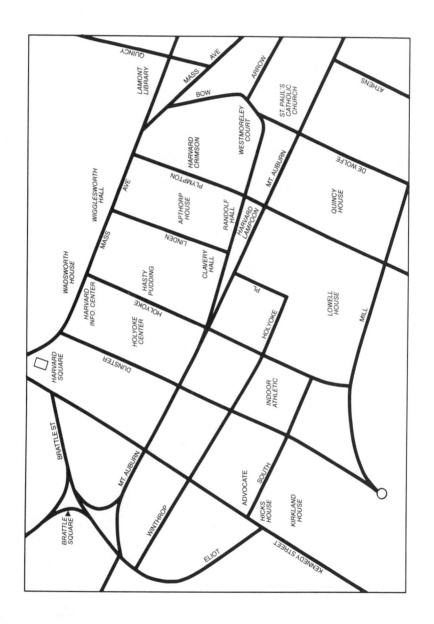

The appearance of the houses along Cambridge's small grid of eight short streets in the town's earliest years has been vividly pictured by some who saw it all develop.

Deputy Governor Thomas Dudley, the founder, who would begin building his house here in spring 1631, has told how the settlers sought to avoid mistakes made in the prior summer by newcomers to Boston.

In a letter Dudley sent early in 1631 to England to the Countess of Lincoln, whose family he had served as steward, he said an order had been adopted that in Newe Towne—Cambridge's name until springtime, 1638—"no man there shall build his chimney with wood nor cover his house with thatch." In Boston too many destructive fires had started in their wooden chimneys. Even the house of a magistrate had just gone up in flames, and he was going back to England in the *Lion*, the ship that was carrying Dudley's letter.

Two years later, in 1633, Newe Towne was visited by William Wood, a colonist, who would publish in England in the following year the first printed book describing the Puritan settlements he had seen in New England. By the time Wood came here, Dudley and the ten other families who had joined him in building their dwellings had their number increased by about 100 men, women, and children. The group was called the Braintree Company—from that part of England—who first tried settling on our own South Shore, there organized the first church when, in 1633, they were joined, as they had agreed back in England, by the renowned preacher, Reverend Thomas Hooker.

Wood was high in praise of what he saw that year. To him the small grid and its eight lanes represented "many handsome contrived streets." True, six of the lanes, as we can still see, were straight, quite in contrast with Boston's winding streets where, so legend says, the surveyors followed the tracks of wandering cows. To Wood, Newe Towne was "one of the neatest and best compacted towns in New England, having many faire structures. . . ." He found most of the inhabitants "very rich and well stored with cattell." To protect those cattle the settlers built a mile and a half of fencing, "a pallysadoe," enclosing 1,000 acres around Newe Towne to protect those cattle "from the wilde beasts."

Kennedy Street, now before us, is one of the four original north-to-south lanes along with the roughly parallel present Dunster and Holyoke Streets to our east, and to our west, curving Brattle and Eliot Streets, which formed original Creek Lane. Kennedy Street had several earlier names: Wood Street, its original name; Brighton Street because it led there; and Boylston Street. After the first bridge across the Charles River, the "Great Bridge," was built in 1663, the future Kennedy Street was for a century and a half—until the West Boston (Longfellow) and Craigie (Charles River Dam) bridges were built—the start of the eight-mile-long principal route to Boston.

We will see several reminders about John F. Kennedy along Kennedy Street. On our left is the Wursthaus at 4 Kennedy Street, now on much of the site where Dudley's son-in-law Simon and his poet wife Anne Bradstreet built in 1631. The Wursthaus ("that's bologna in German," said the genial host) was begun as a small delicatessen back in World War I by a Harvard student who gave up college so that he could have a store like his folks did in New York.

The host, and also owner, Frank Cardullo, took over in World War II and greatly enlarged the enterprise long popular with students, faculty, and public officials. He told of Kennedy eating here as a student and recalls meeting him on visits after voters had sent the young war hero to Congress and the U.S. Senate. Kennedy's favorite, said the host, was hot pastrami. On the walls are scores of photographs of luminaries and friends of the host. Kennedy's is "the biggest in the house," as Cardullo put it, signed by J.F.K. when the voters made him president.

Just a bit farther south, about mid-block on our left, a meeting in 1635 of two classmates from Emmanuel College, Cambridge University, England, tremendously changed the early history of Newe Towne and Harvard College. Here, the next dwelling to the Bradstreet's, was the home of Reverend Samuel Stone, and here, a couple of days after landing in the New World with his company of potential settlers, came Reverend Thomas Shepard, who would be credited later by Cotton Mather as the reason why "Cambridge rather than any other place was pitch'd upon to be the seat" of Harvard College.

Reverend Stone, as part of the Braintree Company, had come with his pastor, Reverend Hooker, and when Reverend Hooker founded the first church here, Reverend Stone became its teacher. By 1635 Reverend Hooker and his flock were planning to leave Newe Towne to obtain more land for their big herds of cattle. The colony had in the prior year voted them additional land, including "Little Cambridge," later Brighton, on the south side of the Charles River. This expansion still left them a feeling of being hemmed in between Watertown and Charlestown, both of whose boundaries were then much closer than now. "Little Cambridge" was not enough to hold the settlers.

All three clergymen, Hooker, Stone, and Shepard, were close friends. All were graduates of Emmanuel College and, all, as nonconformists in England, had been suspended, reprimanded, or silenced by King Charles I's formidable Archbishop William Laud, intent on hounding dissidents out of England. Soon, following their get-together at Reverend Stone's, a friendly agreement was made under which Shepard's flock purchased houses—the "many faire structures"—and land of the Braintree Company.

In the ensuing year Reverend Hooker, Reverend Stone, and about 100 colonists, with their cattle, goats, and swine, started along the old Charlestown–Watertown Path, the King's Highway, 100 miles overland to Hartford, where Reverend Hooker would become "The Father of Connecticut."

On the opposite, west side of Kennedy Street, again at about mid-block, long flourished Cambridge's most famous public house, the Blue Anchor Tavern.

For nearly the first century of its existence (1654–1737), it was located at the northeast corner of present Kennedy and Mt. Auburn Streets, which we will see shortly. In 1737 the owner (the tavern has had several) moved the Blue Anchor signboard diagonally across to the west side and soon the tavern, plus its stables and livery, was called Bradish's, after owner Ebenezer Bradish. In our Revolutionary War era it was the rendezvous of patriots. Minutemen gathered here; so too did members of the Provincial Congress who created them and, also using the old meeting house for sessions, members of the 1780 convention who drafted our precedent-setting State Constitution, dined and slept here.

Bradish's sheltered some patrons, who, at least at first, felt miserable about their accommodations: "Gentleman Johnny" Burgoyne, British general and dramatist, and his staff of officers, including six other members of Parliament and Baron von Riedesel, major general of the "Hessians," actually a contingent from Brunswick. Burgoyne and his officers found no arrangements made for them when, just a month following his surrender after the battle of Saratoga, turning point of the Revolution, he arrived in Cambridge.

A German officer called Bradish's "a gloomy hole." Burgoyne himself, who had found the bad roads en route too much for his "shattered constitution," protested to the Continental Congress of being quartered "in a dirty small miserable tavern, lodging in a bedroom together, and all the gentlemen of our suite lodging upon the floor in a chamber adjacent, a good deal worse than their servants had been used to."

Major General William Heath was sympathetic, and worried that the British might reject the surrender agreement. Local residents were more opposed to the British than the German officers, but highly appreciated the solid gold coin in which they paid their bills, even while denouncing the charges as excessive. General Heath finally moved Burgoyne to one of the best mansions in Cambridge, Apthorp House, which we will soon see.

By the time Christmas came, Burgoyne's officers had come to enjoy Bradish's as much as the local selectmen when they met to do business and, as their records show, paid in pounds, shillings, and pence for "flip and cheese," "dinners and drinks," "punch and eating." Mrs. John Winthrop, wife of the famous scientist and regular correspondent with John Adams's wife, Abigail, told of a merry and big Christmas party at Bradish's, her next-door neighbor. The British officers, she observed, seemed now to love the place, for "the British officers live in the most luxurious manner possible, rioting on the fat of the land."

In 1796 Bradish's got a new proprietor, Israel Porter, and the tavern for four decades—or until he died in 1837 at ninety-nine—was known as Porter's. Although the Fourth of July had become the number 1 holiday, commencement time at Porter's was just like the days when it was the Bay State's number 1 public festival, with the streets thronged, fancy chariots, chaises crossing the bridge, and heavy family coaches and grandees arriving at the tavern. Colonel Thomas W. Higginson, a lifelong Cantabrigian, recalled that his grandfather would engage quarters at Porter's and "keep open house with the punch bowl."

Porter's became increasingly a resort for students, for relief, some said, from dry studies. On Class Day seniors would meet at Porter's for their class dinner. In the early years, the Porcellian Club members, wearing the club badge hanging from green and white ribbons around their necks, marched here with music to do some feasting. Despite devotion to pots of steaming Indian meal, the Hasty Pudding members in their early decades shifted their Washington Day celebration and marched to Porter's for banquets. James Russell Lowell tells how President Kirkland decided to investigate why Porter's flip was so attractive to students. Kirkland came, called for a mug of it, drank it, and said:

"So, Mr. Porter, the young gentlemen come to drink your flip, do they?"

"Yes, sir—sometimes."

"Ah, well, I should think they would. Good day, Mr. Porter."

The Winthrops' house was on the northwest corner of Mt. Auburn and Kennedy Streets, with a dignified portico, shrubs, trees, and garden; a beautiful dwelling facing the old Marketplace that fifty-five years after Professor John Winthrop's death would be named, in his honor, Winthrop Square. Professor Winthrop, a great-great-grandson of Governor John Winthrop, was twice offered the presidency of Harvard but stayed with his mathematics, natural philosophy, and scientific correspondence with other great scientists, including Benjamin Franklin and Count Rumford.

All the greater men of Winthrop's day came here to visit with him: John Hancock, John Adams, James Warren. Madame Hannah Winthrop, his wife, left touching stories about the panic and plight of terrified women and weeping children, herself among them, pausing near Fresh Pond in one of her brother's houses on April 19, 1775, the day the Redcoats landed in Cambridge and Lord Percy with his forces and cannon moved right along present Kennedy Street past the Winthrop dwelling. Correspondence exchanged by pen pals Hannah Winthrop, Mercy Warren, and Abigail Adams preserves fascinating scenes of the Revolutionary era.

The nearly two-centuries-long history of the Blue Anchor Tavern began on the opposite (east) corner when Andrew Belcher, whose wife was a daughter of Deputy Governor Thomas Danforth, treasurer of Harvard College, got in 1654 a license "to sell beer and bread for the entertainment of strangers." Andrew Belcher, Jr. swapped the Blue Anchor in 1682 with his brother-in-law for a house, now a mansion and showplace on Tory Row, the Henry Vassall House at 94 Brattle Street. A year earlier, Andrew Belcher, Jr.'s son Jonathan was born here. The father would become a wealthy merchant. Son Jonathan would become governor of three colonies—Massachusetts, New Hampshire, and finally New Jersey.

On the south corner, at 44 Kennedy Street, facing Winthrop Square, is the 1906 brick-ender, home of the Fox Club, an exclusive final club founded seven years earlier as the old Greek-letter Digamma Club. Its location on Mt. Auburn Street positions it as a sort of sentinel, with the main street of Harvard College club life running currently along Mt. Auburn Street from here to the picturesque, some think whimsical, *Lampoon* "Castle" on its conspicuous mid-street triangle of land.

This stretch was part of the Old Gold Coast and most of the clubs, following the lead of the luxury apartment houses, came and built here in their heyday around the first decades of the twentieth century. The river view southward then was mostly of salt marshes. There was no Memorial Drive, no river embankment, and President Lowell had yet to fill the marshes and spread the many structures of his House Plan along the Charles River.

The House Plan, with its numerous social amenities, along with wartime and depression, brought changes and decline in the roster of clubs from the early 1900s when the Gold Coast plus the final clubs proffered a social ladder to invitees. On the west side of Winthrop Square—and we will see another example of change just a block south of us—is an imposing 1908 building, this one of red brick and gray stone, currently popular Grendel's Den at 89 Winthrop Street, but no longer—indeed not since the 1960s—ocupied by its builder, the Pi Eta Club, founded more than a century ago.

More recently the unexpected publication of the club's secret newsletter belittling women, despite an apology from its president that it was a jest that misfired, has had the historic effect of severing the all-male Harvard clubs from the College that has grown completely coeducational since women and men students first joined in classrooms during World War II. Presidents of both Radcliffe and Harvard had a decisive role in this landmark severance from these clubs, and we will come to its inception five blocks along Mt. Auburn Street, where Pi Eta moved when it combined with another club.

Grendel's Den has also been the site of a landmark legal action, this time by the U.S. Supreme Court. For more than a decade the restaurant's effort to get a liquor license was defeated by its proximity—within the state's then 500-foot limit—to a church, its neighbor immediately to its north at 100 Mt. Auburn Street, the Holy Cross Armenian Catholic Church. The Court held that the state law violated the Constitution and Grendel's Den celebrated with wine, balloons, and "We won!" signs hung on the side wall, still bearing Harvard birthmarks inserted by the Pi Eta.

The church itself is on a most historic site. John Haynes, who in 1635 would succeed Dudley as governor, arrived two years earlier with Reverend Hooker. Here he built a large two-and-a-half-story house, with a huge midhouse chimney, rooms with high wainscoting and big oak beams in the ceilings, which faced the marketplace and, with additions, stood until the mid-nineteenth century. Haynes left Cambridge with Reverend Hooker and Reverend Stone and in 1639 became the first governor of Connecticut.

The owner of the first printing press in North America, the widow of Reverend Jose Glover, a wealthy nonconformist who had died at sea en route to joining his friends in the colony, took over this dwelling with her five children, many servants, and beautiful furnishings. Two of her daughters married sons of Governor Winthrop and, a year after Henry Dunster became Harvard's first president, Dunster married the Reverend Glover's widow. Some impression of the splendor of the new Dunster household is Harvard's oldest piece of silver, "the Great Salt," given by widow Glover's brother, Richard Harris, who joined Dunster as a tutor and lived in a ground-floor chamber of then new first college hall in the Old Yard.

Young Ralph Waldo Emerson, taking his final studies in theology, knew this building well. His mother hired quarters here from the family of one of Emerson's Divinity School classmates, so that Emerson could have room to run another school for boys preparing to enter college. It was spring 1826, and Emerson was twenty-three. Among his twenty pupils was future author Richard Henry Dana, who felt Emerson was "a very pleasant instructor." Another pupil, John Holmes, a writer like his brother Oliver Wendell Holmes, said Emerson was "every inch a king in his domain," though "rather stern in his very infrequent rebukes." Emerson closed the school, which would be his last, in the fall when he was approved for preaching.

Winthrop Square land was originally allotted to Sir Richard Saltonstall to build a dwelling. But Saltonstall, who had founded Watertown at the present Gerry's Landing on the Charles, less than a mile away, went back to England early in 1631 with three of his children. And so the early proprietors designated the land "The Marketplace."

The seeds of abolition were planted nearby in the early days in Cambridge. Selectman and constable Peter Towne, a cooper by trade and son of the sexton of the first church, who lived at the south corner of Winthrop and Kennedy Streets, in 1705 gave freedom and funds to his three black slaves and arranged that no part of his estate would go to a cousin unless the cousin also would give his slave money and freedom.

Across Kennedy Street from the park at the southeast corner of Winthrop Street was, for four decades, the dwelling of Harvard's first Hebrew professor, Judah Monis. Monis, born in Italy and famed as a Hebrew scholar, came to Boston in 1720 and became a close friend of Reverend Increase Mather and President John Leverett. In that same year Harvard gave Monis the first M.A. degree awarded to a Jew. The College had long sought a qualified Hebrew teacher and in 1722, just after he was baptized in the College hall, he began teaching at the College. In 1735 he published a Hebrew grammar, the first Hebrew book published in America.

For three unhappy weeks, Baron von Riedesel, his wife, and their three little girls, after leaving the Blue Anchor Tavern, lived here "sleeping on straw in one room and a garret," with servants living in passageways. Personal belongings they deposited on the Common, on arrival in Cambridge, were stolen. At last they were happily shifted to an abandoned Brattle Street mansion, we will see, though to make it habitable they had to buy everything from tables and chairs to beds and cooking utensils.

The other former clubhouse, mentioned above, is the three-story gambrel, now headquarters of the Harvard Athletic Department at the northeast corner of South Street. It was built in 1929 as a fraternity house, for Sigma Alpha Epsilon, and was called Shannon Hall. The College bought it in 1942. Work-study students come steadily here for paychecks for their help in running the University's many athletic facilities. Staff in the office handle scheduling of games and recreation of all sorts: football, basketball, hockey to women's lacrosse, yoga to squash, karate to scuba diving. For tickets the place to go is Harvard Hall basement office.

South Street, where we will turn left, was the southernmost lane on the small grid of Newe Towne's original street plan. Just a few feet south of us, the stream that started in the old Yard and curved through Eliot Street shot east across present Kennedy Street and along the far side of South Street. There were salt marshes—called the Ox Marsh—beyond South Street all the way to the river. South Street quite naturally was called Marsh Lane. A causeway, which would be the lower part of the present Kennedy Street that we will visit later, was built from here to the "Great Bridge" when it was raised in 1663 to span the river and replace the ferry.

The Son of Liberty who built the 1762 three-story gambrel now standing behind the white picket and old granite post-and-rail fences at the south corner of South Street, John Hicks, grabbed his musket on the fateful night when William Dawes galloped through Cambridge shouting alarm. Hicks was actually "an exempt" because of his age. He was fifty, father of ten children, and one of these sons would be a regimental surgeon in the war then beginning.

A little more than a year earlier Hicks had joined in the Boston Tea Party, helping to dump those heavy chests into Boston harbor. When he did not come home on the afternoon of April 19, 1775, his wife sent their fourteen-year-old son to find him, and he did. Hicks's body was by the roadside near Watson's Corner, a good mile north of Harvard Square. He, and other patriots killed there, had formed behind a barricade of empty casks in a blacksmith's yard to fight the retreating Redcoats, but were surprised from their rear by British flankers.

This Hicks house was one of the houses used as a headquarters during the 1775–76 seige of Boston by "Old Put"—General Israel Putnam—when it used to stand a block away. It was moved here in 1930 to contribute ground for the big brick Indoor Athletic Building just ahead of us, which President Lowell built as part of his great House Plan. Since then, Hicks House has provided a genuine eighteenth-century setting for the library of Kirkland House, with which it is connected on its south side by a covered passage.

The two-story gray clapboard with white trim on our left at 21 South Street, as the winged-steed seal on the pediment proclaims, is the *Harvard*

Advocate, a student periodical founded in 1866, the College's oldest extant literary publication. Though now it is associated with famous writers, it was nearly stillborn.

It first appeared as the *Collegian* but was suppressed by the faculty for disparaging compulsory prayer in College chapel. It reappeared as *The Advocate*, and its staff has managed for well over a century to avoid threatened expulsion, though, as author Norman Mailer, an entranced staffer while in college, has said, its good reviews, essays, short stories, and poems have barely spared it from immersion in what he called a "cauldron of debt."

In Mailer's college years *The Advocate* had five small rooms on the third floor over some stores at 40 Bow Street, directly across the street from a one-time rival, the *Lampoon*. To Mailer, whose World War II experience was background for his novel *The Naked and the Dead,* which brought him fame at age twenty-five, happy life on *The Advocate* was, as he observed it, "probably what I enjoyed most about Harvard."

Its editors have ranged from future professors like George Lyman Kittredge to writers who, like Mailer, would be famous. *The Advocate* printed in one issue three poems of E. E. Cummings when he was a sophomore. It printed the early poems of Edwin Arlington Robinson, of T. S. Eliot, who became an *Advocate* editor, too, and poems of his College mate Conrad Aiken. And in the late 1950s it published the writings of Radcliffe students, who then joined in getting out *The Advocate*.

NEWE TOWNE'S "MAIN STREET"

On our right, as we walk now to what was the main street of Newe Towne, the present Dunster Street, is the red brick new section added during the House Plan building in 1930–31 to form Kirkland House. On arriving at Dunster Street we have ahead of us on our left the Indoor Athletic Building (students call it the I.A.B.), and on our right the open space called the Winthrop Triangle. Around it, or just off it, are the three original 1913–14 freshman dorms built by President Lowell as an initial step he hoped, once he could get funding, would lead, as they did in 1930–31, to his new House Plan.

Those pre–World War I days saw a small percentage of the student classes living, like cream on the milk, in the luxury of Gold Coast private apartments and then, in larger numbers, indulging in the comforts, social events, and exclusiveness of their secret clubs. Lowell's aim in his House Plan was to democratize and mingle, not split, the student body, and thereby improve the educational community.

Diagonally across the open space are two of these 1914 freshman dorms, Standish Hall and, to its immediate east, Gore Hall, combined in 1930 to form Winthrop House. The third of these pioneer freshman dorms is on our right, the 1914 Smith Halls, which in 1930 became the main quadrangle of Kirkland House. We will see more of them when we walk along the Charles River and lower Kennedy Street.

The founder of Cambridge, Thomas Dudley, built his "great house"— as Governor Winthrop described it—on our left at the west corner of South and Dunster Streets. As we will presently see, just about all the basic community needs of the pioneer town were provided by the buildings along the present Dunster Street. Its name then, as might be expected, was Water Street. The stream from the Eliot Street direction curved at this corner, flowed southward past the present Kirkland House, and, just to the west side of the present Winthrop House, flowed on into the river.

About the first community project in Newe Towne, after laying out the street grid, was to have this creek dredged 12 feet deep and widened to 7 feet so that larger craft could come to the town wharf on the east bank of the creek just forward of Kirkland House. This spot also became in 1635 the ferry landing for the passage across the river, the regular charge a penny, but only half that on weekly lecture day in the meeting house.

The College, as it grew, had its own wharf on this creek and a legend-like college sloop, named *Harvard*, which went down East to Maine to fetch wood for the fireplaces in the old Yard. The poet Lowell said that wood "gave to winter life at Harvard a crackle and cheerfulness" the warmer anthracite could not provide.

The sloop's delightful passages came abruptly to an end in the later 1820s when the great navigator and mathematician Nathaniel Bowditch joined the Corporation. Bowditch was a penny-pincher and the Common-wealth had just about ceased grants of money to the College. To Bowditch the old sloop was too costly; indeed, he even managed to enforce so many (probably unavoidable) cuts that a great president like John Kirkland, for whom Kirkland House was named, handed in his resignation.

Dudley, who came to live here in 1631, stayed until he completed his 1634–35 term as governor, then, along with his kin living nearby and friends, went off to live in Ipswich, of which John Winthrop, Jr. was the founder. In 1650 during one of his many subsequent terms as governor of the Bay Colony, Dudley signed the Harvard Charter. It was in this house—rather than Simon Bradstreet's—that later lived the first treasurer of Harvard, Herbert Pelham, before he went back to England in 1649. On a walk in Cambridgeport, we will see an important crossroads long called for him, its owner, Pelham's Island.

On the opposite corner from Dudley's house, where we now see the I.A.B., was the home of John Bridge, the quintessential Puritan whose bronze statue we saw on the Common. He served as deacon, selectman, in the General Court, and, not least, supervised Cambridge's first public school, established a block from here in 1635.

The earlier site of John Hicks's house was the northwest corner of the I.A.B. The high, round top windows mark the two floors required for the large swimming pool used by the students. On the third floor are facilities for wrestling, fencing, boxing, special exercises, and on the top floor a gym plus three courts for volleyball and basketball.

After crossing Winthrop Street we have a fine view, to our right, of the

Lowell House Tower looking like a delightful twin of Independence Hall in Philadelphia.

The Dunster Street block just ahead of us was the center of Newe Towne's community life, with its first ordinary (public house) and First Meeting House. Looking on, from the opposite, east side, were prominent citizens. America's first bookseller, before he shifted to Boston in 1645, had his dwelling at the northeast corner of Winthrop and Dunster. Hezekiah Usher was the agent for the London sponsors of Samuel Green, the elder, printing the Indian Bible, psalter, and catechism of Reverend John Eliot in the Indian College building in the old Yard.

Just north of Usher's house, at midblock, was the dwelling of Cambridge's first schoolmaster, Elijah Corlet. A graduate of Oxford, Corlet ran "the faire grammar schoole" (whose site we will presently see on Holyoke Street) from 1642 until his death in 1688. Though the authoritative "New Englands First Fruits" of 1643 highly praised Corlet for his "abilities, dexterity and painfulnesse in teaching," he was found to be so "very poor" in his old age that the General Court voted to give him 500 acres "where he can find it." He finally did—miles away in Worcester County!

The lawsuit won by Grendel's Den is brought to mind by the dwelling that once stood at the northwest corner of Winthrop and Dunster where we now see, at 53 Dunster, the mid-nineteenth-century structure currently the residence of the Master of Harvard's scattered facility for commuting students, Dudley House.

Harvard College's first steward, Thomas Chesholme, a tailor by trade, bought the large house that stood here in 1635 and became deacon of the First Meeting House, his immediate neighbor, at the northeast corner of this block where we now see the D. U. Clubhouse, 45 Dunster Street. In the following year, Chesholme was licensed to "keep a house of entertainment." By 1640 Chesholme was allowed "to draw wine"—right beside the church. Eventually, just like Governor Dudley's "Great House," Chesholme's former tavern went up in flames.

Plainness characterized the meeting house built here in 1632, with its simple lectern, rows of benches, the faithful summoned by drumbeat, and, some years later, by a church bell. Reverend Thomas Hooker, as he had agreed back in England, arrived in the following year to take care of his flock with Reverend Stone as teacher. A few months before they left for Hartford, their recently arrived friend, thirty-year-old Reverend Thomas Shepard, a splendid preacher, began here his ministry in February 1636, with Governor Winthrop, as Winthrop recorded, present along with Reverend John Cotton, who came out from Boston to extend the right hand of fellowship.

Events, crucial in the development of the Bay Colony, many of them right here in the Meeting House, followed fast after Winthrop defeated young Vane in the spring 1637 election by the oak tree on the Common. Little more than a week later came victory at Mystic and an end of the Pequot War.

In August the clergy of the New England colonies held their first synod here and, with Anne Hutchinson and her followers in mind, condemned "erroneous opinions." In November a newly elected General Court, dominated by orthodox Puritans, with Governor Winthrop presiding, met in the Meeting House, first banishing Anne's brother-in-law, Reverend John Wheelwright, and then banishing Anne.

Anne Hutchinson on trial has left an imperishable memory of a valiant woman. Mother of fifteen children, again pregnant, she was permitted to sit in a chair during the proceedings. Herself the daughter of a minister, she had been a parishioner of Reverend Cotton, a nonconformist, and followed him to America. She held the liberal views of her father, who had been imprisoned for attacking the bishops' inflexible orthodoxy. She was against formalism in the church.

Even Governor Winthrop, again presiding, admired "her ready wit and bold spirit"; still he voted that Anne be banished, being profoundly concerned about the division she was creating in the colony and "the danger of her course amongst us." She would flee to Rhode Island and on to New York, where she and all but one of her children would be killed by Indians.

Reverend John Harvard came here to the meeting house on that November 2, 1637 when the newly elected General Court assembled. He had been only five months in America, was a clergyman in Charlestown, and was seeking admission as a freeman of the colony. He was admitted on that day and may have even attended later proceedings before the court which in that same November, with war over and Anne banished, again took action on creating a college, ordering on November 15th that the college "be at Newe Towne." On the following May 2 it was ordered that Newe Towne "be called Cambridge." Four months later, John Harvard, only thirty years old, passed away.

The D.U. Club, formed in 1881 as the Delta Upsilon Fraternity, has long been known for staging old Elizabethan dramas in the springtime. In its earlier clubhouse on Harvard Street, still standing, it had the help of Professor George Baker, of "47 Workshop" fame, in these productions. To carry out its original aim of "furthering good fellowship," the club, in its present 1930 home, has a fine library, good bar and dining room, big upstairs hall, and garden with tables to entertain guests. It has always sought to win top scholars as members, a large number of whom have been Phi Beta Kappa.

Before turning right at Mt. Auburn Street we can get a good impression of how Dunster Street appeared for many years just ahead of us. Large carbarns were along most of both sides to house the successive varieties of vehicles that transported Cantabrigians to and from Boston. Notice the three arches in the corner building just across the street at 79 Mt. Auburn. When they were not so bricked in, their opening accommodated both cars and horses for a forerunner company of the present "T."

Some Gold Coast buildings, of course, in the final years of the nineteenth century, replaced part of the carbarns and livery stables. One of these was the birthplace of Dudley House, which finally made commuting students feel part of the growing community. This was Dunster Hall, built privately in 1897 about midway up the east side of Dunster Street.

Bought by Harvard in 1918, it was renamed Dudley House in 1930 to shift the name of Harvard's first president to the new House Plan's Dunster House on the Charles River. President Conant, soon after taking office, had eating, commons, and social facilities provided—all of which are currently more amply furnished in Lehman Hall, in the old Yard, where they were moved when Dudley House was demolished to make space for Holyoke Center.

This southeast corner of Dunster and Mt. Auburn, on our right, is an intellectual summit of the College community, with the Signet Club at 46 Dunster and its neighbor, the Society of Fellows, a creation of President Lowell, in the small 1839 house at 78 Mt. Auburn. Neither is a final club.

The Signet's two-story clubhouse goes back to 1820. It bought the building in 1902, had it refitted, and put the Signet's motto carved in wood over the entry: some words of Plato, "Work and ply the Muses." Besides the two Roosevelts already mentioned, T.R. and F.D.R., the club has had Harvard presidents and a long list of distinguished professors and graduates, Nobel laureates, and Pulitzer winners in its membership since it was founded in 1870. President Conant avowed that his interests were more broadened by the "highly sophisticated level" of conversation around the Signet's luncheon table than by all the lectures in the College courses that he took.

The Signet has annual dinners, Christmas dinners, and strawberry nights, but the members have mostly praised the regular Signet luncheons and the enjoyment of listening to or talking with celebrities—William James, George Santayana—whose poem to Signet was mounted in the library on the club's centennial—newsman Joe Alsop, Samuel Eliot Morison, Robert Frost, Archibald MacLeish, governors, judges. The list could go on and on. David McCord, poet, long editor of the *Harvard Alumni Bulletin*, thought that no other college organization in the nation could produce so distinguished a membership list as Signet. To John Mason Brown the Signet was Harvard's "Conversational Paradise."

Back in Newe Towne days the Signet site was occupied by the dwelling of Reverend Samuel Dudley, a son of Governor Thomas Dudley, who married Governor Winthrop's daughter, Mary.

Membership in the Society of Fellows, as in the Signet, is based on merit. Fellowship members have won as many as four Nobel prizes in a single year. President Lowell, who gave openhandedly to the University, made endowment of this fellowship his last major gift. Eight fellows are chosen each year from literally the most brilliant and promising students in the world. They cannot personally apply; instead they must be nominated.

Those who remain for the final round come here in the lovely old parlor, with its lounges and fireplace, at 78 Mt. Auburn, for the screening that decides the eight winners. This building, the Society's headquarters, has offices and workshops for the members, though, as we will see, the Fellowship's central gathering place is off M entry in Eliot House by the river, where the Fellows and their faculty advisers meet for their weekly supper of fine food and fine wine. There are no speeches. Conversation, ranging illimitably, inspires, as Lowell hoped, ever greater benefits to mankind.

TO WADSWORTH HOUSE AND ITS OLD NEIGHBORS

Ten-story, city block-size Holyoke Center, directly across Mt. Auburn Street from the Society of Fellows, brings us to the era of Harvard's first high-rise structures, undertaken by President Pusey because the growth of the University exceeded the availability of land. Holyoke Center, completed in 1966, was conceived by an architectural group of the dean of Harvard Graduate School of Design, Jose Luis Sert, whose associates were then building dormitory towers more than double this height by the Charles River.

The midblock, south entry to Holyoke Center leads to the arcade, a pleasant walkway, which connects the University health services on the south end of the center, 75 Mt. Auburn Street, with the many University administrative offices on the north end, 1350 Massachusetts Avenue. In earlier years students in need of health services had to make their way for about a mile out Mt. Auburn Street to Stillman Infirmary, opened in 1901, near the city's Mt. Auburn Hospital. Now everything is handy here for students, including the Stillman beds, emergency medical, dental, and counseling services, and even an underground garage for parking.

A short way along the arcade is the pharmacy, with its posted promise to fill prescriptions in seven minutes, and low prices, including "contraceptive products at much less than retail prices." Reverend Edward Holyoke, for whom the center was named, the seventy-five-year-old president who led the battle to save nearby dorms when old Harvard Hall went up in flames, would certainly think times have changed. But then, Reverend Holyoke, who served longer than any other president save Eliot, was quite a liberal for his times, which were also packed with far-reaching changes of all sorts.

A brief scan of the listings, at either bank of elevators, of all the activities in Holyoke Center is impressive. From the mail room in the basement to news-gathering on the top floor, they give directions on where to pay College bills, raise loans, catch up with University planning, personnel, purchasing, registration, and even raising multimillion-dollar Harvard Funds.

Even more impressive is taking the elevator to the Penthouse, a conference room, number 1000, on the top floor, to get matchless views of

Cambridge. The river view is breathtaking—straight across to central Baker Library in the Business School, the panorama takes in, from left to right, a downriver prospect of the bridges spanning the Charles to Soldiers Field, and closer in the great tower of Lowell House with its gilded weathervane.

The arcade is named for one of the University's most foresighted and generous benefactors, Edward W. Forbes, long the director of the University's art collection, who enriched it with great original paintings and sculpture. Forbes and his friends, early in this century, before the 1910 Charles River Dam stabilized the water at high-tide level, purchased many acres, from Mt. Auburn Street's Gold Coast to the shore, scattered houses, mud flats, and salt marshes, so that the area would be available to the College for an expanded Yard. The Plaza ahead, as well as the arcade, is also a memorial to Forbes.

Just before we come to the Plaza there used to be, in pioneer Cambridge years, a small body of water, called the Town Pond, where townsfolk watered their cattle.

On our right, among the bookstores and shops and just off the arcade, is the Harvard Information Center. Drop in; there are up-to-the-moment pamphlets and booklets on University doings, Harvard and Radcliffe maps gratis, and in an adjoining section tickets for sale to student productions and a chance to see a large diorama of Harvard University (1976), which used to be in Radcliffe's Byerly Hall, now used as an admissions office for both Harvard and Radcliffe. Those student productions and entertainments are often staged in the dining common and other rooms of the University dormitories.

Forbes Plaza, with its tables, seats, and raised and railed part, but particularly the inviting open area, is a popular gathering place, meetingplace, and showplace for street performers, musicians, break dancers, and acrobats. Buildings, right to the sidewalk edge, long occupied this north side of Holyoke Center.

On the east half of the Plaza, to the corner of Holyoke Street, was old Holyoke House, a five-story red brick built in 1870 by President Eliot as student housing with retail stores on the street level. On the west side were two three-and-a-half-story buildings, first built in 1854 and called Little's Block. Poet T. S. Eliot lived in old Holyoke House in his junior year. The five seniors who formed Harvard's Glee Club in 1858 held their first meeting in old Holyoke House in the room over the corner grocery.

George Santayana gave Little's Block quite a boost when, compared with the way President Eliot found dorms in the Yard, Santayana observed that Little's Block actually had "a bathroom on each floor." Most likely, though, the facility most associated with Little's was "Widow Nolen's," or simply "The Widow's." This was a cramming service set up by a summa cum laude 1884 graduate, William Nolen, to help casual students assure themselves of passing college exams by eleventh-hour prepping and shrewd analysis of prior exams. This practice of permitting short cuts to diplomas was finally done in by the faculty in the late 1930s.

As we have seen, in the earliest years of Cambridge there was located on this site the homestead of William Bordman and family who, from father to son to grandson, served Harvard as its steward for a century and a half, and served the town as town clerk and other officials for more than fourscore years. The Bordmans became one of the largest Cambridge land owners, with more than 100 acres in East Cambridge.

A granddaughter of William Bordman, raised in this homestead, married Reverend Benjamin Wadsworth, who, as Harvard president, was the first to live across the street (1726–27), in Wadsworth House, one of the city's most historic buildings. In fact, President Wadsworth wrote, he and his wife Ruth, with winter coming, moved in when the house, now Harvard's second oldest, "was not half finished within."

The building is most of all associated with General George Washington. He slept here for a dozen nights after he arrived on July 2, 1775 to take command of our Revolutionary forces. In the living room, just to the left on entering the front door, between the two windows on the west wall, is a print likeness of Washington by Gilbert Stuart and, on the opposite wall, a copy of the Harvard honorary degree given the General, signed by President Langdon and five fellows, including Professor John Winthrop.

Across the corridor is a conference room where General Washington, as he indicated in his letters, had troubled moments, enduring sleepless nights as he and his staff tackled monumental difficulties and shortages. After Washington moved his headquarters to Brattle Street, the commissary, constantly beset by food problems of a growing army, took over Wadsworth House as well as Harvard Hall.

Here Harvard College commenced in the first dwelling on this site, the house of an original Newe Towne settler, William Peyntree, who had left for Hartford with his neighbor, Reverend Thomas Hooker. In summer 1638, Harvard's first principal, Nathaniel Eaton, began teaching nine students living with him, his wife, his children, and his servants. Despite Eaton's seeming fine credentials the College was shut down a year later because Eaton, basically, was a scoundrel.

Eaton was described later, by one of his students, as "fitter to be master of a house of correction than an instructor of Christian youth." Eaton had come over with a much older brother, a noted man, who would become a founding governor in Connecticut. He had also come on the same vessel with Reverend John Harvard, a college mate at Cambridge University. Though seemingly friends, their characters were profoundly different.

Neighbors of Eaton's, in summer 1639, including Reverend Thomas Shepard, who had succeeded Reverend Hooker in the parsonage immediately east of the Peyntree House, came running when they heard screams. Eaton had got into an argument with his new assistant and was repeatedly cudgeling him, as Governor John Winthrop described it, with a "walnut tree plant big enough to kill a horse." Eaton had the gall to press charges against his victim.

The magistrates, however, found Eaton guilty of "cruell and barbaros beating" and fired him. Students testified about beatings they had suffered and especially about the stingy, miserable food served them in Peyntree House. Mistress Eaton, saying she now felt shame, admitted that her servants served mackerel "with guts in them and goat's dung in their hasty pudding," and bread and beer were denied students "betwixt meals." Food problems at Harvard certainly got an early start.

Eaton's friendship with John Harvard was, however, a blessing for the College. Eaton had barely started his classes in Peyntree House when, after making a last-minute oral will giving the College his library and half his estate, John Harvard passed away. His largesse was apparently influenced by the association with Eaton, for it is not known if John Harvard ever had time to visit the infant College.

After Eaton fled to Virginia it was found that he had left big debts and had made off with some of John Harvard's bequest. His wife and all but their eldest son perished when the ship they were taking to join Eaton was lost at sea. Eaton would finally die in debtor's prison in London. The son left behind was generously reared by Harvard's first steward, Deacon Chesholme, in Newe Towne's first tavern by the Meeting House site we visited.

College simply came to a halt for a full year. To revive it, thirty-year-old Reverend Henry Dunster was named president in summer 1640, only three weeks after arriving in the New World. He took over Peyntree House, got back the students, completed construction of the Old College, and in it held the first commencement, in 1642. Meantime, roughly a year after his taking over, he married Reverend Jose Glover's widow and lived in the luxuriously furnished mansion she had purchased overlooking the present Winthrop Square.

Beside Peyntree House and the Hooker-Shepard House immediately to its east there was only one other house, standing also with its cowyard in back, in Dunster's era on the Yard side of the present Massachusetts Avenue. This dwelling, directly west of Peyntree, was left by the town constable when he departed with Hooker. Dunster obtained it in 1652 as an additional dorm for the growing College and, after its then owner, Edward Goffe, it was called Goffe's College.

A tale about Dunster and a neighbor shows how different his disposition was from Eaton's. Across the road on the site of old Holyoke House lived Sister Bradish, grandmother of the Bradish who would run the Blue Anchor Tavern.

When complaints were made about her, Dunster wrote to the Court in her defense, saying she should "bee encouraged . . . in her present calling for baking of bread and brewing and selling of penny bear, without which she cannot continue to bake." Further, he said, she was really "promoting of the weal publick," observing all orders, and students were not "unseasonably spending their time and parents' estate," paying "at any time above a penny a man nor above two shillings in a quarter of a year."

Reverend Thomas Shepard, renowned preacher whose voice, said Cotton Mather, was "a silver trumpet," took over the parsonage that had been built in 1633 for Reverend Hooker. Relations were most cordial; indeed Reverend Hooker's eldest daughter became Shepard's wife. Shepard lived here during all thirteen years of his ministry in the First Meeting House in Dunster Street. Shepard was an orthodox Puritan, was present at Anne Hutchinson's trial in his church, and thought her guilty of "gross and fundamental errors."

A few days later in that November 1637, Newe Towne was chosen for the College seat "rather than any other place," said Mather, "in respect to the enlightening and powerful ministry of Mr. Shepard."

The three units of the present Wigglesworth Hall stretching between Wadsworth House and Lamont Library, with eleven entries facing the Yard and four gates between or through these dormitories, mark the completion, in 1931, of President Lowell's plan to cloister the Yard. The Hall takes its name from two of Reverend Shepard's successors in his parsonage, which stood partially on the site of the Wigglesworth unit beside Wadsworth House and the McKean Gate. This gate, as two boar heads under *Veritas* at the tip of the arch both streetside and Yardside indicate, honors Reverend Joseph McKean, founder of the donor of the gate, the Porcellian Club.

Reverend Edward Wigglesworth held Harvard's first endowed professorship, a chair of divinity created in 1721 through the bounty of the Hollis family. Both he and his son, his namesake who followed him in this Hollis chair, lived here, as had President John Leverett, who had appointed the father. Leverett's presidency saw the College in transition from orthodox Puritanism to Unitarianism and liberalism, changes strongly advanced by Leverett and the Wigglesworths.

When General Washington arrived at Wadsworth House it had coach house and stables in the rear, and in the front a lovely "lilac-filled front courtyard," cut off when the street was widened and tracks installed for streetcars. A half dozen presidents following Wadsworth lived here. His immediate successor, President Edward Holyoke, called this home for thirty-two years. President John Kirkland, who was a friend of Ralph Waldo Emerson's deceased father, had young Emerson as a "freshman orderly." Kirkland's study was in an upstairs rear room just above the lodgings of fourteen-year-old Emerson and Kirkland's nephew. A rap on the ceiling from upstairs brought young Emerson promptly.

"Old Quin" is also remembered because of his five daughters—quite an attraction—who lived here, too, and left diaries. Few, if any, houses in Cambridge have had so many famous guests, including U.S. presidents. The girls, dining in a back parlor where the band played, told of over-hearing the talk and laughter of important visitors and guests at beautiful spreads or banquets in the front parlor—and afterward, coming in to enjoy the ice cream and fruits still on the table. One daughter, Eliza, helped her father write his celebrated history of the College, and all of them pitched in at commencement, tying degrees with blue ribbons.

Edward Everett, the orator, was the last president to live here, for him an experience in misery for three years between his being Bay State governor and U.S. senator. His dignified bearing seemed to encourage College pranksters, one holding cock fights in his dormitory, another staging midnight parties for some "females." Everett likened the presidency to being "the sub-master of an ill-disciplined school."

Henry Adams, the writer, Mrs. Everett's nephew, seemed to have shared his uncle's sentiments about "the factory of the Muses." He put it plainly in his *Education of Henry Adams;* he said he "detested school" though he liked the lectures, in particular those of naturalist Louis Agassiz.

When Henry Adams came back to this country after serving as secretary to his father, our Civil War ambassador to Great Britain, President Eliot offered Henry an assistant professorship teaching medieval history. Adams came to live in Wadsworth House, which had become a boarding house. He recalled, in a talk with Eliot, his first visit to his aunt and uncle when he was nine years of age, and that he was now renting rooms that had been their drawing room and kitchen. It was Adams's custom to assemble his students here for discussions.

Wadsworth House by 1871 was no longer for rent. The Harvard bursar, equivalent of the old stewards, took over the first floor and the College printer the second. After compulsory daily prayer ended in 1866, a preacher's room was provided in Wadsworth House for the five preachers on the board to meet with the students.

Currently Wadsworth House is alumni terrain, a center for handling alumni activities, keeping alumni records, coordinating some 125 Harvard Clubs worldwide, and holding delightful receptions in the drawing room. The poet David McCord for nearly four decades handled alumni doings, especially as editor of the magazine. From his office in Wadsworth, his facile pen, in letters and brochures, has kept contributions flowing into Harvard, and, for the classes after 1976, the Harvard–Radcliffe Fund he directed to keep abreast of the needs of the University.

PORCELLIAN, PUDDING, AND ALONG HOLYOKE STREET

Take notice of two buildings on the south side of Massachusetts Avenue before we walk down Holyoke Street.

Directly across the avenue from the McKean Gate is the Porcellian Club, the four-story brown brick at 1324 Massachusetts Avenue, with its Palladian window on the second floor and dormered top floor. In the building just left of the clubhouse is the close-to-legendary Leavitt & Peirce smoke shop at 1316 Massachusetts Avenue.

Tobacco displays, gridiron heroes, Harvard greats in the store's windows are sure-fire clues to the socializing and clublike perks students, faculty, and many celebrities have enjoyed here since the days when the student body was forbidden to smoke in public. In their rooms there was no taboo. Their favorite, still for sale, has long been L & P's fragrant "Cake Box Mixture." A friend of those who began the store in the 1883 horsecar years, the well-known tobacconist David P. Ehrlich, took over after World War I.

Among their many fans over the years have been discerning Lucius Beebe, Bernard De Voto, historian Samuel Eliot Morison, and "Copey," too. There has been a poem from Robert Hillyer and praise from John Updike. The place gave the clubless a club, but now the upstairs billiard table and the easy leather chairs nearby are gone. Still there's the ancient cigar-store Indian, pipes of all sorts from carved meershaums to clay churchwardens, and scents galore.

The Porcellian Club, founded in 1791, is outranked in continuous life at Harvard only by the scholarly society, Phi Beta Kappa. The club first settled on this site in 1833 and in 1890 decided to replace those quarters with this present one. When future clergyman-professor McKean started in college in 1789 there was a dining society, "the Argonauts," which he joined. He became the founder of the present Porcellian, when, entertaining his fellow Argonauts, he put on a showy meal of a roasted young pig. His new club was promptly called "the Pig Club," but soon tried "The Gentleman's Society" before settling on its present name in 1794.

In the early days the club members marched to nearby oases for their sumptuous, merry fare, to long-gone Moore's Tavern north of the Yard, and on the south side, the Blue Anchor. Sociability was the foremost aim but a fine library was assembled, now in the present, lavishly furnished quarters along with such amenities as a billiard room, lounge, and huge dining room. Social position and wealth have accented the club's choice of members, and in 1983 the Porcellian finally became the last of the "finals" to include a black member.

The Porcellian's private blue book has included social names from Appleton to Saltonstall, two Jerome Napoleon Bonapartes of Baltimore, Agassizes, Lodges, some professors, some authors, William H. Prescott, Richard Henry Dana, Owen Wister. Future President F. D. Roosevelt was unhappy that he was not invited. Earlier, future President T.R. had been; and the tale is often told of how, in letting the German Emperor know of daughter Alice's coming marriage, T.R. emphasized that both he and the groom, future national Speaker Nicholas Longworth, were members of the Porcellian.

The present Holyoke Street, first called Crooked Lane, was the easternmost in Newe Towne's small grid of streets. The name Crooked came from the lane following partway a stream that wiggled southward to the river from the Town Pond. A glance down Holyoke Street shows that the twists have all been removed.

The current Yenching Chinese Cuisine, on the corner beside the Porcellian on our left, is a vivid mark of the internationalizing in recent years of this area. University Book Store, once on this site, was owned in 1849 by famous bookman John Bartlett, who began in 1833 as a clerk when he was sixteen and rose to be the proprietor. He got out the well-known *Bartlett's Familiar Quotations*. Bookselling has played since early times a steady part in College life. Nowadays roughly two dozen bookstores, of all varieties, all fascinating, lie within a block or two of the south and southwest edge of the Yard.

At 12 Holyoke we come to one of Harvard's best-known clubs, the venerable and liberal Hasty Pudding. "Upstairs at the Pudding," as the sign in the front tells, offers both men and women an opportunity to enjoy the large, attractive top-floor club dining facilities since 1982 when hostess and chef, the owners, took over this service as well as catering meals to the

Pudding's members. The popularity and age of the Pudding are attested by another sign on the landing outside the second-floor lounge on the way up. On it are pictures of five Pudding members—John Adams, John Quincy Adams, Theodore Roosevelt, Franklin D. Roosevelt, John F. Kennedy—captioned "From the Pudding to the Presidency."

The Pudding, founded in 1795, was joined in 1924 by the even older "Institute of 1770," and is sometimes called the nation's oldest college club. General George Washington was still president of the United States and the Pudding founders met on the eve of his birthday to honor him. Meetings, in members' rooms, had the joy of savoring steaming Indian pudding spreading its aroma from the fireplace.

By 1844 the club's entertainment shifted to the theatrical, staging a junior's *Bombastes Furioso*. This innovation led on in 1882, to national fame when the club played *Dido & Aeneas,* an operetta written by Owen Wister, then a senior. Performances of it in Boston, New York, and Philadelphia followed, and the custom of the Pudding's annual musical burlesques was established.

Theatrical shingles recalling the annual shows adorn the club walls. The "Institute of 1770," formed for the "practise of oratory," went on also to have its shows, and so the combination of the clubs was natural. The Institute brought with it an inner group called the D.K.E. or "Dickie," composed of the first grouping of sophomores selected annually, but best known for its rugged initiations.

The present clubhouse was built by the Pudding membership in 1888. Many stars of Hollywood, Broadway, and television have come to the club's impressive theatre for the annual show and presentation of miniature Hasty Pudding pots to those the club picks as the man or woman of the year, accompanied, of course, by a far-from-quiet street parade.

Apley Court, the five-story building next on our left at 16 Holyoke, was built a decade after its neighbor, the Pudding. It was put up for Gold Coast devotees, and here T. S. Eliot, who changed quarters along this Coast in each of his college years, lived as graduate student before leaving for Europe, where he would spend most of his life. Harvard purchased Apley Court just after World War I, and it was later used for Dudley

House nonresident students and tutors as well as administration. The last was shifted to Lehman Hall in 1964.

Directly across the street we can see an incised stone in the sidewalk locating the site of Cambridge's first schoolhouse, and also where printing was first done in North America. Wealthy widow Glover, soon to be the bride of Harvard's first president, beside the Governor Haynes mansion, bought the dwelling here of man who had been ordered out of the colony after being punished at the whipping post and having his ears cropped.

James Luxford, a forger, had felt that the ocean was wide enough to conceal the fact that he had left a wife in England when he took another here. He had to sell his house to pay his fine. Governor Winthrop remarked in March 1639, "a printing house was begun" by Stephen Daye. Here it continued until President Dunster moved the "great presse" into his new presidential house, where Massachusetts Hall now stands.

This former Luxford House, with the help of President Dunster, who gave some land, too, became the first schoolhouse, probably (the date is uncertain) in 1642. "New Englands First Fruits," printed in England in the following year, had the highest praise for the schoolmaster, mentioning him in the distinguished company of Dunster and John Harvard. Master Elijah Corlet, it said, ran his school fitting "young schollars" to be received "into the colledge" for more than four decades until his death, at seventy-eight.

The location near the pond—good for bathing—was pleasant for the youngsters. The stream out of the Town Pond ran southward right behind the schoolhouse, then beside it to zig-zag down Crooked Lane. Two later schoolhouses followed on this site. After Harvard reestablished a printing press in 1761, the University Press was here for more than a century. In a way, medical service for students at Holyoke Center had its beginnings in another building here that was acquired by the College in 1931 when its tenant, the Spee Club, suffered a severe fire. Harvard swapped some property farther down Holyoke Street and here installed a handy hygiene department with clinics and labs.

For many years after the split in the town's First Parish, the Congregational followers of the Reverend Abiel Holmes, father of Oliver Wendell

Holmes, occupied a church they built on the northwest corner of Mt. Auburn Street, just below the site of the first schoolhouse. The land was a gift of a member of the Dana family, an heiress of one of Cambridge's large land owners, Judge Edmund Trowbridge, whose dwelling stood where we now see, on our right, the south entrance of the Forbes Arcade.

Judge Trowbridge had built an office earlier on this church site and, in those pre–law school days, his helpers—actually pupils—included famous lawyers and jurists of the future, among them his nephew, future Chief Justice Francis Dana, Harrison Gray Otis, Chief Justice Theophilus Parsons, and Governor Christopher Gore, generous benefactor of Harvard College. After the congregation built its new Shepard Memorial Church on Garden Street in 1871–72, St. Paul's Catholic parishioners worshipped here until 1915, when they moved eastward along Mt. Auburn Street to their new church, whose magnificent, tall campanile we can see just beyond, towering over the *Harvard Lampoon's* "Castle."

Before crossing Mt. Auburn Street, notice the brick building on the northeast corner, built in 1927 by the century-old Manter Hall School, a prep school. The founder back in 1886 was the same creative William Nolen, who two years earlier had provided cramming services for students seeking to conquer Harvard entrance or other exams. Manter School, like "the Widow's," moved a few times as it grew, took its present name in 1923 when it was located in the old Manter Hall building on the north corner of this block next to the Porcellian Club.

On crossing Mt. Auburn Street we have, on the southwest corner, the walled garden and brick Spee Club house at 76 Mt. Auburn—an attractive swap for its prior fire-charred quarters at 15 Holyoke. This was future President John F. Kennedy's club. A fellow member, who had painted J.F.K. from life, gave the portrait to hang over the fireplace in the club library. Jack's brother Robert, graduated eight years later than he, was also the victim of assassination—a most shocking occupational risk in seeking or attaining our American presidency.

The Spee, which was founded in 1852, started, as did almost all Harvard clubs, as a Greek-letter fraternity (Zeta Psi). Like other secret societies it was twice banned by the faculty in the mid-1800s, but survived. Few clubs in land-hungry Cambridge have their own garden areas. Some members have reportedly felt that Dean Sert's high-rise Holyoke Center has invaded their garden's privacy.

A first-hand impression of what some of the club building is like inside, too, became available in the mid-1980s, when Schoenhof's Foreign Books, which started in Boston in 1856 and had been on Massachusetts Avenue across from the Yard for four decades, rented at 76A storage space on the ground floor and the entire basement for its interesting stock. Nice setup.

On the southeast corner, at 74 Mt. Auburn, is the former Iroquois clubhouse of World War I vintage that since 1979 has been the Riesman Center for the Harvard–Radcliffe Hillel B'nai B'rith. The attractive dining room serves kosher food. Three rabbis on the staff conduct Sabbath services Friday nights and Saturday mornings.

Hillel's neighbor at 72 Mt. Auburn is another World War I brick clubhouse, the Phoenix-SK Club, on the site of the celebrated wooden "Gas House," built in 1885 by wealthy members, including J. Pierpont Morgan, Jr., for their newly formed Delta Phi fraternity chapter when they found they had not been invited to join a final club.

"Gas House" or "the Gas," as it was called, was just wit and whimsy. The lighting was actually by electricity, then fairly novel, but the steward was so enamored of his new domain that he kept lights ablaze—especially in the windows—hence, its nickname. The Phoenix-SK is a combination of about half a dozen clubs back to the Sphinx of 1897. These clubs involved many locations, including the old John Hicks House and the *Lampoon* site, before buying the "Gas" and building here.

As we proceed down Holyoke Street we have ahead, on our right, the east side of the 1930 Indoor Athletic Building, renamed in 1986 for Peter L. Malkin, Harvard 1955, a New York lawyer who was behind the $6,000,000 fund drive to "modernize" the old I.A.B. Two future U.S. presidents resided on this block while in college. President Theodore Roosevelt's lodgings were on the northeast corner of the I.A.B. lot and President Hayes's near the southeast corner. Hayes could not be included in the Hasty Pudding roster because he was a graduate student and the Pudding enrolls only undergrads. Hayes did, though, find life very congenial at Mrs. Ford's rooming house with some fellow students from Ohio.

At graduation, T.R. jubilantly observed that he had "lived like a prince" in his college years. He had been a winner in just about everything, friends, clubs, athletics, and, in love, had won the sweetest of girls, "my own best-loved little queen" Alice, to whom he was married just after his graduation. Almost eighteen when he came as a freshman to live in a two-story clapboard house at 16 Winthrop Street, T.R. lived there until graduation. On the first floor, also with four side windows looking across the salt marshes to the river, was his classmate and closest friend, Richard Saltonstall, who introduced T.R. to Alice, Richard's cousin, on one of their many social visits to the Saltonstalls' Chestnut Hill estate.

"Bamie," T.R.'s eldest sister, always devoted to her "Teddy," furnished his quarters. At first he wanted to be a naturalist and acquired birds, antlers, even live snakes and turtles that he kept in his living room, study, and bedroom. Health deeply interested him. He was neither a smoker (a promise he made to his father) nor a drinker. He loved roaming Cambridge woodlands, swimming, rowing, wrestling, and boxing. Club life appealed strongly to him. He was in Porcellian, Hasty Pudding, and many others, as well as being an *Advocate* editor and making Phi Beta Kappa. The princely aspect included banquets with guests at the Porcellian and riding about Cambridge, and to Chestnut Hill, driving his favorite horse and cart, later a fashionable tilbury.

The great East Asia expert John F. Fairbank, in whose honor Harvard's Center for Asian Research was renamed in 1977, relates in his 1982 memoirs his delight in the 1845 yellow frame dwelling on our right at 41 Winthrop Street, across from the I.A.B. He first rented it from the College for $50 a month when he began teaching history at Harvard in 1936. Here for decades he greeted his students at open-house gatherings and teas on Thursdays and often entertained famous visitors. Fairbank students included Theodore H. White and Arthur Schlesinger, Jr.—in the same class.

Professor Fairbank's greatest joy in his old, often remodeled, modernized, sometimes enlarged Cambridge residence has been its proximity to

Widener Library, only a couple of hundred yards. He figures it has saved him a half a year's time that could have been lost in commuting. And over the years of his tenancy, when finding space to plant lilacs and an apple tree was not easy, demolitions on either side of the old house—one of a clubhouse—have provided expansiveness now ever scarcer in land-short Cambridge.

Before heading into Holyoke Place, let us recall that with the present Holyoke Street, originally the easternmost of Newe Towne's small grid, ahead of us, there was —even in T.R.'s era—almost entirely river marshland to the south of the present Mt. Auburn Street. On the southeast corner, where we now see the west side of Lowell House, was a bit of a rise in the marshes, on which Dudley and the first settlers had planned to protect the town with a fort, but never did.

On the northeast corner, where at 30 Holyoke we see the handsome quarters of the Owl Club, lived a close and wealthy friend of Reverend Thomas Shepard, Joseph Cooke, local official and captain of the town's first train band (local militia). He owned so much river marsh and land hereabouts that the town in 1636 ordered him to "keep the ferry," the penny one, at a ha'penny on lecture days at the meeting house.

Old President Edward Holyoke, who in his long term was the College's greatest colonial builder—New Harvard Hall, Hollis, and Holden Chapel— wanted a place for his wife should she outlive him. She did. The house he bought was a successor building to Joseph Cooke's and was built in 1668. It stood here until 1905. In that year the Owl Club, a final club then only nine years old, built on this site.

We go along Holyoke Place toward the great tower and entry of Lowell House. Lowell, the largest, is one of the three original House Plan dormitories built completely new, and one of the first two—the other is Dunster House, which we will see by the river—that were ready for master, tutors, and students in fall 1930. This was just two years after one of Harvard's greatest benefactors, 1897 Yale man Edward S. Harkness, offered to pay for all seven dorms that President A. Lawrence Lowell had long been eager to build.

Harkness, like Lowell, took profound interest in every step of this construction. It was on a walk Lowell and Harkness took one day from the Yard to where we entered that Harkness, as Lowell related it, took Lowell's arm and asked for his only favor. Would Lowell allow this dorm to be named for himself?

Lowell, who was as averse as Harkness to having gifts bear his name, congenially agreed that he would—if Harkness would follow suit on another of the new dorms. Lowell told how Harkness, who, in a lifetime of giving far more than a hundred million dollars, kept his name from any gift, drew away from Lowell as though Lowell had proposed conspiring in a crime.

On the far, south side of the large Lowell House quadrangle (a second, smaller quadrangle is to our left) is the dining hall inside the row of five big arched windows with two bay windows on either side of the ground floor. Here Harkness and Lowell shared one of the happiest days of their lives, the first high-table (academic head-table) dinner in Lowell House. On going in the east entry to the left of the windows, immediately on the left in the corridor is a comfortable common room and on the right is the large dining hall.

Over the dining hall's ample fireplace and around the walls are portraits of members of the Lowell family, for whom the house was named, back to John Lowell, class of 1721: merchants, judges, educators, benefactors of both Harvard and M.I.T. President Lowell's sister, Amy, the poet, and brother Percival, the astronomer, have portraits, along with his. And just inside the east door of the dining hall is a splendid portrait of the renowned philanthropist Harkness, seated, wearing red academic robe, a likeness made by F. O. Salisbury seven years before Harkness's death in 1940.

On going back across the big quadrangle we have a fine view of the Lowell Tower, with its blue dome, now close enough to see clearly some of the seventeen various-sized bells of the carillon that came from a monastery in Moscow.

To our left, on the north side of the quadrangle, just below the library on the second floor, is a bronze bust by Daniel Chester French of another member of the Lowell family, the poet James Russell Lowell. A well-known family member, the poet Robert Lowell, had his quarters in Lowell A41 when he came as an eighteen-year-old freshman in 1935. Still another modern writer, John Updike, spent his middle years at Harvard (1951–53) in Lowell House E51 and 53.

The open land on our left, as we go toward Mt. Auburn Street, adds to the beauty of this approach to Lowell House, particularly with the old-fashioned Yard type of enclosure of granite posts and rails. The patrician red brick building with six-pillared entry on our right, on the east corner at 2 Holyoke Place, is the Fly Club. It has had many famous members besides both Presidents Theodore and Franklin Roosevelt since it was chartered in 1836 as a Greek-fraternity chapter (Alpha Delta Phi). Poet James Russell Lowell, then an eighteen-year-old sophomore, was a charter member, and President Lowell, also a member, often dined—as did another member, President Eliot—in this 1902 clubhouse's grand dining room.

President Lowell, known so fondly for his democratizing House Plan, bringing students and faculty together in group study and living, wished to get away from the divisiveness of Gold-Coast luxury. He and future President Woodrow Wilson even consulted on terminating College clubs, but Lowell felt that would be unnecessary and excessive.

The Fly Club gave up its old charter and adopted its present name in 1906. Parties in its adjoining garden have long been regarded as one of its top attractions. Outstanding members have included Law Dean C. C. Langdell; Bishop Phillips Brooks; economist Professor Frank Taussig; Justice O. W. Holmes; Larz Anderson, whose gifts included a popular bridge to the stadium that we will shortly see; and Henry Lee Higginson, who gave Soldiers Field, where the stadium was built.

Ahead of us, the wider triangular street area in front of the *Lampoon*'s "Castle" is familiarly called Freedom Square, a Poonster's (or Poonie's) playground for merrymaking under the *Lampoon*'s mascot, the ibis, right atop the tower. On the 1910 dedication day of this beloved landmark, playfully designed by one of the *Lampoon*'s founders, President Gluyas Williams led his fellow Poonsters out the tower entry—with Lampy's purple, yellow, and crimson on the door—in a dance through the square and all around the building until they poured back in for more fun and liquid refreshment in their new Great Hall.

The *Lampoon* (it was nearly called the *Harpoon*) is the nation's oldest college humor magazine. The founding group in 1876 included future architect of the "Castle," Edward M. Wheelwright, also a future founding editor of *Life* magazine and an *Advocate* editor so disappointed about the

Advocate's turning down his sketches that he wanted to join in begetting a comic paper.

Until William Randolph Hearst became business manager and provided a Brattle Street sanctum in 1885, the members met in their student quarters around the Yard to enjoy themselves cooking up and working out their comic notions. Beside providing a sanctum with armchairs, long tables, and all the illustrated comic papers in the world exchanged for Lampy, Hearst brought in advertising ample to lift Lampy well out of debt and provide some joyful banqueting.

The *Lampoon* had several humbler quarters in this area, one as a neighbor to the Pudding, before acquiring the Castle. Architect member Wheelwright loaded the décor with pictorial Delft tiles from the Turkish baths in the basement given by Hearst up to the Great Hall, with its oak-beam ceiling and gargoyle-like light fixtures along the walls. The furnishings range from lavish to strange: a desk once owned by Leonardo da Vinci, Japanese suits of armor, precious gifts from famed collector Isabella Stewart Gardner, to later gifts Hearst had first intended for his grandiose San Simeon mansion.

Where a jester's stick is a symbol of editorship there's bound to be tomfoolery galore, pranks, practical jokes, and boisterous fun. Hazing of initiates in Phool's Week is said to have included creeping on knees up the tower staircase to revelers in the Great Hall and standing upright in a fireplace. A human fly might have trouble climbing up to the ibis—yet it has been stolen several times, with suspicion falling instantly on rival editors of the *Crimson*, the Crimeds.

One time, in 1953, the ibis was given to the Russian delegation at the United Nations, until talked back to Cambridge. Another time five Crimeds were kidnapped and confronted with a bread-and-water diet until the ibis was returned. Springtime and sap flowing can signal that new pranks are afoot.

Springtime 1985 found Pooners and Crimeds at it again. Swatting back for the disappearance of caricatures of Crimson presidents from their editorial floor, Crimeds with mountaineering gear fetched the copper ibis from its perch, only to meet surprise arrest by Cambridge police. All was settled next day, with news and television cameras alerted, when smiling *Crimson* editors returned the sacred mascot to their *Lampoon* counterparts at the Castle.

Lampy's seven founders are beautifully memorialized on a panel in the sanctum. The roster of Poonsters who have won fame is much longer and still grows. In the early days there were Owen Wister and George Santayana, who said being invited to join Lampy was a "decisive event" in his College life. He did not even write for it; at the urging of his classmates dining in Memorial Hall, he got in by submitting a cartoon.

The usual entry, on the north side at 44 Bow Street, was a familiar goal in its first decade to cartoonist Gluyas Williams, witty Robert Benchley, authors John P. Marquand and Robert Sherwood, and still later to John Updike. Over the years, two unusual Poonsters were poetical president Thayer, who wrote "Casey at the Bat" and John Reed, only American buried in the Kremlin, who wrote editorials and concocted *Lampoon* jokes.

At several places in our walks we will see major street developments that originated in a fierce three-year battle over attracting the new, growing traffic flowing from the west through Cambridge and across the new bridges to Boston. Freedom Square is one of these places. The rivals, each trying to get this traffic to go past his own estate and over his own bridge, were developer Andrew Craigie, living in the present Longfellow House on Brattle Street, builder of the Craigie Bridge at the present Charles River Dam, and Chief Justice Francis Dana, living a half mile east of here at Dana Street and Massachusetts Avenue, builder of the West Boston Bridge where the Longfellow Bridge is today.

In 1808, after intensely bitter, wavering town meetings, lawsuits, and some violence, the town built Mt. Auburn Street from near the Watertown line and across river flats to Brattle Square, renamed old Spring Street Mt. Auburn Street, and extended Mt. Auburn Street from Holyoke Street and east through Freedom Square to Massachusetts Avenue. Dana, favored by the town, had won, and early nineteenth-century traffic from western communities flowed along here for years. It was this victory that left the pie-shaped piece of land on which we see the *Lampoon*'s Castle.

Just a glance along the north side of Mt. Auburn and Bow Street confirms that we are in the heart of the old Gold Coast.

Directly across from Holyoke Place is Claverly Hall, with its grand entrance and towerlike corner bays, which in 1893 was the first of the Gold-Coast luxury dorms to be completed on Mt. Auburn Street. Ridgely Hall, just to its left, was built a decade later, and just down the alley between them is the 1898 three-story brick Senior House of Claverly Hall. All three of these buildings provide living quarters for Harvard undergraduates for whom nearby House Plan buildings have insufficient rooms.

Once a bastion of the Gold-Coast era, five-story Randolph Hall, built in 1897, occupies the entire north side of Bow Street across from the *Lampoon*. Its large swimming pool, still in use, was among the envied advantages of Gold-Coast living. Now, of course, this and other pools, like that in the I.A.B., are available to all the students. Randolph Hall was the main structure that Harvard acquired in 1916 in its swap for College House in Harvard Square. Most of Harvard's acquisition of other Gold-Coast dormitories went on during the lack of patronage these buildings encountered during or just after World War I.

Randolph Hall became part of Adams House in 1931. Like three other of the seven houses financed by Mr. Harkness, Adams was formed by combining some existing structures with new ones, as we are about to see. Among the units included in Adams House is one of the oldest and most interesting mansions in Old Cambridge, Apthorp House, which began life in 1761 and came under heavy criticism of a still Puritan-background colony because it might be intended for a "Bishop's Palace."

APTHORP, *CRIMSON*, ARROW STREET

Going up Linden Street with Randolph Hall on our right until, at its north end, we come to a gateway into a courtyard, back of Randolph Hall, in which stands Apthorp House on a still-elegant terrace. Before using this gateway to the courtyard, let us look at two structures on the west side of Linden Street.

Just beyond Claverly Hall on our left at 9 Linden Street, the patrician structure with two pediments and four-pillared porch with neatly polished brass knocker on its blue door, is the Delphic Club. The members built these grander quarters in 1902 when they vacated "the Gas." The building they displaced here was a private house in which future President A. Lawrence Lowell lived during his years in both College and Law School. He loved athletics, from boating to polo and walking, and to keep in shape would, starting from Linden Street, run at least a mile before bedtime, often in the river area, where he would in time carry out his House Plan.

Lowell's successor, President James B. Conant, was also a Linden Street resident in his College years. His quarters were in the neighboring house, the four-story gray clapboard with white trim at 5 and 7 Linden, now a Harvard facility, then a rooming house known as "Mrs. Mooney's." A fellow lodger, future journalist-novelist John P. Marquand, had a top-floor room where he kept a parrot. Both Conant and Marquand covered their College courses in three years, both majored in chemistry (though Marquand did not pursue it), and they were lifelong friends. Marquand, who intensely envied the Gold-Coast living he could not afford, had his imaginary H. M. Pulham reside in the affluence of nearby Randolph Hall.

We enter now the gateway to Apthorp House. On our left are the College squash courts that, along with Randolph and other surrounding buildings, have made Apthorp a prisoner of progress. Originally, Reverend East Apthorp, scion of a wealthy Boston family, acquired six acres here for his dwelling, which he got under construction in 1760 at the same time as he and his new Tory Row parishioners were building Christ Church, of which he had been made rector. There was then neither Linden Street behind us, nor Plympton Street, just ahead of us. Reverend

Apthorp's six acres included just about all the land east of Holyoke Street to the next mansion on Bow Street, and had an unobstructed view across the marshes to the river.

The top floor was added, for servants, by a later owner; otherwise the mansion appears much as it did when twenty-eight-year-old Reverend Apthorp moved in, in 1761, with his lovely bride, a niece of future Royal Governor Thomas Hutchinson. Controversy arose over the mansion's grandeur, and Apthorp himself later agreed that its central pediment, pilasters, ornamentation, and interior elegance did indicate "too much show and expense." A pamphlet war followed, with Boston clergymen distressed by rumors from London that Apthorp was to be named a bishop. By fall 1764, Apthorp took off for a parish near London, and the mansion was sold to another wealthy Tory, who fled to Boston with the Tory Row Vassalls, his cousins, on the eve of the Revolution.

Currently, Apthorp House is again like a private residence, as the dwelling of the master of Adams House. In the intervening years it has had well-known occupants. The patriots confiscated it and it was used as a barracks by militia responding to the April 19th alarm.

General Israel Putnam and his staff used it for a time as headquarters, until he moved to the Inman House near Central Square, closer to the enemy cannon to thwart any hostile breach of defense posts along the river. It was here that General Heath arranged quarters for General Burgoyne and his officers. Burgoyne, however, had to borrow furniture and fireplace equipment and pay rental that he declared exceeded what would be asked "for a palace in the dearest metropolis of the world."

The land boom after the opening of the West Boston Bridge in 1793 led later owners to mark out Linden and Plympton Streets and divide the Apthorp land into house lots. Apthorp descendants, in the family line of architect Charles Bulfinch, reacquired Apthorp House, used it as a private dormitory, and built Randolph Hall in the Gold-Coast era. Apthorp, as well as Randolph Hall, became College property in 1916.

Adams House was the residential affiliation of Bernard Francis Law, Harvard class of 1953, who in 1985 became Cardinal in Boston of America's third largest Roman Catholic diocese. Although Apthorp

House never did become a bishop's residence, its Harvard master has had full responsibility for Adams House, which served as quarters for a future prince of the church, Harvard's first cardinal. The future cardinal, after living his freshman year in the Old Yard, lived in Claverly House for a year, then as a junior and senior lived in Adams B46 (1951–53).

Following graduation, Law studied for the priesthood in the south and was ordained in 1961. He often communicated to his classmates his happiness in the ministry. During his years in the Mississippi diocese he opposed racial segregation and has worked over the years on ecumenical and interreligious affairs. When he arrived in Boston in 1984 as archbishop he was welcomed at the airport by the Harvard Band, even wore a band cap as the musicians joyfully played "Ten Thousand Men of Harvard."

We head now around the east end of Apthorp House to the Plympton Street exit, where we can see the *Harvard Crimson,* the College newspaper, directly across the street in the two-story building of brick with stone trim.

The *Crimson* student officers since its founding in 1873 have included three future presidents of the United States, both Roosevelts and Kennedy; future presidents of the College; students who became famous; and literary, newspaper, and public figures. First, though, let us see other buildings, part of the Adams House that we have been seeing.

Russell Hall, with its cupola and gold dome on the corner of Bow Street to the south of the *Crimson,* thanks to the Harkness largess, replaced in 1931 a Gold-Coast private dorm of the same name. Entry C, through the iron gate and down a few steps to the red doors near the north corner of Russell Hall, is the main doorway to the 1931 structure. Different from its Gold-Coast predecessor, Russell House now has, on our right, music and lounge rooms, and in the basement a tunnel that goes underneath and across Plympton Street for lucky residents to enjoy the Adams House swimming pool in the basement of Randolph Hall.

Entry C leads also to a large dining hall with genteel oak wainscoting. The one-story, templelike south side of this hall, with pediment, pillars, and three high arched windows, can be seen from lower Bow Street. It stands between Russell Hall and Westmorly Court, still another former

Gold-Coast private dormitory which is part of Adams House and which we will see presently.

The two-story brick structure on the left of Entry C contains a lower Common Room on the ground floor and an equally comfortable Upper Common Room on the second level, with a bust of President John Adams on the mantel over the fireplace. Robert Frost, the poet, sitting by this fireplace, had here one of his favorite spots to meet with students crowding in for his lectures and informal talks during the 1938–1942 years before he returned to Amherst.

Notice the *Crimson*'s center window above the 14 Plympton Street entrance. Just inside it, the chief focus of the large sanctum is the high-back 1906 chair used by the *Crimson* president to preside over all *Crimson* doings, from editorial confabs, to presenting celebrated visitors, to merrymaking clublike cocktail parties. With its delightful outdoor patio in the rear of the second floor, it is as exciting to student news sleuths as the newsrooms on the ground floor and the pressroom in the basement.

On the back of the tall chair are metal plates with the names of all the student presidents since 1906, among them President Reagan's well-known Secretary of Defense, Caspar Weinberger, class of 1938, and the first Radcliffe student to become president, Gay Seidman, class of 1978.

The *Crimson* has had several homes since its birth in Stoughton 22 in 1873, before its profitable operation made it possible to purchase land here in 1914, build this structure in 1915, and hold a big housewarming in the following springtime when the sanctum was completed.

The most important contribution to this success came back in 1883, just a decade after the *Crimson*'s birth, when the editors gave up being a merely literary endeavor, which had led to the demise of a long string of predecessors, and started publishing a newspaper. It grew stronger and stronger as it went on to covering sports, getting out extras, and acquiring in 1919 the old *Harvard Illustrated Magazine* so that it could issue its own pictorial supplements.

A fascinating sidelight on all this enterprise was the editors' getting out an early extra when games were played north of the Yard in old Holmes Field, now Harvard Law School terrain. Editors watching the game from the top back row of the bleachers put rocks with their intermittent copy, dropped it to runners below, who sped on their bicycles across the Yard to the printing plant, then in the basement of 1304 Massachusetts Avenue, in the Porcellian block. As the fans made their way from the game they were met by the boys selling their sports extras. All this action proved sport, too, for the Crimeds, sport as jolly as rival pranks with the Poonsters, like making off with the ibis.

The Crimeds, who have included many besides national and College presidents—Owen Wister, Cleveland Amory, Thomas W. Lamont, for a few—have not always been quick with the right answers. Future President Conant had to try twice to become a Crimed, although he had been editor-in-chief of his high school papers and would make Phi Beta Kappa. His classmate John P. Marquand competed without success to join the Crimeds. Their verdict on Marquand: "does not know how to write." At one time the Crimeds even denounced President Lowell's greatest educational reform, the House Plan.

Future President Kennedy, though a Crimed (he served on the business staff) took issue as a senior with a *Crimson* editorial urging neutrality in 1940. He had visited England, where his father was United States ambassador, had seen how British opposition to rearmament would mislead Hitler into precipitating war, and had just written his thesis that would become a bestseller, *Why England Slept.* Kennedy defended President Conant, who was assailed in a *Crimson* editorial for urging United States armament that would eventually lead to Hitler's defeat. When Hitler unleashed his attack a few months later the *Crimson* came around to the thinking of Conant and J.F.K.

On our right as we head up Plympton Street we see part of the bookstore wonderland that thrives near the Yard: the Grolier Book Shop, with its thousands of poetry titles and cassettes; the Harvard Book Store's law annex beside the *Crimson;* and Harvard Book Store itself, which has been providing a selection of new books for more than half a century.

On the west corner, as announced by the club emblem of a bull on the elaborate doorway at 1 Plympton Street, is the A.D. Club, which for decades has been regarded as in a class with the Porcellian. Like the Fly Club,

A.D. traces its beginnings to the Alpha Delta Phi chapter, instituted in 1836. It built this building in 1900, moving from the 1820 house where we saw the Signet Society quartered.

The rest of this block facing the Yard is now occupied by a five-story 1985 office-retail building, 1280 Massachusetts Avenue, which displaced some bookshops that had been here for decades, Schoenhof's, which we saw on Mt. Auburn Street, and Pangloss, a delight of scholars, diagonally across Mt. Auburn Street in Harvard College's Ridgely Hall.

We turn right at the Harvard Book Store, on the ground floor of a 1902 former Gold-Coast dorm, and we are a few steps east of where the East Gate, an opening in the original palings protecting Newe Towne and the cattle from wild animals, was located in midlane. Across from us, in the Yard, stood the 1670 parsonage of the First Parish Meeting House, just beyond the Dexter Gate and archway through Wigglesworth Hall.

The Old Parsonage, which was demolished by the College in 1843, was the dwelling of several distinguished Cantabrigians. Reverend Urian Oakes, who arrived from England and took over the parish in 1670, served several years as both parson and College president. Reverend William Brattle, scion of a prominent Boston merchant, was a Harvard tutor (when it had only two), served as College treasurer as well as parson, and was the progenitor of the Brattle family in Cambridge. The last of six resident parsons was Reverend Abiel Holmes.

We have on our right, as we head for Bow Street, two more contemporary attractions of the late-twentieth-century Harvard Square vicinity. Opposite the east end of Wigglesworth Hall at 1246 Massachusetts Avenue has been, since 1960, popular Mr. and Mrs. Bartley's gourmet burger shop, next to its neighbor, reminiscent of Yenching Cuisine next to the Porcellian, the Hong Kong Restaurant. The Bartley's epicure cooking, using high grill temperature to seal in juices of the ground beef, has attracted many fans, including Jackie Onassis and other Kennedys and celebrities.

Before we walk down Bow Street, notice a memorial to the founder of Newe Towne, Thomas Dudley. It is across the street in the rear of Lamont

Library, but is accessible only when the Class of 1880 Gate, on our left with its curved retaining wall, is open. On the wall are the names of President Theodore Roosevelt and his classmate, Secretary of State Robert Bacon. This Dudley memorial remains from the 1915 Dudley Gate, formerly at the north driveway entry to the President's House on Quincy Street. Dudley is hailed on the memorial by his poet daughter, Anne Bradstreet, as:

> True patriot of this little Commonweal,
> Who is't can tax thee ought, but for thy zeal.

The upper curve of Bow Street was part of the original "way to ye oyster bank" on the Charles River in early Newe Towne. That "way" then turned east, passing along the present Arrow Street, and in front of St. Paul's Catholic Church we can see down Bow Street. The short, straight stretch of Massachusetts Avenue from the head of Bow Street to the east end of Arrow Street dates from the era after Cambridge got its 1793 West Boston Bridge across the river, its first to Boston. The triangular four-story building opposite us at the northeast corner of Bow Street is the 1892 former Gold Coast's Quincy Hall.

On our right as we go down the curve of Bow Street we come to the former Gold-Coast bastion, Westmorly Court, with its terraced entries facing down Arrow Street. Westmorly, built in 1898, became a unit of Adams House as part of Lowell's House Plan. Westmorly 27, decorated by his mother, was future President Franklin Delano Roosevelt's quarters during three years of seeking his A.B. degree in history and economics and a fourth studying law.

President Teddy Roosevelt, his cousin, was his model, which had the future Democratic leader joining the Harvard Republican Club and marching in a Cambridge torchlight parade for T.R. Twenty-one years old and early in his final year, F.D.R. fell in love with a distant cousin, a niece of T.R., and married her in the year after he left Harvard, with uncle T.R. giving away the bride. Franklin's "worst disappointment in his youth" was failure to make the Porcellian, a club of both his father and

T.R. His greatest joy was his activity on the *Crimson,* which he served as writer, managing editor, and president.

St. Paul's Catholic Church is the new edifice, built by the parishioners in 1915 on land they had obtained when they moved from the old church, which stood a few blocks west at the southeast corner of Holyoke Center. The cathedral-like church makes an impressive visit, especially when filled with the magnificent tone of the organ on the right of the main altar.

Just east of the church, at 20 Arrow Street, is the Harvard-Radcliffe Catholic Student Center, open to all the members of the University community. These buildings are on the site of the old Phips mansion, with its ample grounds and a clear panoramic view of the river, just like that of the Apthorp House. The main entrance through the surrounding Phips enclosure was guarded for years by brightly colored, life-sized wooden Indians armed with bow and arrow, still recalled in the local streets' names.

Lieutenant Governor Spencer Phips had enormous holdings of land, owning all of East Cambridge and a northeast section of Cambridgeport. He was the nephew and adopted son of Royal Governor Sir William Phips, who had won knighthood and wealth finding a sunken ship loaded with treasure.

Spencer Phips in 1714 bought the residence here of Major General Daniel Gookin, commander of the militia and close friend of Reverend John Eliot, the Apostle to the Indians. Here ten of Phips's children were born. Life in the mansion seemed always joyful. Phips may well be called the progenitor of old Tory Row, which we will presently visit, for his children married into most of the families that dwelt on Tory Row: Lee, Lechmere, and Vassalls.

In 1811 the old Phips estate was purchased by William, youngest son of eminent scientist Professor John Winthrop. William, long known as Squire Winthrop, built a new house, had a wharf on his river land called "Squire's Wharf," and served Cambridge in local and state office. This house was long used by the Sisters of St. Joseph, serving St. Paul's Church.

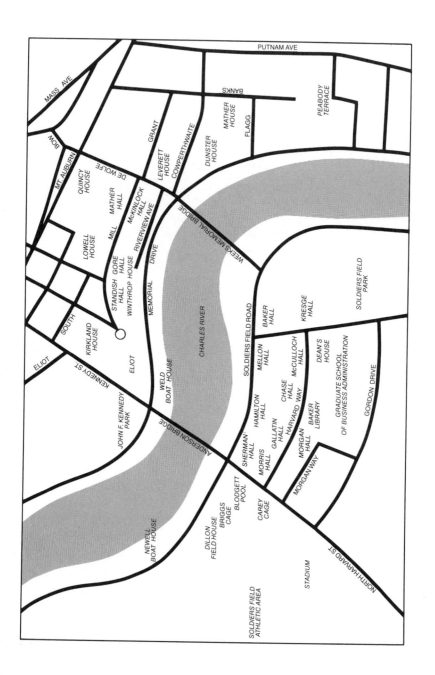

DEWOLFE ROUTE TO RIVER HOUSES

DeWolfe Street, once meant to be transformed into the main portion of a tree-lined boulevard between the river and the Yard, starts with a short stretch from Bow Street to Mt. Auburn Street on the southwest side of St. Paul's. This project did not materialize, but it had the support of Edward W. Forbes, grandson of Ralph Waldo Emerson, and aroused his interest in acquiring riverside land to enlarge the Yard.

Forbes, future director of the Fogg Art Museum, which he would transform into one of the greatest in America, was in his late twenties when he and his friends in 1903, as he expressed it, started buying some land between Mt. Auburn Street and the river for "the benefit of Harvard." His endeavor would make possible the location of President Lowell's other House Plan buildings that we will see on this walk. A couple of decades later President Lowell gave Forbes an honorary degree for having acquired land and works of art, saying that Forbes had "achieved the incredible."

The neat, two-story, dark, gray clapboard house with white trim and one-story brick addition, on our right, marks the east end of Mt. Auburn Street's club row. Here, joined with the Speakers Club, is the old Pi Eta Club, whose resplendent former clubhouse, the present Grendel's Den, we first encountered on the west end by Winthrop Square. Pi Eta, founded in 1865, was a rival to Hasty Pudding, staging its own musical farces and member-written plays, even acquiring its own playhouse. It has in recent years played, as we have seen, an unsought role in putting an end to the University's ties with all Harvard's secret final clubs.

In fall 1983 the Harvard Dean of Students shut down this 45 Mt. Auburn Street clubhouse for a month following a late-night initiation that put ten students in emergency care at the University Health Services after they were reportedly force-fed beer through a garden hose after swallowing shots of alcohol.

The crisis in University relations was provoked in the following spring and had dozens of students protesting and picketing the clubhouse. A paper that was printed, said the apologizing club president, as "a parody of our club newsletter," was inadvertently sent to a woman student. In it women were called a "bevy of slobbering bovines fresh for the slaughter."

Coeducational Harvard-Radcliffe, through both presidents, called the letter shocking, and when all nine of the final clubs insisted on remaining all male, the University in mid-1985 called off the few remaining direct ties with the clubs: low-cost steam heat and use of the University's mailing lists and telephone system.

Not all the students in F.D.R.'s College era felt so unhappy as he did about not making a favorite club. Future architect Buckminster Fuller, Harvard class of 1917, though an eighth-generation Harvard man whose great-grandfather helped found Hasty Pudding and whose grandaunt was Margaret Fuller, came up with a solution.

He and some other classmates who were not invited founded their own club, the HCKP Club. That stood for the subway stations—Harvard, Central, Kendall, Park Street—their route to enjoyable oases in Boston; before the days of the Charles Street station, which might have made it the HCKCP Club. The social amenities of the House Plan, available to all Harvard-Radcliffe students, have led to times more in tune with carefree Mr. Fuller, more widely remembered for his great geodesic-dome structure at the 1967 World's Fair in Montreal.

Legendary Club 47 was on our right, a few steps beyond the Pi Eta, at 47 Mt. Auburn in the one-story building now a Sage, Jr. Store. Fans used to line up around the block to get into the small coffee house, to enjoy the delightful soprano folksinging of Joan Baez, beginning her ascent to musical fame from this "Jazz Club," as she called it. Diagonally across Mt. Auburn Street, on the southeast corner of DeWolfe, the attractive brick building is the rectory of St. Paul's Church.

On our right as we head down DeWolfe Street toward the river is Quincy House, with its courtyard on the west side facing toward Lowell House. Quincy, built in 1959 under President Pusey and named for "Old Quin," went up after a gap of three decades after President Lowell got the House Plan's first seven houses under way. Quincy's seven stories mark President Pusey's move toward taller structures, and a break with President Lowell's Georgian style, in favor of contemporary design with greater use of concrete and glass.

We come presently to Mill Street, on our right, along which President

Lowell took the first hopeful steps toward his still far-in-the-future House Plan by building four freshman dorms that we will see. Curiously, though they would be Harvard's first buildings along the river, their main and most-used entries face the Yard.

Entry locations had a decisive part back in the hectic, disorderly Vietnam War period when Secretary of Defense Robert S. McNamara, in fall 1966, arrived in Mill Street to lunch in Quincy House with students of the John F. Kennedy Institute that he was to address. Some 800 antiwar demonstrators blocked his University Police car. He agreed to answer some questions, did so from atop the auto, then said he had to leave for an appointment across the river.

That brought intensified yelling, catcalls, jeering. The police escorted McNamara into McKinlock Hall, on our left. Then they stationed a decoy automobile outside Quincy Hall and passed a rumor that McNamara would go through a tunnel and depart from Quincy House. The crowd dashed around the corner. Crowds, it seems, can be easily led or misled; for when Mill Street was left empty the police escorted McNamara out of McKinlock Hall and calmly on his way.

Lowell began moving toward the House Plan, a fundamental change in the University life of students, in 1902 when President Eliot appointed Lowell to a committee on student housing. Lowell had recently given up law practice and had been named by Eliot to a professorship in the science of government. Lowell strongly believed that Gold-Coast living was a "great danger," and that "democratic feeling . . . ought to be at the basis of university life."

Soon after Lowell was inaugurated president he proposed construction of freshman dorms, a stupendous endeavor that would require four buildings each capable of housing at least 500 students if, as planned, they were to accommodate the entire freshman class. By 1913, with old bequests and new funds raised by alumni, Lowell was able to start—on land provided by Forbes—three of the freshman dorms farther up Mill Street, completing them in the following year. The fourth, McKinlock on our left, named for a class-of-1916 graduate among alumni who gave their lives in World War I, had to wait for funding until 1925.

Three years later Lowell received a letter of the sort that makes dreams come true. He had heard that a Yale graduate, Edward S. Harkness, had offered to build for Yale—as an example to other large universities—exactly what Lowell had been trying to do for Harvard: provide dormitories with dining rooms, lounges, and libraries where students could commingle in a scholarly society with tutors to give the nation "the best type of citizens."

Harkness's letter expressed his desire to talk about something that he hoped would meet Lowell's approval. Lowell's guess proved right, and, when Harkness came to Cambridge and made his offer, it is said that Lowell's acceptance was instantaneous. Harkness, like Lowell, had no children, and both wished to make mankind their heir.

Three years later in 1931 all seven houses were complete, some even sooner. Lowell, most often with his dog, roamed construction sites, climbed scaffolding, kept an eye on everything, and, as he had given his ideas on the freshman dorms to the distinguished architect, Charles A. Coolidge, he did the same on all planning for the houses.

McKinlock, with additions, became a unit of present Leverett House, named for President John Leverett. A wing with large dining room and master's house was added on the DeWolfe Street side and Mather Hall, at the southwest corner of Quincy courtyard, was erected, both thanks to Harkness's gift. Joining the orthodox Mather name with liberal Leverett's might not have sat well with either of the principals in their day.

But Mather Hall, now called "Old Quincy" by the students, became part of Quincy House when the latter was built in 1958 along with the Quincy House Library, the pavilion on round stilts we see from Mill Street.

Before heading back to DeWolfe Street, notice the detail of units in the Leverett House diagram on the wall on the left of the entry to McKinlock Hall. Instead of old Mather Hall (Leverett House since 1961), it now includes Harvard's first high-rise structures, Leverett Towers, built under President Pusey.

On returning to DeWolfe Street and going toward the river we see this new portion of Leverett House on our left. Including the basement,

Pusey's skyward trend since Quincy House reaches twelve levels here in each of the two towers of dormitories and related facilities. Leverett House Library is at the southwest corner of Leverett's courtyard (called Tower Courtyard), and is reached by an easy, winding stairway to the house library on the second level.

We turn left at Cowperthwaite Street, at the library, go past the back part of Dunster House (we will see it better from its splendid river view), and come to two more of President Pusey's modern high-rise dormitories.

Mather House, at 10 Cowperthwaite Street, built by Pusey in 1967 to help house a University student body that grew in his presidency from 10,000 to 15,000, was named for Harvard's first native-born President, Increase Mather, father of Cotton Mather. President Mather, because of his many other activities, was only a part-time president of the College, but he was a top figure in the Puritan period when the colonial clergy had the prestige of aristocracy and he, virtually on his own, was able to promote one of his parishioners as royal governor of the Bay Colony.

The tower, including the utility floor, soars twenty stories. The interior is very modernistic. Walls in the dining hall and library are variations of cement and red brick, but there are delightful views through great plate-glass windows to the river, tennis courts, and nearby, the equally modern Peabody Terrace.

We can get a good view of Peabody Terrace as we walk around Mather and along Flagg Street to Memorial Drive. Peabody's three twenty-two-story towers are the peak in Pusey's high-rises. They were among his most fervent undertakings in order to furnish married students affordable apartments as close as feasible to their instructors. Completed in 1964 by Jose Luis Sert's group, who did Holyoke Center, the complex was named for Reverend Francis G. Peabody, professor and preacher, who helped in 1886 to make daily religious service at the College voluntary rather than compulsory.

The acreage of Peabody Terrace devoted to tennis courts, trees, playgrounds with swings for children, and brick courtyards on which we see youngsters pushing around on tricycles and kiddie carts, are all benefits made possible by Pusey's decision to involve less land by constructing high-rises.

The Peabody complex, instead of House Plan amenities like libraries and dining halls, emphasizes family living, with its own nursery school, "tot-lot," convenience store, laundries, and parking spaces for unloading groceries, and a big garage, all to service some 500 apartment dwellings comprising studio apartments, and one-, two-, or three-bedroom apartments, all with kitchen.

On our way upriver along Memorial Drive we pass, at the corner of Flagg Street, the Dunster House master's house on the small east court and come then to the very attractive main courtyard. Harvard's arms embellish the central pediment. As Lowell House's blue dome is copied on its entry doors, Dunster's red dome sets the color for its outer doors. The high, rounded windows on its second floor beneath the clock tower locate the library, reached through Entry F.

The five similar big windows on the ground floor on our right are part of a room that has been considered one of the University's finest, the pine-paneled dining hall with its many portraits. It has none of Harvard's first president, then thirty-year-old Henry Dunster, for no likeness exists. But just inside Entry J, by the dining-hall doorway, are some tracery stones given in Dunster's honor by Magdalene College, Cambridge, England, where Reverend Dunster got his M.A. in 1634, two years before the founding of Harvard.

Norman Mailer, fresh from Brooklyn, found his top-floor quarters in Dunster House enjoyable, though views of the river reminded him of his failure to make the crew. He entered Harvard before World War II, in which he would serve as an infantryman and acquire background for his Pulitzer Prize–winning works. His freshman hope had been to be an engineer, but reading literature for English A had soon made him want instead to be a writer.

Mailer's greatest joy in College, the *Harvard Advocate,* was then opposite the *Lampoon* on the third floor of the squarish old building at 40 Bow Street. Life there was a bit shabby, yet merry—especially when Somerset Maugham was invited in springtime 1942 to an *Advocate* cocktail party that drew an overflow of Harvard grandees (Mailer called them), and all was highly exciting as he told it in the *Advocate*, though it was not learned until the next day that Maugham had actually telegraphed that he would not be coming.

Another Pulitzer Prize winner, Thornton Wilder, a Yale graduate, was not overjoyed with quarters assigned him in fall 1950 when he came to take over Harvard and Radcliffe students for a professor who had died. Wilder thought that his Dunster room was even too small to fit in his jar of blackstrap molasses.

But Wilder loved doing things, working so steadily on his lectures, and accepting such a flood of invitations to speak and to go to parties with friends like T. S. Eliot, that by the following spring he had a breakdown. The poet Robert Lowell, who lived life ruggedly, despite his psychic and physical problems, came back teaching for the last time at Harvard early in 1977 and lived on the third floor of Dunster House with a grand view of the river. He died a few months later from a heart attack while riding in a taxi during a visit to New York.

Continuing along Memorial Drive we come, on our left, to a foot-bridge that friends erected in tribute to the many years of public service of John W. Weeks, who rose from mayor to Congress to the cabinet. His son, Sinclair Weeks, also served in the U.S. Senate and as Secretary of War. This Weeks Bridge, along with the Anderson Bridge, next upriver, conveniently link the Harvard buildings south of the Yard into a river campus.

Weeks Bridge, built in 1926, carries concealed above its three arches utilities for the comfort of the Graduate School of Business Administration, then under construction. The boundary between Cambridge and Boston is roughly in midriver, also midbridge, where it is possible to stand with one foot in Cambridge and the other in Boston while enjoying impressive panoramic views of the buildings and the river. Depending on the season, activity on the river ranges from skating to rowing, and may include races, a regatta, or, on gala occasions, even a fireworks spectacle.

Riverview Avenue, more a pathway than a street, which we follow now past McKinlock Hall, used to be called Dyke Street. The name goes back to decades when the Charles River was tidal, when a coal wharf and woodyard were near the site of Standish Hall, just ahead of us, on our right, and even earlier when the old sloop *Harvard* used to deposit firewood for students at the nearby College wharf.

The white house with the pillared porch at the west corner of Plympton Street and Riverview Avenue, like scattered residences adjacent to or linked with the House Plan structures, provides quarters for Winthrop House tutors. Winthrop House itself, though dating back only to 1931, comprises two of the original freshman dorms President Lowell built in 1914.

Gore Hall's name, through alumni gifts, keeps current the gratitude of the University to an early Bay State governor, Christopher Gore, a benefactor whose bequests financed old Gore Hall in the Yard, the Gothic library that was for more than seven decades the intellectual center of the College. Present Gore Hall, with its quadrangle facing the river, has the most poignant student association of all Harvard buildings. Both John F.

Kennedy and his brother Robert, future victims of assassins, lived here as undergraduates.

Jack came in his junior year from Weld Hall in the old Yard and lived in Gore F14. Robert, a decade later, lived diagonally across the hall in Gore F13. Notice, on the west side of Gore quadrangle, the central limestone section of the façade around F entry. The four ground-floor windows in the red brick section to the right of the entry belonged to the quarters J.F.K. occupied with classmates. The rooms, now called the "Kennedy Suite," are used by the John F. Kennedy School of Government to house its guest speakers.

Life here was a happy one for J.F.K. despite the football injury that gave him difficulty the rest of his life. Student politicking, though, strangely for him, was an uphill effort. Thirty-five classmates ran ahead of him when as a freshman he entered the race for class president. As a sophomore he missed in a run for the student council, but as a senior came in fifth in seeking one of the six places on the permanent class committee.

He took trips to Europe, visiting his father, then Ambassador in London to the Court of St. James. Here in Winthrop House he enjoyed student social activities, house dances, even led the "Big Apple." He was on the swimming team, a future boon to his crew when his torpedo boat, PT 109, would be hit by a Japanese destroyer at Guadalcanal in the World War II struggle for the Solomon Islands.

Both Jack and Robert lived in other rooms in Winthrop House. In his senior year J.F.K. moved across the Gore Courtyard to Gore I-21 on the second floor with his three roommates, all on the varsity football team. Here and at Widener, J.F.K. worked on his thesis that would win him honors at graduation. Getting his manuscript typed produced an unusual scene in Gore Courtyard. He bought an ad and named the hour when he would interview applicants. To his astonishment, and the annoyance of the Winthrop faculty, fully five dozen young women appeared in the courtyard outside his room.

Riverview Avenue seems about at an end as we reach the gateway between Gore and Standish, the two dorms of Winthrop House. The rearing red lionlike figure in the overhead grillwork of the gateway, according to resident students, is a griffin, a fabled creature that is the "mascot of Winthrop House." The Griffin Gate, however, was a gift in 1914 from the Fly Club (the attractive one we saw in Holyoke Place) to the then-new dorms in gratefulness for "friendship made in college."

The dining hall of Gore on the Mill Street side has quite a high ceiling because it includes both the ground and first-floor levels. Future Harvard President Pusey, then a poor freshman from the Midwest who got to college via a scholarship, recounted for drama critic Brooks Atkinson how his Harvard experience began on the day he sat in the nearest empty seat in this dining hall in fall 1924. The conversation of other freshmen at his table ranged back and forth about Nietzsche, Ibsen, and Shaw to Katherine Mansfield and James Cabell, making Pusey "at once amazed, terrified, excited and pleased."

Standish Hall, on our left, has a similar dining-hall space, but when Harkness funds made it part of Winthrop House it was converted into a beautiful house library. Around the high-ceilinged room are some dozen and a half portraits of members of the Winthrop family over the years, among them Governor John Winthrop, who brought the Bay Charter in 1630, and his great-great-grandson, Professor John Winthrop, for whom Winthrop House was named.

On display by the fireplace is a telescope that Professor Winthrop, à la Galileo, used to study the planets and other heavenly objects. Standish Hall was mainly the gift of a descendant of Captain Myles Standish, the pilgrim stalwart and friend of Governor Winthrop.

The path between Standish and Gore Halls is like a continuation of Holyoke Street. From the path at Mill Street we turn left. Across Winthrop triangle from us is the elaborate, pilastered entry to Smith Halls, the last of President Lowell's 1914 freshman dorms, this one named for the family bequest of an alumnus. With newer Bryan Hall to its right and the old 1762 Hicks House Library linked by a covered passageway, these halls comprise Kirkland House, named for a great Harvard president of the early nineteenth century, John T. Kirkland.

The path curves leftward now toward the traffic circle at the end of both Dunster and Mill Streets, and to the main entry of Eliot House and its great hexagonal courtyard. To the right of this entry, and beneath its commanding, 230-foot-high tower, with its light turquoise dome and clock, is the dining hall, which is graced on its east wall by a huge, full-size standing portrait of President Charles W. Eliot, painted by John Singer Sargent. Outside the eight large, arched windows on the courtyard side of the dining room is a terrace with a fine bronze bust of Eliot that is sometimes concealed by the neighboring shrubs.

One of the greatest tributes here to Eliot, however, is the honor President Lowell reserved to his predecessor for having in some instances created, in others imaginatively developed, Harvard's array of graduate schools. When Lowell, through the Harkness liberality, was completing Eliot House in 1931, he set aside and beautified with oak paneling two rooms off Entry M—immediately left of the main entry to Eliot House—for Lowell's Society of Fellows.

This was to be Lowell's last of many gifts to Harvard. Only when he died in 1943 did it become known that when he had been unable to obtain the Society's financing he gave $1,500,000 himself "in a kind of desperation although it took nearly all I had." It was given in the name of his wife, Anna, who had died in 1930.

Lowell felt that completion of the House Plan was the opportune time to begin his long-maturing idea of a Society of Fellows that would bring together the most exceptional of young students to pursue study and research or writing on their own, without the routine academic requirements of classes and examination, with stipends, quarters, and all the facilities of the University available to them.

They would be called junior fellows and would have "the guidance and companionship of professors," including the College president, who would be called senior fellows. President Lowell has said that this goal is what poet (and relative) James Russell Lowell had in mind in his Alumni Day Oration in 1886 when he referred to fellows in English colleges who had sharpened "their wits in training by continued fencing one with another" and by "frequent social commingling" at meals and postmeal gatherings.

The young fellows, including women since 1972, are selected for three-year terms from students worldwide. President Lowell had the help of others in shaping the program, in particular Harvard benefactor Alexander Agassiz, renowned philosopher-mathematician Alfred North Whitehead, and Professor Lawrence J. Henderson, distinguished biological chemist. Sole requirement for the fellows is that they join with their senior fellows around the U-shaped table in their Eliot House dining room on Monday nights. There are no set speeches, just conversation over wine and food. Often there are celebrated guests.

Back on September 25, 1933, when these gatherings began, Lowell felt that they "should carry intellectual contagion beyond anything now in this country." They have indeed, if Nobel Prizes—and Pulitzers too many to count—are a measure of excellence.

The Harvard community up to the early 1980s could list twenty-six Nobel laureates. The Society of Fellows alone, junior and senior, by then had thirteen, with one junior fellow, physicist John Bardeen, having twice won Nobel Prizes and the society alone, three junior and one senior fellows, having won four Nobel Prizes in 1981. This prize activity ranged over many fields, including chemistry, economics, physics, medicine, and psychology.

There are many eminent, familiar names among the fellows who have met here at Eliot House: psychologist B. F. Skinner; former Harvard Dean McGeorge Bundy, who served in two presidential cabinets; historian Arthur Schlesinger, Jr.; linguist Noam Chomsky; poet Richard Wilbur; sociologist E. O. Wilson; and Daniel Ellsberg, whose airing of the Pentagon Papers sped United States withdrawal from Vietnam. President Pusey expressed joy in the fellowship's being a rewarding source of recruitment for faculty posts. Fully one fourth of the fellows have served on the Harvard faculty.

Before heading back through the Winthrop-House path to Griffin Gate we think of a distant cousin of President Eliot who lived in Eliot House, T. S. Eliot, the poet. He had rooms in Eliot B11 when, for the first time in seventeen years, he returned to the United States in 1932 as a Charles Eliot Norton professor and to give lectures on literary criticism and a course on modern writers.

He was already famous for his poem "The Wasteland," and ahead of him was a Nobel Prize as a dramatist, as well. For Eliot it was personally a difficult period over the breakup of his marriage, but he had many relatives he could visit in this area, among them his three sisters who lived in Cambridge. Each week he held a tea-party discussion session with his students in his Eliot House quarters.

On coming out of Griffin Gate we turn right past the Standish Hall courtyard. The original Town Creek, a decisive factor in Newe Towne's location, used to enter the Charles River between the sites of Standish Hall and Eliot House, flowing past the old College wharf. Soon, on our right as we pass Eliot House, we come to a great gate that, along with openings in the metal fencing, affords a fine view across the Eliot courtyard to the tower and the terrace, just outside the large dining hall.

At times, especially at night, University gates are padlocked for security. As we approach the corner and Kennedy Street, still another Eliot House Gate offers yet another courtyard view. Above this archway gate, reached by Eliot's Entry C in the courtyard, is the Eliot library on the second floor, an amenity indicated by the white pilasters and five big, round top windows.

On the riverbank beside Anderson Bridge is Weld Boathouse, its attractive red tile roof making it a prominent part of the panorama we have been seeing while walking along the river since we arrived at the foot of Flagg Street. Rowing is the University's oldest athletic sport. The early clubs were named after their eight-oared shells, and Harvard's Oneida Club won the first Harvard-Yale boat race in August 1852.

By 1869, Harvard Boat Club had a boathouse on the riverbank near the foot of Flagg Street that was used until 1900. Meantime, in 1890, an enthusiastic oarsman, George Walker Weld, Harvard class of 1860, built a two-story wood boathouse here for Harvard students not members of varsity crews. In 1907 it was replaced with the present Weld Boathouse by trustees of Weld's estate. Currently, it is used by all Harvard house crews, women's novice and varsity teams, both sculling and sweep rowers, and for recreational programs.

Weld Boathouse with its big ramp was a triumphant setting for the windup of the University's celebration of its 300th anniversary, with thousands crowded along either bank and on both bridges for the "Illumination of the River," with its spectacular fireworks. The Harvard Band, which had been entertaining from its barge, festooned with Japanese lanterns, landed at the boathouse ramp amid a thunder of applause and cheering.

SOLDIERS FIELD TO "BAKER BEACH"

Anderson Bridge's concrete with brick facing was designed to conform to the architecture of its Weld Boathouse neighbor. A special act of Congress had to be passed in 1911, closing the Charles River to navigation, so that the bridge could be built without a drawbridge. "To a father by a son" capsules the devotion of Larz Anderson, famed diplomat, minister to Belgium, ambassador to Japan, who gave the bridge in memory of his father, also a Harvard graduate, who, by twenty-seven years of age, had been promoted to major general during the Civil War.

Anderson Bridge replaced a wooden drawbridge, last of a succession of bridges back to the first "Great Bridge" of 1663, which was then the largest bridge in the Bay Colony. This was the way, in 1775, by which patriot Dawes galloped to spread the alarm and Lord Percy came with his detachment to try to rescue the Redcoats after they were driven back from Concord and Lexington battlegrounds.

Again, in midbridge, Boston is a step away. Once, all the land, as far as the present Brookline, was part of Cambridge and was called "Little Cambridge." In 1807, the same year in which West Cambridge became Arlington, "Little Cambridge" became Brighton and, by 1874, this town of Brighton was incorporated with Boston. One of the earlier names of Kennedy Street was Brighton Street.

For a time in its earlier period the bridge was called the Stadium Bridge as the way to the University's new riverside sports and recreation area, a successor to two earlier playing grounds we will see north of the Yard, Holmes and Jarvis Fields, acres now covered with many structures of the expanding Law School and the University's scientific and high-tech laboratories.

With the sensationally successful Harvard Business School and Stadium so close, we take a brief walk to see their chief attractions prior to heading back along Kennedy Street.

Before leaving the bridge, notice another boathouse to our right on the south bank. Newell Boathouse is devoted to University varsity teams and, they hope, training for the U.S. Olympic team or pursuing the Grand Challenge Cup Prize in England's Henley Royal Regatta. A gift in 1900 of the New York Harvard Club, it replaced one the club began building here about a year earlier that was destroyed by fire.

Dedication was in the name of a beloved, widely admired Harvard five foot seven, all-around athlete, Marshall Newell of the class of 1894, who rowed on all his College crews from freshman to varsity; played football too, on every team; was chosen all-American tackle each year; was good in his studies; was chosen marshall on Class Day; and shocked all his admirers on Christmas Eve three years later when, at only twenty-six, he was struck and killed by a train.

While crossing the Charles it seems appropriate to recall the important association between the river and the University color. It was from the river here in June 1858, that future president Charles W. Eliot and others in the Harvard Boat Club six-oared shell rowed downstream to a landing at the foot of Boston's Beacon Hill to participate in the Boston Regatta. To be sure that spectators and particularly his fiancée, Ellen, could identify them, Eliot hurried into town and bought six silk handkerchiefs to tie on their heads; they did win, in record time. The color of the handkerchiefs was crimson.

Just inside Gate 1, the main gate to Soldiers Field Athletic area, there is on our right a marble memorial shaft commemorating Major Henry Lee Higginson, banker and generous benefactor of Harvard, dedicating Soldiers Field to six friends and kinsmen who gave their lives in the Civil War. He served along with them in the cavalry and was wounded in battle. Major Higginson is also well known as the founder of the Boston Symphony Orchestra. We shall presently see that he played an important role, too, in ensuring creation of the Harvard Business School.

The two Lowells mentioned on the memorial shaft were brothers, and nephews of poet James Russell Lowell, a close friend of Higginson's. The four lines are a quatrain called "Sacrifice," written by still another friend, the poet Emerson.

Harvard acquired sixty-acre Soldiers Field over two decades beginning in 1870 when the poet Henry Wadsworth Longfellow and friends gave not only the present Longfellow Park we will see on the other side of the river but also twenty-one acres on this side. Some small gifts and acquisitions were followed by the large gift of thirty-one acres by Higginson in 1890. Major Higginson gave the land with no restrictions on its use but the hope that it would be used as a "playground for the students." Currently facilities are there for just about every recreational or competitive sport.

The big building like a backdrop to the memorial shaft is Blodgett Pool, one of the three sports buildings built on the field in the late 1970s. The entrance to the pool is on the south side; the pool is of Olympic size, some 55 yards long and 25 yards wide. It is considerably larger than the I.A.B. pool.

Both building and pool seem truly immense, and, with 2,000 spectator seats and lots more room for standees, they provide an exciting setting for intercollegiate, national, and international swimming events. The diving well is fully 15 feet deep. Blodgett Pool, opened in 1978, was one of many gifts to his alma mater from John W. Blodgett, Jr., class of 1927, scion of a distinguished Midwest logging and milling family.

We walk now along the east (street) side of Blodgett Pool, and on our left is a memorial rock with a bronze plaque depicting the great Harvard athlete H. R. "Tack" Hardwick making a high kick. The plaque tells of his spectacular record as a star in three varsity sports, football, baseball, and track.

On coming abreast of Gate 2, which we will presently use, we turn right and past Blodgett Pool to the next building on our right, the Briggs Athletic Center, used mainly for basketball. Built in 1927, the cage was named for a popular and distinguished educator who believed in a health-producing relationship in the right combination of education and sports. Professor LeBaron R. Briggs even made time to head a committee regulating sports in a strenuous career that included being dean of Harvard and president of Radcliffe College (1903–1923).

Next on our right, Dillon Field House, is on the site of about the first major structure of Soldiers Field, the old locker building built by alumni in 1893. It burned down in 1930 and was replaced by this building, a gift from Clarence Dillon, who, with a 1905 classmate, founded a major New York banking firm. Here are provided showers, lockers, offices for the coaches, supply and medical rooms, and a lounge for easy socializing with visiting teams.

From in front of Briggs' Cage there is a fine view southward of the Stadium, the showpiece of Soldiers Field. Celebrated architect Buckminster Fuller said that when it was built in 1903 it was America's—and maybe the earth's—first colossal reinforced-concrete structure. A fiftieth-anniversary plaque affixed in 1953 at the Stadium's northeast corner tells the tale. It was, of course, the country's first huge college stadium, and, with the colonnade added in 1910 it has, despite its open U shape, the atmosphere of Rome's ancient Colosseum.

Holmes and Jarvis Fields, each with five acres, had by the 1880s proved inadequate to accommodate the open-air sports of President Eliot's rapidly growing College. Longfellow's gift had shifted attention to the marshes on the south side of the Charles that could be filled, an interest intensified by Higginson's gift. Alumni responded to appeals for building and equipment.

The Class of 1879 started a new tradition by picking its twenty-fifth reunion to make a major gift, as a starter $100,000—about a third of the cost of the Stadium. The tradition won permanence a year later when the Class of 1880, Teddy Roosevelt's, gave still another $100,000 at its twenty-fifth to boost an endowment for the Stadium.

When, in alternate years, the Harvard-Yale football game is played here, temporary stands are erected between the goal post and the parking area just in front of us. The Stadium, normally seating 30,502 on the colonnade and concrete, can then seat 40,410. This capacity includes temporary seats on the track, roof seats on the visitors' (Yale) side, and 500 standees, also on the roof.

The Stadium's early years coincided with the sports wizardry of Percy D. Haughton, who became head coach in 1908. The big annual show was the Harvard–Yale football game, alternating here and in New Haven. Haughton in a dozen years won all but two of these games, one, in 1915, by a score of 41 to 0.

The Harvard–Yale series, intercollegiate football's oldest, goes back to 1875, in which Harvard won, only to lose many of the following games to

Yale. Haughton's football was under the new rules to make it a "gentle-manly sport," after many years when the faculty had to ban it more than once for being "brutal and dangerous," more like mayhem-on-order than sport.

For years seats in the Stadium were at a premium as fans, many in fash-ionable raccoon, flocked to the games, particularly alumni and their friends. Partying went on before the kickoff, at half time, and post-game. Tailgate picnicking, music by the Harvard Band, cheerleading, wild cheering, singing, shouting, yelling were all part of the merry scene, with glee reigning supreme. The arrival of professional football times has done some tempering, but the old College spirit still does well.

Football, of course, was not the only sport in mind when athletics shifted here. A baseball cage was designed for just west of us, in line with the present Newell Boathouse, and there was a quarter-mile cinder track, and courts for tennis and cricket. Nowadays just about every indoor and field sport can be pursued here.

On our right are two more late 1970s buildings, the Bright Hockey Center and the Gordon Indoor Track and Tennis Facility, sometimes also used for class-reunion buffet-luncheon parties before the Harvard–Yale game. Beyond, on Longfellow's former river flats, are facilities for rugby, lacrosse, soccer, Frisbee, an outdoor track, and tennis courts.

We head now back to Gate 2. On our right just before we come to the gate is Carey Cage, a former baseball cage, named for an alumnus who gave an athletic building on old Holmes Field. To replace it, Harvard gave and named this building in 1898. It has had many uses, but in recent years has been mainly used for Business School meetings and activities, espe-cially basketball.

On the south end of this Tudor-looking building, with its own entry, is the office and lounge of the Harvard Varsity Club. To be closer to athlet-ics, it left its own building near the Old Yard in 1982 and now holds its functions in the Carey Cage or nearby athletic buildings when its former varsity players gather.

On crossing North Harvard Street (the "North" comes from being in the northern section of Brighton), we come to Harvard Way, which runs through the center of the Graduate School of Business Administration and leads to all its main buildings.

The complex of impressive, numerous Business School structures before us seems astonishing, even miraculous, on reflecting that at the time Major Higginson gave Soldiers Field, on a College map about the only significant structure here was a coal wharf with lumber sheds near the old wooden bridge and just across from where we have seen the present Weld Boathouse.

We have, at University Hall, mentioned the small beginning of the Business School in fall 1908. Its birth actually came about years earlier when President Eliot observed the increasing number of graduates going into the business world. The beginning in 1908 was to open a five-year experiment that was nearly put off, at the eleventh hour, by the damper on fund raising clamped by the Panic of 1907.

Economics Professor Frank W. Taussig, a top fund raiser for President Eliot's project, has told how his worry ended when he got an urgent, early morning phone call to come see Major Higginson. Taussig did, and Higginson told him to tell President Eliot that an anonymous but financially reliable person would guarantee the money that remained to be raised. Taussig did and Eliot was able to get the experiment started on schedule under its first dean.

The school's celebrated dean, Wallace B. Donham, a top Boston banker, took over just after World War I. Donham had been a student of President Lowell when Lowell was giving courses in government. The postwar boom brought such a flood of students that all the College facilities were overcrowded. Business School classes were still being held in catch-as-catch-can space, and the school had neither its own community nor a campus.

To get the original thirteen buildings we see here—the big Morgan administration building and Baker Library on our right, the Dean's House ahead, and all but the four small insert office buildings of the fourteen buildings in the two big quadrangles between Morgan, Baker, and Dean's

House and the river—Donham became executive chairman of an unprecedented Harvard Fund drive in 1924.

Bishop emeritus William Lawrence, a cousin of President Lowell, added to his many other services, including University preacher, by being chairman to raise $10,000,000. That figure nowadays may not sound huge, but it was Harvard's largest fund-raising goal up to that time. This sum was to provide $5,000,000 to build the thirteen buildings, and another $5,000,000 for the equally needy and growing departments of fine arts and science. The alumni had recently been canvassed to provide other educational improvements sought by Lowell, and so Bishop Lawrence and Donham decided to try for big individual donations.

Just about the most distinguished man in New York's Wall Street was its dean, George F. Baker, with his mutton-chop whiskers, a philanthropist, then in his mid-eighties. Baker, who had started work at sixteen as a clerk in the New York State banking department, achieved his immense success in banking and railroads. The bishop, who knew Baker personally, called upon him in New York and expressed the hope that he would head the list of donors with a contribution of $1,000,000 to America's first graduate school of business. Baker said he would reflect on it.

Roughly a dozen weeks went by and then, by telegram, Baker said he would come to see Bishop Lawrence, who was visiting his daughter in New York. Baker, alone, rang the bell at exactly the time he had set. No, he would not give the $1,000,000—but he would give $5,000,000 if, as he told the Bishop, "I could have the privilege of building the whole school." Baker thought that the new school would lead to better business standards and he would like to be its founder. Dedication of the buildings came in June 1927.

At Dean Donham's suggestion to Baker, the main dormitory buildings on the large and small quadrangles on our left were named for Secretaries of the Treasury. The one immediately on our left, Morris Hall, was named for a signer of our Declaration of Independence, Robert Morris, Philadelphia financier who, like Baker, began on the bottom rung of the business ladder and handled our national finances during the period of the Articles of Confederation. Well-known Secretaries of the Treasury for whom dorms were named include Alexander Hamilton, Albert Gallatin, Salmon B. Chase, John Sherman of antitrust fame, Carter Glass, and Andrew Mellon.

The four smaller buildings, like the brick-trimmed, stucco brick-ender Anderson with 10 Harvard Way over its entry, were truly inserts added later as enrollment of the school grew. These four forming the four sides of the small quads were, however, included in the original design. Steps on either side of them lead down to small courtyards that, as we can see, emphasize how the school grounds throughout have been gracefully landscaped. These insert buildings, like a later building, Cotting Hall of 1967, immediately on our right as we entered Harvard Way, are used mainly for offices. Growth of the school even forced the dean in fall 1984 to do as President Lowell had done early in the old Yard, close the campus to traffic.

Names of the two large buildings ahead, on our right, Morgan Hall and Baker Library, also had Mr. Baker's warm approval, given to Dean Donham. Morgan was a memorial for a close lifelong friend of Baker's, J. Pierpont Morgan, another Wall Street grandee and philanthropist.

Morgan Hall is chiefly occupied by administrative and faculty offices. Aspirants come here from literally all over the earth to enroll for the school's M.B.A. (Master of Business Administration) degrees. Radcliffe students have attended since after World War II, during which joint Harvard-Radcliffe classes had been held in the old Yard.

Information is available in the lobby of Morgan Hall along with a one-page map of the buildings on the Business School campus. In the lobby is also a much larger version of the map. A still larger open-air, bronze display of this helpful map is, however, just a few steps away in the delightful, restful memorial garden area between Morgan Hall and Baker Library.

Just south of this garden-lounge area are tennis courts and, on the left, a recent building (Teele), where the school has its own annex of the Harvard Coop on the first floor and upstairs are the quarters of the prestigious *Harvard Business Review,* founded in 1922. Its reports on business, including research, development, and new goals, printed in eleven languages, reach a genuinely international readership in more than 125 nations.

Baker Library, next along Harvard Way, is the heart of the school. The expansive lawn of the main quadrangle, stretching in front of Baker from the flagpole seemingly to the river, is affectionately known to the students as "Baker Beach."

The bell in the tower beneath Baker's gold dome is kin to the bells of Lowell House. It was part of the Russian carillon purchased by a former minister to China, Charles Crane, on hearing that the Soviets were to smelt them down for armaments. When Crane gave them to Harvard in 1930, President Lowell assigned this one to Baker Library. It is rung only twice a year, once as a test and once at June commencements. "Sounds just like Big Ben," remarked a student from London, "just one more bong and I'll have my M.B.A."

Portraits of several prominent Business School professors can be seen in the spacious lobby. Most interesting of the likenesses is the impressive bronze bust of George F. Baker at the head of the lobby, just outside the stacks. It was originally a gift back in 1917 in Baker's banking days from a longtime friend, Henry Clay Frick, a couple of years before Frick's death. Frick had also begun his career as a clerk and rose to the mountaintop of wealth as head of Carnegie Steel. He was, too, a celebrated philanthropist and, on his death, left his Fifth Avenue mansion with its great art treasures as a public museum.

On the left (east) wall, as we enter, is a bronze plaque telling of the 1927 dedication and Baker's desire "to promote knowledge and integrity in the art of finance, industry and commerce." This message, at the suggestion of Baker's equally philanthropic son and namesake, was written by President Lowell.

The Baker Library has, for some years, been the largest, most comprehensive business library in the world. The school, from its beginning, followed the successful case-study technique of the Law School, but had to start from scratch in acquiring library material. Nowadays, the library has in its collection, cared for by its excellent archives and manuscript section just off the lobby to our right, business records of the medieval business giants, the Medici, and the records of famous Slater Mill, America's first cotton-manufacturing plant, to correspondence in modern times of world-wide commerce and corporations.

Acquisition of the special Kress Library of Business and Economics, which is reached on the second floor by the stairway just off the left side of the lobby, illustrates the difficulties of starting great libraries from scratch.

Dean Donham, determined as he said that the Business School would have "one of the great libraries of the world," learned in 1927 of a collection that had been started in 1875 by a London economics professor and, through an agent, personally committed himself to purchase it on the professor's death, but that came in 1936, deep depression times, when raising funds was a close to hopeless task.

New York financier Claude W. Kress, chain-store executive deeply interested in economic research, financed not only the purchase but also the cost of its present quarters, adapted to treasures like first editions of Adam Smith's *Wealth of Nations,* literally the birth of modern economics. The library has received many additional treasures since it was opened in 1938.

The staircase off the lobby on the right leads to a recreational reading room on the second floor, the Aldrich Room, which is comfortably furnished in the clublike spirit of the Farnsworth Room in the old Yard. On approaching the main reading-study room of the Baker Library on the third floor we see a fine portrait of Dean Donham and one of several large portraits of George F. Baker in the building, this one with him wearing academic honors.

The reading room, reserved for scholars and researchers, is magnificent in size, running the full length of the building, some 240 feet. Resources are easily accessible for study and research into every aspect of business, with corporate information on microfilm, computer facilities, current periodicals, and even printouts to keep subject content up to date.

Resuming our walk along Harvard Way we have two major additions to the Business School that were completed in 1953, Aldrich Hall on our right and Kresge Hall at the east end of Harvard Way. Classrooms were improvised in Baker Library, for by World Warr II the school enrollment under Dean Donham had more than doubled to nearly 1,100. Donham's successor, Dean Donald K. David, interested John D. Rockefeller, Jr. in donating $5,000,000, which friends of the school matched to provide the exceptional thirteen classrooms of Aldrich Hall, which is connected on its west side with passageways to the library.

At Rockefeller's suggestion, the hall was named for Mrs. Rockefeller's father, Nelson W. Aldrich, Rhode Island financier and United States senator. The classrooms are horseshoe shaped with semicircular, theatrelike ascending tiers of seats to provide easy communication between teachers and students. Each classroom can accommodate 100 students, and along the corridors are small sitting spaces, where students, in little groups, can further pursue their discussion.

On our right, near the end of Harvard Way, is the house of the dean of the Business School. It was the first addition made to the buildings originally planned and was built, 1928–29, to meet the express wish of Mr. Baker to provide suitable quarters. The first occupant was Dean Donham, both classmate and close friend of Mr. Baker's son, George F. Baker, Jr.

President Conant, in one of his final acts before leaving to be U.S. High Commissioner in postwar Germany, presided in June 1953 at the joint dedication of Aldrich and Kresge, then Harvard's largest building program since World War II. Kresge Hall has ample, indeed luxurious accommodations in its large lounge, for dining, meetings, and conferences. The semicircular cafeteria downstairs can seat 660, and the top floor has a faculty lounge and dining rooms. Kresge is located at a bend in the Charles River and offers splendid, sweeping views from all its riverside windows.

In the lobby is a portrait of merchant prince Sebastian S. Kresge, who, like George F. Baker, started his business life as a clerk, went on to selling tin and hardware, and then owned a chain of nearly 1,000 stores around North America. Kresge Hall was the gift of a foundation he established. Dining now at the school beats by far the early days, when dining rooms in six of the dorms were served via tunnels from the basement kitchen in McCulloch Hall. And for current fast food there is the "Galley," a grill on the first floor of Gallatin Hall and, adjoining it, "the Pub," where one may have beer or wine with a sandwich.

On either side of Kresge Hall we see recent Business School expansion. To the right (south), set a ways back from the Dean's House, is Burden

Auditorium, given in 1971 in memory of New York industrialist William A. M. Burden and the Burdens of his and three other generations who studied at Harvard. The complex of seven- and eight-story red brick housing, just east of Burden Auditorium, is used for graduate students of the Business School and of John F. Kennedy School of Government, which we will see presently on our return to Kennedy Street.

To the left of Kresge Hall are two dormitories, Baker Hall and McCollum Center, built in 1969 to help accommodate the fastest-growing courses at the Business School, the Advanced Management Program, and later, the similar Management Development Program, started midway through World War II. Baker, the school's second building to bear this name, is for George Pierce Baker, who served as the school's dean from 1955 to 1969, son and namesake of the eminent Harvard and Yale professor of drama and inspirer of famous playwrights, but unrelated to George F. Baker.

This executive education program's most popular field is providing thirteen- and fourteen-week courses for corporate executives and managers, everywhere, to get them abreast of the latest research and ideas in their various fields, or for training prospective corporation and business executives. Baker Hall, recently renovated, has seen so much coming and going of enrollees that it is described by many students as a campus motel.

En route back to Kennedy Street a most pleasant path is along Harvard Way and through the large courtyard of Hamilton Hall, named for our first Secretary of the Treasury, Alexander Hamilton. The careful landscaping, the trees and lawn, give additional elegance to the school's structural combinations of red brick and stucco. Two exit archways on either side of Sherman Hall get us back to North Harvard Street and the Anderson Bridge.

At midbridge the views upriver or down are among the best in Cambridge, especially from the turquoise dome of Eliot House to the red dome of Dunster House, the high-rises of Peabody Terrace, and beyond, the background of Boston's midtown and downtown skyscrapers. With sun shining on both the river and the riverfront structures the vistas are even more striking.

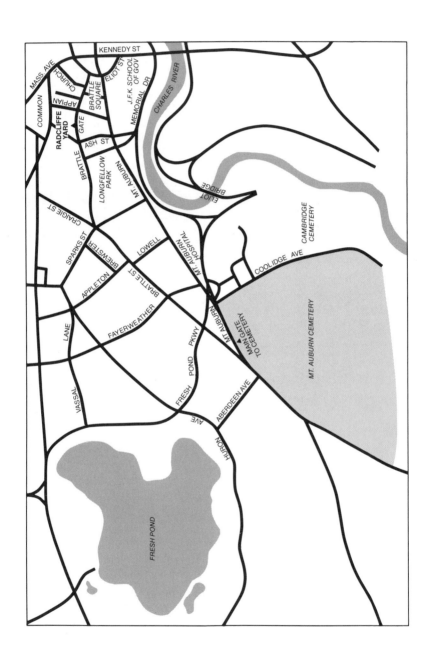

J.F.K.-LAND, ELIOT, AND BRATTLE SQUARE

John F. Kennedy Street, from Anderson Bridge to Eliot Street where we are heading, began life as a causeway across Ox Marsh. This marsh, not really filled in until after the Civil War and the building of a dike, extended on the west side of Town Creek from Winthrop House to Windmill Hill at the foot of the present Ash Street, which runs southward from Brattle Street to the Charles River; because of the causeway this stretch of Kennedy Street was long known as "the causie."

When workmen were dredging in 1913 to locate the Cambridge-side pier for the new Anderson Bridge, they discovered, deep in the river mud, logs believed to have been part of the original causeway constructed to the first "Great Bridge" of 1662. It was so costly an affair to maintain that the colony made it a toll bridge. This plan was quite productive in revenue because the bridge was along the popular route to Boston, which, as the old milestone in God's Acre tells us, was fully eight miles distant by this way. The bridge was, for those times, soon rebuilt after it was swept away by high tides in 1685.

For many years at the site that now holds Eliot House on our right was a huge generating plant supplying the Boston Elevated Railway Company (now the Massachusetts Bay Transportation Authority [M.B.T.A.] or "T") with electricity. That was before President Lowell's House Plan era.

And, on our left, all the land from Memorial Drive, the entire site of the J. F. Kennedy School of Government up to Eliot Street, and westward as far as University Road, was acreage, on its western portion, used for decades for horsecar and livery stables and, after the coming of electricity, for electric-car yards; and, after the 1912 opening of the Harvard Square to Park Street subway service, for storage and maintenance yards for the subway trains. This expansion eliminated three or more of the area's short streets and working folks' dwellings.

Sports fans still recall times when Saturday crowds poured from the subway trains' temporary Stadium Station at the west corner of Kennedy Street and Memorial Drive to make their way across the river to football games, especially the Harvard-Yale classic. That station site, now mostly open land between the J.F.K. School and the river, is to be converted into a memorial park to President Kennedy.

The reader, on leaving Anderson Bridge, may have noticed the Metropolitan Park Commission's signboard appeal to help save the sycamore trees along Memorial Drive. Ironically, and fortunately, in 1963 when the Metropolitan District Commission (M.D.C.) wanted to cut down these trees to build an underpass like the one on the south side of Anderson Bridge, the trees were saved by Cambridge women who chained themselves to the tree trunks in a "Save the Sycamores" campaign—and won.

From Anderson Bridge the fascinating views certainly include, at 980 Memorial Drive, adjoining the projected J.F.K. Memorial Park, the Chapel of St. John the Evangelist, built in 1936 in the early Gothic style. It is regarded as one of the most attractive small churches in Cambridge. It was added to the decade-earlier, equally attractive Episcopal monastery with its delightful cloister and garden. President Kennedy's daughter, Caroline, and other family members participated in plans for the park on this 5.5-acre site, once intended for the J.F.K. Presidential Library that now stands on Dorchester Bay across from the *Boston Globe*.

The park, as foreseen in 1985, was designed for passive recreation, a grassy area for walking or sitting with a simple water fountain reflecting J.F.K.'s love of sailing and naval service. The area is indeed the Kennedy-land of Cambridge, with street, park, and graduate school named for him, and visible from the front steps of the school is Winthrop House, in which he and other family members spent undergraduate years.

The John F. Kennedy School of Government comprises the two buildings on our left: the Littauer Center of Public Administration, built in 1978, and the 1984 addition at the corner of Eliot Street, the Belfer Center for Public Management. To meet the school's steadily increasing needs still another addition was under construction in 1985 in the rear of the Littauer Center, for more conference and seminar rooms and offices for faculty and fellows.

The J.F.K. School got its start back in 1936, the year Kennedy entered Harvard as a freshman, with a large gift from New York congressman, manufacturer, philanthropist, and close friend of President "Teddy" Roosevelt, Lucius N. Littauer, widely known for his Littauer Foundation grants "to better understanding among all mankind." The first Littauer

Center, whose portico makes a classic backdrop north of Harvard Square, was dedicated in 1939 and in 1966 became the John F. Kennedy School of Government. The school moved to this new Littauer Center in 1978.

On entering the school the visitor is almost at once in the middle of one of its best-known activities, "The Forum," a program of the school's Institute of Politics, which brings distinguished speakers to lecture, debate, or participate in panel discussions of public affairs and problems. The Forum's central, four-story atrium with leisurely seating off the open stairways, and a screen for movies or television, can accommodate an audience of 600.

Typical Institute speakers, all talking on major issues of the day, have included all seven candidates for the 1984 Democratic presidential nomination; President Reagan's arms negotiator Paul Nitze; atomic-bomb scientist Edward Teller discussing the advisability of deploying nuclear weapons in star wars; director emeritus of the congressional budget, Alice Rivlin, talking on the perplexing difficulties of making government work.

Just inside the main entrance is a very fine likeness of President Kennedy by William F. Draper. Kennedy is smiling most warmly as he looks out on the Forum and toward a side doorway that leads to his memorial park. The Institute does not give degrees. Its purpose is to bring together the worlds of politics and education, but the school has courses, programs, and research work that lead to doctorates in public policy, city and regional planning, and public administration.

Executive programs are among the fastest-growing J.F.K. activities, and have newly elected mayors and Congressmen attending one- and two-week courses. Other executive courses range from three- to thirteen-week programs for senior managers of local, state, and federal services. Here, as at the Business School, the case technique is used, with scholars able to hear visiting speakers, who include prime ministers, cabinet officers, generals, authors, newsmen, distinguished professors, and top public officials. The J.F.K. School's goal, as seen by its dean, is "excellence in public problem solving."

Robert Alexander Belfer came in 1942 from Poland, for generations the family's homeland, when he was seven years old, was naturalized at twelve, got a law degree at Harvard at twenty-three, and went into manufacturing and petroleum in New York. At the dedication of Belfer Center, one of the many gifts from him and his wife, he told President Bok and the audience, "I consider myself to be blessed beyond words to live in this great country."

Belfer Center's five floors provide offices for students and faculty, but mainly, one above the other, it has theatrelike lecture halls, and the two top floors are devoted to the school's Center for Business and Government, with its own lecture hall. The lower halls were named by their corporate and individual donors for two inventors, Alexander Graham Bell and instant-camera creator Edwin H. Land, with a larger 200-seat auditorium named for the longtime president of the Littauer Foundation, Harry Starr, lawyer and Harvard overseer.

As we turn left at Eliot Street and begin walking along its curve we are following, upstream, the course of the ancient town stream that originated in the Harvard Yard and once flowed through Harvard Square. The bed of this Town Creek was, as we will presently see, much lower than the present Eliot Street.

Back when the subway tunnel was built to Harvard Square, an extension was added under the curve of Brattle Square and Eliot Square that required digging roughly down to the original level of the stream. We can see that tunnel's exit and entrance to the former elevated caryard at the next corner on our left, where Murray Street, which runs parallel to J.F.K. Street, comes into Eliot Street and Square.

Just go a few steps along Murray Street and look back and down and you can see "Boston Elevated Railway Company 1911" over the tunnel. This corner was for nearly seven years (1979–85) the site of the temporary Brattle Station (though it was in Eliot Square) that was used while the Harvard Square underground station was being enlarged and the subway service was being extended to Alewife in North Cambridge.

How long we will be able to see that 1911 inscription over the end of the tunnel becomes uncertain as we look across Murray Street at the largest of the area's many expanding contemporary developments,

$100,000,000 Charles Square. The inner courtyard alone is fully an acre in size. The development, built 1983–85, covers all of the space to the west of Murray Street, once a compound of carbarns and sheds, extending from luxurious Charles Hotel with its opulent public rooms, big ballroom, gourmet dining places, swimming pool and sauna, garage, handy boutiques, shops, and office space, down to nearly 100 condominiums at the foot of Murray Street, a stone's toss from the Charles River.

To see first-hand evidence on the depth of the old Town Creek we go a few steps up Winthrop Street, next street off Eliot Street on our right, after we reach the beige clapboard with white trim (106 Winthrop Street) at the corner. Between this house and its neighbor, at 98 Winthrop, both dating from around the first years of the 1800s, is a retaining wall that originally gave the number 98 lot added elevation above the old creek. Filling in the creek began around spring 1808, not long after these two old houses were built.

Just across Winthrop Street was the site, partly on land of Grendel's Den, of the first jail, built to replace a private dwelling on the east side of old Crooked Lane (Holyoke Street) that the county had purchased, with cattle and corn, for a jail in 1655 and engaged its owner as keeper. The jail here was several times altered and enlarged, particularly during the witchcraft craze, and was used until 1816, when functions of the jail as well as the court were moved to East Cambridge.

Having community services, like the jail, in this section of old Cambridge close to the marketplace was a natural choice. On our returning to Eliot Street, notice the Harvard Motor House between Bennett and Mt. Auburn Street. Here for sixty years was an 1874 three-story mansard brick structure with a clock tower, replacing both the first 1864 district police station on Church Street, which we saw up Palmer Street from the Coop, and the first city fire station, which once stood a few feet to the east of the old police station.

The fire station, called Cambridge I, did not get its first horse-drawn steamer until 1862. In the new 1874 city building there was also a police court and, on the top floor, large armory quarters, used at times for community activities. Directly across Mt. Auburn Street where we see a bank at the corner of Brattle Street was, in the early decades of this century, the local post office.

The 1808–1809 filling of the creek that we just mentioned concluded nearly three years of lively town-meeting debate. A series of close votes, first for one side, then the other, ended in a May 1808 vote to build "at once" an extension of Mt. Auburn Street in part across the river marsh from Elmwood Street to Brattle Square. This was a victory for Judge Francis Dana's West Boston Bridge instead of feeding Boston-bound traffic from the west to Andrew Craigie's more recent bridge from Lechmere to Boston.

To make their action more decisive, the town meeting, a mere four months later, made the highway here another crucial spot in the all-out Dana-Craigie struggle that gave Cambridge most of the streets that are still its main west–east thoroughfares. The town meeting later changed the name of Newe Towne's Spring Street to Mt. Auburn Street after connecting Mt. Auburn Street directly with the present Massachusetts Avenue at old Putnam Square. We will see on a later walk how Craigie, near Harvard's Memorial Hall site, continued his expensive battle (he would die nearly bankrupt) struggling to compensate for the town's favoring Dana.

Spring Street had, of course, been the original lane to the Town Spring on Brattle Street just to the west of the CWT (Cherry, Webb & Touraine) store we see on our left. All this loop of land between Mt. Auburn and Brattle Streets was part of the extensive Brattle estate. Recent improvements along Eliot Street and in Brattle Square—red brick walks, 20-foot-wide sidewalks, benches, bike racks, artistic decorations, finishing touches that went along in 1984–85 with completion of the subway extension—contrast sharply with the way the area looked to the first settlers. The first improvement came in 1636, when the town voted just to build a small wooden footbridge over the creek to the Town Spring.

Even at the time of the Revolution there was little change. The Square area got its first beautifying when the last Brattle estate owner, Thomas Brattle, a lover of horticulture and hospitality, returned here from England after the Revolution and made this loop portion and pond near the Spring such an attractive park area, with trees, plantings, shrubs, and walks, that town folks and lovers who used it as a promenade to the river called it Brattle's Mall.

After his death (he left no children), the land was sold, and in 1849 it became the site of a large, wooden five-story structure with big four-pillared portico facing Brattle Square and was called Brattle House. It was too big for leisurely, rural Cambridge and was not a success, but for three decades (1865–95) it served as the University Press. William Dean Howells, editor of the *Atlantic Monthly,* has told how he and his neighbor Henry Wadsworth Longfellow often met at the University Press. Longfellow, said Howells, liked to "bring his proofs back to the printer himself" and *The Atlantic* used to be printed there.

Before we start walking along Brattle Street, notice the plaza on the north side of Brattle Square. It was named for Joseph Austin de Guglielmo, first Cambridge mayor of Italian descent and a key figure in J.F.K.'s first winning a seat in Congress. De Guglielmo, Harvard class of 1929, had a law office in Central Square and served as an associate justice of the Boston Municipal Court. After dedication of the plaza some 250 friends gathered at the nearby Wursthaus to celebrate as J.F.K. and "deGug," J.F.K.'s nickname for his close friend, used to do.

The brick staircase on the plaza leads down to the elaborate new Harvard Subway Station. Harvard's first president, Dunster, while living by Winthrop Square after his 1641 marriage, used to have six acres of land and a barn here on the north side of present Brattle Square, partly back of the "deGug" Plaza.

FAMOUS DOINGS ON BRATTLE'S ACRES

Brattle Street—old Tory Row—which we now join, on our left, is the most historic and prestigious street in Cambridge.

That prestige dates back to the pre-Revolutionary days, when it was also known as "Church Row," a reference to its residents' building and attending Christ Church, across from the Common. In those times all the land from Brattle's to and even beyond Elmwood Avenue, slightly more than a mile ahead of us, was divided into seven estates, each with a mansion that we may still see.

When Thomas Brattle died in 1801 his estate included all the acres in the loop and along the south side of Brattle Street to, and including, the former Greenleaf mansion, now the residence of the president of Radcliffe, with all Brattle's land just west of Story Street to Ash Street, running down to the Charles River. He also owned many acres on the north side of Brattle Street, which included much of the land that is now Radcliffe Yard. The Town Spring was on the east side of the grand courtyard of his mansion, where we now see the Brattle Theatre. The spring, which eventually became just a well, flowed from under a stone arch, later replaced by curbing, to the Town Creek.

Brattle Theatre, 40 Brattle, originally Brattle Hall, was built in 1889 by the nonprofit Cambridge Social Union, headed by local civic leaders, for holding amateur threatricals, lectures, musical comedies, and dances. Professor George Pierce Baker was the group's first artistic director, and before World War I also acted here, before he set up his famed 47 Workshop. Many outstanding names have been associated with performances here over the years. T. S. Eliot acted on its stage. Dramatic companies performed before and during World War II. Paul Robeson played here his celebrated role as Shakespeare's Othello.

After World War II the theatre was sold to a private group, which made a summer-stock playhouse and, beginning in 1949, for fourteen years the Brattle Theatre Company acted here with world-famous performers Eva Le Gallienne, Jessica Tandy, Hume Cronyn, Hermione Gingold, and Zero Mostel. In 1953 the theatre began featuring great foreign and classic films. The success of Humphrey Bogart and Ingrid Bergman in *Casablanca* still attaches to the theatre with the basement, via the old porte cochère, and other shops and cafés offering popular Club Casablanca.

The community-minded Cambridge Social Union of 1876, back in 1889, also bought the original Brattle mansion next to the theatre at 42 Brattle, where it carries on its many programs providing high-quality instruction for adults who desire to improve "their best potential." In 1938 the Union changed its name to the widely patronized Cambridge Center for Adult Education.

Time, with growth in population, has mightily crowded this mansion house that was built in 1727 by future Major General William Brattle, commander of all the militia of the province and one of the wealthiest men, if not the wealthiest man in Cambridge.

The three-story gambrel buff clapboard with traditional white trim and green blinds is even more crowded than we saw Apthorp House, though Brattle's was once the proud center of acres so broad that it had farm buildings, barn, hen house, and dairy spread around its service court, and William's only surviving son, Thomas, in trying to cut the loss of Harvard students to drowning, built a bathhouse for them on his river land far ahead of us at the foot of Ash Street. He also built one of America's first greenhouses.

Thomas Brattle and his father were naturally partial to the College where Thomas's grandfather served as a renowned tutor before becoming pastor of Cambridge's First Church. William, who was born in the parsonage, married Connecticut Governor Saltonstall's daughter, mother of Thomas. On the eve of the Revolution, William fled with other Tories to Boston and soon died, still denying Tory sympathies. Thomas, on his return to America, was proved to have been helpful to Americans imprisoned in England, cleared himself of all charges, and regained his estate.

Many great Americans have used the projecting entry to the Brattle mansion, most of all General George Washington, who did so many times. When one of Washington's aides, future Pennsylvania Governor Thomas Mifflin, came to live at Brattle House as the army's commissary general, the thirty-two-year-old fighting Quaker, in charge of feeding and clothing the soldiers, Mifflin's young wife made the Brattle House a social center for Washington's staff, officers, and their wives.

Life there has been vividly described by Mary Morgan, wife of Dr. John Morgan, the patriot army's surgeon general. It was at a social gathering that Washington, as she told it, had one of his happiest breaks in his long weeks of worry about getting fighting supplies for his warriors.

An express rider, who had galloped much of the way, late in 1775 dismounted outside the entry and delivered the terrific news that a British ordnance transport had been captured at sea and moored in Gloucester harbor, Cape Ann, by Captain John Manley. Pleasure beamed on the countenance of Washington and all his major generals present, Horatio Gates, "Old Put," Charles Lee, as Washington himself ecstatically read the prize ship's cargo: 2,000 muskets, "with bayonets, scabbards and steel rammers," 100,000 flints, tons of musket shot, round shot, mortar beds, two brass six-pounders, and the immense brass mortar that "Old Put" would promptly call "The Congress" at that christening on the Common, where we have already visited.

General Washington promoted Manley, a former sailor in the British Navy, to be Commodore of the fleet that Washington called "Our little squadron," four armed vessels of the pioneer U.S. Navy, created October 5, 1775, by Washington to wage war at sea as well as on land.

John Adams told of dining here with his wife Abigail, and visiting here again when he was on his way to Philadelphia to sign the Declaration of Independence. Abigail was a visitor in Cambridge, where she knew many of the patriot families, but most of her time she spent caring for her children in Braintree. After one of her early visits she wrote to her husband, who was foremost in getting the Continental Congress to make Washington commander-in-chief, that the choice had brought "universal satisfaction."

In later years, Margaret Fuller, future feminist champion, and ill-fated Marchese Ossoli, came at age twenty-three in 1832 with her father, Timothy Fuller, to live here with her sister and six brothers in the Old Brattle House, then owned by her uncle. Fuller had devoted so much time to public life as state legislator, speaker of the house, and in four terms in

Congress, that his law practice had about vanished. When President Jackson was reelected, ending Fuller's prospects of a federal appointment, Fuller left for Groton to try to support his family by farming. He soon died and Margaret, who took over the family's support, tried to carry on the farm but shifted to the editing that brought her fame.

It was here in the old Brattle mansion in the early days of the Cambridge Social Union that community leaders formed the distinguished Cambridge Historical Society in June 1905, with the author's only son, Richard Henry Dana III, presiding. The group included old Cambridge neighbors, historian Albert Bushnell Hart, author Thomas Wentworth Higginson, and, always an active community worker, Alice Longfellow, daughter of the poet.

Church Street, entering Brattle Street on our right, was a familiar route of the poet and his family to the church whose spire we can see down the street. Alice Longfellow often went this way alone, for she taught Sunday School in the old parish house, now replaced by the attractive stone 1902 structure back of the church. Back in August 1834, when nineteen-year-old future author Dana, too troubled by impaired eyesight to try to continue at College, left for *Two Years Before the Mast,* the Danas were living in a house on a large lot at the north corner of Church and Brattle. Here he said goodbye to his father, the poet, and went to Boston to board the *Pilgrim,* a brig.

In the next lot east of the old Dana corner lot, the 1827 traditional buff with white trim clapboard at 53 Church, for decades in the mid-1800s was the home and later just the office of one of Cambridge's most admired and beloved doctors, Dr. Morrill Wyman, a founder of Cambridge's first city hospital. President Eliot credited the skill of Dr. Wyman, his family physician, with saving Mrs. Eliot's life when she was desperately stricken (and other doctors at their Mt. Desert summer place had given up) by dashing miles by horse and wagon to the rescue.

Eliot also praised Dr. Wyman's abhorrence of doctors who overcharged patients. For doctors to do so, said Wyman, was an unethical violation of the Hippocratic oath they had taken. Eliot was far from alone in his admiration. Bishop Lawrence called Wyman the "Nestor of physicians, a genius in diagnoses." The doctor kept up his practice until his late eighties, dying in 1903 at age ninety-one.

In most of the space between Wyman's house and the old red brick ex-police station was once a convenience loved by the local gentry—Pike's stables, where Teddy Roosevelt in his College years kept his favorite horse, buggy, and fashionable tilbury gig. Pike's supplied hacks for every sort of occasion and, for winter's snow, put them on runners (in this form they were called booby-hutches), which were drawn by a pair of horses.

Continuing along Brattle Street we see, at the east corner of Farwell Place, a big apartment house. This is where Washington Grammar School, a three-story brick building, stood from 1852 to 1905. A brown stone tablet once told that this school was a "descendant of the Faire Grammar School," Cambridge's first.

It was the seventh since that first school that once stood on the present Holyoke Street, but it is especially known for three famous pupils: artist Daniel Chester French, ornithologist William Brewster, and civil service reformer Richard Henry Dana III. All were youngsters together when they took lessons here, went on bird walks in the woods, shooting and trapping, fishing ventures at Fresh Pond, and became permanent friends.

Probably best remembered is how they handled a school bully. It took more than they had learned in snowball fights with boyhood rivals from other parts of town. Dick Dana's father taught him how to box and he passed that on. Sure enough at a noon recess in the yard, back of the school, the bully struck again. Dick's nose spurted blood and he saw stars, but he hit back. When the bully found blood gushing from his own nose he wanted to quit. A teacher appeared, saw that the bully was getting his comeuppance, quickly decided it was a lesson overdue, and let it go on. The bully struck no more, at least, not at Washington Grammar School.

Farwell Place in those times was known as School Court, with good reason. Back of Washington Grammar School's yard was once Auburn School, of special interest because of its proximity to Cambridge's first women's college, now a block away. The grammar school where girls in

1826 were first admitted to the class, though they had to sit in the rear, was on nearby Garden Street within the present Radcliffe Yard.

Auburn School, a wooden structure, was built in 1832 when the earlier school became crowded. Auburn School was used at first for girls only, but in 1845 became a high school for both girls and boys. Auburn School was moved away in 1851 and later served, until 1927, as the parochial school of St. Peter's Church on Concord Avenue.

On our left as we go along Farwell Place, just beyond the Gutman Library, are two old wooden buildings that once stood facing Brattle Street but were uprooted to make room for the library. The early nineteenth-century Nichols house at 11 Farwell Place once stood on the east corner of Brattle and Appian Way. The more ancient and better-known Read house, now beyond and diagonally back of the Nichols house, stood at the west corner of Brattle and Farwell Place.

The two-story Read house, with its pedimented entry, green door, and two dormers in the attic, was built long before the Revolution by a family whose progenitor arrived in Cambridge in 1725. The Reads in 1760 sold the northern part of their garden for £16 so that their Tory neighbors could complete assembling, with some town land, the present site of Christ Church at the far end of Farwell Place.

When the Revolution came, the Reads, different from their neighbors, had two young sons, one a Minuteman, the other a volunteer, who fought against the Redcoats. Levi Farwell acquired the Read property in 1826 and a year later sold the house to Harvard's notorious would-be medical professor John Webster, who lived in it from 1827 to 1834 and moved to where we will again meet him when he was arrested for a sensational murder.

Returning to Brattle Street, we see in midblock on the south side, at number 56, one of Cambridge's most beloved sites, the home of the village blacksmith, Dexter Pratt, immortalized by his neighbor, the poet Longfellow. The 1808 house, buff with white trim and green blinds, set end to the street, was acquired in 1972 by the Cambridge Center for Adult Education and is called Blacksmith House, modernized and used as a bakery with outdoor terrace and café. Among its specialties are items that might puzzle Dexter Pratt—tortes, quiche, croissants, all most natural for the Cambridge Center, which offers fully fifty courses in cooking.

The spreading chestnut tree under which Longfellow met Dexter Pratt, despite Longfellow's and neighbors' efforts to save it, was chopped down when Brattle Street was widened and straightened by the municipal authorities in 1870. Cambridge schoolchildren on his seventieth birthday gave him an armchair made from some of the chestnut cuttings.

The poet was so fond of walking along Brattle Street that he even gave up going to Nahant's seashore during summer months. Students loved to walk the street to and from Mt. Auburn woods and Fresh Pond. It was enjoyed, as well, as a great resident bikeway. Residents did not take kindly to modernization. They delighted in the old horse-drawn cars, whose conductors would obligingly stop at a patron's front door. They fought so mightily in 1894 when electric cars were to replace horsecars, bringing wires and electric poles, that the trolleys were put instead on Mt. Auburn Street and later on Concord Avenue. But old-fashioned horsecar service on Brattle Street did not survive.

Between Dexter Pratt's house and Hilliard Street, where we now see the seven-story Brattle Arms at 60 Brattle Streed, once lived William Hilliard, early publisher of the University Press, for whom Hilliard Street is named. Hilliard bought the land from the Brattle estate and began printing on Hilliard Street, which until 1852 was called Woodbine Lane.

His work was soon engaged by the College and the 1802 commencement program saw his name credited along with, for the first time, the University Press. He built his large brick house in 1809, its end toward Brattle Street, and sold it to the College in 1829. Here, from 1829 to 1845 when he was in Cambridge, lived Supreme Court Justice Joseph Story, first Dane professor of law, intimate friend as well as associate of Chief Justice Marshall and credited by Harvard President Josiah Quincy with being "the real founder of the Harvard Law School."

Hilliard Street has seen many famous residents besides Justice Story. Philosopher George Santayana, while he was still an assistant professor at $2,000 a year, came to live in the old Story house and while here had his salary doubled in 1904 on becoming a full professor. He has told how he had his "walls covered with Arundel prints." Professor George Lyman Kittredge, famed teacher and authority on Shakespeare, lived for many years at 8 Hilliard Street on our left down the street.

And in a couple of houses farther down Hilliard Street, on our right, at number 13, author John P. Marquand lived as a youngster with his grandmother Fuller while going to Cambridge Latin School. The Fullers, including Margaret and Buckminster Fuller, were of a longtime Cambridge family; and it was at 13 Hilliard Street that the future author learned Cambridge ways and got the nickel that launched him on his sarsaparilla spree in Harvard Square.

APPIAN WAY TO CREATIVE MR. GILMAN'S GATE

Appian Way, directly across from Hilliard Street, brings us to both the border of Radcliffe Yard and the birthplace of Radcliffe College. Gutman Library's 6 Appian Way entry was the address and site of the two-story wooden dwelling with pitched roof and attic, named Carret house after its most obliging owners, where twenty-seven young women of the first Radcliffe class began their courses in two rented, improvised classrooms in fall 1879. President Eliot, in his inaugural address in the First Unitarian Church, had strongly favored higher education for women. Now, with his hearty approval given for Harvard professors to furnish the instruction, the new venture was launched with the Carret family acting more like academic helpers than landlords.

Classes started in just two of the rooms, but more had to be engaged, almost squeezing out the Carrets. Soon a library was put in a house directly across the way, which, we will presently see, became a Holmes residence. Another house on this street provided a lab, indeed "about all extra rooms" in Appian Way were utilized. Enrollment in the school popularly called "Harvard Annex" continued to grow so steadily that after only a half dozen years famous Fay House, on Garden Street across from the then vigorous Washington Elm, was purchased from its highly cooperative owner, Maria Fay. This purchase, in 1884, marked the beginning of the Radcliffe Yard, which we will presently visit.

Appian Way, with but few of its old houses still here, in recent years has developed as the center of Harvard and Radcliffe's Graduate School of Education. The five-story Gutman Library was built in 1972, two years before the death of Monroe C. Gutman, a magna cum laude 1905 graduate who became a partner in the New York brokerage firm of Lehman Brothers. It was planned to provide materials for the study of all aspects of education.

Longfellow Hall, just ahead on the left, once Radcliffe offices and classrooms with a big legislaturelike lecture room, is devoted to the School of Education and is the office of the dean. Besides big Larsen Hall just ahead on our right, the school includes three smaller structures on or near Appian Way.

A fascinating tale of Appian Way is told about one of poet Longfellow's young granddaughters on a first visit to Rome. On coming to its most celebrated highway her face beamed on being told the name and exclaimed, "Why, there's an Appian Way in Rome, too!"

Besides giving birth to many educational projects, the local Appian Way has had many celebrated residents. Directly across the way from the Carret house lived, at 5 Appian, John Holmes, witty, antiquarian brother of Oliver Wendell Holmes. John spent the remainder of his life here after the historic 1737 house north of the Yard in which the Holmes brothers were born was demolished in 1883. In John's last years he was told that a neighbor had died the previous night while in her easy chair. "My," exclaimed John, "a death like that makes my mouth water."

The white clapboard house still standing at 10 Appian Way is a reminder of poet John Berryman's living in the ell in back of this midnineteenth-century structure. He called it 10½ Appian Way, felt it was tiny yet hard to heat. At the time he and his fellow poet Delmore Schwartz, who won fame when only twenty-six, were English instructors at Harvard. So many of Berryman's students kept dropping by that Berryman took his beloved red leather chair and moved to Boston's Beacon Hill.

The modernity, height, and amplitude of Larsen Hall, next on our right, proves that the Graduate School of Education has left behind the financial leanness of its earlier years. President Bok, in announcing the success of Harvard's recent unprecedented six-year campaign to raise funds, included Roy Edward Larsen, a Harvard 1921 grad who rose to be head of the Time Inc. enterprises, among the top few he commended by name. This 1966 structure, with faculty offices, studies, labs, and lounges, was just one of the many large Larsen gifts.

Fund raising, with educators receiving small incomes, was so difficult in the 1930 depression years that President Conant feared it would result in killing "the kitten," the separate graduate school that the old division of education became in 1920. Conant came up with a new degree idea, "my invention," he called it, shifting emphasis to achieving better education through school principals and superintendents; and Boston businessman A. Lincoln Filene became the school's continuing benefactor. President

Pusey, a great fund raiser in his day, encouraged building of the Gutman Library to make it a leader in the field of providing research materials even for experienced professionals renewing or updating their studies, and had presided at the dedication of Larsen Hall.

Where now we see Longfellow Hall, named for the always community-minded eldest daughter of poet Longfellow, Alice Longfellow, a founder of Radcliffe College, was in 1883 the birthplace of Browne & Nichols, new path-blazing preparatory school. An experimental prelude to the school's 1883 opening took place in a three-story squarish wooden house then at 11 Appian Way.

Stocky George H. "Daddy" Browne, on being graduated from Harvard in 1878, started at once as a high school teacher but soon felt a better system would be to train young people to observe and think rather than just memorizing old courses. Two of Browne's Harvard instructors, "Stubby" Child and Charles Eliot Norton, both with sons to be educated, recalled what a skillful pupil Browne had been and agreed with his ideas. In 1882 they got Browne to take their three sons and two other lads to instruct them in rooms in old Felton Hall, then back of Cambridge Latin School.

Near the end of the experiment Browne met accidentally with a classmate, Edgar H. Nichols, scion of a long line of Unitarian ministers. Nichols, a tall, thin fellow who was a whiz in college in math and science, would prove to be a brilliant teacher and administrator. He agreed to join Browne, prepared an announcement, and when they started classes at 11 Appian Way they had seventeen boys. Growth came fast.

In 1885 they acquired, from the father of one of their first pupils, a larger building at 8 Garden Street, next to famous Fay House, which we will see shortly in Radcliffe Yard. By 1894 they had to build a big four-story wooden schoolhouse back of 11 Appian Way. Only three years later they traded all three buildings with Radcliffe College, which was also expanding, and Browne & Nichols built itself a new three-story brick schoolhouse two blocks west at 20 Garden Street, which would be its home for just over half a century.

Longfellow Hall, built in 1930, replaced not only Browne & Nichols's first building but the big 1894 four-story wooden classroom building that would be used as Radcliffe classrooms for more than three decades.

On the north end of Longfellow Hall's site was still another large dwelling, built at 15 Appian Way around the end of the eighteenth century that, in deference to its age or occupants, was saved by being moved more than a mile west to Coolidge Hill. It had been at different times the dwelling of Elizabeth Dana, sister of Richard Henry Dana III, English poet Arthur Hugh Clough, and historian Albert Bushnell Hart.

At this far end, 18 Appian Way, philosopher William James lived from 1882 to 1885 in a small house he bought after his mother died and his father and sister moved to Boston. James, along with future Radcliffe President LeBaron Briggs, was among those who gave classes at the other end of Appian Way in the Carret house where Radcliffe began. James got a lot of his writing done here, but when the second of his two sons born here died from pneumonia James and his wife moved around the corner to his mother-in-law's house at 19 Garden Street.

Nichols House and Read House, both of which we saw while walking in Farwell Place, are part of the School of Education, the former in psychology and Read in community programs. Also part of the School is a former doctor's house and office on the corner, facing Garden Street, called Westengard House, used for offices and research.

Here also near the corner at 22 Appian Way once stood the home of a professor of Latin whose enthusiastic support helped to create Radcliffe College, James B. Greenough. In harmony with Appian Way's being birthplace of many educational ventures, it was Harvard Professor Greenough's son who was a founder of well-known Noble & Greenough Preparatory School. And it was Professor Greenough who made his house available for amateur theatricals so that the Cambridge Dramatic Club, which had a big part when the Cambridge Social Union was building Brattle Hall, would get its start in 1876.

On returning to Brattle Street we have, diagonally across the street, the Loeb Drama Center, at 64 Brattle. Had President Lowell been able to provide such practical, not to mention attractive, theatrical facilities as we see in this 1960 structure, no doubt former Professor George P. Baker would never have left Cambridge. There are actually two theatres, the major 556-seat one, and back of it an experimental theatre with room for 120 seats. Also off the lobby is a refreshment patio with a delightful outlook on a garden area between the theatre and the dwelling of Radcliffe's president.

Besides the Harvard-Radcliffe Dramatic Club, presenting classic and original plays, the theatre has been the residence of the American Repertory Theatre since 1979, bringing a legendary array of stars and plays to its stage. In the lobby is a plaque stating that the theatre was the gift of New York broker and banker John Langeloth Loeb, Harvard 1924 graduate, whose son and namesake (Harvard 1952) was at the head of President Bok's list of donors with his gifts totaling $9,000,000 to the recent campaign.

Continuing along Brattle we have on our right two of Radcliffe Yard's three oldest houses, both of them former family dwellings the College purchased early in this century. From the children's playthings and sandbox in its yard we quickly observe that the first, the 1838 Putnam House, initially utilized as a Radcliffe dormitory and offices, is now a care center for the youngsters of student mothers. The second, another survivor of a former row of old dwellings, 1821 Buckingham House at 77 Brattle, used for offices, career services, and various study projects, was named for its last owner, Harriet Buckingham, Radcliffe College teacher and secretary, from 1911 to 1937.

Right beyond Buckingham House we come to the brick gate named in honor of the founder of Radcliffe College, Arthur Gilman, editor, author, educator, first secretary, and later regent of the new College. Gilman and his wife Stella were eager for a college education for their children, in particular their daughter Grace. Gilman talked over his ideas with neighbors and Harvard professors, often visited and was encouraged by Professor Greenough.

Late in 1878, Gilman wrote a letter to President Eliot on his proposal to make a Harvard education available to women, predicting that though it might have a slow start, "it will grow." Gilman requested permission to use the services of Harvard professors. The very next day, the day before

Christmas, Eliot appeared at Gilman's house in midblock, 5 Phillips Place, just one house north of the future Radcliffe Yard, and gave Gilman his enthusiastic support.

With Gilman acting as secretary to receive responses at his house, he and seven women issued an announcement on February 22, 1879, offering "Collegiate Instruction for Women" and promising that "no instructor will be provided of a lower grade than that given in Harvard College." Because the College had no dorms, the women offered to help students "secure suitable lodgings."

Heading the ladies was future first President Elizabeth Cary Agassiz, widow of Professor Louis Agassiz. The six other signers included Mrs. Gilman, three wives of and two daughters of Harvard professors, including Alice Longfellow and Mrs. Greenough. To 6 Appian Way that fall came "the intellectual emancipation of women" that President Eliot had sought in his inaugural. As seen by future Radcliffe President LeBaron R. Briggs, the Annex, "a dream of Arthur Gilman and his wife," came true.

On our left as we enter Radcliffe Yard is a bronze statue with upraised arm called *The Oracle* in honor of the first dean of what is now called the Bunting Institute. The location of *The Oracle* is of special interest because it was here on a parcel of old Brattle land, part of the future Radcliffe Yard, that Gilman came up with a second educational creation for the community, the Cambridge School.

This 1886 preparatory school did so well that he, as its director, was able only a decade later to get a larger new classroom building a third of a mile away at 34 Concord Avenue. Gilman himself was always so busy that although he changed residences he kept them always near the Radcliffe Yard.

The map of the Radcliffe buildings, on the post on our right near Buckingham House, shows the positions and relationship of the five other Radcliffe buildings we see in the Yard.

RADCLIFFE YARD AND OLD ASH STREET

Fay House, directly ahead, built in 1807, is the oldest of the buildings in the Radcliffe Yard and for nearly all the life of the College has been its administrative center. Its address, 10 Garden Street, reminds us that it was built facing the Common.

The experiment at Carret House prospered so well that the "Society for the Collegiate Instruction of Women," incorporated in 1882, chose Mrs. Agassiz as president, and by 1885 purchased already historic Fay House. Indeed, Maria Fay, the owner, delighted with the increasing number of students at the "Harvard Annex," had gone on her own to visit the Gilmans to offer her house and land. Fay House was then also known by the nickname "Harvard Annex" or sometimes simply as "Annex House."

With almost a decade of continued growth behind them, petitioners with President Eliot in the forefront went in 1894 to Beacon Hill, and the College obtained its incorporation. Along with this document came agreement that its diplomas would be signed by the presidents of both Radcliffe and Harvard. Mrs. Agassiz was now chosen president of Radcliffe College, with Arthur Gilman as regent and her son-in-law, philanthropist Major Henry Lee Higginson, as treasurer. Mr. Gilman recorded that in that fall the College had a dozen times as many students as it had started with in Appian Way.

The new Radcliffe College name was adopted at the suggestion of Mrs. Agassiz in deference to the widow of a Lord Mayor of London, Lady Anne Radcliffe Mowlson. Back in 1643 Harvard College, still in its infancy, had fielded a committee in England seeking to raise funds. Lady Anne gave £100 to establish a scholarship, Harvard's first. Giving gifts for education came naturally to her and her late husband, who had founded "a faire school" in his birthplace at about the time Harvard was born. President Agassiz warmly and generously favored using Lady Anne's maiden name for the College even over her own.

The Fay House of 1885 was an impressive mansion but much smaller than the structure that we now see. The prosperous man who built it was impoverished by Jefferson's embargo and it was sold to Harvard Professor Reverend Joseph McKean, founder in his undergraduate years of the

Porcellian Club. Silvery voiced Edward Everett, another clergyman who would be governor, president of Harvard, U.S. senator, and orator at Gettysburg along with Abe Lincoln, was a later resident here while professor of Greek at Harvard.

Judge Samuel Fay, eminent townsman and Harvard overseer, bought the house in 1835 in time for the 200th anniversary of Harvard, which brought here one of its best-remembered visitors, the judge's brother-in-law, Reverend Samuel Gilman. It was in the second floor northwest front room off the hall that Reverend Gilman, as guest on the commencement eve, wrote the lines to his famous ode "Fair Harvard." The room is now the office of the secretary to Radcliffe's president.

Enlargements that doubled the size of Fay House within a few years after Radcliffe acquired it included a new auditorium on the Mason Street side, classrooms, and an entire third floor for a library, supplied by Alice Longfellow. Arthur Gilman kept his eyes on every step of this expansion, intently watching the Corinthian columns being put up in the entry to the big new library.

Among early College events in Fay House, Mrs. Agassiz, in the original oval drawing room, held her midweekly afternoon teas for students, faculty, and friends; the big doors to the hallway were left open to provide space for the first commencement here, with President Eliot taking part; Radcliffe's early Idler Club, founded for recreation, staged its first play here in Fay House with women, imitating Hasty Pudding, playing all the roles.

Byerly Hall, just east of Fay House, is the most recent structure in Radcliffe Yard. Built in 1933, just after Longfellow Hall, it was named for the first Harvard professor to get on Mr. Gilman's list of prospective instructors at the new College in Appian Way, math Professor William E. Byerly, who went on to serve Radcliffe in many major capacities. The building at first had, besides lecture halls, several laboratories, for it was chiefly intended for instruction in the sciences

Emphasis on use of Byerly Hall for sciences shifted after Harvard, fully coeducational with Radcliffe since President Mary I. Bunting's 1969 merger proposal to President Pusey took effect, got its new big Science

Center in 1972. Currently, for both young men and women seeking admission to Harvard-Radcliffe, Byerly Hall is where applications have been made since admissions offices were merged in 1974.

How different it all was back in 1849 when a young woman, a fine scholar, applied to Harvard President Jared Sparks. Harvard College, he told her, was arranged for young men only and it would be inexpedient for a "solitary female mingling . . . promiscuously with so large a number of the other sex." He did, though, say it was all a misfortune and looked forward to a more intelligent and liberal future to end "this deficiency." Now admission is open not only to the Colleges, but to all ten graduate schools, too.

Byerly does have lecture halls, offices, and other services, and in particular it is the center for Harvard-Radcliffe group tours, each taking a bit more than an hour, which are conducted by students. Visitors who have taken them say enthusiastically that they are informative and highly enjoyable, particularly for prospective students. Many attractive, historic displays are to be seen in the Center, which also has maps and related material available near the ticket office.

The three buildings in the northwest part of the Yard, all connected by covered, porchlike walkways—Hemenway Gym, Agassiz House, and Schlesinger Library—date from the turn of this century. The oldest, originally a gym built in 1898, was Radcliffe's first gift of an entire building. The site in part was where Arthur Gilman experimented with his Cambridge School for Girls before getting his own first schoolhouse on the site of the *Oracle*. The donor was Harriet, a sister of Bishop William Lawrence, whose husband, Augustus Hemenway, member of the Harvard Class of 1875, gave Harvard its first Hemenway Gymnasium only three years after his graduation.

Use of Hemenway has entirely changed since a new athletic center was built in 1979, a few blocks up Garden Street near the Radcliffe Quad; the latter is a complex of dormitories that we will be seeing. The pool installed here in the basement in 1900 is now used for storage. The renovated main part, once for gymnastics and other athletic facilities, is now the Murray Research Center, created in 1976, which came here in 1981 for its expanding study of women's lives in order to understand the effects on them of social changes. The top floor, once a basketball court, was converted into the Radcliffe Dance Center, with access via Agassiz House and the connecting covered walkway.

Few people have had a happier eightieth birthday than Radcliffe's first President, Elizabeth Agassiz. To celebrate it, her family and friends raised funds to grant her fondest wish by building (1903–1904) Agassiz House, with its striking white-pillared portico, as a student center.

The Gilman Room, first on the left off the main hallway, a room named in memory of Arthur Gilman, is still used for meetings, lectures, and forums. The beautifully comfortable student lounge, first on the right off the hallway, a pleasure now available in common rooms of the Radcliffe Quad dorms, was replaced by the busy Office for Arts at Harvard and Radcliffe, a clearing-house for the entire College community's art programs. There is also a splendid ballroom for receptions and social events.

Most famous in Agassiz House, though, is its 350-seat theatre, in the amphitheater style, with rising tiers of seats. A foretaste of its fame can be seen at the end of the main hallway, in the enlarged 1909 photograph of the all-female cast of Shakespeare's *Merchant of Venice*, which was put on here by the Idler Club.

The Idler, Radcliffe's first club, was merged years later with the Harvard Dramatic Club, founded back in 1908, the first Harvard Club to admit Radcliffe girls as members. The stage is especially associated with Professor George P. Baker, who used it for performances of his 47 Workshop. Even earlier, Baker in 1904 had begun his English 47 course—he called it "dramatic composition"—here at Radcliffe a year before extending it to Harvard.

Many celebrated women have used the stage: Amy Lowell the poetess; Jane Addams of Hull House; Gertrude Stein on her 1934 lecture tour, when she found Cambridge so different from her student days ("it was as if I had never been there"); and Eleanor Roosevelt as a guest of the Radcliffe Phi Beta Kappa chapter, which held all its early gatherings here after it was formed in 1914.

The Schlesinger Library, the nation's foremost research center on the history of American women, is a successor to Radcliffe's undergraduate library, which occupied this building when it was completed in 1908 through the fund raising of Radcliffe's second president, Harvard Dean LeBaron R. Briggs. Back then, Radcliffe students were mainly commuters. By 1966, when the undergraduate library moved out Garden Street to the new Hilles Library in the Radcliffe Quad, most Radcliffe students lived in the Quad's dorms, which have since gone coed, as have those in Harvard Yard.

Schlesinger Library was known simply as Women's Archives in 1943 when the first president of the League of Women Voters, a leader in the long struggle for women's suffrage, Maud Wood Park, 1898 Radcliffe grad, gave the papers, manuscripts, books, and photographs she had assembled over the years in her Woman's Rights Collection. Women's Archives continued collecting in just about every field of women's endeavor under the guidance of Arthur M. Schlesinger, Sr., Harvard professor of history and even longer a Radcliffe trustee; he was eager to show the role of women in our nation's history. When he died in 1965 the Archives was renamed Schlesinger Library for both him and his wife, Elizabeth.

Photographs, autographed letters, and documents from the original Park collection are on display in the library. Most prized gems of the archives include family papers of Harriet Beecher Stowe; papers, letters, and manuscripts of Susan B. Anthony, Elizabeth Cady Stanton, Julia Ward Howe, Lucy Stone, pioneer aviatrix Amelia Earhart, Betty Friedan, Dr. Elizabeth Blackwell, and many other eminent women; and 200 boxes of the Lydia Pinkham company, including unopened bottles of her "vegetable compound," which, according to an old song, she made because of "her love for the human race."

Collecting still continues, including, since 1976, an oral-history project to assemble the history of black women in America. The collection has grown so greatly that it was to be moved in 1986, along with the also expanding Bunting Institute (which had occupied the top two floors since 1967) to new quarters nearby at 34–40 Concord Avenue.

On returning to Brattle Street via the Gilman Gate, we see on our right, where James Street slants into Brattle, a handy small wooden house where Radcliffe alumnae have long held meetings and sometimes stayed overnight. The big six-story former apartment house just west of it has helped meet housing needs of the ever-growing graduate student body in Cambridge.

Directly across from the Gilman Gate, at 76 Brattle, is three-story Greenleaf House, the official residence of Radcliffe College presidents since President Briggs in 1913, and the College's first full-time President Ada Comstock (1923–1943), to Matina Horner, whose presidency began in 1972. President Horner and Harvard President Bok just about completed merging the two Colleges with their 1977 agreement on financial arrangements, faculty appointments, and Harvard-Radcliffe instruction.

Greenleaf House was built in 1859 by James Greenleaf, son of distinguished early Harvard Law School Professor Simon Greenleaf. James Greenleaf was spectacularly successful in selling and manufacturing cotton before the Civil War. Frequent travel to New Orleans made him fond of its French mansard-style mansions, which he copied.

To preserve the handsome grounds around his dwelling he removed his father's impressive three-story Federal-style house to nearby Ash Street; it is a house famous in Cambridge for its many distinguished visitors and Professor Greenleaf's friendly relations with students and his neighbor, Justice Story, who had got him to come to the Law School and whom he succeeded as Dane Professor of Law.

James Greenleaf, a cousin of poet John Greenleaf Whittier, was married to Mary, the sister of Henry Wadsworth Longfellow, and, like the Longfellows, was born in Maine. Their families' combination of similar backgrounds in Maine and professorships in Bowdoin and Harvard Colleges led to Greenleaf House's repute for a happy social life.

For James Greenleaf, who died at the end of the Civil War, this pleasant life ended after only a half dozen years, but it continued into the twentieth century for his widow, joyfully known as Aunt Mary to several generations of College students, and in delightful family get-togethers of the Greenleaf, Longfellow, and Dana relatives hereabouts. Convivial gatherings have gone right on in both the dwelling and its spacious gardens.

Long remembered when President Comstock retired was her wedding, in 1943, to a Yale history professor, in the mansion's living room.

Cronkhite Graduate Center, the big, long three-story brick building at the corner of Ash Street, was built in 1956 and named for Bernice Brown Cronkhite, who served Radcliffe for nearly four decades as dean of the College and first dean of the graduate school. That school, long her goal, was the first collegiate women graduates' center and was merged in 1963 with Harvard Graduate Schools. It serves as residence and restaurant, and fills many other graduate needs, with wings added so that the building, with its main entrance at 6 Ash Street, extends a block down Ash Street and has another wing parallel to Brattle Street, all forming a beautiful courtyard looking toward the west side of Greenleaf House.

At the northeast corner of this courtyard (accessible from Brattle between Greenleaf and Cronkhite) is a monument linked to one of Radcliffe's best-known graduates, Helen Keller. The monument's braille dots on the plaques and the water of fountain and pool had special significance for Helen Keller, a 1904 Radcliffe graduate, who at nineteen months of age had been left deaf and blind by illness. At her graduation, held in Harvard's old Sanders Theatre, she was handed honors she had won and, a little more than a half century later, in 1959, President Pusey gave her the first honorary degree given by Harvard to a woman.

The woman who helped patiently to make Helen Keller's achievement possible is also honored by this monument; she was Anne Sullivan, who, as the monument tells, began this "miracle" with the word "water," which she first imparted to young Miss Keller. Miss Sullivan, who was "half blind herself," was engaged by Helen's family to be her companion-teacher when Helen was only six years old.

Ash Street, originally called Windmill Lane after Windmill Hill and its windmill, to which the lane led at the river, was the western path of the Newe Towne's 1632 "pallysadoe." A town order of this period says that this structure, which enclosed the town's roughly 1,000 acres, was built of "sufficient posts and rails" with Deputy Governor Dudley in command. Governor Winthrop wrote that six months later the windmill was moved to Boston because "it would not grind corn but with a westerly wind."

It was on the same windmill site that Thomas Brattle built the boathouse for the College students. This spot was on the westernmost part of his land, which, like the eastern part, ended in a loop and curving path west of Windmill Lane that was long called Bath Lane.

Harvard Square and Harvard Yard first got gas for their street lamps by pipe in 1853 when the new Cambridge Gas Works, with a big stone wharf for coal freighted upriver by barge and a big, round, conical-top gas house, was completed at the foot of Ash Street. This was one of many local enterprises, including the first horsecars to Harvard Square, initiated by Gardiner G. Hubbard, whose mansion, now gone, once stood as the centerpiece of six acres at 146 Brattle Street.

When the gas operation was moved away, a group of neighborhood men, in 1882, with poet Longfellow's artist son Ernest as leader, set up a bit farther west a boathouse, tennis court, and bowling alley they called the "Casino," which would lead to founding of the Cambridge Boat Club in 1909.

All these activities on Ash Street and thereabouts have vanished, along with Windmill Hill. Still, Ash Street has some buildings of note: the second house south of Cronkhite Center, 14 Ash Street, at the bend where T. S. Eliot lived in 1913–14 while teaching at Harvard before going abroad; and, near the northwest corner of Mt. Auburn Street, at 19 Ash, where we can still see Professor Simon Greenleaf's 1823 mansion.

E.D.S., VASSALL, AND LONGFELLOW-LAND

W here we see Mason Street enter Brattle there was in the early days of Newe Towne a gate in the pallysadoe known as Westgate, which corresponded on this side of town to Eastgate, whose location we saw on Massachusetts Avenue near Linden Street.

Westgate gave access to Newe Towne's oldest passageway, the Charlestown–Watertown road, the future King's Highway, which crossed the old Common, came along Mason Street, and followed westward out the future Brattle Street. Town records mention in spring 1634 an early burying ground "without the Common pale" that was succeeded in the following January when the ground we know as "God's Acre" was ordered "paled in."

This temporary Newe Towne cemetery was on the grounds, on our left, of the twenty-two-room 1883 mansion at 90 Brattle, designed by the famous architect H. H. Richardson for the mother of historian John Fiske, Mrs. Edwin Wallace Stoughton. Mrs. Stoughton's husband, a half dozen years earlier, in 1877, had become the U.S. Ambassador to the Court of Czar Alexander II, a ruler mostly remembered for having freed the Russian serfs and being assassinated. Fiske, who was also very popular as a lecturer, had had a house built for him nearby at 22 Berkeley in the year Stoughton became ambassador, but shifted his residence here in 1900 after he made this mansion even larger to adapt to his big library.

Near the opposite corner on part of the site where we now see St. John's Memorial Chapel, the first building of the Episcopal Divinity School (E.D.S.), was once the dwelling from which the young artist Daniel Chester French headed for the old Washington Grammar School near Farwell Place. Daniel French's wife tells of the sketch of a bird Dan did when he was only five. Dan was thirteen when, after an 8-inch fall of snow he and his older brother made a snowpile in the front yard, in which they carved two lions, one big, one small.

Folks homeward bound from church, including poet Longfellow and his children, paused to smile and pour out praise. And in the dwelling, with its long-remembered lilac hedges, kept "comely clept" by her father, Dan at sixteen was making statues in clay that his dad, a lawyer and judge, had fetched home from Boston.

St. John's Memorial Chapel was completed in 1869, less than two years after the seminary, with a $100,000 gift from Boston philanthropist Benjamin Tyler Reed, who opened temporary quarters near Mt. Auburn. The stained-glass windows on the west side were reduced in size when a new door, now the main entry, was added in 1970. Its interior, with freestanding altar, wood trusses, red chair seats, and original stained glass, is quite beautiful.

The old-style-looking buildings of pudding stone were all built in the late 1800s, next left of the Chapel as we look toward the campus, in a partial quadrangle formed by three of these older buildings. On the west is big Lawrence Hall (1873), always a dormitory, a gift from industrialist Amos A. Lawrence, father of the seminary's future dean and bishop, William Lawrence. Father Lawrence would not permit anyone to put his name on the hall until after his death; then, as he desired, a tablet was installed saying that the hall was "In remembrance of God's Great Goodness," which, Lawrence explained, was thanks for his "wife and seven children—and not one of these has ever caused me an hour's pain by any misconduct."

The other two stone buildings in this quad include Reed Hall (1875) at right angles to Lawrence Hall, and Burnham Hall (1879) at right angles to Reed, both now dormitories. In early years Reed provided classrooms and offices; Burnham was the first refectory. Now large Washburn Hall, built along the Phillips Place side in 1960, amply provides refectory space and an auditorium.

On St. John's Road, which begins in the rear of Lawrence Hall, is still another pudding stone dormitory, Winthrop Hall, built in 1893 under Dean Lawrence. Along the curve of St. John's Road are several faculty residences, among them three early 1800 dwellings that were moved here to make space for the tall Larsen Hall, which we saw on Appian Way, and the Loeb Drama Center.

Most modern of the seminary's buildings is the one built in 1965 on the Mason Street side—Sherrill Hall, named for Bishop Henry Knox Sherrill. The present multiplicity of buildings demonstrates the growth of the seminary that had but a dozen students annually in its early years. In striking contrast, right forward of Sherrill is the fairly small Wright Hall, now used for administration, which was ample, when built in 1911, for a library.

Currently, along with Sherrill Hall library, with 250,000 books, all students now attending here through the seminary's affiliations with Harvard, in addition to those from nine area theological schools, have access to one of the world's greatest sources of theological knowledge.

Just across from Sherrill Hall, on the corner of Mason Street and Phillips Place, in the white wooden building, is one of the two Jesuit seminaries in the United States, the Weston School of Theology. Its students share jointly with the E.D.S. students in the Sherrill Library. Back in 1974, when it was merged with the Philadelphia Divinity School, the Episcopalian Theological School, more than a century old, became the Episcopal Divinity School.

Because the seminary has combined its facilities with Roman Catholic, Greek Orthodox, Anglican, and Protestant theological schools, the campus has become an ecumenical participant in a property that the school itself describes as "a unique venture in cooperation." The ecumenical spirit extends along Mason Street to the Congregational Church, near the Common, where the Jesuits have held commencement exercises.

Returning to Brattle Street we see on the south side, opposite E.D.S.'s Lawrence Hall, a Tory Row landmark, the Henry Vassall House at the east corner of Hawthorn Street. The mansion in Henry Vassall's pre–Revolutionary era was much enlarged from its oldest parts, the 8-foot-square stack chimney with cement for its bricks made from oyster shells, and the kitchen and dining room adjoining it, when the original builder left in 1641 for Ipswich as a follower of Governor Dudley.

Henry Vassall, who acquired the estate in 1741, had land that comprised the next large estate west of Brattle's. It extended from Ash Street to the present Longfellow Park and down to the water. Before Brattle Street was widened in 1870, Vassall House had 30 feet more between it and the King's Highway. In this space was an imposing brick wall, an acacia hedge, and dozens of locust trees.

The grounds were just as ample in that time, with accessory buildings and gardens extending to the river marshes over land where a later owner developed Hawthorn and Acacia Streets. Where we see Hawthorn Street was the mansion's cobblestone-paved courtyard with stables. Near where we see Acacia Street was a large carriage house for chaises and chariots.

Before Vassall's time, future Royal Governor Jonathan Belcher, who would inherit the property, spent his childhood years and later went to Harvard. His older sister married into the Oliver family, well-known Tory sympathizers. The real heyday of high living on Tory Row, which would enthrall Baroness von Riedesel with its many intermarriages of highly placed Tory families, began when the estate was bought by John Vassall, of an immensely rich and large family of West Indies plantation owners.

John, at twenty-one, had married a daughter of Lieutenant Governor Spencer Phips and wanted to be near the Phips mansion, whose site we saw at Bow and Arrow Streets. Living was merry, carefree, and lavish for John and friends until his young wife died in bearing their third child, and John sold the estate, in 1741, to his younger brother Henry, who took up residence here with his bride.

High living resumed with Henry, who at age twenty had married eighteen-year-old Penelope, daughter of Isaac Royall, a very wealthy West Indies sugar plantation owner and honored benefactor of young Harvard College. Henry served in the legislature, was a prime supporter of new Christ Church, and became a lieutenant colonel in his neighbor William Brattle's First Middlesex Militia. But Henry, though he entertained innumerable high-society friends in opulent fashion, had a great weakness: gambling for high stakes.

Henry died young and insolvent, and so Penelope, with her own and the family's funds, satisfied his creditors. As the Revolutionary crisis came she left Cambridge and eventually reached her estates in the West Indies. Vassall House was taken over for use by the patriot forces, but was not confiscated because Penelope was never a foe of the Sons of Liberty.

The mansion's twenty rooms, with nine of those upstairs rooms a hospital, became the first center of the patriot army's medical corps. Besides the house, the doctors got Penelope's family medicine chest, a private apothecary shop in effect, one of only two in the entire colony at the outbreak of war. The Provincial Congress had given Penelope permission to take any possessions with her except the medicine chest.

Vassall House medical center was the focus of one of the greatest shocks to the patriots in the early months of the war, because of the arrest and confinement here of Dr. Benjamin Church, director general of the hospital and surgeon general, a man on the most secret patriot committees, on a charge of treason. He was taken off to trial in a chaise under guard with fifes and drummers playing "The Rogue's March."

George Washington sent word to President John Hancock of the Continental Congress that Church, by means of a "woman kept by Dr. Church," had forwarded a letter Church wrote in cypher to an aide of General Gage in beseiged Boston. In that letter Church had urged that the aide "make use of every precaution or I perish." Church did perish. There being then no patriot law on penalties for treason, Church, after some confinement, was exiled to the West Indies, and sailed on a ship out of Boston that was lost at sea. From his early jailing in the middle front rooms on the second floor there remains in Vassall House the inscription "B. Church Jr." that he carved with penknife on a closet door panel.

The patrician residence across the highway at 101 Brattle Street, long known locally as the "Bishop's Palace," was acquired by the Episcopal Divinity School in 1950 and is used as a faculty house and offices. Built in 1844, it was acquired by future Bishop William Lawrence, who had come in 1884 to teach at E.D.S., when he became dean in 1888. He told of enjoying the clear view to the river across present Longfellow Park area, then Longfellow's meadow, to the marshes, the river, and the Brighton hills.

From his study the Bishop wrote that he could see schooner masts slipping along the river "as if it were Holland." In 1893 he succeeded his friend Phillips Brooks as bishop, and was also Harvard's University preacher. Among "the great days of my life," as he expressed it in his memoirs, was commencement, 1905, when Teddy Roosevelt, buoyed by the big electoral majority that kept him in the White House, came for his 25th class reunion.

The Roosevelt and Lawrence families were long friends. Teddy lodged here, his secret service contingent using the Lawrence Hall dorm. He loved the quiet, early breakfasts, though he talked of making another try (which would succeed) to end the Russo-Japanese War. Teddy and his Secretary of War and trouble-shooter, future President William Howard Taft, "worked hard" in Lawrence's study on problems of constructing the Panama Canal before commencement-night supper. A few years later Bishop Lawrence, seeing new building crowding in between the old houses, and street noise on the increase, felt "another era was setting in." In 1911 he left for a smaller dwelling in the Blue Hills, but he kept up his close association with the University as tireless fund raiser, helping his cousin, President Lowell.

Tory Row's most historic house is the next one on our right at 105 Brattle Street, Longfellow House, a wedding gift to the poet and a gift from his children to the public. Across its threshold have passed many of the most renowned persons of Cambridge, indeed, of the nation and the world, particularly George Washington, who lived here nine months while winning the first patriot victory of the Revolution. General Washington at that time branded the Redcoats' fleeing Boston "an inglorious retreat." The National Park Service now administers mansion and grounds as a historic site where visitors may see the gardens, old carriage house, and Victorian and family furnishings arranged by the poet and his wife during their residence.

The mansion was started in 1759 by twenty-year-old John Vassall, Jr., in anticipation of his marriage to the sister of the province's last Royal Lieutenant Governor, Thomas Oliver, in 1761. Through the Phips family, John Vassall, Jr., a grandson of Lieutenant Governor Spencer Phips, had a blood uncle, aunt, or brother-in-law living in all the five other Tory Row mansions on estates that occupied all the land along the old King's Highway westward of the Brattle estate to and much beyond Elmwood. John Vassall, Jr.'s domain, where he lived joyfully and his seven children were born, stretched on the south of Brattle Street almost to Elmwood and on the north as far as Sparks Street, taking in the present hill of the Harvard Observatory on Concord Avenue. When confiscated, in 1778, after loyalist Vassall fled to England, it comprised 116 acres.

Like other Tory mansions, this one became an improvised hospital to treat soldiers wounded in the Battle of Bunker Hill. Colonel John Glover next quartered his Marblehead Militia here, and by July 15, 1775, General Washington, who had moved from Wadsworth House, was recording in the account book that he ever scrupulously kept that he had paid £2 10s 9d "for cleaning the house" as his headquarters. Among some happy moments was December 11, when Martha arrived from Mt. Vernon in a coach with postilions drawn by four horses. On Twelfth Night they held a party to celebrate their wedding anniversary. Yet his makeshift army's lack of weapons and gunpowder gave the Commander-in-Chief, as he recorded, "many an unhappy hour when all around me are wrapped in sleep."

Still, he had glorious moments. From here he dispatched the then heroic Benedict Arnold to try to capture Quebec. The wilderness march, though unsuccessful, remains among the finest in military history for the soldiers' fortitude. Here General Washington welcomed Benjamin Franklin and his committee members from the Continental Congress, seeking, successfully, to solve the crisis threatening the rebuilding of the army, and here General Washington delightedly greeted twenty-five-year-old, 250-pound Henry Knox, future Secretary of War in Washington's first cabinet, and made him a Colonel and head of the army's artillery after Knox delivered the cannon with which Washington clinched his victory.

Less than four months later, the founding fathers triumphantly proclaimed our Declaration of Independence and the birth of the United States.

Dr. Andrew Craigie, who would be famous for building the 1809 Canal Bridge, later Craigie's Bridge, at Lechmere's Point, set out to buy and develop all of early East Cambridge. He bought this former Vassall estate in 1793 from an interim owner, a wealthy Boston merchant. In that year thirty-nine-year-old Craigie, apothecary general during the Revolutionary War, married the beautiful twenty-two-year-old daughter of a Nantucket clergyman, Elizabeth, and brought her as a bride to her new mansion.

To accommodate his lavish entertaining, he enlarged portions of the house. Washington had used the southeast front room as a study, the room back of it for his aides, and Martha had used the southwest front room as a drawing room. Craigie's biggest change was to expand the aides' room into a paneled banqueting hall, where he was host to Prince Edward, Duke of Kent, father of Queen Victoria. He built the first ice house in Cambridge on an island in a small pond once 100 yards west of the mansion.

Elizabeth, on Craigie's death in 1819, had to cut her staff of servants to two helpers and rent out rooms. Craigie had been so beset by debt near the end of his life that to avoid arrest he had left his house only on Sundays. Elizabeth drew some prominent lodgers, among them future Harvard President Jared Sparks, then working on an edition of Washington's letters and using the bedchamber above Washington's study, where the General had slept. Another was future statesman and Harvard President Edward Everett. Later, in 1837, then youthful-looking, unbearded Henry Wadsworth Longfellow was nearly turned away until he assured widow Craigie, "But I am not a student. I am a professor."

To begin with, Longfellow had two rooms on the east side of the second floor. He used the front one as a study and soon got the front one across the hallway for a dining room. Charles Dickens, on his first American visit in 1842, had breakfast in that room after Longfellow showed him Washington's headquarters, and they came up the stairway and passed the big clock that is still on the landing.

Longfellow had been courting beautiful Frances "Fanny" Appleton and writing her poems since they met in Switzerland when she was only sixteen. They married six years later in 1843. Here they brought up two sons and the three daughters of "The Children's Hour—grave Alice, laughing Allegra and Edith with the golden hair"—all of whom used to skate in the winter on the little pond.

Dickens came back in 1867, a quarter of a century after his first visit, during his only Thanksgiving Day in America. Longfellow greeted him at the front door and now, with the entire place his, Longfellow led "Boz" to the big dining room down the hall. Fanny had perished in flames in that hall six years earlier when her light summer dress accidentally caught fire from drops of hot sealing wax.

Dickens wrote back home to his son Charles that he "could not get the terrific scene out of my imagination. She was in a blaze in an instant, rushed into his arms with a wild cry, and never spoke afterwards."

The diary of Longfellow, who was ever hospitable, is crowded with names of visitors "who lifted the knocker on his door." These were his fellow professors, neighbors, literary and family friends, the Lowells, Danas, and Howells, eminent publisher James T. Fields, Thackeray, Trollope, Bret Harte, future King Edward VII when Prince of Wales, close friend Charles Summer, who came often, when away from Washington, to see him and take walks in the "beautiful Cambridge" that Longfellow loved.

Two sad tales of letters long hidden in the mansion were told by the poet's grandson. Craigie, in wartime Philadelphia, had had a daughter he never acknowledged. The high-society parents of his loved one, for religious reasons, would not let her marry twenty-five-year-old Craigie.

The child, Mary, who in later life became head of a religious teaching order and was called "Sister Polly," in letters she wrote addressed him as "dear Uncle." Long after his death her letters to him dropped one after another from a secret compartment over the cellar stairway. The poet had even taken Dickens down to show him the secret hiding place.

Mrs. Craigie, when young and single, had fallen in love with a young man who sailed off to seek a fortune. He found it but did not return. She burned his letters, long kept in the attic, just before she died. Craigie was buried in the old Vassall tomb that was part of the estate he had bought. Mrs. Craigie, who died in 1841, was buried in a lot she selected in Mt. Auburn, with only a quote from Voltaire, whose philosophy she admired, for a marker.

Longfellow's son-in-law, Richard Henry Dana III, in 1913 drew up a deed of trust through which his wife and the other Longfellow children gave the public Longfellow Park to preserve his beloved view across his meadow to the river. His son Ernest describes how his father, bareheaded, would sit on his front steps, gaze across the meadow, and hope that the view would always be there.

It was with this view from the poet's study, said Ernest, that, as his father sat at the round table between the windows of his second-floor study, he wrote the poem that first brought him fame, "The Psalm of Life." That was in 1838, soon after he came to the mansion.

A short way down the park, along the way Longefellow used to go in his early years here to bathe, is a monument wall with steps down either side. On the river side of this wall sculptor Daniel Chester French in 1914 made a bronze bust of the poet, on a pedestal in a small garden, and behind it a fascinating bas-relief depicting Longfellow's great poetical figures, among them Evangeline, Myles Standish, Hiawatha, and the Village Blacksmith.

The park neighborhood has become a religious center. On the west side is the Friends Center, started in 1916 in the dwelling of one of Longfellow's granddaughters, to which the brick Quaker meeting house was added two decades later. On the park's east corner at Brattle since 1955 is the gathering place, offices, and recreational facilities of the Church of Jesus Christ of Latter-day Saints. Around the corner, now at 15 Hawthorn Street, is a house, nearly a century old, which was moved to make room for the Mormon Church, and is now a Jesuit dormitory of the Weston Jesuit Community.

The Longfellows developed a neighborhood of their own family houses to go with the mansion that became the residence of "grave Alice," the oldest girl. A founder of Radcliffe, she made it a "helpful, pleasant" gathering place for Radcliffe students. In 1870, her brother Ernest, the artist, built the house on the west corner of the park at 108 Brattle. A fine portrait he painted of his father was placed on an easel in the poet's study. Ernest said the family considered that 1876 likeness the poet's "best portrait."

The next two houses just west of Longfellow House were built in the same year, 1887. Richard Henry Dana III ("Dick"), whose family house was in back of Longfellow's, had been engaged to Edith "with golden hair" since his last year at Harvard Law, and built at 113 Brattle. His brother-in-law, who was married to Annie "laughing Allegra," the youngest daughter, built the house at 115 Brattle.

Richard Henry Dana III, lifelong friend of Daniel French, was a big fund raiser for Harvard, leader in civic-improvement drives, civil service reform, and the successful fight that saw Massachusetts adopt the secret ("Australian") ballot in 1888. He was a close friend of Teddy Roosevelt, a guest at the White House, and several times host here to T.R. when he came earlier as Federal Civil Service Commissioner to speak at Harvard and M.I.T., then in Boston. Theodore, said Dick, was "overflowing with humor and delightful stories" and surprised all at breakfast by taking his coffee "with five to seven lumps of sugar."

The 1844 house on our right, at 121 Brattle, also has links to the Longfellow neighborhood. The well-known dictionary compiler Joseph Emerson Worcester, Yale Class of 1811, married Professor Joseph McKean's daughter and resided along with Professor Longfellow in Craigie House. On Mrs. Craigie's death, Worcester had also bought much Craigie land west of the Craigie House, he and his wife sharing Craigie House with Longfellow until their dwelling was built.

Part of Worcester's purchase included the small pond where the Longfellow yongsters would skate and in summer swim and picnic. Though friend Worcester sometimes chased youngsters away, Longfellow fondly referred to it as "Worcester's Pond," and drew a map of the pond with three little bridges. The stream that came from present Observatory Hill—site of Craigie's garden house—long fed the pond but ran dry in later years, ending a heavenly Brattle Street playplace.

SPARKS STREET TO ELMWOOD

Sparks Street, at this triple, busy intersection with Brattle and Craigie Street, until shortly before the Revolutionary War was the dividing line between Cambridge and Watertown. The short distance we have walked from Harvard Square is evidence, if any is needed, of why Thomas Hooker and early settlers took off for the fertile Connecticut Valley in 1634. They felt that Newe Towne was just not large enough for their cattle and crops.

After 1754 the Cambridge boundary was extended westward beyond Gerry's Landing, partway over the Coolidge Hill, and included Fresh Pond.

Sparks Street, on our right, goes over something scarce in Cambridge, a ridge. Before continuing along Tory Row, we notice some interesting sites along and off Sparks Street. Behind the cedar fencing and hedge at the corner of Sparks and Craigie, at 27 Craigie, is a mid-nineteenth-century house that was the home of outstanding chemistry Professor Eben Horsford, whose daughter Lillian, like Alice Longfellow, helped found Radcliffe College. Professor Horsford, deeply interested in Norse history, came to believe that Leif Ericson, the discoverer in A.D. 1000 of Vinland, actually built his shelter on the site of Gerry's Landing. Horsford even paid for a stone marker once to be seen there.

Robert Frost came to live on the first street off Sparks Street, on our left, when President Conant got him to continue his lectures and sessions with Harvard students. Frost came in spring 1941 to the three-story house, about midblock at 35 Brewster, to enjoy more room than he had on Beacon Hill for his books and writings, his friends, and his dog "Gillie." In the following year his new book of poems won him a fourth Pulitzer Prize. Friends recall Frost's walks through "Brewster Village" with Gillie. One neighbor told of going at Frost's request to forward him an academic hood, to an attic closet and finding it jammed with hoods of academic honors that Frost had amassed.

Highland Street, next on our left up Sparks Street, goes along the ridge to Reservoir Street at the peak of Reservoir Hill, where Cambridge in 1855 built its first reservoir, with water pumped up from Fresh Pond. At the start of this century the reservoir was filled in and houses were built on the fill.

Charles Eliot, celebrated landscape architect and son of President Eliot, lived in the big three-story clapboard mansion on the north corner of Highland at Sparks Street at 1 Highland Avenue. Across the road at 74 Sparks Street, now back of number 76, was the residence built by one of Harvard's distinguished librarians, Justin Winsor, an editor of the four-volume *Memorial History of Boston* celebrating that city's 250th anniversary. Winsor's granddaughter wrote of often seeing President Charles Eliot and his wife bicycling past the Winsor house to visit their son. President Eliot, who appointed Winsor, called him "the most eminent librarian in the U.S."

At 80 Sparks Street lived a close friend of Winsor, Charles Deane, who dwelt in this 1859 mansion where, after his retirement from business, he became a historian. It is to Deane that America owes recovery of Governor William Bradford's *History of the Plimouth Plantation,* which had disappeared from Old South Meeting House when the Redcoats fled Boston. Deane, while browsing in bookstores, came across a footnote citing the Bradford manuscript as in the Bishop of London's palace library. It eventually came back as a gift from England to the Commonwealth of Massachusetts.

Governor Alvan T. Fuller, who built a fortune as an automobile dealer, had his residence here in the 1940s. In 1949 Fuller sold the mansion to growing Buckingham School for use as its upper (high) school. A classroom wing was added in 1969, five years before all the school's buildings combined to form present Buckingham Browne & Nichols School. It is now BB&NS combined middle (junior high) school.

Opposite the old Deane estate, also with barn, gardens, and extensive grounds, once stood at 79 Sparks Street, after the Civil War, the residence of one of Cambridge's most popular physicians ever, Dr. Morrill Wyman, whose untiring work helped to create Mt. Auburn Hospital. Cambridge also has a road and a square named for his gratefully remembered family.

Always interested in his fellow beings, Wyman, not to disturb his less scientifically interested neighbors, built a shed, but hid it in his seven acres of woodlands, for his study of pleural pneumonia. He even made the Fourth of July such a neighborhood event that Deane's granddaughter recalled her playmates gathering on the Deane roof and eating ice cream while they watched Dr. Wyman's fireworks display.

The Wyman estate was part of the old Lechmere confiscated acres and reached to Vassall Lane, which began as a pathway to Fresh Pond, a road at first called "Highway to the Great Swamp." The land on the east side of Sparks Street was part of John Vassall, Jr.'s estate, most of it along here his orchard.

Being on the edge of town the road had the reputation of being a lover's lane. Roughly on future Deane land, then on the outskirts of the early village, was the quarters of a man named Gibson, who conducted a house considered to be a den of iniquity. Records do not show he had a license, but he made midnight partying available for wealthy students. He was brought to court, banned by the College for bringing liquor into the Yard. A better side of Gibson was that he served as a private in King Philip's War.

Returning to Brattle Street, we see on the northwest corner of Sparks Street the 1961 Holy Trinity Armenian Church, on former Lechmere land. The building immediately to its west at 145 Brattle, now the Holy Trinity rectory and offices, was built in 1887 on the site of the 1762 house. Richard Lechmere, who married a daughter of Lieutenant Governor Spencer Phips, built to be near his Phips relatives, a house we will next see that was moved a block west.

The 1887 house was the home of ornithologist William Brewster, the boyhood chum of Daniel French and Richard Dana. Daniel's bird hunting drew Brewster to the trio ranging the woods and to taxidermy. At fourteen, Brewster, who would later build his own museum on his then ample grounds, started America's finest collection of mounted birds. He gave it to the College and it is now in the Harvard Museum.

At the west corner of Riedesel Avenue, most of the original structure confined to its second floor, is the much-altered 1762 Lechmere House that was moved here in 1886. Lechmere, wealthy Boston distiller, sold the estate in 1771 to Jonathan Sewall, the last provincial attorney general under George III. Sewall and his friend John Hancock had married sisters of the Quincy family. Sewall was also a friend of John Adams, but Sewall was as firmly in the Tory camp as Hancock and Adams were with the patriots.

Sewall is well remembered, though, for a slave case he eloquently conducted in 1769 as a lawyer against Lechmere. The suit, financed by descendants of pioneer John Bridge, whose monument we saw on the Common, freed a slave and helped establish the principle in Massachusetts that "all persons born or residing in the province" were free. In fall 1774 citizens, angered by Sewall's support of Governor Hutchinson and General Gage, surrounded the house. Following gunfire and window smashing, Sewall, his wife Ester, and their family fled to Halifax, Nova Scotia. Eventually the house and forty-four acres were confiscated.

An enchanted admirer of old Tory Row, Baroness von Riedesel and family, who had come to Cambridge in November 1777, with dejected, ailing General Burgoyne's 5,300 Redcoats and German mercenaries after defeat at Saratoga, took up residence here after a short, unhappy period at the Blue Anchor and in a dwelling on the present Kennedy Street.

Her husband, the baron, was a major general in command of his contingent from Brunswick, and their life here was quite in contrast to that of the poorly clothed "convention troops" who had marched in stormy weather over bad roads from Saratoga. Most of the officers were housed in Cambridge but their troops were crowded into old barracks on Prospect and Winter Hills in the present Somerville (then part of Charlestown).

"We lived very happily and contented in Cambridge," said the baroness, referring to her household here, her husband, and their three young children. She held suppers and dances, and had military servants and musicians. Stories of the earlier families in their mansions on Tory Row entranced her as the most "agreeable situation" she had ever chanced upon. She described vividly in her memoirs their carefree existence in words that have long epitomized Tory Row living.

> [The owners of the] farms, gardens and magnificent houses . . . were in the habit of daily meeting each other in the afternoon, now at the house of one,

and now at another, and making themselves merry with music and dance—living in prosperity, united and happy, until, alas! this ruinous war severed them and left all their homes desolate. . . .

At 153 Brattle is a 1799 dwelling that old Judge Joseph Lee, a few years before he died, built so that his nephew would be near the judge's own house at 159 Brattle, now a couple of houses away. On the way, notice at 152 Brattle across the street the large house that the widow of author Richard Henry Dana, on her return from their residence in Italy where he was buried, built for herself in 1887 to be near the family.

Old Judge Joseph Lee, who married the youngest of Lieutenant Governor Spencer Phips's daughters, Rebecca, was warmly regarded by the Sons of Liberty for promptly resigning—as he confirmed to the crowd at the steps of the old courthouse in Harvard Square—thus spurning his unsought appointment to the mandamus council of military Governor Gage. Lee had purchased this house in 1758 and lived here till 1802. He had no children, but one of his nephew's daughters became the wife of the eminent Dr. Benjamin Waterhouse, whose ancient house we will see still facing Cambridge Common.

The judge's house, in part, is one of the oldest in Cambridge. Similar to the Henry Vassall House, this one's huge stack chimney, 12 feet square, is held together with a cement composed of clay and oyster shells, going back to the 1680s. It still has some low, studded ceilings, but the judge considerably enlarged the farmhouse and converted it into a mansion.

In 1919 William Emerson, New York architect and cousin of his 1895 classmate Edward W. Forbes, grandson of Ralph Waldo Emerson, was invited by M.I.T. President Maclauren to head M.I.T.'s School of Architecture, and bought the old Lee House. Emerson served as dean for two decades and on his death gave the house to the Cambridge Historical Society, which took over in 1957. As in the Longfellow House, the public now can see some treasures of a society that has magnificently striven to preserve the history of one of the nation's oldest, most interesting communities.

Kennedy Road, next on our right off Brattle, relates, not to President

Kennedy, but to the head of a cracker-manufacturing firm in Cambridge-port, Frank A. Kennedy. Kennedy Road once led to the rear of a mansion that the cracker-maker built on the ridge, 48 Highland Street. That mid–Civil War structure was replaced a few years after World War I by an architect's dwelling, a change typical of the hill and the area to Fresh Pond as the rise of contemporary houses cut the once big Tory Row estates down to city-lot size.

On our right, just beyond Kennedy Road, 163 Brattle has been the residence for decades of the widely known inventor of instant photography, Edwin H. Land. The Land camera he announced in 1947 was the second of his major inventions. Back when he was still of high school age he became engrossed in trying to polarize light and, while in his second year at Harvard, at only eighteen years of age, left to work on his invention in his own cellar lab.

By 1937, at twenty-eight, Land founded his Polaroid Corporation, producing polarized products. The instant-camera idea struck him when he took a picture of his young daughters, Jennifer and Valerie, and they asked "where's the picture?" His camera revolutionized photography. He quit his Polaroid Corporation after forty-five years as its chief, but continued research in other fields in still another lab, near the Charles River.

The next mansion on our right, at 165 Brattle, was built in the 1870s by Cambridge bookseller John Bartlett, who ran the College bookstore, as successive editions appeared of his *Familiar Quotations,* which he first got out in 1853. Poet Lowell, Bartlett's neighbor, joined fairly regularly in Bartlett's weekly whist parties and wrote a poem to pay tribute to his friend Bartlett's skill as a trout fisherman.

Across Brattle, at number 168, is the mansion built on the once-large estate of Edwin A. Grozier, former *Boston Globe* reporter and editor of Pulitzer's *New York World.* Grozier developed his own newspaper, the *Boston Post,* on Boston's old Newspaper Row, which became the largest-circulation morning newspaper in America. The next mansion west, at 170 Brattle, a mid-nineteenth-century building, was moved here from Phillips Place by the Episcopal Divinity School to make space on the E.D.S. campus for the seminary's new Sherrill Library.

On the west corner of Channing Street, at 174 Brattle, is the residence built by William E. Russell, governor of Massachusetts (1891–94), and in earlier years one of Cambridge's most distinguished mayors (1885–88). Russell was a classmate at Harvard of Frederick H. Rindge. Through Russell's efforts during his mayoralty, Cambridge obtained princely gifts from Rindge that provided land and buildings we will see in Cambridgeport, in particular the Cambridge Public Library and the City Hall, which Russell was able to get underway in the final months of his successful administration.

Directly across the highway is a Tory Row landmark, Fayerweather House at 175 Brattle, whose record of patriot occupants makes "Tory" appear inapplicable. The house was built in about 1760 by Amos Marrett, a descendant of Harvard's first president. Marrett moved to Lexington, became a member of Captain John Parker's Minutemen, was on Lexington Green on April 19, 1775 with his musket when Parker, faced by the Redcoats, called to his men, "If they want to have a war let it begin here!" It did.

In 1771 Marrett had sold this property to a planter from Jamaica, George Ruggles, who married John Vassall, Jr.'s aunt Susanna. In 1774 Ruggles sold in turn to Thomas Fayerweather, son of a Boston merchant who made it available as a military hospital after the Battle of Bunker Hill. We have been given quite a glimpse of this property's scattered farm sheds and shelters by Fayerweather's sister Hannah, wife of scientist Professor John Winthrop of Winthrop Square, who fled this way with alarmed women and children past Fresh Pond when the Redcoats swung through Cambridge on that April 19th.

A later owner, William Wells, in 1827 bought the house and its sixty acres after his publishing building was destroyed by fire. He then started a boy' school here, in which he helped train some Cantabrigian youngsters who would become prominent in later years, Judge Story's son William, a future sculptor and writer, and three others of literary bent, Richard H. Dana, Sr., Thomas W. Higginson, and James Russell Lowell, a nearby neighbor. Wells, who taught Latin and Greek, was a firm maintainer of discipline. Higginson described Wells, with "always a rattan in his hand or handy on his desk," but said, outside of Boston Latin, Wells's School was "the best place" in which to prepare for college.

The old King's Highway turned left and went along present Elmwood Avenue, where on the right, at 33 Elmwood, is the westernmost of the Tory Row mansions. Thomas Oliver, legatee of two big West Indian fortunes, acquired ninety-six acres, reaching from about Gerry's Landing to the shores of Fresh Pond, and built the mansion in 1767. He had married Elizabeth Vassall, sister of his Harvard College schoolmate John Vassall, Jr., who married Thomas's sister. It was Elizabeth Vassall's mother's death when Elizabeth was born that interrupted merry life on Tory Row. The Olivers, with their six daughters born here, however, had luxurious living to the hilt with servants, carriages, and interfamily partying and picnicking.

Thomas's trials began as his living turned from social to political in 1774, when King George III named him Lieutenant Governor and head of General Gage's mandamus council. It could all have been a mixup, with Thomas Oliver mistakenly named instead of one of the Boston Oliver family, who had held many top posts in the province and were related to Governor Huchinson. Thomas Oliver was no relation to those Olivers or Hutchinson, who had suggested Thomas Oliver's name to the king.

Neither that nor Thomas Oliver's stopping General Gage from sending Redcoats to Cambridge, when the Sons of Liberty swarmed to Harvard Square in outrage against General Gage's getting the county's gunpowder and cannon, saved Oliver two days later. On that September 2, 1774, some 4,000 irate citizens gathered around this mansion and forced Oliver to resign his office. A few day later he fled with wife and daughters to Boston and in the spring to England. Mansion and land were confiscated.

Word of the Lexington alarm had hardly reached New Haven when Captain Benedict Arnold responded at the head of his finely uniformed company of Minutemen. On the way, Arnold joined Israel Putnam, also headed this way. On arrival this mansion was assigned to Arnold and here, with his company in tents on the grounds, he laid his plans to try to capture the British cannon at Fort Ticonderoga. After Bunker Hill, the mansion here was also used as a hospital, and soldiers who died of wounds were buried near Brattle Street until moved later to God's Acre.

A signer of our Declaration of Independence, Elbridge Gerry, bought the estate in 1787 and enlarged its acreage, adding some nearby farms, barns, and outbuildings while living here, having guests as prominent as John Adams and his son, John Quincy Adams. Gerry was twice elected governor of Massachusetts, and in 1812 was elected vice president for President James Madison's second term. Gerry died in office. Debts of a friend he had helped fell to Mrs. Gerry to satisfy, and she had to sell the property.

The father of poet James Russell Lowell, Reverend Charles Lowell, bought the portion to the south of Brattle Street in 1818 and named it Elmwood for the elms that enclosed the forecourt. Poet Lowell was born here a year later and would live here almost all his life, being mainly away after the death of his first wife and the eight years, by appointment of President Hayes, that he was America's ambassador in Spain and Great Britain. He is most warmly remembered as editor, the earliest, of the *Atlantic Monthly,* and as a professor, succeeding to the chair held by his friend Longfellow.

Author Henry Adams had few "likes" while at college, but he and many other students loved their evening a week at Elmwood. They met in the library and tell of Lowell, smoking his pipe, tongs in hand, stirring the wood fire, and talking to his students like an old friend. His guests included fellow professors, literary neighbors and writers of the era, as well as Thackeray, during his 1853 lecture tour, and Dickens, in his final appearance on the American lecture circuit.

Elmwood is presently the official residence of Harvard's president. Lowell died at Elmwood in 1891. His family sold it in 1925 to an authority on Romanesque art, Yale Professor Kingsley Porter, who, on President Lowell's invitation, came to teach at Harvard. Along with funds for maintaining the mansion and the lovely grounds, where Lowell occasionally gave picnics for students, Porter willed them to the College on the death of his widow. His wife agreed, saying it was "fitting" that Harvard should be the last owner.

President Derek Bok, who got his degree at Harvard Law School in 1954, joined its faculty in 1958, became dean a decade later, and has lived here with his family most of the years since assuming the University's presidency in 1971. He has become known for his analytical, forward-looking observations. A champion of keeping Harvard a center for free speech, in recent years he has criticized our American legal system as "grossly inequitable and inefficient," told how Harvard can blaze "a new pathway" in medical education, even questioned whether computerizing education improves it.

Supremely striking in Bok's term has been his unprecedented success as a fund raiser for the University, now in its 350th year. Bok said, when his recent five-year campaign was in the home stretch, that Harvard started with one teacher and a dozen pupils and now had about 17,000 men and women seeking degrees. The $350,000,000 goal was the highest ever targeted by a university.

For contrast, little more than a century ago, at the time of the Great Boston fire, President Eliot dashed to Boston's financial center to save the College endowment funds. They were, in toto, $2,508,000. When Lowell became president they were $22,000,000, and the student body's graduating class numbered only 170. When Bok's predecessor, in a 1957 drive, raised $82,500,000, it was described as "gigantic." Bok exceeded his 1985 goal by almost four times the amount that Eliot braved smoke and flames to rescue.

FRESH POND, MT. AUBURN, AND GERRY'S LANDING

A short way from Elmwood are three attractive, charming places intimately connected with the lore of Cambridge: Fresh Pond, Mt. Auburn Cemetery, and Gerry's Landing. Once all three were entirely in Watertown. Mt. Auburn Cemetery, save for a comparatively small rectangle of land at the west corner of Coolidge Avenue, still is in Watertown. To take them all in, briefly, would require only about as much walking as we have already done from Brattle Square.

On the way for a view of Fresh Pond, we return to Brattle Street and turn left (westward). This extension of Brattle Street was built in 1812 by the county authorities, who favored Craigie, who was eager to attract traffic from Watertown to his bridge across the Charles. We will see presently at the south end of Elmwood Avenue what the town did earlier to attract this same eastbound traffic to Judge Dana's rival bridge.

A close friend and brain-truster of President Franklin D. Roosevelt, Harvard Law School Professor Felix Frankfurter lived on our left at 192 Brattle and would walk from here to his classes. Frankfurter, a summa cum laude graduate of the school, while on the faculty was a severe critic of the controversial Sacco-Vanzetti trial. Though President Lowell was on the opposite side, he did congratulate Frankfurter after F.D.R. appointed him in 1939 to the Supreme Bench. Frankfurter, in tête-à-têtes and afterward as a live-in guest at the White House, had advised F.D.R. on the economic ideas of John Maynard Keynes as the New Deal's best bet to lick the Great Depression of the 1930s.

Other distinguished educators have lived nearby. Directly across the street, in the mansion at 195 Brattle, was the home of the creator of 47 Workshop, Professor George P. Baker. The pleasant open, landscaped area on our left, Lowell Memorial Park, through which Fresh Pond Parkway was made at the turn of the century, was part of poet Lowell's Elmwood estate. And in the northeast corner, where the Parkway crosses Brattle Street, behind the serpentine brick wall around 17 Fresh Pond Parkway, was the retirement home (1910–1926) of President Eliot. He lived in this much-altered, enlarged early nineteenth-century farmhouse of the Wyeth family, from whom he bought it. Athletics for sportsman Eliot then became his bicycling, which so interested his neighbors or weightlifting on rainy days.

Much of the land around Fresh Pond belonged to the Wyeths. Just ahead, on our right, the fabulous post-Revolutionary shipowner William "Billy" Gray acquired many acres. Gray was one of the greatest of the builders of our Far East and Russian trade when British ports were closed to our shipping. He still stoutly supported both Jefferson's embargo and "Madison's War," quit the Federalist party, and moved from Salem to Boston. Here, in 1808, he had got his summer home and was elected lieutenant governor on the ticket with his neighbor, Governor Elbridge Gerry.

Grays Hall, on the south side of the old Harvard Yard, was named for Gray's sons and grandsons, lavish donors to Harvard, who helped him surround his summer home, "The Larches," with magnificent grounds. Son Horace was one of the leading sponsors of plantings that started Boston's beautiful Public Garden. The Larches, which, set off by unusual fencing, still stands at 22 Larch Road, next road off Brattle on our right, was moved early in this century to adapt to development of this Larchwood section. The extensively altered 1801 Wyeth farmhouse, once part of The Larches and once used as a servants' wing, was moved to 36 Larch Road, just north of The Larches, which has been occupied by several descendants of the Gray family.

On the next street to our right off Brattle is Fresh Pond Lane where, at 57 Fresh Pond, Bay State Governor Charles F. Hurley had his residence for many years until his death in 1946. He was a Cambridge realtor who served six years as the Commonwealth's treasurer prior to his term as governor from 1937 to 1939.

To get a view of Fresh Pond we turn right at Aberdeen Avenue to Huron Avenue, which runs, in this area, a short distance from around the pond. At Huron Avenue, turn left to cross the bridge over the railroad track and on the right is a pathway down to the pond at its southeast shore.

A municipal golf course is on the west and some of the south shore, and so walkers along the shore should watch against stray shots. Land surrounding the pond, some of it from neighboring Belmont, was completely acquired by the city, about 170 acres, in the 1880s, and all private structures were removed to ensure a protected source for Cambridge's water supply. It was from here that the pumping station, one of the municipal services on the east shore, once maintained the now-vanished water setup on Reservoir Hill, nearby but 75 feet above the pond.

Most tales of Fresh Pond are far happier than that of the panic-stricken women and children on the day the Revolutionary War began. On the east shore, in the present Kingsley Park, Jacob Wyeth in 1796 built the Fresh Pond Inn, which was run by the family for several decades. Oliver Wendell Holmes gives us a merry account of what he and his chums in the famous class of 1829 did on their commencement eve to celebrate their impending escape "from the thraldom . . . of college government and college duties."

They marched out to Fresh Pond, where Mr. Wyeth, "who will ever flourish in our recollection . . . gave a most superb supper." There were claret, champagne and madeira, toasts, singing, and they marched back late "in pretty good order." The new owner of the hotel put in bathing and athletic facilities, and there were sleighing parties, a livery stable, and boats for hire.

Some Cantabrigians just liked the walk, the water, the woods. William James walked here Sundays with William Dean Howells. Young Winslow Homer, who felt that his first art copying job was like imprisonment, got up early mornings so that he could walk here to fish, a lasting hobby of his, before walking back to Harvard Square to catch the omnibus to his work in Boston. Young Professor Longfellow writes about the loveliness of the lake, of taking a boat and floating away "rocked in dreams." Student Teddy Roosevelt, always champ of the strenuous life, defied frostbite late into the evening, skating in fierce wind and cold, but calling to a classmate, "Isn't this bully!"

Frederick Tudor built his fortune here. The famous "Ice King" got the idea that he could cut the pond ice in blocks and sell it in the tropics. People laughed when in 1805 he sent off his first shipment in a brig to Martinique. But Tudor prospered, along with another Wyeth, "Nat" Nathaniel

Jarvis Wyeth, far-West pioneer who in 1832 would lead the first expedition to settle the Oregon Territory, as manager of Tudor's ice houses, which sprang up on the north and east shores of the pond.

The railroad was especially put in here to replace ox teams and haul the ice to the wharves. "Fresh Pond Ice" signs became a world item from Havana to Calcutta and Bombay. In 1888, when Cambridge cleared the land around the pond, the hotel was removed, and the ice houses and old summer places used by workmen as lodgings were demolished. Nature resumed sway, as when young Will Brewster and his pals had come looking for birds and fun.

On going back along Aberdeen Avenue to Mt. Auburn and turning left, we can see diagonally across the highway—at 580 Mt. Auburn—the Egyptian Gateway designed by Dr. Jacob Bigelow, founder of Mt. Auburn Cemetery, the first garden cemetery in America. Dr. Bigelow was a man of many accomplishments, a popular writer on botany, Harvard Professor of Medicine, a founding supporter of M.I.T., and he even originated the term "technology" while teaching in still another field, mechanics. Many growing parishes no longer had room for cemeteries around their churches, and Dr. Bigelow was opposed to continuing the use of church cellars for burials.

Mt. Auburn Cemetery was the creation of Bigelow, combining the need for more burial ground with his love of botany. He recruited, at sessions in his Boston residence, helpful, like-thinking friends, especially George W. Brimmer, who had been acquiring these woods and farmland for a summer estate. Members of the Stone family had utilized them since Simon Stone, an early Watertown settler, began farming here back in 1634.

Stone's Woods, as they were called, were also known as "Sweet Auburn" to College students and many illustrious Cantabrigians, who have told delightedly of their strolls here, after their walks along the old King's Highway past fragrant rows of lilacs. Brimmer turned the seventy-two acres over, at cost, to the Massachusetts Horticultural Society, which had been formed two years earlier with Dr. Bigelow as secretary. Mt. Auburn was opened in fall 1831 as a nondenominational cemetery under auspices of the Horticultural Society, which in 1835 transferred it to the Proprietors of Mt. Auburn, who still maintain it.

Be sure to visit the cemetery office, diagonally inside on the left when you come through the granite gateway. Visitors are welcomed and, along with other literature, they may have gratis two most helpful maps, one locating and naming all the plants, flowering shrubs, and trees, both native and of worldwide origin, beautifully landscaped over 170 acres, and another map locating graves and monuments of the cemetery's distinguished dead. Longfellow came often, selected, then looked quietly as workmen dug his future resting place. The grounds were so beautiful, he said, that he could look at the grave-digging "without any dread."

So many outstanding women and men are interred here—statesmen, artists, actors, authors, professors, and college presidents—that it has been called a bucolic Westminster Abbey. Here are the graves of nearly all past Harvard presidents since Kirkland and "Old Quin," and here with them are the founders of Radcliffe, Arthur Gilman and Elizabeth Agassiz, Tufts' first president, Reverend Hosea Ballou, M.I.T.'s founder William Barton Rogers, and the great M.I.T. president Richard C. Maclaurin, who brought M.I.T. to Cambridge. Mt. Auburn, as a visitor quickly finds, is an irresistible attraction to nature lovers and camera fans who come, alone or in club groups, to enjoy the landscape, to be the first to see blossoms in springtime, to watch or listen to birds.

Very special sights should not be missed. The path straight ahead from the entry is Central Avenue, and, on the left, right back of the cemetery office, a chapel dedicated to the man who gave the 1831 dedicatory speech, Justice Joseph Story, the proprietors' first president. A short way along Central Avenue, on the right, encircled by Lawn Avenue, is a beautiful fountain and garden named for famed botanist Asa Gray. A special specimen in it is a tall ginkgo tree. Farther along Central Avenue, on Chapel Avenue to the right, is a gothic chapel designed by and later named for Dr. Bigelow. In front of it is, in two tongues, the Sphinx Memorial to our Civil War dead, by sculptor Martin Milmore.

Above all, continue along Central Avenue to Walnut Avenue and Mountain Avenue to see still another creation of Dr. Bigelow, the tower on the 125-foot hill in the cemetery, Mt. Auburn Hill. The sweeping panoramic view above the treetops, with the stadium as a focus, is well worth the further climb up the 60-foot tower via Mr. Bigelow's circular staircase of stone.

Possibly the most monumental memorial in Mt. Auburn is Mary Baker Eddy's, with its high crown of eight fluted columns and steps down to a beautiful gem, Halcyon Lake. It is near the northeast corner of Mt. Auburn. It also can be seen from Coolidge Avenue, toward which we head by turning right along Mt. Auburn Street on leaving the Egyptian Gateway.

Coolidge Avenue for most of its length up and over the hill is the east boundary of Mt. Auburn Cemetery and the boundary between Watertown and Cambridge. Land on the east corner of Coolidge Avenue and Mt. Auburn, with his house about opposite Elmwood, belonged in Revolutionary times to Colonel Samuel Thatcher, Minuteman who succeeded to the command of General William Brattle's Middlesex Regiment at the time of the Battle of Bunker Hill. Colonel Thatcher had rallied his Minuteman company and was in action all day April 19, 1775 when word came to him here that the Redcoats were landing in Cambridge and heading for Lexington.

Elbridge Gerry purchased Thatcher's land in 1793 when he was expanding the old Oliver estate. Josiah Coolidge of Watertown, who would acquire most of the area that is now called Coolidge Hill, in 1821 started with the Thatcher farm and, though most of the hill was sold off more than a century later, descendants still live on the hill.

Bay State Governor Robert F. Bradford, tenth-generation descendant of Plymouth Colony's Governor William Bradford, eminent lawyer, graduate, and honored benefactor of old Browne & Nichols School, which we will see presently near Gerry's Landing, lived many years on the hilltop at 106 Coolidge Hill Road, first street on our left off Coolidge Avenue. Bradford's was the second house on our right.

Farther down Coolidge Hill Road, on the south slope on eight acres of former Coolidge meadowland, purchased in 1925, is the delightfully situated Shady Hill School, with its many fine buildings, classrooms, and play facilities, at 178 Coolidge Hill Road. We will be seeing Shady Hill's birth-place and other locations in later walks.

Return down Coolidge Avenue, turn right along Mt. Auburn Street, and turn right again on another section of Coolidge Hill Road to see the big 1822 homestead built by Josiah Coolidge. It is the fourth house from the corner on our right, at 24 Coolidge Hill Road, moved from its original location facing Mt. Auburn Cemetery and enlarged for double residences by some later descendants of Josiah.

Famous Radcliffe graduate Helen Keller lived in this house when it was at 14 Coolidge Avenue, before it was turned in 1915 and moved 100 feet to this location. She and her dog, named Sir Thomas Lipton for the cele-brated yachtsman, its donor, would roam Coolidge Hill, sometimes need-ing guidance from neighbors. Most of all, though, Miss Keller had the companionship of her wonderful teacher, Anne Sullivan, fourteen years her senior, who opened for deaf and blind Helen ways of reading and con-versing.

Continuing along Mt. Auburn Street to the parkway and curving to-ward Gerry's Landing, we have on our right a height of Coolidge Hill where Emerson's grandson, Edward W. Forbes, Director of Fogg Art Museum, who assembled riverside land for President Lowell's House Plan, bought all the east part of the Coolidge Hill land for himself in 1910. On top of the hill, overlooking the Charles River, he then built, where Coolidge farm once had a field of squash, the big three-story mansion at 30 Gerry's Landing Road across the parkway from Clark House, old nursing school on the grounds of the Mt. Auburn Hospital.

Still farther along to our right, opposite the Eliot Bridge crossing the Charles, is the Buckingham Browne & Nichols upper (high) school, play-ing grounds, hockey rink, tennis courts, and gym, the extensive south part of the Coolidge farm, hill, meadow, and cowpasture that Browne & Ni-chols began purchasing in 1912.

Beside the main buildings, facing the river, are the Bradford and Almy buildings. Bradford honors Governor Bradford's devotion to the school as president of his alma mater's corporation from 1924 to 1960. In its lobby is a splendid likeness of the governor. From the lobby a visitor can enter the Almy Building and the beautiful library, gift of Bradford's neighbor, friend, and fellow B&N alumnus Charles Almy, Jr., long the B&N board chairman, builder of a large Cambridge chemical company. From the library there we have a grand view across athletic fields and westward up Coolidge Hill to the more than a dozen buildings of BB&N's neighbor, Shady Hill School.

Along the river to the west and up to Coolidge Avenue on the hill is the Cambridge Cemetery, which the city began to acquire in 1854 so that it could close the increasingly inadequate Cambridgeport cemetery. It did so in 1865, and moved remains from there to this cemetery and converted the old one into the present small Sennott Park at Broadway and Norfolk Street. The cemetery comprises the large area bought first from the Stone farm and another eleven acres purchased at the close of the Civil War from the Coolidge farm.

The Metropolitan Park Commission bridge across from BB&N School was named in honor of Harvard President Eliot and his son Charles, distinguished landscape architect and both apprentice and associate of famed Frederick Law Olmstead, whose "emerald necklace" through city and Back Bay fen gave Boston America's first metropolitan park system. Young Charles Eliot and friends of his, eager to save scenic areas for the public, were able in 1892 to have the state establish the Metropolitan Park Commission, to which he was an adviser. Eliot sought to improve the banks of the Charles River and Cambridge parks, efforts cut short by his death in 1897 at age forty-one.

Just downriver from Eliot Bridge is the Cambridge Boat Club, formed by some Cantabrigians in 1909 at the home of Richard Henry Dana III, a successor to the 1882 casino near the foot of Ash Street. The clubhouse had to be moved here in 1947 from its location between here and Ash Street to make way for the extension of Memorial Drive along the river. Besides being a well-equipped boathouse, it is a Cambridge community and social center.

A few steps farther downriver, beside the boathouse, is a monument marking Sir Richard's Landing, the beginning of Watertown in mid-1630, when Sir Richard Saltonstall, his five children, and others who had come in John Winthrop's *Arbella* flotilla, arrived from Charlestown to this area that would long be known, in recollection of Elbridge Gerry, as Gerry's Landing.

With Sir Richard was the first Watertown minister, Reverend John Phillips, who, with his parishioners, built a meeting house and parsonage near the present Elmwood, up meadowland between the present Coolidge Hill and the much cut-back Simon's Hill, where we see the Mt. Auburn Hospital. Five years later the Watertown pioneers shifted upriver near the present Watertown Square, leaving allotted land to farmers who stayed, including Simon Stone, for whom Simon's Hill, first site of Watertown's town building, is named.

John Vassall the elder, who had been the first Vassall on Tory Row but left after his wife's death and turned 94 Brattle over to his brother Henry, came back after a second marriage. His residence again had an unhappy ending. He built a house near Gerry's Landing, a long-vanished structure about which little is known, and died here in 1747 at forty-four, just after the death of a daughter.

We walk now back to Mt. Auburn Street, which runs in front of the main hospital building at 280 Mt. Auburn, where "T" buses are available back to Harvard Square for our next walk, along Garden Street.

The extension of Mt. Auburn Street along here in 1808 was a key factor in the struggle of the Dana vs. Craigie camps to attract Boston-bound traffic to their rival bridges. Three times, starting in 1805, the town reversed itself, for Craigie had offered to build and pay for the road to go from the foot of Elmwood Avenue across his land to Mason Street. The final order, in 1808, was to build the present route past the river to Brattle Square. Poet Lowell describes it well: as a lad he often rode his pony this way.

Simon's Hill, location of Mt. Auburn Hospital as well as of Watertown's first meeting house, was part of the sixteen acres of rough pastureland originally granted to Sir Richard. The hill itself was cut back in 1808 to provide fill along Mt. Auburn extension, particularly in the lowland at the curve of the river long known as "the Marsh."

Two of the buildings in the hospital complex, Parsons, the hospital's

1886 red brick building at 330 Mt. Auburn, its first, and Wyman, the building in back of Parsons, attached to the newer main structures, recall two individuals, both tirelessly devoted to the welfare and well-being of other people, who were mainly responsible for Mt. Auburn, Cambridge's first community hospital.

Emily Parsons, though left lame by a childhood illness that impaired both her eyesight and hearing, volunteered as a Civil War nurse in battle areas and suffered further from the malaria that affected many of the soldiers. She was a granddaughter of famed Chief Justice Theophilus Parsons, and a daughter of his namesake, a Harvard Law School professor.

After the war she tried to fulfill the desperate need of many Cambridge people, especially the poorer citizens, for a hospital and opened a small house in Cambridgeport in 1867 for women and children; when it was forced to close, she raised more funds and reopened in 1869. By 1871 she had gained still more support for the sick and disabled, and Cambridge Hospital was incorporated. She died at fifty-six in 1880. Bequests, proceeds from a fair run by Cambridge women, other helpers, and particularly Dr. Morrill Wyman, who wished to see realized "the dearest wish of her heart," got the present Parsons Building under way in 1883 and opened in 1886.

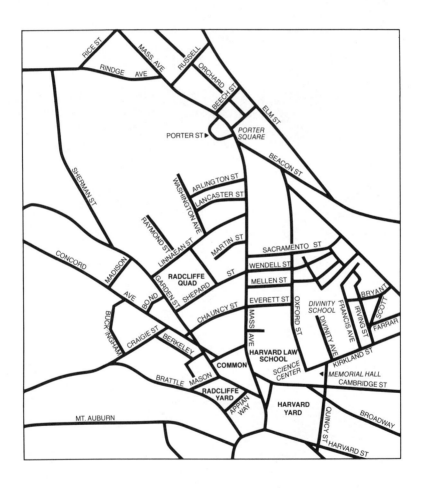

GOD'S ACRE TO WASHINGTON ELM

On passing the old Unitarian Church, opposite the main gate to the Harvard Yard, we see on our left Cambridge's oldest cemetery, long known as God's Acre, graciously and respectfully bestowed by the poet Longfellow from an "ancient Saxon phrase."

Despite the closeness of the graveyard to so busy a crossroads as Harvard Square, a chain and padlock usually bar this entry because of damage vandals have inflicted on God's Acre.

Back in less urban, more bucolic days literary friends of Longfellow came in unimpeded. Young Thomas Higginson tells how he and his pals, sometimes after listening to lectures in the old Lyceum, "went often" to God's Acre "exploring and translating the Latin epitaphs and calling up old associations." Young Oliver Wendell Holmes, who lived just off the Common, went often and wrote a poem. Young James Russell Lowell recounted how he came one Halloween and sat on a table tomb to catch sight of any ghosts.

The kindly sign on this gateway is assurance that entry is still possible with help from the sexton of Christ Church, at the west end of the graveyard, which we will visit presently along Garden Street. Meantime let us take note of prominent points of interest that we can see from the sidewalk. From the gate we can discern the usually overgrown red brick path and the clear white obelisk near the far end of the cemetery.

About halfway to the obelisk is an irregular grouping of graves of the altar type to the left of the path and opposite the gold-tinted stone parish hall and Crothers Chapel of the First Unitarian Church. These altar memorials mark the graves of early Harvard presidents. Here, as, most often, long Latin inscriptions relate (when decipherable), are buried eight—some say nine—of Harvard's early presidents, the ninth being Reverend John Rodgers of Ipswich, who served only a year back around 1683 when the small, new College was having a hard time luring a preacher to give up his parish and accept the presidency.

The others include the first president, Reverend Henry Dunster, who got Harvard its 1650 charter. Though forced out, Reverend Dunster so loved Cambridge that he asked to be buried here. His original stone, fragmented, was later embedded in a larger stone on a granite base. Two other eighteenth-century presidents' graves are here, Dunster's immediate successor, Reverend Charles Chauncy, and Reverend Urian Oakes.

In the grove, too, were buried John Leverett, who brought liberal thinking to Harvard; Reverend Benjamin Wadsworth, for whom venerable Wadsworth House was built; Reverend Edward Holyoke, who trained the fathers of the Revolution, fought the fire in old Harvard Hall, and built the present one; and Reverend Samuel Webber, whose election in 1801 underpinned the University's shift from orthodoxy to Unitarianism. On higher ground to the right of the Chapel, best sited of all in the College vault, is the tomb of Joseph Willard, who started the Medical School and welcomed new U.S. President George Washington to the Harvard Yard in 1789.

Immediately inside the metal fencing, to the right of God's Acre main gate, is the Dana tomb, with a memorial in the form of a cross beside the row of brick vaults. Intermarriage with old and prominent Cambridge families can be seen in the names on the memorial cross, names we will see presently on streets that divide the once great estate of Chief Justice Francis Dana, patriot of the Revolutionary era, builder of the pioneer West Boston Bridge.

There have been recent family burials here, but most remembered in this tomb are family members, including Judge Edmund Trowbridge, the artist Washington Allston, and, still earlier, Royal Governor Jonathan Belcher, who wanted to be buried with his College mate and cousin Judge Jonathan Remington, whose remains were dug up and moved here. Author Richard Henry Dana describes his being at the burial here of a young cousin and how "All the family went down into the tomb. . . ." Author Dana himself, who died abroad, is buried in Rome, near the graves of Keats and Shelley.

On turning left at the old milestone, we head along Garden Street, once called "the highway to the great swamp," where brooks ran into Fresh Pond, and later Washington Street. It was renamed in the mid-1800s as the way to Harvard's Botanical Garden. A few more steps and on our left is a showpiece, the Vassall tomb of five stone pillars supporting an altarlike slab, on which was cut only the family's heraldic emblem of a vase (*vas*) and the sun (*sol*). Here, distinct from the later family crypt that would be built in Christ Church, was buried John Vassall, Sr., who died in 1747 at Gerry's Landing, along with his first young wife, who had died in child-birth.

The mound just inside the railing, about midway along the cemetery fence, demonstrates that many gravesites are no longer identifiable. Even now we can see stones broken or sinking into the earth. The earliest extant grave goes back to 1653, nearly two decades after God's Acre was ordered "paled in," in 1635. Among the known Cantabrigians buried here whose graves are no longer marked are those of Reverend Thomas Shepard, credited by Cotton Mather for having Harvard College located in Newe Towne; the nation's first printer, Stephen Daye; and the first Cambridge Grammar School teacher, Elija Corlett.

On a number of graves the groove cut in stone to hold the metal identity plate of the departed is gone, and only the cut remains, an unintended catchbasin for rainwater. Most of the missing metal was melted down by General Washington's soldiers to furnish desperately needed bullets for their muskets.

A bit in, just to the right of the mound, can be seen a raised, coffinlike memorial surrounded by railing, with the lengthy epitaph on the top long gone; but the occupant is known. He was called "English Thomas" Lee, who was actually on the patriot side and a College benefactor, to distinguish him from his neighboring Lees. A very wealthy merchant, he came to Brattle Street during the Revolutionary War and lived in the Lechmere-Sewall House for almost a decade.

Next along Garden Street we see a shaft of a granite-based brownstone on a grassy mound, which the city erected in 1870 in memory of the six men of Cambridge (Menotomy, the present Arlington, was then a parish of Cambridge) who gave their lives fighting the Redcoats on the first day of the Revolutionary War.

Some of the Sons of Liberty who were wounded at Bunker Hill and died in the improvised hospitals along Tory Row were buried here and commemorated on a dark stone, now in a clump of trees, a few steps more along Garden Street. Several skulls with bullet holes were found during digging for these monuments. The graves of fifteen Revolutionary War soldiers buried here up to 1830 are known, among them two black patriots, Neptune Frost and Cato Stedman, buried with their owners' families.

Turn left at the west end of the cemetery railing and a few feet farther, on the left across from the entrance to Christ Church, is the back gateway to God's Acre. The sexton, always obliging, can be found either in the church or the parish house immediately west of the church.

The cemetery has many other attractions. The white obelisk we saw from the main entrance, its message now defaced, was erected to the memory of the family of Selectman-Deacon and first school supervisor John Bridge, whose bronze statue is the Puritan we saw on the Common. Some of the family were buried nearby. A visitor may see where Dexter Pratt, the village blacksmith, was laid to rest.

Or look, in the grove of Harvard presidents, some paces forward of the Unitarian chapel, for a grave of a great early friend of the Indians, Major-General Daniel Gookin (the stone cutter carved it "Gookings"); or the almost-effaced tomb of legendary tutor Henry Flynt, who taught Harvard lads for fifty-five years and died at eighty-four in 1760, still serving the College.

And nearby is still another multiple burial of friends. Reverend William Brattle, also a beloved tutor and minister of the First Meeting House, who died in 1717, is buried with his wife in the tomb with his classmate and close friend, Dr. James Oliver (carved as Jacobi Oliveri) in the Brattle tomb.

Christ Church, Cambridge's oldest house of worship, was created by the nabobs of Tory Row, some of whom found Boston's King's Chapel, a dozen miles distant, too long overland and, by ferry in stormy weather or winter, too "troublesome and sometimes impracticable." Henry Vassall acted as their leader, and he had the enthusiastic help of wealthy young Reverend East Apthorp, back from his religious studies in England at twenty-six, engaged to the niece of soon-to-be Royal Governor Thomas Hutchinson and building Apthorp House, as we have seen, for himself and his bride.

Reverend Apthorp and the Tory Row sponsors got architect Peter

Harrison, who had designed King's Chapel, to send them plans, from Newport, Rhode Island, which would include "no steeple, only a tower with a belfry." The town pound was removed and new Royal Governor Francis Bernard, who would design the present Harvard Hall, and be knighted, laid the cornerstone in 1760. First services were held in fall 1761.

The elegance of the Apthorp House, completed in the same year, brought Reverend Apthorp under attack by Boston's orthodox clergy. Their leader, Reverend Jonathan Mayhew, had been tipped off by none other than Thomas Hollis, a Harvard benefactor who sent liberal literature to our future patriots, that Reverend Apthorp was to be named a bishop. A pamphlet war, Mayhew vs. Apthorp, followed, and Reverend Apthorp, who had turned down being a leader of New York's new King's College—which would soon be renamed Columbia University—so that he could head Christ Church here, went off to England three years later. Most of the Tory Row folks followed on the eve of the Revolution, leaving Christ Church on its own.

Sons of Liberty who marched from Wethersfield, Connecticut, at the outbreak of the war, Captain John Chester's company, had quarters here. General Washington, who attended services with most of his troops in the old meeting house in Harvard Square, had Christ Church refurbished when Martha asked to have their divine services here on the last Sunday in 1775. Their pew's location can still be seen, the third pew from the front on the left-hand window side. Colonel William Palfrey, of the General's staff, filled in as preacher. Colonel Palfrey wrote to his wife that he prayed for God to bless the Continental Congress and the Commander-in-Chief to overcome all enemies. The prayer, he told her, "was much approved."

The church suffered from neglect, desecration, weather, and vandals during the war years. The savage gouge of a bullet can still be seen, about seven feet up, just to the right of the main door of the church, inside the porch. Worst damage, smashing of the pulpit and even the pipes of the fine organ that had been built in London, came from aroused townsfolk when the church was opened in 1778 for services for a young British officer shot by a sentry while Burgoyne's convention army was in Cambridge.

The bitter onslaught struck while mourners were below putting the body in the Vassall crypt. Neglect continued until the mid-1790s, when a subscription led to the reopening with lay ministers.

Growth in the congregation led in 1857 to the enlargement, with an added 23 feet on the altar end. In 1861, for its 100th anniversary, the church belfry got the Harvard chime of thirteen bells, still with a delightful ring on Sundays and for special events that bring additional churchgoers to the lovely interior with its white pillars, red-cushioned seats, and crystal chandeliers. This was the way it was when the elder Senator Henry Cabot Lodge was married here, the Danas attended, and Teddy Roosevelt, while a College student, came to stoke the furnace and teach Sunday School.

An eerie scene came about in the church cellar in 1865, when city authorities ordered that the only tomb there, Henry Vassall's, be sealed. Henry, chairman of the church's building committee and public and military official, had many friends, who had come in white silk stockings, laced coats, and cocked hats, and alighted from their coaches to attend his burial, descending the flight of stone steps to the crypt.

Two prominent doctors were on hand just before the flight of steps was filled with earth: Dr. Morrill Wyman and Dr. Oliver Wendell Holmes. They came to examine the remains in the ten coffins in which lay family members, the young British officer buried in 1778, and ninety-two-year-old Darby, son of the Vassall slave-coachman, who died in 1861. Amid the bones the doctors found cherry pits with their kernels eaten out by mice.

Set back on the west side of the church is the 1897 parish house, and, behind it, the greater parish facilities of the larger one, built in 1949. Next along Garden Street is the Christ Church rectory, an 1820 structure, acquired in 1916 by the growing congregation. The next two buildings, also of gray clapboard and white trim like the rectory, are early and mid-nineteenth-century structures, once the dwellings of members of an old Cambridge family, the Howes, and now owned by Harvard University. The Episcopal chaplaincy, serving both Harvard and Radcliffe students, is also located at 2 Garden Street, which, in earlier times, was a residence for students, among them future orator Charles Sumner, who boarded here.

Projects of the Graduate School of Education occupy 3 Garden, on the corner.

On going by Byerly Hall in the Radcliffe Yard, we recall that here, as we noticed on our walk in Farwell Place, was once a one-room 1769 public grammar schoolhouse, where coeducational instruction—precursor of the service that Harvard and Radcliffe now provide in Radcliffe Yard—began in Cambridge in 1826. The few girls who came had rear seats on the street side of the classroom. It was in an 1832 successor school on this site that Professor Charles Eliot Norton (in 1847) began Cambridge's first evening school, which he ran for several years.

Children and grandchildren of Radcliffe's first president, Elizabeth Cary Agassiz built in her memory the third gateway on our left, into Radcliffe Yard. It leads to the original entry, in the north semicircular bay, of Fay House. Students most often use the side (east) entry. Inside, in the large lobby, with a stairway on its south end, are some delightful wall exhibits and pictures of early Radcliffe, including a view of the once-flourishing elm tree on the highway just outside when General Washington took command of his army on July 3, 1775.

East of present Fay House, in a dwelling now gone, lived young painter Winslow Homer. His father, a merchant who lost his fortune at the time of the 1849 gold rush, could afford to send only Winslow's older brother to college. Winslow, as a youngster, went via Appian Way to the Washington Grammar School, described earlier, on Brattle Street. Young Winslow did sketches of his brother Charles's 1857 Class Day at Harvard and of Charles playing football with his classmates on the Common across from their dwelling, all before Winslow, at twenty-three, went off to New York to pursue his career in art.

Before crossing Mason Street, glance up at the steeple of the First Church in Cambridge, Congregational, formerly called the Shepard Memorial Church. The cockerel weathervane was placed atop the steeple soon after the church was dedicated in 1872. Prior to that this 172-pound, 5-foot-5-inch cockerel, created by Deacon Shem Drowne, who also made Faneuil Hall's famous grasshopper vane, was put atop Boston's Hanover Street Meeting House in 1721. There Royal Governor Hutchinson had been a parishioner and Ralph Waldo Emerson was pastor for four years. It was moved to another Boston church, where an 1869 gale blew down both cockerel and church steeple.

This church was built by the trinitarian members of Reverend Abiel Holmes's parish a few years after their separation from the Unitarian parishioners, who built the 1833 First Parish, Unitarian, which we saw across from the main gate of Harvard Yard.

The Washington elm stood about in mid-Garden Street on the west side of the old King's Highway, which came eastward along Mason Street and across the Common. Oliver Wendell Holmes saw the tree alive, and he saluted it in poetry as "the grand old tree!" under which "our fathers gathered in arms" and swore to "fight till the land was free." Deacon Josiah Moore's wife, whose house was then on the site of the church, said that she saw the ceremony in the shadow of the tree while looking from her window. Deacon Moore was a sergeant in Captain Samuel Thatcher's Minuteman company.

Cambridge trees, both here and gone, have frequently been commemorated. The old Whitefield elm stood in mid-Garden Street just beyond Waterhouse Street until removed in 1871 to accommodate increasing traffic. While standing beneath its branches in 1745, revivalist Reverend George Whitefield, assailing increasingly liberal Harvard and like-minded New England clergy, urged upon a throng of eager listeners a reawakening of piety and morality. In response, Harvard's honored, future firefighting President Holyoke called Reverend Whitefield's remarks a "wicked and libelous falsehood."

To see the oldest structure still facing the Common, we go along Waterhouse Street on our right. To get an idea of how pre–World War I dwellings appeared along here we need know only that where we now see the six-story apartments of number 1 Waterhouse, they were preceded by only two private dwellings on this entire triangle of land. Concord Avenue, which we now cross, opened as a toll turnpike across the Common in 1807, was extended to the West Boston Bridge. Presently, to the east of the Common, we will see what Andrew Craigie did to try to attract its traffic.

When Harvard's Charles T. "Copey" Copeland retired after nearly three decades on the top floor of Hollis Hall, he came to the high apartment house, the second door down on the right, 5 Concord Avenue, to a four-room apartment on the fifth floor. He had a sunporch and delighted in his views of Cambridge, and particularly mentioned his seeing the cross on the steeple of St. Peter's Church on the hill up Concord Avenue. He lived here for his last two decades, still having sessions with friends, taking walks to Fresh Pond, and giving occasional readings for students, as on Easter and Christmas, for those who were still in Cambridge.

The innovative educator Arthur Gilman, who founded Radcliffe College in 1879, came two years later to live for his remaining decades in a dwelling he built on the east corner at 5 Waterhouse Street. In a few years he had his office in Fay House as secretary of the developing College, and he was also busy directing the growing Cambridge School for Girls, which he had got under way in 1886; it was soon offering, in his ads, "Preparation for Radcliffe and other colleges." We shall see presently how that school grew a little way up Concord Avenue. He left his dwelling shortly before his death in 1909 to be in a milder climate, and died in Atlantic City.

Dr. Benjamin Waterhouse's dwelling, the two-story gray clapboard with white trim and picket fence at 7 Waterhouse Street, was just recently redone. It dates from the mid-eighteenth century, and became the residence of William Vassall, John Vassall, Sr.'s younger brother and one of the three Vassalls (the third was Henry) who were graduated from Harvard. William, with his large family, came back fifteen years after his 1733 graduation, got himself a mansion on Boston's Pemberton Hill, and used the dwelling we see here as his summer home. He became high sheriff for Middlesex County and was among those named to General Gage's mandamus council. He did not quit the post, but instead took off for England with his family. He was banished and his property confiscated.

After the Revolution the dwelling was acquired by Dr. Waterhouse. Harvard's Medical School got started under Dr. John Warren in fall 1872, and a month later Dr. Waterhouse was selected to teach theory and practice, with actual instruction beginning in the following year. Shortly before he died, at ninety-two, Waterhouse wrote in his journal: "I cut the claw and wings of smallpox." That was his greatest achievement.

Back in 1800, Waterhouse got some "vaccine threads" from Dr. Edward Jenner, their discoverer, with whom Waterhouse had studied in Europe. Waterhouse first vaccinated his own children, thus introducing vaccination to America. When Waterhouse sent some of the threads to his friend, President Thomas Jefferson, he, too, vaccinated his family.

Dr. Waterhouse kept a journal that gives fascinating glimpses of life in Cambridge in his era. When a hearty eighty-two, he enjoyed all the exciting events of Harvard's 200th celebration, almost outside his front door. Artist Washington Allston, as a student, lived here with him.

It seems amazing, in our land-scarce days, that the doctor's food came from his crops on "eight acres of good land in the rear" of his house. He gives a glimpse of the heyday of ice harvesting on Fresh Pond, when, in springtime, blocks of ice would pass, from daylight to sunset, "incessantly . . . in 6-horse teams without an interval of half an hour, quantities absolutely incredible." Dr. Waterhouse was also a pioneer lecturer, warning against physical damage caused by smoking tobacco, but that advice was heavily overshadowed by his triumph over smallpox.

ALONG GARDEN STREET TO RADCLIFFE QUAD

The Commander, fashionable hotel ahead of us as we return to Garden Street, was named in honor of General Washington when it was built in 1928. In the landscaped area in front of its portico is a splendid life-sized bronze reproduction of Jean Antoine Houdon's statue that the Commonwealth of Virginia placed in its state capitol in tribute to the greatest of Virginians.

Houdon, one of Europe's most distinguished sculptors, came from France and spent two weeks at Mt. Vernon with our future first President to ensure the perfection of the likeness. In the lobby is a depiction, in a diorama, of Washington taking command of the Continental Army nearby under the Old Elm.

As we turn left at Berkeley Street to see some literary sites, we recall that the old corner house replaced by the Commander was the one William James came to (his mother-in-law's) after the tragic death of his young son in Appian Way. While living here, James was promoted to a full professorship (in 1886) and was able three years later to build his most remembered residence, which we will see on Irving Street.

Just beyond where Berkeley Street turns right, on the corner at 9 Phillips Place, was the residence, for his last two decades, of eminent librarian John L. Sibley, who died here in 1885. In his retirement he produced his celebrated biographies of Harvard graduates, starting with the first nine commencers of 1642.

Across the street, beside the extensive lawn on the corner, at 4 Berkeley Street, we see the clapboard house, buff with white trim, which author Richard Henry Dana built on land he had purchased in 1851. He laid out this street, which he named after British philosopher Bishop George Berkeley, whom he admired. Dana's first visitor, when he moved in at springtime 1852 with his wife, four daughters, and one-year-old son, was his neighbor and friend Henry Wadsworth Longfellow. Recording that fact in his diary, Dana added "May it be a good omen."

A quarter of a century later that young son, Richard Henry Dana III, married Longfellow's daughter, Edith. For some years now the Dana House, with a large wing on the west side replacing a Dana porch, has been the Episcopal Divinity School dean's residence, and the former Sibley dwelling became an E.D.S. faculty house.

In 1870, William Dean Howells, then working with famed publisher James T. Fields on the *Atlantic Monthly*, came to live in the neighboring house at 6 Berkeley. The magazine was then printed in Cambridge, and Howells found he "could more conveniently look over the proofs." His place was a center for the contributors, among them Longfellow, who, through an opening in "the high board fence," in back, gave Howells "an easement across that old garden" behind Longfellow's mansion.

John Fiske, who had been a neighbor of Howells in his earlier Cambridge home, followed Howells here and lived across Berkeley Street from Dana's house. Howells, as we will see a short way off, used this house at 6 Berkeley as a model for one he soon built for himself on Concord Avenue.

Returning back along Berkeley Street to Garden, we have, on the west corner, the brick building at 20 Garden that the American Trial Lawyers Association built in 1956. This building, bought a decade ago by Harvard, is used for the University's administration of its extension and summer-school functions.

This building is on the site where the growing Browne & Nichols School built a three-story brick schoolhouse when it moved here from Appian Way in 1897. Here the school stayed until it moved in 1948 to Gerry's Landing. That move had been a hopeful dream of the school for half a century during which, beginning in 1912, it began assembling the ten acres of the old Coolidge cowpasture and meadowland it now enjoys near the Charles River.

Property acquired here by the growing school included its neighboring building at 22 Garden. Back in the mid-nineteenth century this was where Dr. John W. Webster lived after moving from Farwell Place in 1834. Webster was arrested here for the sensational 1849 murder of wealthy banker George Parkman, uncle of historian Francis Parkman. It was at Webster's trial that Harvard President Jared Sparks, in his testimony, made the oft-quoted observation, "Our professors do not often commit murder."

A weird tale has been told about a dinner Dr. Webster gave to a dozen or so friends in his house a year before the Parkman murder. Charles Dickens, on his final American visit in 1868, was so intrigued by the murder that he went one morning to the scene in the old Harvard Medical School laboratory in Boston.

At a gathering later that day, the poet Longfellow, who had introduced Dickens, on his 1842 visit to Cambridge, to several Harvard professors—including Webster—told how Webster had the lights turned off at his dinner and placed a bowl of flaming chemicals on the table. As his guests stared into this odd light they were shocked to see Webster hold a noose-like handkerchief around his neck, put out his tongue, and drop his head to the side as though he had been hanged.

At the north corner of Follen Street and Concord Avenue, on the former grounds of the old State Arsenal, is the Longy School of Music, in the three-story stone mansion at 1 Follen, built and first occupied by Edwin H. Abbot in 1890. In Harvard Square we saw the Abbot Building, a later creation of his. Abbot, along with his 1855 classmates, Henry Lee Higginson and Alexander Agassiz, became immensely wealthy in the boom years after the Civil War. Abbot's special field was extending railroads across country to the Pacific.

This granite mansion has been called his "castle," with its large rooms, immense fireplace, expensive furniture, and two acres of garden, designed by the son of his lifelong friend, President Charles W. Eliot, and enclosed by a stone-capped brick wall.

The Longy School of Music was founded in 1915 by Georges Longy of the Boston Symphony Orchestra, widely regarded as the world's foremost oboist. The school took over Abbot castle in 1937. The faculty has consisted of prominent members of the Boston Symphony Orchestra and distinguished musicians from all over the world, among them Nadia Boulanger and Sarah Caldwell. The adjoining Edward Pickman Concert Hall, named for the president of the School's trustees, was built at 27 Garden in 1968. The hall, with seating for as many as 275, along with the school's concert calendar, student groups, and great visiting artists performing here, continues the neighborhood's long cultural tradition.

The large building at 29 Garden, at the corner of Chauncy Street, is the former Continental Hotel, built in 1929 but currently used by Harvard for married-student lodgings. Just around the corner, on Chauncy, on the lower floor, is a station of the Harvard University Police. The former hotel building stands on the site of the old Arsenal's 100-foot-long, three-story-high brick main building, built in 1818. There had stood a storehouse for munitions almost back to the outbreak of the Revolution and the state, when war threatened with France, built an arsenal in 1796.

All were on land of which Dr. Waterhouse became owner, land that was later purchased by Abbot. The old cannon we saw on the Common, captured from the French and British forces, were stored here before the state built a new arsenal in Springfield in the 1880s. Only Arsenal Square, with its monument to Spanish War veterans, dedicated in 1947, now recalls the old Arsenal, one of whose final occupants, in the 1870s, was the new Cambridge Social Dramatic Club, whose members converted it into a neighborood theater and gave performances there.

We go now along Concord Avenue and, just beyond Craigie Street on the left, at 34 Concord Avenue, is the girls' preparatory school, to which Arthur Gilman in the 1890s moved his Cambridge School for Girls, from the present Radcliffe Yard. This was the period when Helen Keller went to the Cambridge School (1896–1898) in preparation for Radcliffe, which she entered in 1900.

The three similarly stuccoed buildings around the parking lot on the west side of number 34 were purchased as the school grew. For a time the buildings were part of the Lesley School for Children, part of the present Lesley College, but these were purchased in 1984 by Radcliffe College.

After renovation of the four buildings, Radcliffe's growing Bunting Institute was to be located here by mid-1986. This Institute, which used to share part of Schlesinger Library in the Radcliffe Yard, was established in 1960 to help educated women at home to get back into their professional life. It began as Radcliffe Institute, but its name was later changed in tribute to its originator, President Mary I. Bunting, under whom coresidency began at Radcliffe in 1971.

Just across the highway, at 37 Concord Avenue, is the house that new editor-in-chief William D. Howells built with the help of royalties in 1872.

His warmest friends included Longfellow, Lowell, and fellow Westerner Mark Twain. Richard Henry Dana III tells how Howells, in a visit in later life to the Longfellow House, at the poet's death, said that when he first came to Cambridge as a young man "he trembled at the very thought of meeting its 'great literary set.' "

While living here Howells often had visits from Lowell and Longfellow, and often took walks with both. So much social life developed that Howells, to get more time for writing, built farther out Concord Avenue on "Belmont Heights" and soon gave up his editorship to devote himself to being an author.

Sixteen-year-old Helen Keller came to reside at number 37, right across the street from Gilman's school, when she took her entrance exams, based on old Harvard College exams, to become a pupil. She continued to live here when admitted and enjoyed, she put in a letter, being where Howells had lived. For Miss Sullivan, her companion here, the task of teacher was additionally hard because the books Helen needed for Gilman's classes were not as yet printed in Braille.

We return along Concord Avenue to go down Craigie Street, a street of old estates and buildings. Soon, on our left, is the west end of Berkeley Street. The second house down on the right, at number 22, a big pink-tinted mansard, was built by his mother for Howells's old neighbor John Fiske, who moved here from the house opposite Dana's. Across from here, at 23 Berkeley, lived a man long honored in Cambridge, Edward Abbot's older brother Henry, who trained at West Point under Robert E. Lee, was wounded at Bull Run, served throughout the war, and became a brigadier general.

At 19 Craigie Street a modern structure, quite different from its nineteenth-century neighboring mansions, is on the site where historian Albert Bushnell Hart used to live. Expanding Buckingham School built it in 1969 for a kindergarten and lower school, only five years before combining with Browne & Nichols. The attractive play area is contiguous in back with other buildings of the school in Buckingham Street.

We continue now along Craigie Street and turn right at Buckingham. Soon, on our right, at short Buckingham Place, are four earlier Buckingham School buildings. The 1982 building on the west corner is the Markham Building, named for the school's founder, Jeanette Markham, who had held her first classes up the street in a kind friend's house. Mrs. Richard Henry Dana III, who had her own youngsters to be taught, erected this building for the school in a pear orchard once here that Mrs. Dana had purchased. The brick buildings and extensions and the Kelsey House, next down Buckingham Place, were, like the mansion we saw at 80 Sparks Street, later expansions.

On coming back to his native Cambridge in 1878, after the death of his first wife, Reverend Thomas W. Higginson, antislavery crusader, Colonel of the first regiment of freed slaves in the Union Army, author, discoverer of poet Emily Dickinson, came to live at 29 Buckingham Street, the big hillside house on the left up the road at the second bend.

He and Justin Winsor, living up from here in Sparks Street, put a gate in the fence for neighborly visits. Higginson was also a staunch supporter of equal rights for women. His second wife, whom he married here, was a niece of Longfellow. Young Radcliffe graduate Jeanette Markham was encouraged by Higginson to teach his and other children. She started doing so in 1889 across the street in the Morse House at 74 Buckingham Street, many years later a temporary kindergarten for the Buckingham School.

Gertrude Stein was well acquainted with this area. Radcliffe, then "Harvard Annex," lacked dorms when she was in College, and she lived and boarded at the house that was then 64 Buckingham Street (1893–1897), immediately across from Higginson's house. She went on walks, picnics, and bike rides with her brother Leo, who was going to Harvard, and friends, loved plays and song, joined the Idler Club amateur dramatics, got her first writing published in 1895 while here—a paper she coauthored for her favorite William James's psychology class.

The four-story brick apartment house on the corner at 86 Buckingham Street, across from St. Peter's Parochial School and the enlarged 1849 church of which he was a prominent member, was the dwelling of Governor Paul Dever. His apartment here was long a center of Cambridge and state political activity. Dever, a Navy veteran of World War II, is best remembered for his extensive state highway modernization just after World War II, which took several years.

Directly across Concord Avenue from Dever's apartment is an opening in the wire fence around the grounds of the Harvard Observatory, which was located atop the hill where Andrew Craigie—and Vassalls before him—had a summer retreat and lookout as part of his estate.

Harvard's "Old Quin," staunch advocate of the College's having a real observatory, got his desire in his final year, and a year later, in 1846, Professor William Cranch Bond, the director, moved the astronomical equipment, especially the big 15-inch telescope, from Dana House in the Yard to the completed observatory on the rise that was then called "Summer House Hill." Professor Bond observed, on watching Jupiter and its satellites, "There is an awful and mysterious influence comes over one, standing in the dark dome alone with this huge, gigantic tube."

By going up the steep steps within the wire fence and around Building A to the right you can see the original building, gray-painted brick, and the great 30-foot observatory dome on top. Access for the public to the upstairs level, where Professor Bond watched Jupiter, is limited to one night a month, and that when the weather is clear.

The green doorway in daytime does open to the lower floor, where a huge granite conical pier—right down to bedrock for stability—supports the telescope above. The pier occupies most of the space, but there too are celestial exhibits—nebulas, galaxies, comets, the Milky Way. For the 1986 appearance of Halley's Comet, last seen in its seventy-six-year cycle in 1910, there is a new exhibit showing how the comet, first recorded in 240 B.C., enters the solar system and its route in and out on a parabolic course around our sun.

The many other buildings on the grounds, other than the gym, are for laboratories, offices, and research and joint astrophysical activity with the Smithsonian Institute.

Going back via the steep stairs, we head east on Concord Avenue to Bond Street on our left, named for Professor Bond and his son George, who succeeded him as director. Partway along Bond Street, at the bend, we catch sight of the high recent dorms on the north side of the Radcliffe

Quadrangle. On the corner of the Observatory grounds, on our left, is the 1979 Radcliffe Recreational Center, the gym, just mentioned. It has racquetball, basketball, and squash courts, exercise rooms, and on either side of the Garden Street entrance to the Observatory, outdoor tennis courts.

We turn right at Garden Street to go to Shepard Street on the south side of the Quad. On our way we can see, on the left and above the treetops, the most recent large structure in the Quad, five-story Hilles Library, with its limestone and bronzed-glass façade, completed in 1966.

Just before we come to Shepard, notice on our right the site of the present 54 and 54A Garden Street. These dwellings replaced the early nineteenth-century dwelling of Professor Theophilus Parsons of the Harvard Law School, son of the renowned chief justice. Here was the home of one of Cambridge's most admirable women, Emily, oldest of Professor Parsons's four daughters, who paved the way for the present Mt. Auburn Hospital, built after her death in 1880.

Dedication to others was Emily's way of living, though she lost the sight in her right eye at five, was left deaf by scarlet fever at seven, and was left lame by an accident at twenty-five. Yet she served as a Civil War nurse, and on her return inspired others to build the hospital, where we have seen the building named in her memory.

A few steps after we enter Shepard Street we have, on our left, the open plaza and main entrance to Hilles Library, one of the most, if not the most, attractive combinations of landscaping terrace and building in Cambridge. When the sun is shining into the inner, open courtyard of Hilles, to the cobbled area's stone bowls of small trees and flowers, it is a dreamlike vista. Yet the students, hurrying to their study, mostly use the side entrance. Besides handy access to books, as at Harvard Yard's Lamont, Hilles has reading alcoves and exhibits, and also an art gallery, coffee shop, and commuters' lounge, conference rooms, faculty offices, and cinema seating 120. Hilles is closed in summertime so that the staff can work on projects.

On coming from Hilles's main entrance, turn left along the path past Bertram Hall on our right to the grassed open area village green of the Radcliffe Quad.

The fourteen dormitory halls immediately across the Quad are divided administratively into three houses. Cabot House, formerly South House, is the oldest, with six halls, two of which we see on each of the west, south, and east sides of the open Quad. Bertram, the first of Radcliffe's dorms, built in 1902, actually faces Shepard Street. So too does Radcliffe's second, Elliot Hall, in the southeast corner of the Quad, built in 1907. Bertram, named for her family, and Eliot were both gifts of Mrs. David Pulsifer Kimball, wife of the Boston lawyer and railroad magnate.

As Radcliffe's growth continued, Harvard President Eliot joined with Radcliffe President Briggs and members of the Cabot family in 1911 to get what Eliot called another "hall of residence." Dr. R. C. Cabot stressed that such halls "would enable students from a distance to come to Radcliffe and . . . it is possible for the College to become cosmopolitan."

Whitman Hall went up next to Eliot in the following year. Cabot Hall, next to it, with the present Cabot House dining room between it and Whitman, was the last of these Cabot House dorms to be erected, in 1937. Meanwhile Barnard, next to Bertram Hall, went up, and in 1924 Radcliffe's second president, present at the 1911 fund raiser, LeBaron R. Briggs, was honored with Briggs Hall on our left, next to Barnard Hall.

The focus of the Quad Green, Moors Hall, with its cupola and blue dome like that of Lowell House, built in 1949, became the cornerstone of President Mary I. Bunting's coeducational efforts in 1961 to bring the House Plan to Radcliffe. Moors Hall was connected to Holmes and Comstock, named for Radcliffe's first full-time President, Ada Louise Comstock, built in the 1950s as part of North House. To these was added Wolbach Hall, a former apartment building, immediately to the east of Moors. Dining halls and common rooms came with the Bunting remodeling.

Currier House, whose most recent Radcliffe dorms we saw as we came along Bond Street, comprises four interconnected House Plan dorms, all built by 1970 in the northwest part of the Quad, and all named for Radcliffe graduates: Bingham, Daniels, Gilbert, and Tuchman Halls. Tuchman, named for Barbara Tuchman, author of *The Guns of August*, has also a College convenience of modern times on its Linnaean Street side at number 64, a child-care center, as in Putnam House in the Radcliffe Yard. North and Currier Houses also administer nearby coop residences, and in the rear of North House, also on Linnaean Street, are eight townhouses, known as Faculty Row.

We head north now, between Tuchman and Holmes Halls, to Linnaean Street. The University's Botanical Garden Apartments we see on the north side of Linnaean Street, from Raymond Street to Garden Street, are where plants, shrubs, trees, around springs and small ponds, specimens that had been assembled from all over the world, made Harvard's Botanical Garden famous and gave Garden Street its name. Harvard President John T. Kirkland raised funds and appointed William D. Peck the first Professor of Natural History.

Although Dr. Waterhouse had given some natural history lectures, it was Peck who got the Garden under way in 1807. There was then an upper terrace along the back of the area, toward the present Robinson Street, and here a curator's residence was built in 1810 by Peck. Other buildings gradually appeared along this higher land: conservatories, greenhouses, a gardener's cottage, and a herbarium under Professor Asa Gray, friend of Charles Darwin and greatest United States botanist of his era, who became curator in 1842.

To protect Gray's activity, generous Nathaniel Thayer, who would later give the College Thayer Hall, built a fireproof brick herbarium for Gray's precious collection and library in 1864. President Eliot credited Gray, in giving his seasonal courses here, with having "started the first summer school held at Harvard or indeed in the United States." In later years botanical activity shifted to the University's collecting, and research to the Arnold Arboretum and Bussey Institution's much greater acreage in Jamaica Plain. By the winter of 1948–49 the Garden was replaced by the apartments, with some of the specimens going to the plant or garden clubs of Cambridge.

Gray's 1810 house can still be seen at 88 Garden Street on the southeast corner of Madison Street. To go there, we turn right on returning to Garden Street. Just beyond Fernald Drive, at 79 Garden Street, is Kittredge Hall, now devoted to Harvard University Press, which has had many makeshift offices since its reorganization in 1913. Once it was even in the basement of University Hall; now it is roughly on the original site of the Asa Gray House, which faced Linnaean Street from its terraced garden perch. The house was moved here just a century after its construction for Peck and, after him, for his successor as curator, Thomas Nuttall, a great naturalist who in that era thought the whole house and garden a pretty "remote quarter of the town."

Gray lived here, always active on botanical work until his death in 1888. It was from his house that he carried on the then sensational controversy with fellow scientist Louis Agassiz, famous zoologist, who strenuously opposed Darwin's evolutionary theories. Lois Howe, daughter of President Estes Howe of the Cambridge Gas Company, back in the days of early telephones and electric lightbulbs, tells of coming to the Asa Gray house to take preliminary exams to enter "Harvard Annex."

Dear Mrs. Gray, she said, brought in "lemonade for us." The final exams that got Lois and her friends into the future Radcliffe, were next taken in the Carret's House, Radcliffe's birthplace on Appian Way. To savor more of the flavor of earlier times, look at the old fencing and rear structures of Asa Gray House, on the Madison Street side.

W e go now northward along the route that William Dawes, the Cambridge Minutemen, and Lord Percy followed in 1775 out the present Massachusetts Avenue when the musketry of the Redcoats touched off the Revolution.

From Harvard north, Massachusetts Avenue began life as "the Highway to Menotomy," crossing the Charlestown–Watertown path across the Common. Menotomy was the early name of Arlington, a former parish of Cambridge, which became the town of West Cambridge in 1807. The road led, of course, to Lexington, the former "Cambridge Farms," which became a town earlier in 1713. When Cambridge became a city the road, by then a turnpike, was known as North Street until changed in 1894 to its present name all the way from Boston through Cambridge to Lexington.

Just across the present Massachusetts Avenue from where, on the Common, we saw the site of the old election oak, where John Winthrop defeated Harry Vane for governor, there was on the left of where we see the rear entry of Gannett House, at 1511 Massachusetts Avenue, a short street named Holmes Place.

In the Revolutionary period three houses were on its north side, the middle one a Gannett House earlier than the 1838 one that we see. Beyond the three houses, Holmes Place made a right-angle turn and on its east side, facing south to the College like its neighbors, was the famous, historic, and, like the lane, long-vanished three-story gambrel of Oliver Wendell Holmes's father, Reverend Abiel Holmes, for whom Holmes Place was named. We visit there on our next walk.

Some Brattle lore, which we will encounter more of as we walk north of the Common, goes with the old, prior Gannett House. It was named for Reverend Caleb Gannett, who married Katherine, a niece of Thomas Brattle. Gannett was a Harvard tutor, served as the College steward for nearly four decades (1779–1818), and was buried in the Brattle tomb. The College bought the old Gannett House, demolished it, and on its site late in 1849 appeared a curved-roof railroad station intended, via its link to the main Fitchburg Railroad, to bring faster steam rail service to Harvard Square. This line was abandoned in mid-1855, and ever-generous Nathaniel Thayer provided funds to convert the station into a dining place for students on low budgets. They gratefully dubbed it "Thayer Commons."

On the east side of old Gannett House was the dwelling of a Cambridge patriot, Moses Richardson, College carpenter, who had been a captain in the French-and-Indian War and at the capture of Quebec. Richardson, fifty-three, father of six, grabbed his musket and responded to Dawes's alarm. We will see presently where, within a few hours, Richardson on that day gave his life.

In the dwelling just west of the old Gannett House lived "Yankee John" Hastings, Sr., who, before the Revolution, rented horses to students. He spouted "Yankee Good" this or that so often that the students tagged it on him and used to say that he invented the expression. His son and namesake would become, through Yankee John's purchase, owner of the future Holmes homestead, and serve as College steward for three decades.

The present 1838 Gannett House was built on the homestead site of Yankee John. It was twice purchased by the College. After the first time it was sold to a woman who furnished board to students. Repurchased in 1897, it was later given a quarter turn, facing its four-column portico east toward the developing Law School and scientific campus of old Holmes Field, and was positioned on the "Little Common" just south of the original Gannett House. Little Common, once cowpasture, too, included the triangle of land originally formed by the right angle of Holmes Place. The College got this land in a 1929 swap with the city. Gannett House is currently quarters for the Law School's Law Review and Legal Aid Bureau.

Hemenway Gym, next on our right, is a 1940 successor to the much bigger gym completed in 1880, the gift of Augustus Hemenway, whose wife gave the Hemenway Gym in Radcliffe Yard. The old gym was displaced by Littauer Center, now facing Harvard Square. With athletics shifted toward the river and Soldiers Field, the current Hemenway Gym's exercise facilities and squash and basketball courts are used mostly by Law School students. Hastings Hall, the 1889 dorm next beyond the gym, was a gift from a descendant of the Hastings family, College steward, who used to live in Holmes Place.

As we move now beyond the Common, churches stand on either side of the avenue. Howard-Epworth Methodist Church, on our right, built in the early 1890s, were gifts, both land and building, of the city's munificent benefactor, Frederick H. Rindge.

The First Church of Christ, Scientist, on the west side of Massachusetts Avenue, built in the 1920s and dedicated in 1937, is on the conspicuous site of an early tavern and a Civil War–vintage building, moved in the 1920s to nearby 44 Follen Street, and used there as the Lincoln's Inn Society of the Harvard Law School. The early tavern was the pre-Revolutionary Red Lion Inn, with an old red barn, across the turnpike with access to Holmes Place, for its stable. Reverend Lucius R. Paige, venerable Cambridge historian, says that this building may have been the celebrated Moore Tavern, which was in this area.

A 1793 member of the Porcellian Club, Amos Kent, writing a letter advising his brother to join, described how the "Porcellian or Pig Club" began with a roast-pig feast in 1791 in Abel Moore's public house. The participants had found so much "enjoyment to be derived from eating & drinking" that they thereafter formed "a convivial club" and pledged to repeat it all in another month. Moore had been an innkeeper in Boston for many years, but died only three years after the founding dinner of America's oldest club with the same name. Moore's widow's second husband, however, purchased the Blue Anchor Tavern, and it was often the scene of Porcellian merriment and feasting.

Next beyond Harvard–Epworth Church we see at 1563 Massachusetts Avenue, on the south corner of Jarvis Street, the five-story Pound Hall, built in 1970, the most recent large building of ever-expanding Harvard Law School. It was named in honor of Roscoe Pound, a distinguished dean of the Law School from 1916 to 1936.

Students, or students and professors, meeting in the scattered lounges, made additionally attractive by the modern glassed walls giving views of the grounds, have an unusual extra. Thanks to a benefactor, all may enjoy free coffee, save during summer recess. The classrooms and offices are ultra-modern. In a central lounge area are both a bronze bust and a big Charles Hopkinson portrait of Pound. Otherwise the likenesses of Law School personalities are in photographs along the corridors.

In the main lobby, just off Massachusetts Avenue, is a special glass case, with photographs of some whose portraits we will see on our next walk. Others among them include prominent Law School graduates, Judge Charles Wyzanski, '30; Archibald Cox, '37; Caspar Weinberger, '41; Derek Bok, '54; and Elizabeth Dole, '65. On the fourth floor in Room 405, with a fine view over Cambridge Common, was the office of the first woman to be appointed a full-time Harvard Professor of Law, Elisabeth A. Owens, named by President Bok in 1972. Miss Owens, an expert and author on international taxation, now retired, when asked about her reaction, said, "It was a good idea and about time."

Jarvis Street in Newe-Towne days led to the "Hither Pyne Swampe"—later to become the College's playing field, Jarvis Field. It extended from Jarvis Street, which formerly went as far as Oxford Street, to Everett Street, next street north of us. At the present Jarvis Street, the town's earliest protection, the "pallysadoe," crossed the present Massachusetts Avenue. The last evidence of its site was a row of old willow trees, now gone, which extended to the Hither Pyne Swampe.

We catch up again with Brattle lore associated with the next two streets on our right, Mellen and Wendell Streets. Thomas Brattle, who returned to Brattle House after the Revolution, had two nieces: Katherine, who had married Reverend Caleb Gannett, and Martha, who married Reverend John Mellen. These nieces became the heirs of Thomas Brattle after the death of his sister, their mother, who died at ninety in 1821.

They gave the family names to the large estates they had here when they developed them. Widowed during the Revolutionary War, their mother was long known as "Madame Wendell," so popular a Cambridge figure that her friendship with the Sons of Liberty was a big factor in Thomas Brattle's retaining his huge estate along Brattle Street and the river. Madame Wendell's residence once stood midway between Mellen and Wendell Streets, where we now see the motel built in the 1960s.

Sacramento Street, next on our right, provided twenty-nine-year-old

William Dean Howells with his first Cambridge lodging when, just hired as an assistant to celebrated editor James T. Fields, Howells came with his bride to 41 Sacramento Street in 1866. His nearest literary neighbors, as he recalled, were John Fiske, two blocks north at 139 Oxford Street, and Reverend James G. Palfrey, dean of Harvard Divinity School, historian, and congressman, who lived two blocks south at 94 Oxford Street. To Howells, who had written a life of Lincoln and been named United States Consul in Venice, where he had lived "in a Gothic palace on the Grand Canal," the house formerly here was just "a carpenter's box . . . covered with mortgages." He loved Cambridge literary life and moved, in a couple of years, to the larger place on Berkeley Street that we have seen.

On returning to Massachusetts Avenue we see on our right two buildings of Harvard's scattered Dudley House, which provides College amenities to nonresident students. These buildings, near the corner at 3 Sacramento and, around the corner, the large pilastered mansard at 1705 Massachusetts Avenue, are doubly unusual.

They are cooperative houses, with students taking care of their own cooking and housekeeping chores, and combine undergraduate and graduate students.

At the far end of Martin Street, just across the Avenue, at number 79, was the apartment of author John Updike, Harvard '54, during his senior year, where he wrote some of his best contributions to the *Lampoon.* He had been chosen the Poonsters' president while a junior, and regarded the *Lampoon* as Harvard's best club.

Shortly, on our left off Massachusetts Avenue, we see Linnaean Street, to which the Common extended until Linnaean, long called Love Lane, was put through as a dirt road to Garden Street in 1725. The intervening land, used as a cow common to protect the milch cows at night, had been divided a year earlier into lots.

On Linnaean Street at number 21 still stands the oldest entire dwelling in Cambridge, dating back to the second half of the seventeenth century. Opinions differ on whether Deacon John Cooper, a selectman and at times town clerk, over more than four decades, built it in 1657, or his son Samuel, also a selectman and deacon, built it in 1690. Four Cooper family generations lived in it, as well as Frost and Austin descendants, until the latter sold it in 1912 to the Society for the Preservation of New England Antiquities. Just seeing the period's long earthward pitch of the roof is fascinating, and even more so is a visit to see the several big fireplaces in the huge central chimney, the paneling, and the interior (some of it exposed) beam construction.

On our way back to Massachusetts Avenue, notice how the land north of Linnaean Street rises slowly up Avon Hill and, near Massachusetts Avenue, rises to 90 feet on the prominence that in early days was called Gallows Hill, on Avon's east slope. The unmarked site used to be approached about 200 feet up the now gone dead-end Stone Court, just off Massachusetts Avenue on our left; it ran between Lancaster and Arlington Streets. The gallows was raised in a clay pit.

In a tale of the colony's witchcraft period it is said that "Goody Kendall," a Cambridge housewife, was executed for having bewitched a child to death. Much better documented is Professor John Winthrop's 1755 account of two black servants, Mark and Phillis, being executed by the county for poisoning a Charlestown sea captain, their master, and torching his dwelling. Mark was hanged and Phillis burned at a stake ten yards away from the gallows. Seven-year-old Oliver Wendell Holmes, with his five-year-old brother, witnessed the last execution here in 1817, and got a reprimand for doing so when he got home. The grim name Gallows was soon dropped, and the setting instead was long known as Jones's Hill.

On the east side of Massachusetts Avenue, on land next to where we see the North Avenue Congregational Church at the south corner of Roseland Street, was Deacon Gideon Frost's old (built in 1670) farmhouse. Lord Percy's Redcoats came by here near midday on April 19, 1775. Many of them darted to his curbed well and passed buckets of water to slake their thirst. Deacon Frost's slave Neptune served as a drummer boy in the Revolutionary Army and is buried with the deacon's family in God's Acre. The Congregational Church was built in 1845 as a Baptist Church, on the present site of Littauer Center, sold to the present parish, and moved here in 1867.

On crossing the Massachusetts Avenue bridge over the old 1843

Fitchburg Railroad line we arrive in thriving Porter Square. The 1985 opening of the new, glassy Porter Square Station of the "T" rapid transit from Harvard Square and beyond further boosts development in this area.

The change first got under way when the Middlesex Turnpike, in 1805, came down its present Massachusetts Avenue route to Porter Square and on southeast, via Somerville's Beacon Street, to the still-new 1793 West Boston Bridge. As that bridge, along with Craigie's bridge, combined to speed the growth of East Cambridge and Cambridgeport, the new traffic had similar effects here.

Blacksmiths, carriage and wagon builders, inns, taverns, stables, and shops appeared among the farmhouses. Next came the railroad and its station. Just like the new "T" station we will be using on our way back to Harvard Square to begin our next walk, it was on this same site, and handy to the center of activity that had drawn the businesses here.

Most celebrated of the hotels was the one whose popularity changed the name of the square from Union to Porter. Zachariah Porter of Brighton and his associates, already having links to the cattle market there, in 1837 bought the big three-story 1831 hotel then at the present 1972 Massachusetts Avenue, at the north corner of Porter Road facing Beech Street, and changed the hotel's name to Porter's. This was already a cattle-market area, but the coming of the railroad in 1843 intensely accelerated its growth. Immediately to the north of Porter's, rows of cattle pens were developed down to the railroad track, and nearby were slaughter houses, packing houses, and not far off were tanneries.

Porter's had the best cuts of beef to serve the cattlemen and drovers, a cut still called Porterhouse steak. With tip-top food and a race track, a short way down nearby Rindge Avenue, Porter's became a social center and continued to be one even after the cattle market moved away. College groups, particularly the marching outfits, came here, and here at commencement time was many an open house with ample punch bowl.

The cathedral-like St. James' Episcopal Church, partly on the site of even older, pre-Revolutionary Cooper (later Davenport) Tavern on the corner of Beech Street, is a beautiful landmark on the old Battle Road of

April 19, 1775, which we have now entered. The first column of Red-coats, under stocky Lieutenant Colonel Francis Smith, after landing and making their way through East Cambridge, came via the present Somer-ville's Union Square along Milk Row, the Charlestown–Medford highway (now Somerville's Elm Street) at the far end of Beech Street. In passing the Cooper Tavern some of Smith's men dropped in to refresh them-selves.

The atmosphere was quite different on the way back, with Sons of Lib-erty, most often from behind farmers' stone walls, firing their muskets. Smith was wounded in the leg, many of his men had been killed and wounded, and only the help of Lord Percy's brigade made possible any returning. It was here at Beech Street that Lord Percy carried out his crucial decision.

Earlier in the day on his way to Cambridge, Percy had found that the planks of the Great Bridge over the Charles had been removed, but they had been left on the Charles River's far bank and were easily replaced. By turning here along Beech Street, instead of returning via Harvard Square, Percy's route back would be five miles shorter. Also he was warned, by a Tory mandamus councilor, that the patriots' General William Heath had the planks up again and an ambushing force was waiting for the Redcoats to return.

Furthermore, to try to keep Percy headed toward the ambush, General Heath had stationed sharpshooters at the far turn, where Beech Street en-tered old Milk Row. But Percy's cannon, once the wounded riding on them were removed, quickly cleared his path. Of that decision at Beech Street, Sir Henry Clinton, who would succeed General Gage, told Percy that had he not made it: "There would have been that day an end of Brit-ish government in America."

As we move into territory that folks hereabouts have long known as "O'Neill Land," the buildings tell pointedly of change in this neighbor-hood, from farmhouses to apartment houses, from residences to stores and offices, and the departure of old-time trades. The large five-story brick building we see on our right at Hadley Street, 2067 Massachusetts Ave-nue, illustrates this change. It is called Henderson Carriage Building still, for it was here that a blacksmith, Robert Henderson, opened a small shop in 1841 on a parcel of farmland. He next became a carriage builder, and by 1869 this family trade led to a three-story brick factory here.

When that factory burned down in 1892, it was replaced by this much bigger, fireproof five-story structure, making carriages, wagons, and river barges. Later it became a large automobile dealer's property and showroom. By the 1980s it was recycled for current retail stores and offices with a highly desirable, large parking space in the back, where other factory additions once stood.

In the lobby are interesting displays picturing some Henderson products: panel-top milk and bakery wagons for $130, canvas-sided ones for $87, or even as low as $78.50. They are gone, as the racetrack in 1855 went for a subdivision of workers' houses and cottages, or Porter's Hotel, demolished in 1909 for a row of stores.

The eight-story brick apartment house "Cornerstone Park," at 2130 Massachusetts Avenue, or on our left across from Russell Street, replaces the 1854 Cornerstone Baptist Church, North Cambridge's first meeting house, which burned down in the late 1970s.

Russell Street is the heart of O'Neill Land. The old V.F.W. Hall, at the north end of the Henderson Building, is, as we will presently see, an integral part of O'Neill Land.

Longtime Speaker Thomas P. O'Neill, Jr., was born and lived in this area throughout his public life, which led from local office to the heights of Capitol Hill in Washington, D.C. His dwelling is the post–Civil War mansard, number 26 Russell Street, at the corner of Orchard Street.

Around the corner, to the right, the fourth house from "Tip's" at 74 Orchard Street, his father's house, is where twenty-eight-year-old Tip, who from here had been elected state representative five years earlier, was living when married in 1941. At number 26 Russell, Tip and Millie brought up their five children, one of their sons serving as the state's lieutenant governor. In 1949 Tip became the first Democrat to be chosen Speaker of the Massachusetts House, in 1952 he succeeded John F. Kennedy as congressman, and in 1976 he became Speaker of the national House of Representatives.

As we return to and continue on Massachusetts Avenue we see, on our left, diagonally in front of 2158 Massachusetts Avenue, a stone marker. Here was once the dwelling of Jacob Watson, a blacksmith, when the Redcoats were fighting their way back on April 19, 1775. Three patriots, who had taken firing posts back of casks they stacked in Watson's yard, were surprised from behind by Lord Percy's flank guards, and killed along with a young laborer who was on a fence nearby.

The Cambridge dead here were two Sons of Liberty whose dwellings we have discussed, John Hicks, earlier a member of the Boston Tea Party, and College carpenter Moses Richardson. The third patriot was from Brookline, Major Isaac Gardner, the first Harvard graduate killed in the Revolution.

Rindge Avenue, renamed in the 1840s to honor Cambridge's well-known benefactor, has deep roots in the story of both North Cambridge and Tip O'Neill. Rindge Avenue, the former Kidder's Lane, then Spruce Street, leads down to Sherman Street, once called Dublin Street. Below that was once the Great Swamp along the Menotomy (the present Alewife) Brook, and it was to get the clay beneath the swamp that widespread brickmaking developed there with its yards, sheds, kilns, and brickmakers' cottages springing up on the old racetrack and above Dublin Street—an area with most of the old clay pits filled, where we now see recreational land, public housing, malls, offices, and new industrial plants.

Tip O'Neill's grandfather Pat O'Neill came from Cork in the 1840s during the potato famine, to work in the brickyards. Then he went back and brought his wife. Their son Thomas, a bricklayer, became head of the union and, at the time of Tip's birth, was a member of the Cambridge City Council, and would become superintendent in charge of Cambridge sewers and sanitation, directing 1,700 workmen.

Tip was still fourteen when he got a foot on the political ladder in the Dublin Street district, seeking votes for Al Smith by campaigning "door to door, on street corners, over back fences." Tip got jobs as a night watchman and truckdriver in the brickyards while preparing to go to Boston College.

To Tip, Sheridan Square, where Rice Street enters Rindge Avenue, is "affectionately known as Barry's Corner." Six-foot-two Tip was captain of the basketball team in the parochial school of St. John's Church, the beautiful brick and terra cotta church, with its tall campanile, which we saw a short way farther out Massachusetts Avenue, beyond Rindge Avenue.

Barry's Corner was named for the house that used to stand on the corner, at 149 Rindge Avenue, the home of J. Fred "Jack" Barry, a *Boston Globe* sports writer who, Tip says, "was really the father of basketball in the greater Boston area." The Barrys lived on the first floor, and had a poolroom and cardroom in back where young fellows of the neighborhood gathered. The "young fellows" have continued gathering over the years and still hold their annual get-togethers at V.F.W. Hall near the head of Russell Street.

Along Massachusetts Avenue people and storekeepers, who put up photos of Tip, as we saw in Harvard Square's Wursthaus, tell how Tip has always kept in close touch with neighbors and constituents. Tip has a jovial way of putting it: "I'd rather be leaning against a lamp post in North Cambridge than sitting on a throne anywhere else." First names and friendships, too, last a lifetime with Tip.

In the election that won twenty-three-year-old Tip a House seat, in the neighboring Cambridge district, twenty-two-year-old Leo Diehl, who had at age seven been stricken with polio and forced to use leg braces and crutches, also won a seat. Their friendship has been close over the years, with Leo in high state office and postponing retirement so that he could go to Washington and serve as Tip's chief of staff.

On returning to Harvard Square via the new "T" station in Porter Square, a surprise is the lengthy distance the escalators have to go into the earth so that the "T" tunnels can get beneath the old Fitchburg Railroad bed.

NORTH OF THE OLD YARD

From in front of Johnston Gate we head along Peabody Street, with the impressive Ionic portico of Littauer Center directly ahead. On going around by the curving wall, past Phillips Brooks House on our right, we come to the site of two major decisions affecting the layout of this area.

Notice the busy traffic going into and out of the underpass, no longer a danger to students hurrying between classes to and from the Law School, laboratories, and museums north of the Yard. President Pusey, who put high-rise structures on the College landscape, extended the old Yard area northward with this overpass, built in 1966 through the generosity of a Boston lawyer, George Leverett. Leverett's benefaction is commemorated in bronze in the overpass shrubbery outside Holworthy Gate.

The other major scene-changer was Dr. Andrew Craigie. In an effort to attract Boston-bound traffic from the Concord Turnpike, then moving along Concord Avenue, across the Common, and along the present Broadway, Craigie and friends, at private expense, built Cambridge Street from here (now under the overpass) to his 1809 bridge at Lechmere Point. We can see traffic going from the underpass and continuing that way to the right of Memorial Hall.

The commanding size of the ten-story Science Center (1973) seems to upstage the long-time appeal of the old triangular Delta just west of Memorial Hall, once formed by the junction of Cambridge Street and Kirkland Street. Kirkland, which once ran past Holmes Place to the Common, follows the ancient Watertown–Charlestown Path, along which the Sons of Liberty marched to the Battle of Bunker Hill. The front section of Science Center now covers that part right to the former northern side of the Old Delta. It was on the Delta that Daniel Chester French's statue of John Harvard was unveiled and stood for forty years before being moved to the front of University Hall.

A beautiful, unusual addition to the old Delta between the main entry to Science Center and Memorial Hall is a mist fountain that can have, in sunlight, the effect of approaching the mists of Niagara below the falls. The lichen-covered rocks are spread in a 60-foot-wide circle, with seventy spray jets producing several feet of mist—steam, in winter—in which sunlight produces rainbows. Lights at night have delightful effects, too. Youngsers particularly love it.

Big, modern Science Center has a historic site for its numerous facilities: twenty classrooms, labs, offices, four great lecture halls, a multistoried scientific library on the first floor named for benefactor of both Harvard and M.I.T., Godfrey Lowell Cabot, banker and president of United Fruit Company.

Mostly on the western part of the site was built (1847–1849) the Lawrence Scientific School, a new venture in scientific laboratory education, named for its chief sponsor, Abbott Lawrence, a farm boy who struck it rich in railroading and textiles manufacture, maternal grandfather of future Harvard President A. Lawrence Lowell.

In the first class was future M.I.T. President John D. Runkle. Charles W. Eliot taught chemistry and, when passed over for a professorship, quit and became in 1865 one of the new M.I.T.'s first professors. Four years later he became president of Harvard.

Jolly, personable Louis Agassiz's appointment as Lawrence Scientific School's first professor of zoology and geology so shifted the school's emphasis toward these natural sciences that Eliot later tried to merge M.I.T. and Harvard engineering, because M.I.T. had thereby got an early jump on engineering. The Lawrence School, however, would lead still to the development of Harvard's Schools of Engineering, Architecture, and other applied sciences.

Some scientific instruments from these early, and even earlier, years are in a collection in the Center's basement; and on the ninth floor, with its dome on the tenth, is a grand telescope for instruction linked to Harvard Observatory. And be sure to see in midbuilding, partly open, partly glassed over, "Greenhouse Courtyard."

We go past the portico of Littauer Center that, on its east side, is on the sites of the first (1878–80) Hemenway Gym, then the nation's biggest gym, and, on its west side, the old Holmes gambrel-roofed homestead on Holmes Place. When Littauer was opened in 1939 the intention, as the portico states, was to make it a graduate school of public administration, a function now carried on at the John F. Kennedy School, which we visited.

The center here now houses the economics and government departments. Though both are emeritus, Professor John Kenneth Galbraith and John T. Dunlop still do work in the second-floor, side-by-side offices, a flight over Professor Martin S. Feldstein.

Many tales tell of Teddy Roosevelt seeking to build up his physique. In the still-building gym, T.R., a twenty-year-old junior in spring 1879, was also trying to impress his bride-to-be, Alice, seated in the gallery, by beating the lightweight champ. Suddenly, before the call was given, the champ landed a heavy blow on T.R.'s nose, drawing blood. Teddy generously quieted the hissers who were yelling foul, and said his opponent had not understood the signal. Later that day, T.R. gave a party in his place on Winthrop Street.

In 1737 Holmes House stood in line with the entry to Austin Hall, until demolished, to clear the vista to Austin in 1884. This old residence of the Hastings family, College stewards, became the home of the Holmes family in 1807, and Oliver Wendell Holmes was born here two years later. He loved the memories associated with it and with his having written here the verses that first brought him fame, "Old Ironsides."

This was the headquarters of the first commander of our Revolutionary Army, Major General Artemas Ward, colonel in the French-Indian War, who arrived on horseback on the night of April 19, 1775. Here he planned the fortifying of Bunker Hill, and from here, after prayer at the western doorsteps by President Langdon, the men set out for that battleground. Heroic General Joseph Warren, who would be killed, caught his last nap here before heading to Charlestown. On the night General Washington reached Cambridge, he was given an arrival dinner by General Ward.

Austin Hall, completed in 1883, is where Law School Dean C. C. Langdell, pioneer of the case study, shifted his classes from Harvard Square. The brownstone-limestone building, on the north side of former Holmes Place, was a gift in his brother's memory by Edwin Austin of Boston, who rose from supercargo to be a shipping, cotton, and railroad tycoon.

Austin personally hired H. H. Richardson to make the Romanesque design and, in the pre-Lamont era, paid to get rid of—instead of move, as an obstruction—old Holmes House. The students had a small upstairs moot courtroom in which to practice, the original library, and Langdell and his professors had office-studies with fine paneling and fireplaces. And the students, from the reading room, could formerly enjoy following early football games to the north on Holmes Field. Instead they now have a large moot (sometimes real) courtroom, with high ceiling, hand-carved beams, and a huge open hearth.

Paine Hall, which we see across the campus in back of Science Center but facing Jefferson Lab, was opened in 1914 as a music center. It was named for John Howard Paine, composer, who came in 1862 to be the organist at Harvard's new Appleton Chapel and, with President Eliot's help, set up the first American college department of music, and became its first professor in 1875. The hall has classrooms and, on the two upper floors, a 550-seat concert hall, used by the University's musical groups. The Mason Building addition of 1970 provides lounge and practice rooms and the world's leading academic music library of albums, discs, and tapes.

We are walking on the once-extensive Holmes Field, where Oliver Wendell and his younger brother used to grow their family's vegetables. Save for the music building, the structures on the west side of the old field are mainly of the Law School—the second, after the Medical School, of Harvard's graduate schools. Third was the Theological School that we will see on our next walk, and fourth the scientific schools, which occupy most of the buildings on the east side of Holmes Field.

Jefferson Lab (1884) is a landmark in research, one of the nation's earliest physical-science labs. Connected with it on the north are the much later electronic, molecular, and cosmic research labs, all now linked to the much larger Pierce Hall (1901), with its applied-science labs and classrooms. Scientists north of the Yard have gathered in their Nobel and other prizes seemingly as amply as the Holmes's youngsters once reaped vegetables.

Langdell Hall, bearing names of its famous teachers inscribed in limestone, is the main structure on old Holmes Field, and stands on the big running oval where Harvard and Yale held their first track meet, in 1891.

Besides boxing, T.R. used to trot around the field in a bright red football jersey. The growth of the Law School, with its enrollment nearly quadrupled under Dean Langdell, who had started with only three professors, soon made Austin so clearly inadequate that the southern part of Langdell was finished in 1907. Langdell knew of this monument to him, for ground had already been broken before he died in 1906.

The northern part of Langdell, plus a west wing, was completed in 1928 with a reading room, reached by elevator to the fourth floor, one of the most impressive rooms in all Cambridge. It is fully the length of two football fields, explaining how Langdell houses the largest law library in the world.

Along its walls is a remarkable assemblage of portraits of renowned professors, judges, and lawyers. On the south end is a grand reading lounge, in memory of Elihu Root. Sections are strikingly set off between rows of white, fluted Doric columns, with full-length portraits on opposite walls of Louis D. Brandeis and Daniel Webster in one, and in the other Chief Justice John Marshall and President Rutherford B. Hayes.

A large treasure room on the north end, a memorial to alumni killed in both world wars, has displays of rarities like a codex of Roman law ordered by Emperor Justinian in A.D. 529, and the oldest printed book next after the Gutenberg Bible, and canon law of Pope Boniface VIII (around A.D. 1300). And here, in Robert Peke's famous painting, is wealthy Isaac Royall, along with his family, who used to reside, in pre-Revolutionary days, in a mansion still standing in Medford. Royall's bounty endowed Harvard's first law professorship.

On going from Langdell Hall and turning left, we leave old Holmes Field, where the Law School holds its commencement activities, and see to the north Harkness Commons and its complex of seven graduate dormitories that President Conant dedicated in fall 1950 in memory of the House Plan benefactor Edward S. Harkness. Professor Walter Gropius, of Bauhaus modern architectural fame, designed them and was also present.

The dorms and the social center, with Joan Miro and Gyorgy Kepes murals, modern sculpture, "Back Bench Pub," pool tables, video games, and cafeteria were created to provide for the ever-increasing enrollment in the graduate schools.

Old Jarvis Field, in pre-Soldiers Field days, was, with Holmes Field, the College playground, and here in 1874, under rugby rules, Harvard beat McGill in the first intercollegiate football game. Harkness is also served by the underground passage, "The Tunnel," which links with Langdell Hall and the other major Law School buildings as a helpful, sheltered way in inclement winter weather.

We walk to the right of Harkness Commons, through the courtyard, and to the right of Ames and Dane Halls to Everett Street, once the northern limit of Jarvis Field's football grid and tennis courts.

Diagonally across Everett Street, at number 29, in the living room of her family's residence, Edith Lesley in fall 1909 started training a class of a dozen teenage girls to become Froebel-style kindergarten teachers. Miss Lesley, who had the help of her sister Olive and their invalid mother, thus began as "Miss Lesley's School." Miss Lesley, then thirty-seven, had been a kindergartener in Cambridge for a dozen years and taken courses at Radcliffe. Turning out well-trained teachers, the school grew steadily, and by 1944 became Lesley College, under President Trenwell M. White. By 1981 a graduate school was added, after Miss Lesley, who married an M.I.T. instructor-inventor, but, like her mother, had become invalided, died in 1953.

More than a decade before her death, Miss Lesley and her husband in 1939 changed the school into a nonprofit institution. From its one-room beginning, a room now the president's office, the College has grown into several dozen buildings, currently around forty of them, serving some 2,700 students, starting with neighboring Everett Street houses and expanding into the campus mall along Oxford Street.

The four buildings we saw on Concord Avenue, recently sold to Radcliffe College, had been acquired in 1948 as laboratory schools. The campus here now includes several new classroom buildings, an extensive library, an auditorium, dormitories like four-story White Hall at the corner of Oxford Street, dedicated in 1958 to President White, who cut the ribbon, and the new Students' Center with its dedication in 1985 followed by festivities in Alumni Hall. In that same year Lesley College got its first woman president, Margaret A. McKenna, former head of Radcliffe's Bunting Institute.

Across from Lesley College, on the east side at 46 Oxford Street, is the large 1830 residence of Reverend John G. Palfrey, teacher of Hebrew and dean of the Divinity School, College preacher who became a congressman and author of a well-known history of New England. It was Palfrey's large dwelling, now in a large parking area, which Howells used to see, on Palfrey's once-extensive wooded acreage, from his own honeymoon cottage on Sacramento Street.

South of Palfrey's house, which Harvard bought in 1919 for labs and classrooms, have been the site of some super-modern structures and research connected with a postwar epoch in which man walked on the moon: a cyclotron, in which M.I.T. and Harvard researchers collaborated; a joint electron accelerator of the early 1960s; biomedical research into human genes; and a nuclear lab that has used volts by the millions.

Walking south on Oxford Street we pass, in Conant Hall on our left and Perkins Hall on our right, two dorms built in the late 1890s by President Eliot before dorm construction was being concentrated—as college athletics then were—along the Charles River.

Next on our left is the University Museum, comprising four special museums—Comparative Zoology, Botanical, Mineralogical, and Archaeological—all in a succession of additions to the research collection of Louis Agassiz that, with help of the Commonwealth and friends, formed a museum opened in 1860. Agassiz kept increasing its exhibits with expeditions abroad that made Brazil's Emperor Dom Pedro II a hearty supporter of the museum. But it was Agassiz's son Alexander, fabulously wealthy from the Anaconda copper mines, who lavishly extended the museum building. It had been turned over to the College in 1876 after his father's death. Alexander, too, was a great naturalist.

All seven of the University's museums are open to visitors, some for an admission fee, some a suggested donation, some free. A tip-top attraction at the University Museum here is still the display of the 700 glass models of flowers, made in Germany over half a century, by the Blaschkas, father and son, which started arriving here in 1887. In the museums are materials showing the locations of exhibits, pamphlets listing highlights of the collections, guide service for groups, or rental tapes.

Mallinckrodt Laboratory, next on our left, with its raised Ionic portico, was dedicated in 1928 to give Harvard's chemistry department its first ample laboratory since it outgrew Boylston Hall in the old Yard. The lab was named for the largest donor's son, Edward Mallinckrodt of the St. Louis chemical family, and a bronze tablet to him here was made by Daniel Chester French. Earlier small labs, in pre–World War I days, had been built in back, and it was there that future President James B. Conant became a top-notch researcher in organic chemistry. Smaller Converse Lab was built at about the same time as Mallinckrodt and linked to its east side.

James B.Conant, who had become a full chemistry professor in 1927, had his office in Conant—and his dwelling handy at the then 20 Oxford Street—in April 1933 when President Lowell came to this office to tell Conant that the Corporation had chosen him as his successor and the election would be formally announced in a couple of weeks.

During World War I newly graduated Conant, as an army major, worked on chemical warfare, producing efficient gas masks for our troops and poison gases for enemy forces. His brilliance as a chemist would help develop, as we will presently see, the winning weapons in World War II. Conant Lab, which stood east of the south end of Mallinckrodt, was named for President Conant.

Notice on the path, near the south corner of Mallinckrodt, a pedestal marker that tells us that in 1982 this group of laboratories was named the Cabot Science Complex, in tribute to members of a generous University family, Mr. and Mrs. Thomas Dudley Cabot.

A fascinating tale goes with Gordon McKay Engineering Research Laboratory, across the street from Mallinckrodt. McKay was a wizard at engineering, and as a youth of twenty-one in the mid-1800s, employed dozens of workers in his own western Massachusetts factory. He invented boot and shoe machinery that made him a multimillionaire, gave to Harvard's Lawrence Scientific Center activities, and on his death in 1903 left most of his estate to advance mechanical engineering.

But the bequest's full effects were delayed four long decades, awaiting deaths of beneficiaries. Efforts to share the estate with M.I.T. Engineering were blocked in court. There was a small temporary McKay Laboratory up Oxford Street across from Lesley College, but even this one, which was enlarged a decade later, was not completed until 1952.

Lowell Lecture Hall, on the corner, was, late in 1901, A. Lawrence Lowell's first major gift to the University after he gave up law practice and started teaching constitutional government. He felt that the College needed a large lecture hall, and so this one, opened in 1902, had nearly 1,000 seats, and tutorial rooms in the basement. One restriction went with the gift—anonymity. Until 1959 it was known only as New Lecture Hall. Many graduates of the period long associate with History I lectures of big, thunder-voiced Professor Roger B. "Frisky" Merriman, who, with his fast-motioned ivory-tipped pointer, made use of the entire stage.

On reaching Kirkland Street we are on the route of the patriot army to Bunker Hill, the old Watertown–Charlestown Path, the King's Highway, part of Cambridge's oldest street. Even before Oxford Street was laid out around 1840 this section of Kirkland—as well as the part now covered by Science Center—was called Professors' Row. The only remaining dwelling of that period is the 1838 Jared Sparks House at 21 Kirkland, just east of Lowell Lecture Hall on the corner, but Sparks's House was moved across from Quincy Street to make space for Gund Hall at 48 Quincy, which was built in 1972.

The land along Kirkland Street was divided into five equal lots and sold in 1822 by Harvard to five professors, who built houses of different designs, most of them with two stories, gable, and attic. Two were on the site of Science Center. The one nearer the old Holmes homestead was the birthplace of author-abolitionist-clergyman Thomas Higginson in 1823. He and the Holmes boys played on rainy days in the Holmes's garret, and on bright days, when not roaming the nearby woodlands, they romped on the Delta, then, Higginson recalled, "an open commons . . . with lots of apple trees." Higginson's dad, once a wealthy ship owner ruined by Jefferson's embargo, was the College steward.

The Delta playground and Memorial Hall across old Kirkland Street we will visit on our next walk.

On the west corner site, also covered by Science Center, was in colonial days the mansion of Harvard Treasurer and Deputy Governor Thomas Danforth, who owned 120 acres hereabouts, and a mansion that went up in flames in 1777. The 1822 house is best remembered for its last owners, College preacher Reverend Francis G. Peabody, and its prior resident, Estes Howe, in 1852 president of Cambridge's first gas company, a brother-in-law of poet James Russell Lowell.

Lowell, who had met author Thackeray on shipboard, brought him here as a hearty guest. And when grief-stricken by his first wife's death, Lowell fled Elmwood and came to live with the Howes, taught at Harvard as Longfellow's successor, and did not return to Elmwood until he had married a friend of his first wife.

Until succeeded by New Lecture Hall, the 1822 house on the east corner was the three-story residence of Harvard Law School's Asahel Stearns, named in 1817 its first professor of law, who had been hying over to Harvard Square's College House #2 to teach and carry on also as Middlesex County's district attorney.

Later, when it was named Foxcroft House, for Danforth's son-in-law, young Henry Wadsworth Longfellow, on first arriving in Cambridge in 1836 to teach, came here to board with Mrs. Stearns. His room was above that of future Harvard President Cornelius Felton.

Sparks House, presently the dwelling of University preacher Peter J. Gomes, widely known for his eloquence, is on the site of the 1822 house of a mathematics professor who had been trained as a clergyman. It was well known for the owner's hospitality. And on the site of the museum, at the corner of Divinity Avenue, was once the 1822 dwelling of Reverend Henry Ware, Sr., Hollis Professor of Divinity, who became the first head of Harvard Divinity School when it was established in 1826.

TO NORTON'S WOODS, MEMORIAL HALL,
AND QUINCY STREET

Divinity Avenue, originally called Divinity Hall Avenue, was built off Old Professors' Row through pasture and woods, then extending all the way to the northeastern boundary of Cambridge, to reach the newly built 1826 Divinity Hall we will presently see.

Busch-Reisinger Museum, as a place to exhibit and study German culture, got its start in 1902 when Prince Henry of Prussia visited Harvard and brought casts and other art gifts from his brother the Kaiser. President Eliot, receiving him, remarked that Prince Henry was also a grandson of Queen Victoria.

The collection was first exhibited in Harvard's first gym, once on Quincy Street. Contributions mainly from Adolphus Busch of St. Louis and his family made possible the building at 29 Kirkland, with its fine clock tower, lovely courtyard, and exhibit halls, but its opening was delayed by World War I, and then, sensitively, until 1921. The plaster casts have long since been replaced by precious Northern European art ranging from medieval to modern times.

On the opposite corner, fifteen-story William James Hall is on the site of 1899 Randall Hall, a dining hall that could seat more than 500 students and later was used by Harvard University Press. William James Hall was part of President Pusey's program of high-rise structures to save land space, and was built by 1965 to house the University's behavioral science department. This has been the podium of Nobel laureate B. F. Skinner, celebrated behavioral psychologist who, even when he became emeritus, walked regularly from his Brattle Street dwelling to his office in midbuilding (seventh floor) to get in a morning's work.

The interestingly adorned building at 2 Divinity Avenue, next on our right, now the East Asian Department, with the Harvard-Yenching Institute and library in the back, was built in 1931 as a gift of the former Mrs. Eleanor Elkins Widener, donor of Harvard's big Widener Library. Joining with her in the gift was her second husband, Dr. A. Hamilton Rice, geographer, explorer, and director of Harvard's Institute of Geographical Exploration.

The world map over the entry, showing the relative true size of the continents, and the zodiac symbols, reflect Dr. Rice's lifelong interest

277

in exploration, particularly along the Orinoco and Amazon rivers. Harvard–Yenching Institute, recalling the dragon we saw in the Yard beside Widener Library, gave the two lions on the lawn. Its library in back has the largest Far East collection in the Western world.

Another of Harvard's seven museums is next on our right, the Semitic Museum at number 6, containing photographs and treasures from the Near East, from explorations that go back to 1889 and America's first expedition in the Holy Land. The Museum, dedicated in 1903, was a gift from Jacob Henry Schiff, a banker of New York. After various uses including wartime applications, the displays, some going back to Babylon, Phoenicia, and kings mentioned in the Bible, have been back on display since 1982. Across the street, at number 11, is another entry to the Peabody Museum.

Divinity Hall, once almost alone on most of the surrounding acres, is now nestled, next on our right, in the large courtyard formed on three sides by the biological labs and classrooms, completed in 1931.

Reverend Henry Ware, Sr., coming from his home on Professors' Row, presided, led the prayer, and laid the Divinity Hall cornerstone in July 1825. For the first time the theological school created by President John T. Kirkland was under one roof with lecture room, chapel, library, and dorms. In its early decades it trained renowned students who lived here: Ralph Waldo Emerson, whose ground floor, Room 14, looked toward Norton's Woods (then real woodland), and we will presently visit it; Reverend Theodore Parker the abolitionist, and Horatio Alger, who lived in Room 22 while studying for his Cape Cod pastorate.

In those days several famed residents were training in other disciplines: Charles Sumner during the first year he was in Law School in 1831; Henry Parkman, enrolled in Law School in 1844 but devoting his time more to publishing articles on his forest-roaming and on Indians; and William James, while studying chemistry at Lawrence Scientific School before he gave it up for an 1864 pre-med course. Future President Charles W. Eliot had one of the furthest-reaching encounters of his life here.

Eliot, then doing chemistry work in his lab in his family attic because the College had no chemistry lab, came in his junior year (1851–52) to visit a friend studying to be a clergyman. On the visit he met a Law School resident, C. C. Langdell, eating bread and milk before his fireplace and doing work on "Contracts" for Professor Theophilus Parsons. Eliot came more often because he felt he was "listening to a man of genius." Nearly two decades later Eliot in 1876, remembering Langdell, went to a New York law firm to look him up and ask him to become dean of the law school.

A classic tale has to do with Emerson. In the year after his 1837 Phi Beta Kappa speech in the new meeting house near Harvard Square brought sensational praise, he came to the small second-floor chapel in Divinity Hall for an evening address to the graduating class of 1838. He assailed religious preaching that clung to orthodoxy instead of enlightenment. The audience listened with "profound attention," but even the liberal Unitarian professors were so taken aback by his remarks that Emerson got no invitation back to Harvard for more than three decades.

The hall is now used almost entirely as a dorm, but the famous chapel is still here with its roughly 100 seats, wood-paneled walls, lectern, and organ. Among the marble plaques on the walls, one is Emerson's, recalling his 1837 address with the quotation "Acquaint thyself at first hand with deity."

Turn right around the north end of Divinity Hall and notice at the northeast corner rooms and windows that were Emerson's. Diagonally across, with its two high, brick-faced gables, is the 1888 former Divinity Hall Library, since 1923 the Farlow Herbarium. The Biological Laboratories rhinoceroses flanking the entry were the work (1935–1936) of Katherine Lane, who also did the impressive animal frieze on the upper brick of the façade.

We go back to Kirkland Street and turn left. As we approach Francis Avenue we see, on the west corner, the Nieman Foundation's Center in the large, terraced 1837 structure named for the pundit Walter Lippmann. The widow of the founder of the *Milwaukee Journal*, Agnes Nieman, made it possible for President Conant in 1937 to create these fellowships, which give newspapermen a year's residence of study and academic contacts "to elevate the standards of journalism." The first curator was author and Librarian of Congress Archibald MacLeish, followed, for a quarter of a century, by former *Boston Globe* newsman Louis M. Lyons, long remembered also as a public radio and television newscaster.

As we walk up Francis Avenue, and next down Irving Street (once the driveway) from the present Kirkland Street up through thirty-four and a half acres of woodland to its Shady Hill mansion, we will see that old Professors' Row had many successors when the area was cut up for development in the last decades of the nineteenth century. We will enter an area that was part of Norton's Woods, another name for the estate, when we go past Bryant Street just ahead. But before reaching there we already have a strong academic atmosphere.

At number 7 lived, while he was dean of Harvard Law, James M. Landis, who had headed the National Security Council; humanities Professor Howard Mumford Jones lived at number 14; Abigail Eliot, who lived for more than three decades at number 21, is renowned for founding pre-kindergarten nursery schools; and near the corner of Bryant Street, in the house with pink trim and blinds at number 30, celebrated economist John Kenneth Galbraith took up residence early in 1950. Personable Galbraith, a farm boy who looked for better fields to conquer, became a White House adviser, ambassador to India, and host of one of Cambridge's biggest social events at the garden parties he has given, with big tent and tidbits, on his grounds in Commencement Week.

We seem in a religious campus immediately beyond Bryant Street. Andover Hall, center of this activity with big Gothic tower midsection was built in 1911 with a large chapel on the second floor to accommodate the Andover Theological Seminary on its rejoining the Harvard Divinity School a century after the orthodox Congregationalists had split with the Unitarian direction taken by liberals President Kirkland and Reverend Henry Ware, Sr. Meantime, in 1880 under President Eliot, Harvard's Divinity School had become nondenominational. Relations had always been amicable, but the courts in 1925 decreed a separation and Andover Theological moved to Newton.

The two-story 1960 wing on the south end of Andover Hall houses one of the earth's best theological libraries. The wing replaced the delightful but smaller former 1888 chapel-like building that we saw near Divinity Hall. Rockefeller Hall, at the north end of the school, was built in 1971 and named for John D. Rockefeller, Jr., who made a $1,000,000 gift in his will to the school's endowment.

Opposite the Divinity School, but part of it, is the 1959 World Religions Center, with its own hostel and chapel, where researchers in all religions are accommodated. And, where the avenue bends, at number 44, is a pre–World War I residence, built for a Harvard professor, which became the official residence of the dean of the Divinity School.

The unusual house on the corner, as we turn right into Irving Street, at number 64 Francis, with its gracious, easy-living three courtyards, was built in 1962 by the eminent, modernist designer of Holyoke Center, Louis Sert, dean of Harvard's Graduate School of Design, for his own family dwelling, his students, and his art collection, much of it in the Fogg Museum since Sert's death in 1983.

At the bend a few steps down Irving Street we come to where Shady Hill mansion stood, prominent dwelling of a succession of owners, especially Professor of Fine Arts Charles Eliot Norton, and two other art authorities, Director Edward W. Forbes and his associate, Professor Paul J. Sachs, whose efforts led to creation of the present Fogg Art Museum's main building and converting its collection into one of the choicest in the world of art. The Academy of Arts and Sciences at number 136, founded in Boston in 1780 to promote culture in America, moved from Brookline to the unusual pagodalike center on the site of Shady Hill mansion, which had finally been razed in 1955.

Shady Hill was the name bestowed by the original owner, Bay State Senate president and later Boston's first mayor, John Phillips, who built it in 1807 on its sixty acres as his summer house. It faced the Middlesex Turnpike, opened two years earlier, which gave him quick access from

Boston via Judge Dana's 1793 West Boston Bridge. In 1821, future President Charles W. Eliot's grandfather, prosperous Boston merchant, gave it to his daughter when she married Divinity School Professor Andrews Norton. The house had been turned around by the Eliot family to face the present Kirkland Street, and trees were planted, hence the new name Norton's Woods.

Professor Charles Eliot Norton, President Eliot's first cousin, friend of cultural leaders here and abroad, many of them guests, was born and lived here until his death in 1908. Kindly Professor Sachs, collector particularly of French impressionist paintings, carried on that hospitable tradition. From 7 A.M. to 7 P.M., as signs tell us, visitors may enjoy the actual woods close to vanished Shady Hill. The park, with its benches, is as restful as it is beautiful, and its paths lead to a gateway opening on lower Irving Street, once called Norton Avenue.

Most of the estate remained intact until Professor Norton died, but he did sell some lots to colleagues for building. President Eliot's son, landscape architect Charles, arranged the street development east of Irving Street, where we will pass Scott, Farrar, and Holden Streets, on which houses were later built for tutors and married students.

Going down Irving Street, we again recall a Professors' Row. On colleagues-of-Norton lots there lived at number 104, on the corner of Scott Street, on our left, the poet E. E. Cummings, whose father, while living here, gave up teaching to become a minister; and, on our right, at number 103, the philosopher Josiah Royce lived from 1889 to his death in 1916, his house later the residence of diplomat Paul Child, whose wife, Julia, became a television celebrity as "the French Chef."

On the second lot down on our right, at number 95, philosopher William James also built in 1889 and lived until his death. It was a warmhearted neighborhood. Royce, wrote E. E. Cummings, acquainted him with sonnets. Santayana describes how well philosophy students were welcomed in the James library, stacked floor to ceiling with books. Among them was the future great black leader W. E. B. Du Bois, studying philosophy and for his doctorate, who came here often and said later that his own mother and James had the greatest influence on his life of seeking to serve mankind.

On our left, at the junction of Scott and Farrar Streets, at number 2 Scott, lived the well-known economist Professor Frank W. Taussig, who had a key role in the founding of the Harvard Business School; and at mid–Farrar Street at number 16, until he became dean of the Business School, was the dwelling of Professor George P. Baker, son of the founder of Harvard's 47 Workshop.

As we come to Kirkland Street there was, on our left, the first construction in Norton's Woods other than Shady Hill itself. In 1858 Charles W. Eliot, newly appointed assistant professor of chemistry at Harvard, built a double brick house at numbers 59–61 Kirkland Street. The number 59 house, formerly on the corner, was for his father, who had lost his fortune in the panic of 1857. Still-standing number 61, with its big yard, spacious setback, and high-ceilinged rooms, was for himself and the woman he married in that fall. But the death of two sons and his wife's incurable illness left sad memories, and Eliot departed some months before he was chosen Harvard's president.

A bit farther east, at number 67, lived celebrated Professor Francis J. "Stubby" Child, who had married a sister of Charles Eliot Norton, a homestead long remembered for Stubby's beautiful rose garden and the rose bouquets he gave to the neighbors. Later called "The Kirkland," its fifteen rooms have been for years a guest house for international visitors.

Memorial Hall, both the structure and the site, were gifts from an alumni fund drive. The enthusiastic outpouring of these donations was itself a landmark message to the College that had been through many very lean years: alma mater could, in times of financial need, confidently count on her alumni.

Athletics on the Delta, which was created when Cambridge Street slanted into Kirkland Street in the early 1800s, was shifted from the north end of the old Yard at the time Reverend Charles Follen came to Cambridge in 1824 to teach German. Follen, whose dwelling was on Follen

Street, named for him, set up an open-air gym with ropes, parallel bars, and trapezes.

There were other sports, too, including some baseball, and football tales of plays by young Robert Gould Shaw and others, students who would shortly give their lives in the Civil War. To get the site, the alumni, starting in 1869, bought Holmes and Jarvis Fields, which we have seen, and gave them to the College for playing fields so that Memorial Hall could be here. The cornerstone was laid in 1870 with Reverend Phillips Brooks presiding and the singing of a hymn written by Oliver Wendell Holmes.

The monumental transept, entered by portals on the north and south sides, is the main memorial to the 154 Harvard men who died from wounds on Civil War battlefields or from disease. The names of those battlefields, Bull Run, Antietam, and Gettysburg among them, and the names of the heroic dead are on marble tablets. Some 1,407 men, students and graduates, served, and they were from classes that, up to the Civil War, did not exceed 100.

The great hall in the wide, 164-foot-long nave, at times called Alumni Hall, vividly resembles, with its stained-glass memorial and clerestory windows and art, the cathedral-like atmosphere of high-table gatherings in England's Oxford College. Up to 1925 it was used as a College commons when President Eliot, with enrollment increasing, in 1874 shifted it here from Old Thayer commons and Randall Hall. It has had many uses, from entry and midyear exams to alumni dinners and commencement dances.

Great names galore are associated with apsidal Sanders Theatre, entered by doors at either end of the transept, where commencement exercises were held from 1876 until 1911 when, having outgrown the 1,200 seats, they were moved to Sever Quadrangle. The theatre was named to honor a College steward, Charles Sanders, who died childless and left funds for the theatre and needy students. On the outside are busts of seven orators, from Demosthenes, whose oratory could overpower the roar of the breaking waves, to Burke and Webster. The small stained-glass window above the gallery, like other windows in the hall, was the work of famed John La Farge.

Besides the awarding of diplomas, plays have been staged, concerts given by the Boston Symphony and by college groups, and Phi Beta Kappa has heard its commencement-time orators and poets here. Robert Frost in 1936 and T. S. Eliot in 1950 drew crowds that overflowed to the nave. Future presidents drew big crowds: Taft, who came with Theodore Roosevelt as Secretary of War at T.R.'s 25th reunion; Woodrow Wilson, then president of Princeton, who came in 1909 to give a Phi Beta Kappa address, as did Governor Franklin D. Roosevelt in 1929, three years before winning the White House.

Most unusual, though, was the appearance of Winston Churchill in September 1943 after he and President Roosevelt had completed mid-World War II conferences together with their military leaders. To protect secrecy, the event here was last-minute and vaguely labeled "An Academic Meeting."

Churchill, in scarlet Oxford robe and floppy black medieval cap, was given an honorary degree and hailed by President Conant, to the delight of the packed audience, for having "turned back the tide of tyranny in freedom's darkest hour." At either side of the stage, then as now, were the statues of James Otis and "Old Quin."

Notice the 35-foot-square tower base of Memorial Hall as we head along Quincy Street. In 1897 the tower height rose to 190 feet when, as a postwar class of 1872 gift, clocks facing all four sides were added. Unfortunately, during 1956 restoration work the clock tower was accidentally destroyed when set aflame by a workman's blowtorch; it still has not been replaced.

Earlier, in 1936, when rain moved celebrants to Memorial Hall to hear President F.D.R.'s address on Harvard's 300th birthday, President Conant brought exercises to a close with the traditional adjournment motion "to meet September 18, 2036." But that appointment has, just as traditionally, resulted in no crimp in the University's gearing up for its 350th in 1986.

Sparks House, which, as we saw, was moved to make way for Gund Hall, on our left, used to be the parsonage for the Church of the New Jerusalem on the corner of Kirkland Street. The charming 1901 stone chapel, with its surmounting stone belfry—delightful to visit—was designed by Professor Herbert L. Warren, first lecturer of Harvard's School of Architecture, a school now right beside it.

Gund Hall, where Harvard's Graduate School of Design got new quarters in 1972, provides centralized facilities for architectural departments once scattered, among them the Loeb architectural library, given by the same New York banking family that gave Loeb Drama Center, which we saw on Brattle Street. Walter Gropius, who died in 1969, was head for fifteen years of the department of architecture and had among his students many outstanding modern architects, among them I. M. Pei, who also studied at M.I.T.; Paul Rudolph; and Philip Johnson.

At Cambridge Street we have, on our left at 1737 Cambridge, Coolidge Hall, the former Ambassador Hotel, Harvard's Center for International Affairs, in which scholars and foreign officials study world problems with special interest in Russia, Africa, the Far East, and the Middle East, to help advance world peace. Well-known figures associated with it include Secretary of State Henry Kissinger (1960–69); Ambassador Edwin O. Reischauer; and Ambassador John K. Fairbank, in whose honor the Center's East Asian Research Institute, which he directed from 1955 to 1973, was renamed on his retirement in 1977, with a former student of his, distinguished author Theodore H. White, unveiling the plaque.

The fire station and the fire-department control offices on the southwest corner of Quincy and Cambridge Streets, are on a triangle of land that Harvard in 1929 swapped for a piece of the Common, on which we saw the 1838 Gannett House. It was here, near athletic equipment on the Old Delta, that Harvard had its first gymnasium, the octagonal brick Rogers Building (1860), superseded in a couple of decades by the much larger old Hemenway Gymnasium. Harvard Cadets drilled here during the Civil War. In later years its use ranged from carpenter shop to summer classes, and a beginning in 1902 of the Germanic Museum, when Prussia's Prince Henry made his visit.

The 1985 Arthur M. Sackler Museum, opposite the fire station, with its alternating dozen bands of dark blue and brown orange brick, provides a 300-seat lecture hall, classrooms, and more exhibit space for expanding

Fogg Museum's collection of ancient, Oriental, and Islamic Art. Some call the new museum "Fogg Annex," and efforts continue to link Sackler to Fogg by a skywalk over Broadway.

Quincy Street, ahead along the Old Yard, again recalls Professors' Row. Dwellings of several honored professors were long on both sides of the street, as well as the official residence of Harvard's president. On the corner at our right, on the site of Robinson Hall, was the home of the Law School's great dean and innovator Professor C. C. Langdell, until it was moved diagonally across to make room for Robinson Hall. Opposite, on the corner site of Fogg Museum, was the big mansard home of Professor Louis Agassiz, the eminent naturalist, where he and his wife Elizabeth on their third floor ran a private school for girls (1855–63), which led naturally to frequent meetings here by the founding group of Radcliffe College, and her becoming Radcliffe's first president.

Fogg Art Museum, preeminent among Harvard University Art Museums open to the public, has been well described as their crown jewel. The beautiful red brick building, gracious in appearance and size, was built in 1927 mainly through the fund-raising efforts of its Dean Edward W. Forbes and his associate, Professor Paul J. Sachs, to house the magnificent, growing collection then being assembled. It replaced an earlier, much smaller 1895 building in the old Yard, which stood on part of the site of Canaday Hall.

Besides its art objects the museum has the largest fine arts library in the New World. The largest exhibition gallery is Felix M. Warburg Hall, named for a donor friend of Professor Sachs. Outside the lecture hall below Warburg is a bust of Harvard's and the nation's pioneer professor of Fine Arts, Charles Eliot Norton. Many celebrations have taken place in the main courtyard, among them the Grand Marshal's commencement luncheons for 300 guests, and the luncheon Conant gave for Winston Churchill.

Next on our left is Carpenter Center for the Visual Arts, entered from amid its supporting pillars on its south side, to the lobby, or, excitingly, by the ramp that leads up to exhibit and workspaces on the third floor, among them the Josef Louis Sert Gallery. Another ramp leads down in back, past

Fogg, to Prescott Street. This 1963 cement and glass creation in international style is Le Corbusier's only building in North America; he was an architect ranking with Walter Gropius and Frank Lloyd Wright.

Directly across from the ramp is the gate given in Harvard's Tercentenary year, and named for President Eliot; it finally completed the iron and brick fencing of the old Yard, and now leads past Emerson Hall to Widener. When erected in 1936 it was the north gate of the semicircular driveway that used to lead to the President's House at 17 Quincy, a 1912 gift of President Lowell that replaced an 1860 mansard with curved slate roof that, wrote President Eliot, kept the second- and third-floor rooms roasting in summer. Eliot lived in it for the record forty years of his presidency.

The dignified, three-story brick mansion, now used by the University's governing boards, was the official residence of College presidents from Lowell to Pusey. Distinguished visitors, United States presidents, world leaders, and academic celebrities have been entertained in its most pleasant drawing room. During World War II when Harvard, like other colleges, joined in the war effort, the mansion, as well as other University buildings, was used by the military.

President Conant had joined with M.I.T.'s Vannevar Bush in research that would help America develop the atomic bomb and enter the Space Age. It had all become possible on December 2, 1942, when scientist Enrico Fermi, in a famed test in Chicago, had shown that a nuclear chain reaction was practical. On that day Conant, as scientific adviser to the secret Manhattan Project, received the coded message, "The Italian navigator has just landed in the new world. The natives are friendly." And Conant was present when the first atomic bomb went off at Alamogordo, New Mexico, in July 1945.

Next, on our left, are two granite posts marked number 20 and number 16 Quincy Street. We go between them to circle around the back of number 16, the ancient Dana-Palmer House (1822). The number 16 building on our left is the Harvard Faculty Club (1931) that is on the site of the big, old professor's house that Henry James, Sr. rented in 1866 and to which be came to live with his family.

His celebrated sons, philosopher Professor William James and novelist Henry, Jr. had opposite views of life in Cambridge. William valued Cambridge above any other place "in the known world," and wanted his ashes to rest on the shore of the Charles River among people he loved. Henry, Jr. became so expatriated and Londonized that he gave up his citizenship, but finally directed that his ashes, too, be buried with the family in the Cambridge Cemetery. In 1892 the James House was much enlarged and became the Colonial Club, a business and social group. It was pretty much an early faculty club, enjoyed especially by Santayana for its 50-cent luncheons, which he ate here with faculty friends.

Warren House, next on our left, was named for its professor-donor, but goes back to the early 1800s and a close friend of Professor Charles Follen (they fled together to America), classicist Charles Beck, who became Harvard's professor of Latin in 1832. Beck, always a friend of freedom, served in the legislature, promoted abolition by joining the Underground Railway and installing a trapdoor to a secret, inter-floor room at the head of the Warren House stairway.

The house, since 1899, when given Harvard by Professor Henry C. Warren, has been used by the English department, the longest any University in America has had its English department in the same place. The old Beck house, shifted a bit eastward, once had on its south side his garden, extending to the present Massachusetts Avenue.

Next on our left is the earlier (1911) Harvard Varsity Club, built as a wing on the present Freshman Union's northeast corner, which is now also part of the English department. Inside the doorway to the beautiful main room and opposite the large fireplace is a dedication of the former clubhouse to an all-around, beloved athlete: big, rugged Francis H. Burr, class of 1909, who died about a year later in his first year in Law School. Burr was a good scholar, president of his class, captain of the football team, first marshal on Class Day, with a shining career ahead, cut off suddenly by typhoid fever.

The Freshman Union, with its ample social and dining facilities, like the Varsity Wing, was built in Beck's garden in 1901 as the Harvard Union, another gift from Major Henry Lee Higginson. Higginson's desire, as an offset to exclusive Gold-Coast times, was to provide a comfortable place open to all, where classmates could happily mingle. With the House Plan moving upper classes toward the river, the Union is currently just for freshmen, who mainly live in the Yard.

The great hall is very impressive, with large fireplaces ateither end, busts of George Washington and John Harvard on their mantelpieces, and a sumptuous round, glassed porch on the south side. Over the door to the hall is a dedication to Harvard men who gave their lives in the Spanish-American War.

The basement offers a historic tidbit. In the days when it provided the *Harvard Crimson* an office, future President Franklin D. Roosevelt, as *Crimson* secretary and president, had his office here near his lodgings in Westmorly Court.

Most historic of these buildings is the Dana-Palmer House, the buff clapboard with black blinds and white trim—now with even its brick chimney painted buff with black trim—that was saved by donor Lamont when it was moved here in 1947 to make room for the Lamont Library.

Earlier dwellers at number 16 were philosophy Professor William E. Hocking and his wife, Agnes, daughter of the poet-editor of the Roman Catholic diocesan newspaper, *Pilot,* John Boyle O'Reilly, who founded a children's school here in 1914, mostly for children of fellow faculty members. On succeeding, the school moved to a site in Norton's Woods, thus getting its name of Shady Hill School. To get more space, it was moved in 1925 to Coolidge Hill, where we saw it.

Dana-Palmer House, originally at 11 Quincy Street, became the home of author Richard Henry Dana's father and three maiden aunts after the death of his mother in 1822. Martha, eldest of the aunts, was married here in June 1830 to famed artist Washington Allston. Author Dana spent his boyhood and most of his teens here, loved to sail toy boats on the duck pond of Squire Winthrop on nearby Arrow Street.

In 1839, after its purchase by Harvard, the College put a revolving dome for a telescope on the roof and got its first observatory. Astronomer William Cranch Bond paid his rent by keeping "watch on the stars." Although this building was on the last hill in the old Yard, the setup did not satisfy President Quincy, "Old Quin," until he arranged to get higher land out Concord Avenue, where Cranch moved to the present Observatory in 1844 with the 15-inch telescope.

The Palmer in Dana-Palmer comes from resident philosophy Professor George Herbert Palmer, who took over in 1894 with his honored wife, Alice Freeman Palmer, pioneer in women's education, who had been Wellesley College's second president and, while here, was a major fund raiser for the new Harvard Annex for women. After the building was moved it was provided with several chambers as a guest house for visiting scholars. It may interest them especially that in this house President Conant, going back and forth to Washington to direct wartime research, lived during World War II and entertained Winston Churchill on that midwar visit to Cambridge.

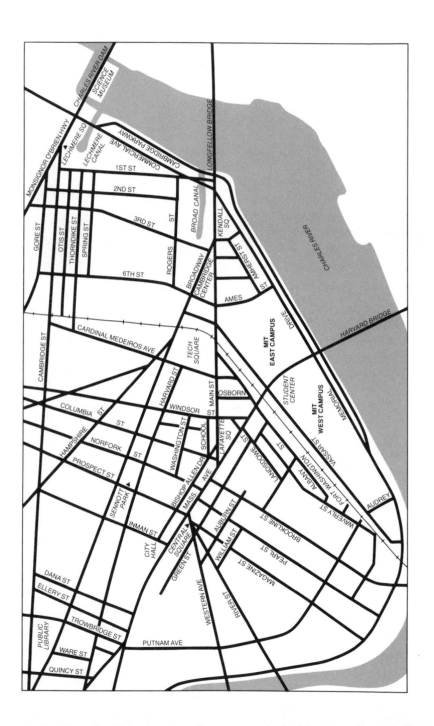

THROUGH CAMBRIDGEPORT TO THE OLD CAUSEWAY

As we head along the old route, via the present Central Square, to Pelham's Island and the 1793 West Boston Bridge, we will meet with many reminders that a large share of the acreage ahead once belonged to one of Cambridge's oldest families, the Danas.

Besides, before Quincy Street was renamed in honor of President Quincy, "Old Quin," it was called Dana Street because it was on Dana land, part of the immense possessions of the largest of the Dana landowners, a Revolutionary era hero, Judge Francis Dana, prime builder of the West Boston Bridge, whose mansion site we will presently see. Streets just ahead of us are named for members by marriage of the Dana family: Remington, Ellery, Trowbridge, Allston, and the present Dana Street.

The triangular land, where we see the gas station between Harvard Street and Massachusetts Avenue, used to be a part of Professor Charles Beck's garden, and when Harvard Street was laid out in 1808 across Dana land—much to the displeasure of Judge Dana—the triangle was called Beck's Park. The direct stretch of Massachusetts Avenue from Quincy Street to Sullivan (former Putnam) Square was laid across Dana land in 1793 to improve the road to the new bridge.

Reverend Abiel Holmes describes land that was then eastward of Quincy Street: swamp, pasture, and woodland bordering the salt marshes and oyster bank of the riverfront, with only Judge Dana's mansion and four other dwellings. It had long been known as "the Neck." Illustrious College preacher Andrew P. Peabody called it all, from bridge to College Yard, a "dreary walk . . . with no lights on our way except dim oil lamps at the toll houses." Even in Old Quin's era, when he drove his high-hung chaise from Boston, sometimes closing his eyes and letting the horse fetch him, he said that from Inman House, near the present City Hall, "there was hardly a house either side until you came to the mansion of Judge Dana," and then to Apthorp House it was only a "short, solitary strip of road through rough pastures."

Beck's Park triangle in 1876 became the site of the first and most lavish creation of the Gold Coast, Beck Hall, with its high ceilings, chandeliers, marble mantels, steam heat, and each resident in a single or double suite, with a private bath. This was the peak of the gold-plated age of high social rank, "gentleman's C," final clubs, private catering, and debutante parties.

Next beyond the attractive 1870 stone Baptist Church we see, at 396 Harvard Street, the former 1916 clubhouse of Delta Upsilon where, as we mentioned earlier, Professor George P. Baker of 47 Workshop fame would come to help the members stage their popular plays. The 7 Ware Street dwelling on our left, now central office of the University alumni publication, lively *Harvard* magazine, was once the residence of kind, tall, brilliant philosophy Professor Hugo Munsterberg, with his strong German accent, who, as in opening the Busch-Reisinger Museum, created an early World War I furor, with President Lowell fighting off any censorship of Professor Munsterberg, who died of a heart attack late in 1916 while lecturing at Radcliffe. For years homeless students or penniless fellow countrymen had freely used his big old house.

When William James, then an assistant professor, married Alice, a school teacher, in 1878, he first came to live in a boarding house at 387 Harvard Street, on the west corner of Ware Street, where we now see a former apartment house converted into a college dormitory. On the east corner five-story Ware Hall, built in 1894, was another of the early Gold-Coast houses before this type of housing generally shifted south of the Yard. We go right, now, and follow Remington Street to Massachusetts Avenue. On the east corner where we see the eleven-story apartment-retail building, young playwright Eugene O'Neill came in 1914–15 to live with two other students on the second floor of the three-story mansard formerly at 1105 Massachusetts Avenue. O'Neill, then twenty-five, still working on one-act trial plays, had persuaded his actor-father to send him to study in Professor Baker's 47 Workshop.

To our right, as we walk east along Massachusetts Avenue, is a street once the fairly short "Little Neck Way" that was renamed for a Revolutionary war hero, General Israel Putnam. Just beyond the second block down Putnam Avenue, on the left at number 62, is a stone marker identifying the site where General Washington ordered Fort #2, soon after his arrival in 1775. This was part of a chain of earthwork fortifications, protecting the Cambridge army campground, which stretched from the river north across the present Dana Hill through Somerville's Union Square to the fort once atop Somerville's Prospect Hill. Little trace remains save of Fort #1, which we will mention later. In the next block below old Fort #2 is a modern Cambridge schoolhouse (1971), replacing a 1904 building that was named for martyred Reverend Martin Luther King, Jr., Nobel laureate and civil rights champion, assassinated in 1968.

On returning to Massachusetts Avenue we go north on Trowbridge Street to see some of the considerable Rindge benefactions to Cambridge. Diagonally northwestward across Broadway, which began as the eastern link of the Concord Turnpike to the 1793 West Boston Bridge, is the library building (now with many additions) and more than three acres of land for public use that Frederick H. Rindge, then twenty-nine and living for his health in California, gave Cambridge in an 1887 letter to Mayor William E. Russell, his Harvard classmate and close friend. The library collection itself, as we will see, traced in part to an earlier gift from the Dana family.

Rindge felt that his kind father, had he lived, would have made such gifts to the community and its people, whom he admired. This land he gave was near the Rindge home that once stood at 334 Harvard Street, and the land was where, wrote Rindge, "I used to play ball and climb the hawthorn for its berries which taste good to boys." Rindge also recalled that in ancient Greece, Rome, and Egypt "didactic" quotations were carved on public buildings. His quotations, like "to know God is best of all," make interesting reading on the tablets inside, which, like the murals on printing, add to any visit. Among those present at the library's June 1889 dedication was President Charles W. Eliot.

Rindge also paid for and long supported an 1888 Cambridge Manual Training School that was on the site, just west of the library, of Rindge Tech, built in 1933 with Mayor William G. Russell's son, Richard M. Russell, who was then mayor and at the dedication. The present park, with facilities for passive recreation, fulfills another of Rindge's desires, that the big tract of land also be used "as a playground for children and the young." Rindge Tech in the early 1980s was joined with old Cambridge Latin School to form a combined citywide high school, Cambridge Rindge and Latin School, using all the school structures around the library, all on Rindge land.

We return now to Massachusetts Avenue by way of Ellery Street, on the east side of Cambridge Rindge and Latin School. After we cross Harvard Street we have on our left two interesting sites. Delmore Schwartz, the brilliant poet, was a young English instructor at Harvard and living at number 20 on the upper floor when in midwinter 1945, big Robert Lowell, twenty-seven, working on his "Lord Weary's Castle," came with his wife as guests. Despite odors from the refrigerator, which Lowell said "gurgled mustard gas," the lodgings were a merry workshop for the fellow poets until, in an alcoholic argument, ill-self-controlled Lowell swung at Schwartz. His wife thereupon took Lowell back to Maine to separate the poetic punch-throwers.

Margaret Fuller in 1842, a year before she went to work in New York on Horace Greeley's *Tribune,* came to live at 8 Ellery. As the oldest of eight children, she had taken charge of her widowed mother and family, seeking to provide a home and education for her six brothers in a neighborhood she had lived in as a teenager.

We turn left at Massachusetts Avenue and soon across the street are two notable locations. At 1000 Massachusetts Avenue once stood the three-story mansard mansion that Henry O. Houghton, founder of the Riverside Press, built in 1857 in Judge Dana's vegetable garden. Handy to him, now about a half-dozen blocks down the later-lengthened Putnam Avenue, was the printing plant he had moved in 1852 from Remington Street into the 1836 brick former Cambridge almshouse by the Charles River between Western Avenue and River Street. This was on the site of Fort #1, part of the Revolutionary fortified line that ran through Fort #2 and across Dana Hill. Only a stone marker now locates the old fort. Houghton had leased from Little & Brown, publishers, who were already there, but as Houghton's printing enterprise grew he came to occupy all of the site for his Riverside Press.

Near Houghton's house, and also across from Dana Street, was once another wooden house with a big portico where six-year-old Winslow Homer's father brought his family to live in 1842 on moving from Boston.

It was not long afterward that father Homer, a frequent mover, found a dwelling he considered better and moved to Garden Street near Fay House.

Dana Street, in the mid-1800s, was considered by the Union Railway Company as the division between Cambridgeport and Old Cambridge, and on passing it the omnibus picked up additional fare. Dana Hill, with the 1785 Dana mansion atop it, used to be much higher before it was used for fill in 1856, when the horsecar tracks were laid. The big two-story wooden mansion, with its central pediment, was seated on terraces midway between Ellery and Dana Street and about 200 feet up from the present Massachusetts Avenue. There were grand views to and beyond the Charles River. Moreover, in 1797, Judge Dana got his neighbor and fellow developer Leonard Jarvis, then owner of the old Inman estate, to agree to keep open a 40-foot-wide strip across Jarvis's land to Pelham Island.

The mansion was known for Judge Dana's hospitality and its important guests. Dana had been a leading Son of Liberty; went on several diplomatic missions—at times with future Presidents John and John Quincy Adams; served in the Continental Congress; presided as the Bay State's chief justice for fifteen years; and was married to the daughter of a signer of the Declaration of Independence, William Ellery. When Dana died, in 1811, former President John Adams was a pallbearer to the burial in God's Acre.

In 1826 President John Quincy Adams came to dinner along with a number of V.I.P.s, just after Timothy Fuller, long a congressman and speaker of the Massachusetts House, bought the mansion. It was while the Fullers lived here, to 1831, that Margaret Fuller attended the nearby private grammar school with future writers Oliver Wendell Holmes and Richard Henry Dana, then youngsters, too. The entire old Dana estate: mansion, coach house, barns, sheds, spring house, went up in flames in mid-January 1839. Among the volunteer firefighters, all handicapped by shortage of water, was twenty-three-year-old author Dana, recently back from his two years before the mast.

We head now along Massachusetts Avenue to see the crowning Rindge gift, City Hall. Down Hancock Street on our left, at 2 to 4 Hancock Place, can still be seen the simply styled, double "Opposition House" that Dana, Jarvis, and friends, eager to divide their Dana Hill land section for mansions, put up almost overnight in 1803 to block the laying out of Harvard Street through land that was then pretty much wooded. The road, before sections of it were closed, was the most direct route from the West Boston Bridge to Harvard Square; it was built anyway. Mansions still followed, particularly on Dana Hill, but later in the nineteenth century apartment houses replaced many of them or covered their terrain. Opposition House, sold by Dana in 1807, was, after an earlier shift, moved to its new site in 1859.

Rindge's selection of "didactic" quotations and their being "over the main entrance," both conditions of his gift, can be seen inscribed in the brownstone of the outside balcony near the flagpole of the 1890 City Hall, with its impressive 27-foot-square, 154-foot-high stone tower. Inside, in the entry, are memorials to Cambridge's famous Civil War Company C, and Cambridge heroes who served and those who gave their lives in the war in Vietnam. Three-term Mayor and Governor William E. Russell, who died quite young, can be seen in a fine portrait in the second-floor Council Chamber. On the third floor is a fascinating, big-model map of Cambridge as it looked in 1776, as prepared for the nation's bicentennial.

City Hall is located on old Inman property. A stone-slab marker can be seen a few steps down Inman Street in front of number 15 Inman, marking the location of the three-story, large wooden mansion, with its semicircular driveway and low-studded, paneled rooms, which Ralph Inman, wealthy loyalist and Boston merchant, built in 1756 on some 180 acres, about half of the later Cambridgeport east of Dana's estate, which Inman bought in that year. He had unobstructed views of Boston across the marshes and the river for the merry guests who shared his hospitality.

The best-known resident, though, was "Old Put," General Israel Putnam, in command of the center of General Washington's 1775 lines besieging the Redcoats in Boston. Here was Old Put's headquarters, and around him in Inman's fields and woods he had many companies of his men encamped. Old Put has often been likened to a watchdog, in front of and protecting the American camp. The Inmans, through the friendship of Mrs. Inman with the patriots, retained the estate. Mr. Jarvis got it in 1792, and it passed to other owners until the mansion was removed in 1873 and later demolished.

Farther north on Inman, at the corner of Broadway, the post–Civil War former Harvard Grammar School, known as the City Hall Annex for half a century, was dedicated "McCusker Center" in memory of men who gave their lives in World War II. On an upper floor are offices of the Cambridge Historical Commission, which has published several architectural and pictorial histories of Cambridge, all printed by the M.I.T. Press.

On our way back along Inman to Massachusetts Avenue we see, on nearing City Hall, St. Mary's Orthodox Church, which was built in 1822 as the first Cambridge Universalist Church and later moved here. It is now, after demolition of two earlier churches, the oldest extant church in Cambridgeport. Famous actor Otis Skinner, born in 1858, was the son of an early rector of the Universalist parish.

Across from Inman Street, where we see the Cambridge post office, was the Cambridgeport private grammar school, which young Oliver Wendell Holmes called the "Port School," where he and his younger playmate, Margaret Fuller, were pupils.

An earlier location of Cambridge's City Hall was in the Cambridge Athenaeum, a two-story structure built in 1851 on the southeast corner of Pleasant Street. The land was a gift from the author's uncle, Edmund Trowbridge Dana, and it was in the Athenaeum, with other contributions, that a library, then called the Dana Library, was opened to the public in 1857. In the following year the city, which had lost its first city hall in a fire, purchased all the Athenaeum property that once was here and used it as a city hall until it took over Rindge's 1890 city hall, diagonally across the avenue.

On reaching Central Square, formerly called Haymarket Square, we have, on our right, Magazine Street, which runs directly down to the Charles River and takes its name from a former state powder magazine on Captain's Island, now connected to the shore with filled marshes, where in early Revolutionary War times General Washington had a gun battery. Diagonally on our right Western Avenue and River Street, also running to the river, were created as roads to Watertown and Brighton. Between them was the now long-vanished farmhouse and barns of the big Thomas Soden farm, opposite present Soden Street, which, with Inman House, comprised the only houses beyond Dana House that Reverend Abiel Holmes reported in all of Cambridgeport when the West Boston Bridge was built. Judge Dana, by then, had owned most of the Soden Farm for several years.

We will find quite a few historic spots along Magazine Street. Near its junction with Massachusetts Avenue, at number 636, Cambridge got its first continuous city newspaper in 1846, the year in which its 13,000-plus population entitled it to cityhood. The *Chronicle* was established by a thirty-two-year-old printer from Scotland in his shop over a corner grocery store. Its growth, like the city's, has been steady, as we see in its current headquarters in the high-rise building across Central Square at 678 Massachusetts Avenue.

The impressively located First Baptist Church, facing Central Square from the junction of Magazine and River Streets, is a successor church to Cambridgeport's then second-oldest church, an 1817 wooden church built here by the Baptist parishioners, later enlarged to include a Sunday school area, which burned down in 1866. Magazine Street is like a church row, with at least four parish churches quite close together. Farther down Magazine on the west side is the Pilgrim Congregational Church, and on the east side are the Greek Orthodox Church and the Grace Methodist Church. In the block south of Grace Church is large Dana Square, a Dana-family gift of land to Cambridge.

We pause at Auburn Street, next street below the Baptist Church block, a street long associated with the Dana family. The celebrated painter Washington Allston, after his marriage in 1830 to author Dana's aunt Martha, came to live in Cambridgeport to enjoy the pine groves he had roamed and the marsh, creek, and river views he had seen in his College days. The Allstons lived for some years in a house once near the southeast corner of Auburn and Magazine Streets. Earlier, in 1831, the artist built himself a studio with a big window to get northern light, diagonally across Magazine at the northwest corner.

More than two years before his death Allston added a new, long-vanished house, finished in 1841, 50 feet across his garden from his painting room. Famous visitors, as well as prominent people seeking portraits, came often. Charles Dickens, who called Allston "a glorious old genius," came on his first American tour to Allston's green studio door, in the building now long gone but then much covered with vines. The Allston section of Boston, across the Charles River, was named in honor of the artist.

Author Dana was a frequent visitor for years. Indeed, the very day that twenty-one-year-old Dana, in fall 1836, returned from the sea he came directly to see Allston and Aunt Martha in their earlier Cambridgeport dwelling. That night Dana went to his Uncle Edmund's nearby house, telling in his journal of "my first wash with fresh water and soap in a basin in two years." Allston loved to sit smoking his cigars before his fireplace, and there he died in summer 1843. His oft-changed huge painting of *Belshazzar's Feast,* at one time revised at Gilbert Stuart's suggestion, was still incomplete, though started in Allston's London studio back in 1817. Author Dana and his wife, before building on Berkeley Street, lived here with Aunt Martha in 1851, and their only son, Richard III, was born here.

In the next block south, on the northwest corner of William and Magazine Streets, lived (1841–43), for the latter two of his four-year residence in Cambridgeport, the great abolitionist William Lloyd Garrison with his family. Though low in funds and in health, Garrison continued on the lecture circuit as leader of the American Anti-Slavery Society, and continued his forceful editing of the *Liberator,* which he had founded in 1835. We return now along Magazine Street to Central Square and go to the right along Massachusetts Avenue to the next street on our right, Pearl Street.

The house in which author Richard Henry Dana was born, in 1815, stood one block south of the northwest corner of Green Street. In later years this was the dwelling, too, of his philanthropic, kindly uncle Edmund, who wished to live near his close friend and brother-in-law, Washington Allston. The house was once designated 5 Green Street. At the southeast corner of Pearl Street and Massachusetts was once the hourly (omnibus) office in an inn where author Dana, while living with Aunt Martha, tells of putting his wife, Sarah, on the omnibus to go to Boston and then, for exercise, "walked in myself."

Across Massachusetts Avenue from the omnibus stop, near the corner of Norfolk Street, was the law office of Cambridgeport's great Civil War hero, James P. Richardson, who organized and trained Company C, the first volunteers to respond to President Lincoln's appeal for troops. Richardson's dwelling was nearby on Western Avenue. He was descended directly from Moses Richardson, who came in 1630 with Governor John Winthrop, and was a great-grandson of the Harvard College carpenter, another Moses Richardson, who was killed by the Redcoats during their retreat on April 19, 1775.

We now go north along Norfolk Street to see earlier sites of Cambridgeport's community services. When we come to Bishop Richard Allen Drive, the former Austin Street, all eleven acres of land west of Norfolk Street as far as Prospect Street, and between Allen and Harvard Streets, was known as the Almshouse Lot, arranged in 1818 for the town by the Austin family. It was here, opposite Worcester Street, just ahead and on the right off Norfolk Street, where the three-story brick 1818 Cambridge Almshouse stood until it was destroyed by fire, killing one of the paupers, in 1836. It was succeeded by the Almshouse at Riverside, by the Charles River.

Just beyond the first almshouse, at the corner of Harvard Street where we now see St. Mary's of the Annunciation, built in 1867 and later enlarged, formerly stood the two-story wooden town hall, designed, with pediment and Doric columns, by eminent architect Asher Benjamin; it was built in 1832. The three villages of Cambridge were split when old Cambridge Village succeeded in winning legislative approval in 1830 to enclose the Cambridge Commons, thus preventing market-bound cattlemen from using it to rest their droves. East Cambridge and Cambridgeport voters combined, and in 1831 picked this Almshouse Lot site "as more central" to the community's population for a town hall.

In 1846 Cambridge's city government was inaugurated here. Mayor James D. Green, in an address in May, said that 13,000 to 14,000 people deserved more efficient government and policing to prevent being "disturbed by riotous noises at night" or having their lives endangered "by the furious driving of horses through the streets." He warned of being on "guard against all unnecessary expenditure," for the tax rate was already 48 cents on the hundred dollars!

A reporter for the *Boston Atlas* said "a glorious gathering" was held in the big, high-ceilinged city hall on a stormy night in September 1848, when a big crowd, preceded by the Cambridge Taylor Club band, squeezed in to hear a congressman from Illinois on a New England speaking tour for the Whig candidate for president, Zachary Taylor. Abraham Lincoln, wrote the reporter, was "six feet at least in his stockings"; offered "no abstract" of Lincoln's speech, which left the crowd cheering "till the rafters shook," but did record that Lincoln was "plain, direct and to the point, powerful and convincing." Late in December 1853, during a heavy snow storm, city hall was destroyed by fire, and the city government later took over the Athenaeum.

Sennott Park, the two-plus-acre public park on our left as we approach Broadway (the old Concord Turnpike), was make a cemetery in 1811 and used until 1865, when the city transferred graves to the present Cambridge Cemetery, adjoining Mt. Auburn. Diagonally across Broadway, on the northwest corner of Elm Street, was where William Lloyd Garrison first lived in Cambridge (1839–41). One block farther east along Broadway, on the southeast corner of Columbia Street, stood the first Cambridgeport meeting house, a two-story brick 1807 structure, destroyed in an 1833 windstorm.

We head now down Columbia Street toward Lafayette Square. Turn left at Washington Street and, in the block ahead on the corner, at 296 Washington Street, was long the dwelling of distinguished Cambridge historian Reverend Lucius R. Paige. A student of Reverend Hosea Ballou, Paige in 1832 became pastor of the old First Cambridge Universalist Church (then in nearby Lafayette Square), which we saw on Inman Street. Because of illness he gave up parish work and became town clerk in 1839, continuing as the first city clerk in 1846, and wrote a history of Cambridge that President Eliot called the "epitome" history of Puritan towns.

We continue along Washington Street, turn right on Cherry Street, and at 71 Cherry, on the corner, is the big dwelling where Margaret Fuller's father set up housekeeping in 1809, and where she and all her brothers and sisters were born. In Margaret's childhood the house had a porch all along the front, big elm trees on the lawn, and a garden back to Pine Street. Currently it is a neighborhood center, providing day care for young folks and tutoring and help to the elderly.

Just across the street, near the south corner of Cherry, once stood, at 55 Cherry, the house in which twenty-six-year-old Elias Howe, Jr., in July 1845, was able to sew two suits of clothes that confirmed he had at last perfected the first sewing machine. He had his lathe here in the low-studded attic, and had been working on his invention ever since he had the idea three years earlier, in a Boston machine shop where he was employed.

Only a few months earlier he had finally hit on the key to his success: use two threads and a shuttle. Howe, with wife and children to support, had found money mighty scarce, but a friend and schoolmate who lived at number 55, George Fisher, small-time local wood and coal dealer, had provided Howe with living space and advanced him $500 for a share in any patent.

Turn left at School and a block away, on the north corner at Windsor Street, was land given in 1802 by Ahdrew Bordman IV, descendant of Lieutenant Governor Phips, town clerk, and large Cambridgeport land owner, on which the town and contributors built Cambridgeport's first small, wooden schoolhouse, which was replaced in 1868 by the large brick one, also named for Bordman.

Bordman, naturally, was an enthusiastic Cambridgeport developer, and some blocks north in 1805 he built himself a great three-story mansion, then surrounded by spacious grounds. Now vanished, the mansion was moved and much altered over the years, became a tenement house, long crowded on its small lot at 96 Hampshire Street by surrounding structures. We continue now down Windsor Street to Main Street, passing on our left extensive New Towne Court public housing, Cambridge's first, which went up in the early years of F.D.R.'s New Deal.

To begin our next walk we will continue along Windsor Street to Massachusetts Avenue, but first we visit another Cambridgeport historic site, just a block east on Main Street at the east corner of Osborn Street.

Main Street, from just east of Lafayette Square to, and slightly beyond Osborn Street, was on the northern edge of twenty-acre Pelham Island. This land in the river marshes was named for one of its first owners, aristocrat Herbert Pelham, who lived in Governor Dudley's Newe Towne mansion. It was from Pelham's Island that Judge Dana and his friends built a causeway almost two thirds of a mile long across the river marshes to the 1793 West Boston Bridge, itself slightly longer than the causeway, to span the river's width long before filling-in took place on both banks.

A bronze plaque on the three-story building on the east corner of Osborn tells how the telephone's inventor, Alexander Graham Bell, talking from Kilby Street, just off Boston's State Street, made the first long-distance telephone call. He did it on October 9, 1876, to his helper, Thomas A. Watson, the same man who had first heard an intelligible human voice over a wire. That was in 1875, in an attic lab overlooking Boston's old Scollay Square. Bell, on spilling some battery acid, blurted, "Mr. Watson, come here, I want you." When Bell formed the Bell Telephone Company in 1877, Watson, then a twenty-three-year-old mechanical wizard, became chief engineer and went on to study at M.I.T. and create his own hugely successful Fore River shipbuilding plant.

The 1876 long-distance feat was carried off in an earlier, similar 1815 structure here that Cambridgeport developer-manufacturer Charles Davenport took over in 1842 and immensely expanded, as his founderies and shops progressed from making carriages and omnibuses to turning out railroad cars.

Notice the yellow metal guards at the curb outside the first door on the left up Osborn Street in the same successor corner building. They stand outside the private first-floor lab of inventor Edwin H. Land, whose success in polarizing light led to his founding Polaroid Corporation in 1937. It was in this lab that he created instant photography, had his picture taken on Osborn Street with his new invention in 1946, and by 1948 had put it on the market. The entire buildings on both sides of Osborn, and all along Osborn, extending to Albany Street and Massachusetts Avenue, are the only part of Polaroid now in Cambridgeport.

A toll booth for the 1793 bridge was near the corner of Osborn Street. Just opposite Osborn, on the New Towne Court land, was the first Cambridgeport building following the opening of the bridge and causeway. This store, near the end of the causeway, belonged to two early Cambridgeport developers, Royal Makepeace and Robert Vose. When Vose died, a decade later, Makepeace was joined by Rufus Davenport, a Boston merchant, in further developing. A tavern was built just east of the store and, on the west corner of Osborn, Vose and Makepeace built themselves dwellings.

"Old Quin," in that high-hung chaise of his, found the drive "a bleak, solitary stretch across the salt marshes before one reached the thickly settled center of Cambridgeport with its numerous big taverns and great square stores mainly filled with country produce and West Indian Goods." Still, taverns, inns, stores, and houses did develop as, James Russell Lowell related, "white topped wagons, each drawn by double files of six or eight horses . . . brought all the wares and products of the country to their mart and seaport in Boston."

But as transportation changed from horse-drawn stages and omnibuses to horsecars, development, especially in filling and making building lots in the river marshes, did not become the immediate bonanza foreseen by the early developers, Royal Makepeace, Rufus Davenport, and later, as we shall see, Charles Davenport, too.

TO M.I.T. WEST CAMPUS: SPORTS AND DORMS

On our way down Windsor Street to Massachusetts Avenue, the main approach to the M.I.T. campus, we can get an overall impression of the great spread and formation of the University's magnificent location along the Charles River, which we will presently visit.

Eastgate, a twenty-nine-story dorm for married graduate students, rises like a sentinel at the east end of the campus. Its tower can be seen, on our left, by looking eastward along State Street. Again on our left, as we go down Windsor and pass beyond the new four-story, tan-colored 1895 Polaroid building, we can see M.I.T.'s Earth Sciences Tower, the University's tallest building, with a big globe on the roof's edge. And on reaching Front Street, again on our left, we get a glimpse of the Great Dome on M.I.T.'s main building. Presently we will see the tower dorms of Tang and Westgate, three quarters of a mile upriver from the Great Dome, and at the west end of the campus.

On our right, in midblock on the present Front Street, although its address is 265 Massachusetts Avenue, is the M.I.T. Museum, established in 1971 to gather and preserve the historical materials and treasures of the University. The museum occupies the entire second floor of the former General Radio plant, with the first and two top levels devoted to storage, offices, and classes. Admission is free. The displays, reached by elevator or an easy twenty stairs, provide a matchless background for our M.I.T. walks, exhibiting epoch-making products of M.I.T. labs that literally have made possible mankind's advance in nuclear, electronic, and computer technologies and the atomic and space age—seedbed of Nobel Prizes.

Here are delightful objects, too, especially for M.I.T. graduates and students. Back of the guard desk, just under the entry, is the large, easy-to-examine 1861 Institute seal with its motto, *Mens et Manus*—Head and Hand. Also on display is the three-foot-long bronze beaver, the beaver being the Institute's mascot and a large bronze beaver the highest alumni award. A portrait gallery displays distinguished M.I.T. leaders, at the end of the entry corridor, and nearby Daniel Chester French's bronze bust of one of M.I.T.'s greatest presidents, its third (1881–97), Francis A. Walker. Walker had firmly opposed recurrent proposals to merge young

M.I.T. with Harvard's earlier scientific department, and he so ably captained the growth of M.I.T. that the eventual move from Boston's tiny campus to Cambridge became inevitable.

In a special display room across from the Walker bust is a large model of the first M.I.T. building, the now-vanished Rogers Building in Boston, a five-story red brick structure with fluted classical columns and pediment. Delayed by the Civil War struggle, the construction was so slow (1863–66) that President William Barton Rogers, on February 20, 1865, began classes (he taught physics) in rented Mercantile Hall of the three-story, 1820 Mercantile Library that, until Boston's disastrous 1872 fire, stood at the east corner of downtown Boston's Summer and Hawley Streets. The first Rogers Building, demolished in 1940, was built near the northeast corner of Boylston and Clarendon Streets in the Back Bay river flats of Boston, which were still being filled.

Most exciting are some of the trail-blazing inventions, on display here, which have been developed at M.I.T. by its scientific wizards. With the push of a button the visitor sees flashes on the device that Harold E. "Doc" Edgerton, father of the electronic strobe light, created. In cases near one another are successive stages of the differential analyzer that Vannevar Bush devised in developing the computer. We can see displays of Jay W. Forrester at work on his magnetic memory core for the high-speed digital computer that won him a place in the Inventors' Hall of Fame. Among the many others is the famous "Mouse in a Maze," Great Britain's Magnetron, which beat Hitler's Luftwaffe, a step in development at M.I.T. of microwave radar. And here is a dynamo, the nation's first, given to M.I.T. in 1887 by an earlier American inventor, Thomas A. Edison, to facilitate instruction in electrical engineering.

On leaving the museum we turn right on Massachusetts Avenue. The part of Front Street on which we have already walked once ran along the edge of the river marsh. Originally, in the late 1790s, Front Street mainly ran from Lafayette Square and was built by an associate of Chief Justice Dana, Leonard Jarvis, who had bought the Inman estate in 1792. When Jarvis was developing building lots, he agreed in 1797 to keep the then 40-foot-wide Front Street unobstructed to preserve Dana's view of the river. Overoptimistic Jarvis, who also speculated in early Cambridgeport canal dredging, went bankrupt.

To attract and service industrial expansion in Cambridgeport, Charles Davenport, the site of whose factories and foundries we visited on Main Street, joined other Cambridge leaders in building a Grand Junction railroad bed across the river marshes to give Cambridge the benefit of rail transportation, linking railroads north and west of Boston. The rails, just ahead of us crossing Massachusetts Avenue between Albany and Vassar Streets, did eventually bring larger industries, but, even though completed in 1855, these were beset by financial miseries within a year and were not used again until 1866, when established railroad operators took over.

The high railroad bed did, as we will presently see, mark an early northern boundary of M.I.T.'s future campus. Charles Davenport, who had been acquiring mud flats, was also a leader in forming the 1881 Charles River Embankment Company, and two years later the present sea wall of granite blocks, beyond the 200-foot esplanade space that eventually became Memorial Drive, was started. The river bottom was dredged to cover the marsh and create a riverside residential area. Progress was slow, beset by bankruptcy and separation of the area from the rest of the city by the railroad and the many factories and warehouses that rail service did attract.

The University currently has 135 acres of land in Cambridge. When it moved here in 1916, though, it had 46 acres; practically all of these 46 were on filled land, and all on the east side of Massachusetts Avenue, and were between the sea wall and the old Grand Junction railroad line. President Richard C. Maclaurin of M.I.T., who picked the site and began acquiring it in 1912, got $500,000, two-thirds of the cost, from T. Coleman Du Pont. This donor of even greater sums to M.I.T. became United States senator, then president of the huge Delaware Du Pont de Nemours Corporation, and was long head of M.I.T. alumni. Du Pont wanted M.I.T. to get at least 45 acres so as to provide for future growth.

Acquisition of land had begun two years after the Charles River Dam, stabilizing the river, was completed in 1910, and two decades after Harvard Bridge and its approaches across the mud flats were completed in 1890. While deciding on the move, President Maclaurin would walk across the new bridge to examine the location. Front Street had been extended in 1889, and was called "Front Street Extension," which was to meet the new Harvard Bridge. Then in 1894 Front Street became part of Massachusetts Avenue, running from the bridge all across Cambridge, the city's longest street.

Notice a few M.I.T. locations as we approach the campus. To handle expansion quickly, M.I.T. has converted a number of earlier apartment structures for College needs. On our right, a block west at 351–355 Massachusetts Avenue, between State and Main Streets, is a five-story M.I.T. dormitory. In part it is a fraternity house, Alpha Delta Phi, and another part was dedicated in 1892 as the Marjorie Pierce House of the Women's Independent Living Group (WILG), formed six years earlier for cooperative living, as in a fraternity. Diagonally across from us, at 282–290 Massachusetts Avenue, is Random Hall, the prior "Cambridge Inn," another M.I.T. dorm. And, as we turn left along Massachusetts Avenue, the three-story triangular block at number 233 is both dorm and fraternity house, Zeta Psi.

With the former mainly industrial areas near the M.I.T. campus shifting to high-technology research and development, the extensive building across the street of the New England Confectionery Company, creator of NECCO wafers, recalls earlier times in Cambridge when pedestrians and motorists enjoyed the aroma coming from about two dozen candy factories that made Cambridge the national center of that industry. Founded in 1847, NECCO came here in 1927 to get more space than it had in South Boston. Most of the other candy factories have vanished or been converted to other uses, but NECCO's famous wafers are still made by billions of pounds a year. On our left, the attractive two-story building on the south corner of Windsor, 211 Massachusetts Avenue, was for more than four decades a laundry enterprise before M.I.T. acquired it in 1947. Currently it supplies M.I.T.'s graphic-arts needs, including offset printing, photo service, and illustration, besides handling M.I.T.'s bulk mail, and, as we will see on a later walk, was in 1953 the birthplace of one of the great building blocks of our high-tech age, the Whirlwind I digital computer.

Ahead of us is an interesting view of the Great Dome of M.I.T.'s main building, seemingly between two Boston high-rises, the Hancock Tower on the left of the Great Dome and the Prudential Tower on the right, back of the oldest extant building on the filled land along Massachusetts Avenue ahead of us, the 1895 Metropolitan Storage Warehouse on the south side of the tracks. On either side of the tracks, a capsule of industrial change in Cambridge, are former warehouses, stables, and factory buildings that M.I.T. has converted for research labs or maintenance facilities. To meet Cambridge's ever-intensifying parking problem, M.I.T. has made parking lots and in the 1960s built three big garages, two on either side of the tracks on and near Main Street and West Garage, just west of old Metropolitan Storage.

The big green gasometerlike structure on our right, at Albany Street, bespeaks unusual activity. There is indeed; here and immediately opposite, too, in the two-story tan-colored building at 155 Massachusetts Avenue, M.I.T. has a high-voltage lab. The green structure is a 1958 nuclear-research reactor, still used by engineering students in the adjoining Nuclear Reactor Lab and classrooms at 138 Albany Street. Just beyond, at 150 Albany, is M.I.T.'s National Magnet Lab, named for M.I.T. physicist-instructor Francis Bitter, who invented a magnet that would make a sensationally powerful magnetic field. The skybridge across Albany Street that connects with a Fusion Center, at 167 Albany, is part of expanded M.I.T. research efforts to make use of the sun and nuclear fusion (in contrast to nuclear fission), so that when the earth's oil is gone, fusion may, we hope, provide mankind with an adequate source of energy.

Albany Street, ahead of us, for ever-keen history buffs, is an easy approach to a Revolutionary War battery, which is all that remains of the fortifications that General Washington built around Boston in 1775 to block the Redcoats and protect his lines. Three old cannon, similar to those we saw on Cambridge Common, are mounted behind earthworks on a land gift from the Dana family that has long been called Fort Washington. Once sited at the edge of the river, it is now cut off by the railroad tracks and ever-increasing high-rise construction. We can see, facing the end of Albany Street, a two-story, white-painted annex of Cambridge Tire, long a Cambridge firm. The fort is near the back of Cambridge Tire and is reached by going a few steps to the right and then left a few steps more on Waverly Street.

The railroad tracks currently came down to just one line as they cross Massachusetts Avenue near Metropolitan Storage, bought in 1962 by M.I.T. and rented out and still used for the Institute as well as private storage. The absence of railroad gates and only one line do not mean inactivity, assured a nearby entrepreneur, "There's traffic lights and a bell, and freights go through often, with horns that hoot like hell!"

We now continue our visit of the West Campus that M.I.T., with its student body heavily increased after World War I, began to purchase in 1924. Next, on our right, is another medieval-looking structure, the National Guard's former Cambridge Armory, with its huge drill hall, built in 1902. The tragic death in 1955 of twenty-one-year old David Flett Du Pont, M.I.T. junior, youngest son of Lamont Du Pont, M.I.T. '01, president of the Du Pont Chemical firm and board chairman of General Motors, who had died three years earlier, provided the major part of the funds that M.I.T. used to acquire the Armory for a gym in 1957. Their funds were also used to build the adjoining Du Pont Athletic Center, on the gym's south side, in 1959. Young Du Pont, though concentrating on metallurgy, was devoted to sports and had willed $1,000,000 "for the improvement of athletic facilities at the Institute." His death came just a month before he was to begin his senior year.

The old, enormous drill hall has space for six basketball courts and even more portable ones. From the front lobby, after entering the huge, castle-like gates, parking-rule offenders climb the creaky stairway to clear up their fines, and all visitors can get help from the ever-courteous campus police, headquartered on the second floor. The top floor, once used for exhibitions, has been divided into a number of modern offices for M.I.T.'s new Center for Real Estate Development, created in 1983, the nation's first such graduate program, with faculty from several of M.I.T.'s schools, among them business, architecture, and engineering.

Departing from the gym, we go right along the cement path, past the plain red brick wall of the 1959 Du Pont Center, which we will visit presently, up the seven steps, and across the terrace-plaza on the Massachusetts Avenue side of the Student Center. The high overhang of the Student Center above us provides additional space for the fourth-floor student activities section and library that occupy the top, fifth floor of the Student Center.

Before we enter the Center, truly the busy hub of M.I.T. student life, we take note across the Avenue of the main entry to M.I.T., the 77 Massachusetts Avenue Rogers Building (1938). This edifice replaced M.I.T.'s first building, the 1866 Rogers Building in Boston, and, as we can read between the four tall, fluted Ionic columns and its fourth-story Dome, was dedicated to William Barton Rogers, founder. We will, on our next walk, see its lofty and busy lobby and stroll what the students call "the infinite corridor."

Looking westward across the Brigg's Athletic Field, we have a commanding vista from between the Student Center and Kresge Auditorium, extending across the playing fields to the high-rise dorms of the Westgate on the right and the new Tang on the left. We enter Student Center by the outside stairways to the Main Lobby on the second floor. The lobby, like the College's largest dining room, to our right on the east side of the building, is of a very attractive two-story height, with the main staircase continuing up to the third or mezzanine level.

Inscriptions tell of the Student Center, completed in 1965, being dedicated to M.I.T. President Julius A. Stratton, M.I.T. '23, second graduate to be elected president. A bust of Stratton is in the mezzanine lounge and a fine portrait is in the library on the top floor. Students had asked that the Center be named for him, and his popularity continues at high tide; the students in 1985 staged a twentieth-birthday party for Stratton Student Center, with party balloons, exhibits, brass ensemble, a play, and other student performances. Stratton, it is warmly remembered, built the Student Center when M.I.T.'s Second Century Fund campaign for $66,000,000, begun after he became president, brought in $98,000,000 in three years.

Student Center, as the wall directories relate, provides beautifully for just about every student service, study, or recreational need, and particularly food. The high-ceilinged dining room, with grand outdoor views of the Institute, was named for a dean of students, Harold E. Lobdell (1929–1946), "known and beloved by alumni everywhere." Near the game room, off the lobby also on the second floor, hot coffee is provided around the clock, and on the third level, along with the television lounge, "Twenty Chimneys," with hot sandwiches for lunch, becomes a steak house at suppertime, 5:00 to 7:00. And nearby are the pinball room, video games, and conference and multipurpose facilities.

The fourth floor is devoted entirely to student activities, from clubs to fraternities, for more than two dozen student organizations. Here in rooms on the southeast part of the floor is quartered *The Tech,* the student newspaper that in 1881 succeeded its short-lived predecessor, the *Spectrum* (1873), and has ever since published student and Institute news. Distinguished editors-in-chief include Arthur D. Little, M.I.T. 1885, industrial research pioneer who made M.I.T. his legatee, and future M.I.T. President James R. Killian, Jr., M.I.T. '26, who went to Washington to be President Eisenhower's science adviser in 1957, when the Russians became the first in space with their Sputnik. A dozen years later the United States would launch the Apollo flights, and Edwin E. Aldrin, Jr., M.I.T. '63 Doctor of Astronautics, son of an M.I.T. '17 graduate, would be one of the first two men to walk on the moon.

Just for students and faculty, the Student Center Library occupies most of the top floor with an open-stack, noncirculating collection of books and materials relating to M.I.T. courses. An unusual collection near the entry desk was given by a friend in memory of a popular, kind humanities professor, Robert E. "Tubby" Rogers, Harvard 1909, whose photo is on display. "Tubby"—he was about five foot and weighed about 200—got widespread publicity when, light-heartedly, his advice to the 1929 graduating class on how to succeed was "Be a snob and marry the boss's daughter." Project Athena, which we will see in other Institute buildings, uses the east end of the floor, providing several dozen computers on which students can write their term papers, study, or practice.

En route back to the campus we can see many other amenities that the Student Center has to offer. Tech Coop, save for the "Lobby Shop," a sort of campus mom-and-pop shop for those who prepare their own meals, occupies the entire ground floor, with acres of books, clothes, equipment, and stationery. And the basement level makes available further services and recreation, from barbershop to tailor shop, and bowling to billiards.

Diagonally across the campus, from the front steps of the Student Center, we see the four-story brick, white stone-trimmed Bexley Hall at 50–52 Massachusetts Avenue. Bexley Hall, currently a coed undergraduate dorm, was built in 1912 with four dozen housekeeping suites, and is one of the oldest West Campus buildings. The University acquired it in 1939 and used it, at first, for faculty housing. A brick wall along the west side of the passage back of Bexley is near the entries to the Institute Chapel, just ahead of us.

The Chapel and the Kresge Auditorium, in midgreensward, are unusual structures designed by the same Finnish architect, Eero Saarinen, built in 1955 and gifts of Sebastian S. Kresge's foundation, which provided Harvard Business School with its impressive, large dining facilities (1953), called Kresge Hall.

The interdenominational, windowless, circular chapel, with 100 plus seats, is illuminated (save in wintertime) by light reflected inside from a circular moat, and has a fascinating, glittering screen behind the altar, a block of white marble. The dome of the Auditorium has the astonishing appearance of resting on three, roughly 12-inch-long metal supports, though they get ample help from the metal struts of the glass walls. The Auditorium seats 1,200, has an organ given by Governor Alvin T. Fuller, Bay State businessman, and, on a lower level, a little theatre seating about 200.

On the west side of Student Center, a sign that we now follow points to Du Pont Athletic Center and Rockwell Cage. The 1939 building on our left, Briggs Field House, with lockers and showers, like Briggs Field, which stretches across most of West Campus, was named in honor of Frank H. Briggs, M.I.T. 1881. Briggs, a Boston leather merchant who lived opposite President Rogers's Back Bay dwelling, took a deep interest in M.I.T. athletics, was first president of its advisory council on athletics, and guided development of M.I.T.'s athletic system.

The main entrance to the lobby of the Du Pont Center, which we now enter, connects with Briggs both the Du Pont gym and Athletic Center and also the 1948 Rockwell Cage. Dr. John A. Rockwell, M.I.T. 1896, a Cambridge physician and close associate of Briggs, devoted more than five decades to M.I.T. athletics. "Dr. John" was so admired that the Cage was named in his honor a decade before he died. It has had many uses besides basketball, volleyball, baseball practice in winter, and graduation exercises. The Centennial celebration was concluded here with a ball and some 1,000 Techmen dancing with their dates. Most memorable was an appearance of Winston Churchill, on a then supersize 15-by-20-foot television screen, during M.I.T.'s 1949 Mid-Century Convocation.

President Harry Truman, unexpectedly detained in Washington by last-minute moves in the Senate to scuttle the Marshall Plan, wrote President Compton his regrets at not being able to come. Churchill, as the windup of his nine-day United States tour, did come, and so many sought tickets that M.I.T., which had opened the Convocation in the Rockwell Cage, presented Churchill to 14,000 in Boston Garden, but carried it all to 4,500, occupying every inch of Rockwell Cage. Television was still in its early stages, and, though millions heard Churchill's address by radio, far fewer saw it on television. This was Churchill's first appearance in the area since he got his honorary degree in 1943 at Sanders Theatre. The Institute gave him its first honorary lectureship. He had high praise for M.I.T. Great Britain, said its wartime savior, had suffered "by the lack of colleges of university rank in which engineering and the allied subjects are taught."

The displays of M.I.T. trophies demonstrate not only athletic prowess but an athletic system that emphasizes individuals participating in athletics beyond fielding teams, though M.I.T. engages in about all intercollegiate sports. The Du Pont Athletic Center provides offices for coaches, on its south, glassed side, and inner courts for all sorts of sports—squash, wrestling, fencing, archery, badminton, and more—besides a health and fitness center, all coed. From Du Pont lobby we go, by the west exit, to M.I.T.'s most recent Athletic Center, next building west of Briggs, dedicated in 1981 to M.I.T. generations past, present, and future, "who espouse the ancient ideal of a sound mind in a sound body." The spacious first floor can seat 4,000, is used for dances, concerts, and banquets, and converts to a hockey and skating rink in the winter. The stairs lead up to four tennis courts, with an indoor running track forming an oval around them.

Just west of the Athletic Center are the outdoor track and bleachers that the owner of the New York Yankees, George Steinbrenner, had dedicated in 1978 to his father, Henry G., a Great Lakes shipowner and track star while at M.I.T. Father Henry, with a "T" on his shirt, is shown, on a nearby plaque, nimbly clearing a hurdle.

We walk west on the river side of the hedge along the Steinbrenner track. Across the football and soccer field we see what the students call "the Bubble," a cover over indoor tennis courts, supported by compressed air. Jasper B. Carr, M.I.T. '16, who formally presented it to President Wiesner in 1971 as part of his class's 50th-reunion gift, played an exhibition match that day, first game in the Bubble, to the joy of his 1916 classmates.

We go through the hedge opening east of the Bubble, then between the outdoor tennis courts, with six clay courts on our left and six all-weather ones on our right, built with Du Pont funds, arriving in Amherst Alley, back of buildings along Memorial Drive.

On our left, particularly notice the building that is considered one of M.I.T.'s most unusual dorms, Baker House, built in 1949 and named for Dean of Students Everett M. Baker (1947–50), who was killed in a plane crash while on an international education mission. The twin exterior staircases, rising in ziggurat V form from the main entry to the upper floors, and also the roof, are all cantilevered. The architect, Alvar Aalto, an architecture professor at M.I.T. (1945–51), gave the river side of the building, as we will see, an equally unusual appearance.

A few strides along short Endicott Street take us to Memorial Drive. On either side of Endicott and in this area are a half dozen fraternity-dorm houses, the largest group of M.I.T. fraternities in Cambridge. The oldest of them, Sigma Chi of 1882, along with about two dozen others, are still across the Charles River in Boston. Greek letters on the buildings and fence doors proudly identify those on our walk.

Large Burton House, next on our right as we continue westward, the former Riverside Apartment Hotel (1927), was bought by M.I.T. in 1947. The three west units were named Burton Hall for Professor Alfred E. Burton, chosen M.I.T.'s first dean of students in 1902. While serving as dean for two decades he continued to teach topographical engineering, took students on an Arctic expedition with his lifelong friend and College mate, Admiral Robert E. Peary, and went on several M.I.T. expeditions to study solar eclipses. The two east units, at 420 Memorial Drive, were named Conner Hall for Arthur J. Conner, New Hampshire industrialist, M.I.T. 1888.

Buildings ahead of us from Fowler Street to Tang Tower bear out why students call the stretch from Massachusetts Avenue to Tang Tower "Dormitory Row." Recurrent raises in tuition during the 1960s did not cut growth in the M.I.T. community as it headed toward its current roughly 16,000 students, faculty, and staff. The rise in incoming freshmen at times led to utilizing lounges in Baker House and cots in main campus buildings.

Ahead of us, MacGregor House, with its nineteen-story tower, named for Frank S. MacGregor, M.I.T. '07, mining executive and large M.I.T. contributor, was added by 1970, New West Campus Houses by 1976, and 500 Memorial Drive in 1981. To accommodate more graduate students, the sixteen-floor Westgate Tower was ready by 1963, with nursery on the first floor and four three-story nearby buildings for graduate students with children. Some 550 single graduate students are accommodated in twenty-four-floor Tang Residence Hall, a 1973 structure, as dedication plates in English and Chinese relate, for the late great civic and industrial Hong Kong developer Ping Yuan Tang, M.I.T. '23.

Pierce Boathouse, on our right as we head down Memorial Drive, part of the big M.I.T. construction of the 1960s, is considered among the best in the nation. Completed in 1966, it was named for Harold W. Pierce, Boston financier and sportsman. Cases of cups, trophies, and bowls proclaim the achievements of the M.I.T. oarsmen, in particular the lightweight crew that in both 1954 and 1955 won the Thames Challenge Cup in England's Royal Henley Regatta. The lounge, outside balcony for onlookers, and the array below of eights, fours, pairs, and single sculls are impressive, but best of all, practice is possible in any season on an eight-person indoor rowing tank that keeps water flowing at a 10-mile-an-hour clip.

The serpentine shape of Aalto's Baker House, diagonally across the way, makes it possible for all riverfront residents to have views, up- or downriver, far more than would have been possible had Baker House been routinely parallel to the street. The two-story structure is a dining hall, with lounge on the upper level.

Green Hall, beside Baker on the corner of Danforth Street, was built in 1901 as a private hospital, served as M.I.T.'s infirmary from 1970 to 1982, and in 1983 became the University's first women graduate students' residence. It was named for Ida Green, wife of Cecil Green, M.I.T. '23, a founder of Texas Instruments, both generous donors whose most prominent gift, the Institute's tallest high-rise, we will shortly see on the main campus.

McCormick Hall, on the east side of Danforth Street, with its distinctive pair of high towers, was M.I.T.'s first dormitory for women students. It was named for the husband of its donor, Katherine Dexter McCormick, M.I.T. '04, wife of the youngest son of Cyrus McCormick, who invented the automatic reaper and founded International Harvester Company. West Tower was built in 1963 and East Tower in 1968, a few months after she died in Boston, where she had first financed an experimental dorm for M.I.T. women students, and willed to M.I.T. an estate that brought her gifts to M.I.T. in excess of $34,000,000.

The west side of the 1900 three-story building, 312 Memorial Drive, purchased in 1963 by M.I.T., provides quarters close to the Chapel for the M.I.T. Religious Counsellors Office. The east side, 311 Memorial Drive, affords a handy convenience for M.I.T.'s Nonresident Student Association, with lounge, kitchen for cooking, and dormitory beds for those working or studying too late to fit in their usual commute home.

Ashdown House, the six-floor graduate dorm with its big courtyard, was also built in 1900, the largest residential structure on the future West Campus, with the hope that the recently filled land would lead to duplication of Boston's fashionable Back Bay. Known later as Riverbank Court Hotel, it became M.I.T.'s in 1937, as its first on-campus graduate-student dorm. It was often used for major Cambridge events, especially a big banquet for the city's 75th anniversary in 1921 with Calvin Coolidge, less than two years before he took over the White House, the main speaker. Cal praised Cambridge as a center of learning, adding "That alone is civilization." In 1965, at the request of the resident students, it was named for popular chemistry teacher and its house master for nearly three decades, Dr. Avery A. Ashdown, M.I.T. Ph.D. '24.

ROAMING THE EAST CAMPUS, M.I.T.

We approach the East Campus along the river to enjoy the best-known, most impressive view of the central main building, with its lofty Pantheon-like dome and wide portico, flanked on both sides of the Great Court by the original 1916 wings.

Despite our entering the era of high-rise structures on both sides of the Charles River, their heights have, as even a quick glance will confirm, in no way upstaged the monumentality of the Maclaurin Buildings in the courtyard that began rising here in 1913 after the plan got the approval of the M.I.T. president for whom these structures were later named, Richard C. Maclaurin.

The architect, like those who created most of M.I.T.'s buildings, had been an M.I.T. architectural student, was Welles Bosworth, who was graduated in 1889 when only twenty years old. He went on to study in France, and would one day supervise reconstruction of the Versailles Palace and design many renowned buildings on both sides of the Atlantic. He took President Maclaurin to see Thomas Jefferson's use of the Pantheon as a model for Jefferson's University of Virginia design, and Maclaurin fully approved Bosworth's also, as Jefferson had done, putting a library, which we will see, high in the rotunda, just under the dome.

Fifty years later President Julius Stratton praised Bosworth as an "architectural genius" and the M.I.T. Corporation, in 1964, on the 75th anniversary of Bosworth's graduation, sent him a resolution crediting his creative vision with having "endowed the Institute with a grand and timeless design."

Several days of jubilation enlivened reunion week in June 1916, when M.I.T. moved to Cambridge. Ever since the turn of the century, cramped on its six Back Bay acres, the University had been talking of a bigger site. This expansion had become Maclaurin's goal from the moment of his inaugural seven years earlier. Then thirty-nine, he became the perfect leader for the task. Born in Scotland in 1870, son of a minister, he was reared in New Zealand, won scholarships as a math whiz to England's Cambridge University, took up law at Lincoln's Inn, became a professor in New Zealand's new Victoria College and dean of its law school, and came to New

York as Columbia's professor of mathematical physics in 1908, and in the following year to M.I.T. He personally, tirelessly led the campaign and solicited the money to pay for the land and the new buildings.

Future President Franklin D. Roosevelt, then Assistant Secretary of the Navy, headed the official reviewing group of power boats, part of a flotilla of craft of all sizes covering the basin, which was surrounded on shore and the Harvard Bridge by crowds of enthusiastic onlookers. The official M.I.T. seal in a gold box and the charter in a gilded chest were borne across the river in a highly ornamental copy of a Venetian state barge, the *Bucentaur,* with Tech flag flying and Mother Technology at the prow with her torch of Progress. Bands played, firecrackers and rockets flared, crowds cheered. On June 14th, the final dedication day, the Great Court was jammed with dignitaries on stands along one side, alumni along the other, and speakers on a platform forward of the colonnade. Maclaurin, in the scarlet gown and gold tassels of his doctorate, dedicated the buildings "to strengthen American industry . . . by fixing it firmly on the solid rock of science."

The two smaller courts, behind the flagpoles, Du Pont Court on our left and Lowell Court on our right, were named for two of the Institute's great benefactors. When Maclaurin, seeking funds to buy the land, was turned down by an eminent fellow Scotsman who was deeply immersed in financing a Pennsylvania college, he sought support from a leading member of the Du Pont family, T. Coleman Du Pont. Du Pont, whose family had sent generations of its youths to study here, all of them generous donors to their alma mater, provided, as we have related, most of the immediate land cost. Du Pont's farsighted insistence that M.I.T. get at least forty-five acres seemed an ample provision then, yet now, not many years later, the University has three times that amount of land.

Harvard President A. Lawrence Lowell, member of the M.I.T. Corporation from 1896 to his death in 1943, spoke at the 1916 dedication in praise of M.I.T. for rendering "a public service with which the world cannot dispense." Lowell Court, faced on three of its sides mainly by the mathematics department, was named in honor of his father, Augustus Lowell, M.I.T. Corporation member from 1873 for nearly three decades and a generous M.I.T. benefactor. On his father's death, Lowell, in 1900, with his brothers and sisters, gave the school a big, new Boston laboratory building, named for their father, to house in 1902 the growing department that would become M.I.T.'s famous and largest, Electrical Engineering, which had already mushroomed from the pioneer engineering classes M.I.T. had started two decades earlier in the thrilling infancy of electric lights and telephones.

The names of Du Pont and Lowell were carved on the original frieze over the central entries at the head of their respective courts, to put them among the world's top scientists, whose names we see cut similarly around wings of the Great Court: Darwin, Da Vinci, Newton, Franklin, and many more.

Small metal plaques on the ground tell about the artists and the titles of the sculptures mounted near the flagpoles: Henry Moore's *Three Piece Reclining Figure* and Michael Heizer's polished pink granite forms. Both, like most other contemporary art we will see around the campus, are part of M.I.T.'s art collection, which was very actively advanced by President James R. Killian, Jr. during his administration in the 1950s. These beautifully located works frequently appeal to more than just eyes, for youngsters love to clamber on them and students, in fine weather, can be seen sunning themselves or reading while perched on a slab of pink prehistoric granite.

To see where an already legendary M.I.T. math genius looked out on Lowell Court from his office, go right on the asphalt path past the flagpole to the south side of the court. Inventor of Cybernetics and father of automation, short, stocky Norbert Wiener long had his office on the second floor, Room 272. Its window is part of the second tall one from Lowell Court's east corner. The son of a Harvard professor, Wiener was graduated from Tufts in 1909 when fifteen, got his Harvard Ph.D. in math when eighteen, taught at Harvard, and joined the M.I.T. math staff at twenty-five.

Tales linger, too, of Wiener the absent-minded professor. One day he was heading down the staircase near his office and suddenly turned around to answer a question. "Forgetting where he was," recalled a colleague, "he turned back and stepped off into space. Lucky Norbert! He broke only an arm."

On the northwest corner of the court, M.I.T. has paid special honor to its first woman graduate, Ellen H. Swallow, M.I.T. 1873, who had been "cautiously" accepted as a science student after her graduation from Vassar in 1870. She was named M.I.T.'s first woman instructor, and headed the department of sanitary chemistry from 1884 to her death in 1911. While becoming an expert in the new field of public sanitation she worked with and married chemistry Professor Robert H. Richards, M.I.T. 1868, M.I.T.'s first class, and the first alumnus to be an M.I.T. teacher. Bronze likeness and portrait, and photos of Ellen Swallow and her times, are just inside the lobby of the entry under chemist Lavoisier's name on the frieze. This lobby, named for her, was in chemistry's first 1916 quarters before most of the department was shifted in recent years to bigger buildings that we will see.

The photo showing Ellen Swallow, the only woman on the chemistry staff, pinpoints dramatic changes and why M.I.T., in 1985, rewrote the Tech tune "Arise Ye sons of M.I.T." (Now it is "Arise all ye of M.I.T.") Ellen Swallow opened the earlier door wider when, in 1876, she took charge of the special Women's Laboratory. Katherine Dexter McCormack's 1963 gift of McCormack Hall led to nearly doubling women's enrollment four years later to 400 when she added the Hall's East Tower. By 1985, President Paul E. Gray, speaking of the need to increase M.I.T.'s endowment as it reached its 125th anniversary, announced that for the first time, women on the M.I.T. faculty exceeded 100 and women made up 30 percent of the undergraduate body.

We now use the corresponding entry on the west side of the Great Court, under chemist Faraday's name on the frieze, to go along the corridor and down the short flight of stairs (between Buildings 1 and 5) to the 33 Massachusetts Avenue exit. Save for the two buildings on our right, Pratt and Rogers, and even they in part, the many buildings of the East Campus frontage along Massachusetts Avenue are units of the M.I.T. School of Engineering. Pratt and Rogers are the seat of M.I.T.'s School of Architecture and Planning. So too is the Visual Studies Center across the avenue at the corner of Amherst Street, a small 1936 one-story structure, predecessor of the big Tech Coop we saw in the Student Center, which was bought by M.I.T. and renovated in 1967 for the new Center, with two-story-high studio rooms to catch the natural light loved by artists.

Plaques tell about the old 1,800-pound anchors from World War II navy ships on either side of the steps to the Pratt Building, which, in 1920, was the first addition to the original 1916 buildings. Charles H. Pratt, Boston lawyer and bachelor, who died in 1912, delighted President Maclaurin with the gift of his estate to build and endow M.I.T.'s Department of Naval Architecture and Marine Engineering. The entry, between the big anchors, is usually closed to allow more space for the Hart Nautical Museum, which we will presently visit.

Watching the heavy flow of students, invariably moving rapidly in and out of the Rogers Building, brings contrastingly to mind the entry M.I.T.'s founder wrote in his diary after he assembled the first class. "Fifteen students entered. May not this prove a memorable day." Eight more enrollees quickly joined. Growth of the student body was pretty steady, but even in 1938, when architect Bosworth's role in this design gave it the imperishable, classical beauty of his larger portico in the Great Court, the enrollment was far less than currently, and most of Briggs Field was still open land.

Nowadays Rogers Building is, even officially, called M.I.T.'s "main entrance." Entering through the three pairs of tall, fluted Ionic columns of the portico and arriving in a lobby rising three floors to a lofty dome can be a truly impressive experience. Students call the Rogers lobby and the long corridor ahead "the Main Drag." It is emphatically the campus crossroads, as affirmed by the crowds and the activities, bulletin boards, large size, lighted campus wall map, banners hanging from the top balcony proclaiming shows, student doings, a blood donation, or a United Fund drive, and a standby counter for hot cups of coffee and snacks.

The memorial bronze, on the north wall, presents a likeness of the Institute's founder, William Barton Rogers, who died in 1882 at seventy-seven. Rogers, member of a prominent family of educators, literally devoted his life to creating and keeping alive a school of technology. After suffering a stroke at a faculty meeting, Rogers turned over the presidency to his dear friend and fellow professor, John Runkle, in 1870. And when Runkle, also worn by the University's financial strains, resigned, Rogers, though weak and ill, resumed the presidency in 1878 during the period that Dean Samuel C. Prescott, in his history of *Boston Tech,* called "the Institute's darkest hour." Rogers had done so provided that $100,000, a sum that seemed gigantic in M.I.T.'s leanest days, could be raised. Three years later he had found and picked a successor, a great leader, General Francis A. Walker.

Joy turned to grief at the May 30, 1882 graduation exercises, at which Walker was to be inaugurated, when Rogers, about to hand out diplomas in old Rogers Building's crowded Huntington Hall, suddenly stopped speaking, drooped, and, as Walker related, "fell to the platform instantly dead."

Immediately on our right, as we entered the Rogers lobby, is the information center, with free maps and other helpful publications. Visitors will quickly become aware that students most often call buildings by their number rather than their name. This custom is an outgrowth of M.I.T.'s "linkage" corridors, and even tunnels, interconnecting the buildings so that students can get most speedily from one to another, a special blessing in stormy or winter weather. The maps explain a typical number like 7-238, which gives first the building number, then the floor, after the dash, followed by the room number. The code 7-238 means Rogers Building, second floor, room 38, which is the architectural library that we will presently see.

Next after the Information Center is the office of the official newspaper, *Tech Talk,* distributed by the M.I.T. administration since 1957. A short way farther along the corridor is the Hart Nautical Museum, where we can see yacht plans of famous designers Nathaniel G. Herreshoff, M.I.T. 1870, and George Owen, M.I.T. 1894, who created many of America's Cup challengers, along with numerous ship models. Beautifully mounted, the models range over the centuries, including Viking vessels, Commodore Stephen Decatur's famous last flagship, Donald McKay's great Yankee clipper, *Flying Cloud,* renowned whaler *Charles S. Morgan,* and modern guided-missile destroyers.

We return to the Rogers lobby and the elevator, in the northeast corner in back of one of the pedestals still awaiting a statue. The Architecture department, formed in 1868, developed from the nation's first college architectural course when M.I.T. began. Called the School of Architecture since 1932, it utilized the Old Rogers Building in Boston until it moved here to the newly completed Rogers Building in 1938. At the time of moving, William Emerson, a relative of author Ralph Waldo Emerson's family, had been dean of architecture for nearly twenty years. Among his bequests was his Brattle Street mansion, now headquarters of the Cambridge Historical Society.

The dean's office is forward on the second floor, and beside it (the 7-238 room mentioned above) is the library for architecture and planning. A giant white plaster head of Michelangelo's colossal David can be seen even before we enter. Just above this library, on the third floor, are its visual collections. And, on the fourth floor around the dome that we saw in the lobby, are students' studios and classrooms, their tables loaded with models and walls covered with architectural plans.

We start now along "the infinite corridor" that, following M.I.T. linkage, traverses seven connecting buildings to the exit we can see at the far end. All along it we will find bulletins, artwork, many interesting photos, and extensive information about M.I.T.'s history and prominent figures, exhibits from the M.I.T. Museum's historical collection.

The clock over the entry to the corridor honoring Harvard President Lowell, a gift from Lowell Institute School alumni, recalls that Lowell Institute relieved some of President Rogers's financial worries by starting in 1872 to pay an annual rental, which it continued for half a century, to hold its free lectures in Boston Tech's old Huntington Hall.

Shortly, on our left and opposite a stairwell, we come to an opening, flanked by two fluted Doric columns, which leads to another Project Athena computer setup. This gathering of machines occupies part of the first floor of a four-story wing in the original building that was erected in 1928, also to Bosworth's design, and named the Homberg Building, an infirmary providing emergency aid until 1982, when superseded by the large Health Service Center that we will see later. Twenty-one-year-old Richard M. Homberg, M.I.T. '23, engineering senior, sports editor of the *Tech,* member of the swimming team and senior crew, died from pneumonia when the shell in which he was competing for the Richards Cup foundered after a crash. His parents were major contributors for the building, now mostly occupied by information systems for all the Institute's computers.

An apple falling on the head of mathematician Isaac Newton, according to Voltaire's tale, led to Newton's discovering the law of gravity. As a gift from the National Bureau of Standards, M.I.T. has a "direct descendant" of Newton's apple tree. Currently it stands about a dozen feet high in a graceful, small park reached by a flight of steps just outside the next opening on our left, again opposite a stairwell. The Newton tree stands at the end of a diagonal path, to the left of the big Oklahoma redbud tree in a stone-edged square, a central feature of the park where students, in good weather, love to lounge, eat lunch, or chat with their friends.

On our left, we go past an attractive meeting room, once part of the laboratory of Vannevar Bush, whose large, five-story building named in honor of this renowned American leader, we will presently visit, and on to the grand lobby of the Maclaurin Building. This is M.I.T.'s memorial center to the Institute's men who gave their lives in our nation's wars. Their names are inscribed on the walls, and for those who made the supreme sacrifice in Korea, 1950–53, and Vietnam, 1965–73, on plaques beside the doors that open on the Great Court and the most magnificent river view on the campus. The 1916 dedication to President Maclaurin, on the east wall, for establishing M.I.T. "in this more ample home," contrasts emphatically when we recall that M.I.T. had left in Boston only seven buildings, the well-known Rogers and Walker Buildings on Boylston Street and, a block away on Clarendon Street just east of the present Trinity Church, the big Lowell and four smaller engineering labs.

In June 1974, the Great Court was renamed Killian Court to honor the first M.I.T. graduate to serve as its president, James R. Killian, Jr., M.I.T. '26, president 1949–1958. Killian was the first science adviser to the White House, serving President Eisenhower (1957–59), handled administration of M.I.T.'s famous wartime Rad (Radiation) Lab that we will see on our next walk, and chaired a national commission that made him known as "the father of public television" for his securing it federal support.

Booths and desks in the lobby, lined up along the path of the busy "infinite corridor," are more student activities, varied as those we saw in the Rogers lobby. Thought is so untrammeled in this United States center of scientific research that it has hosted booths for those who hold antinuke views as mankind advances into the Nuclear Age.

The corridor on the lobby's north side leads past the elevators to the Alumni Center and the Margaret Hutchinson Compton Gallery, part of the M.I.T. Museum, named for the wife of M.I.T. President Karl Compton. Her portrait is on the wall outside the gallery that offers changing exhibits relating to academic activities. As we approach the gallery, we see on our right the office of *Technology Review,* published by the Alumni Association since 1899, one of the best eyewitness sources of M.I.T. history. The wall display, on our right en route to Compton Gallery, is from the Museum's historical collection and among the very best in any of the corridor presentations. It is also a permanent display, presenting the Institute and M.I.T. leaders from earliest days.

Besides courtesy and helpful information, the Alumni Center has other fine attractions, along with a huge metal beaver nipping a stump and a large portrait of President Jerome Wiesner. In the office of the alumni's executive vice president, its permanent director, is a bust of President Killian and a large portrait of the first president of the alumni, big, athletic, much-beloved "Uncle Bobby" Robert H. Richards, active in M.I.T.'s growth until his death at the age of 101 years. He was the M.I.T. instructor who became the husband of Ellen H. Swallow, first M.I.T. woman graduate.

To see some of M.I.T.'s main buildings, use one of the handy elevators. On the second floor, Room 10-250 between the elevators, nostalgically named for old Boston Tech's Huntington Hall, is the largest lecture room in this complex of buildings, a theatrelike room with 525 seats rising from the speaker's platform with its tiers of big blackboards. A short way west on the same corridor, Room 3-208, with its view of Killian Court, is the president's office. Through the door's window, especially brilliant when sun is streaming in from the courtyard, is Thomas Hart Benton's industrial painting, which he made in 1945 as part of the many paintings commissioned by Standard Oil Company, and as a gift to M.I.T., significantly advancing its collection of modern art.

Emma Rogers, wife of M.I.T.'s founder and daughter of a wealthy Boston banker, devoted both herself and her fortune to M.I.T. until her death in 1911. Her portrait can be seen across from the elevator on the third floor. Go to the left from the elevator, on the fourth floor, and you arrive in "Strobe Alley," dedicated to the developer of stroboscopic light and its miraculously fast photography, Harold E. "Doc" Edgerton, M.I.T. '27. Currently in his eighties, and when not traveling, he still comes to give lectures or experiment in microscopic photography in his nearby lab that, in earlier days, was in famous Building 20, the old "Rad Lab" that we will see. Pictures on view, in particular the crownlike splash of a drop of milk, or exploratory underwater photography, are from M.I.T.'s historical collection. On the fifth floor the giant M.I.T. School of Engineering, with its nine big departments, has its engineering library, with its loungelike central reading section right under the Great Dome, which rises 138 feet from the campus. The dome ceiling above the library, supported around the circular sides by two dozen pilasters and Corinthian columns, is a lofty 42 feet above the library floor.

We go back through the Rogers Building lobby to see the remaining buildings on the Massachusetts Avenue frontage of the main campus. Most of these structures north of Rogers and Maclaurin are specialized laboratories that developed within M.I.T.'s School of Engineering. This campus area might well be called Sloanland, for M.I.T.'s greatest financial benefactor, Alfred P. Sloan, Jr., M.I.T. 1895. Sloan was so young when he passed his M.I.T. entrance exams that he was refused admission until he was seventeen, and was graduated at twenty. At twenty-six he headed a manufacturing concern, and when it became part of General Motors he went on to run that and made it the world's largest industrial corporation.

The five-story cement and glass Center for Advanced Engineering, next on our right at 105 Massachusetts Avenue, was opened in 1967, the year after Sloan, ninety years of age, died. Former President Killian, then M.I.T. Corporation chairman, said that Sloan had proposed this "pioneering center," and Sloan's foundation financed it for professional scientists and technical managers to research or catch up on new technologies. The black metal working model of Alexander Calder's *Big Sail* on the front terrace, gift of President and Mrs. Stratton, is a preview of the big Calder we will see in midcampus. The Center here was the building completing this side of the main campus from the river to Vassar Street.

The Guggenheim Building, next on our right, center of M.I.T.'s Aeronautics and Astronautics Research, was built in 1928 through the generosity of the head of the Guggenheim international mining empire, Daniel Guggenheim, who had become interested in aviation through his son's serving as a naval pilot in World War I. To promote aviation and rocketry, the then unrecognized route to the space age, Guggenheim financed Charles Lindbergh's tour of all forty-eight states after his *Spirit of St. Louis* was the first to fly across the Atlantic. He also financed for years Robert H. Goddard, United States pioneer in rocketry, and sponsored research in eight colleges, including M.I.T.

Guggenheim, who died in 1930, would certainly feel his hopes fully realized, for it was this building that saw the beginnings of M.I.T.'s famous Instrumentation Lab, and it was here that Charles S. "Doc" Draper, M.I.T. '26, who invented the guidance mechanisms that would land the Apollo mission on the moon in 1969, had his lab and became head of this department in 1951, where he had started as a research assistant in 1929. On our next walk we will include the world-famous Draper Lab, where he still carries on his research, the former Instrumentation Lab, which he had run along with the Aeronautics Department that under him in 1959 added space-age courses in astronautics. The library, with access to worldwide sources of information, occupies most of the third floor. Research labs, studying space systems, lasers, computation dynamics, and much more, not only use this building but have quarters in five of its immediate neighbors.

The impressive text of the Memorial Stone on the five-story corner building, the Sloan Metals Processing Lab, built in 1952, is only a partial list of his gifts up to that year, which also included professorships and scholarships. A penthouse atop this laboratory, intended for a lounge, is often pressed into use as a conference room. We return now to head via the passageway under the Center for Advanced Engineering, raised on stilts. On our right is the Bush Building, to which we will return, and immediately on our left are the 1952 Wright Brothers Wind Tunnel and more Sloan Laboratories. The latter, beginning as an automotive lab in 1922, has expanded through additions to include research labs on fuel energy, gas turbines, and aircraft.

Turn left, and ahead of us with the roadway under it to Vassar Street, is the six-floor Microsystems Technology Lab that, in 1985, replaced M.I.T.'s computer servicing center, for which it was built in 1968, and which, as we saw, was shifted to the Homberg Building. The building on its west side, built in 1969, furnishes laboratories and offices for the Center for Space Research, x-ray and infrared astronomy, cosmic rays, and interplanetary vehicles, involving several M.I.T. departments. The tall white tanks on the Center's east side, with protective fencing for their liquid oxygen, nitrogen, and argon, were installed for work in the new Microsystems System Laboratory.

Partly back of the tanks and eastward of them are three buildings of the large Electrical Engineering and Computer Science Department. Originally there were the six-story West and the eight-story East units of the Fairchild Building, connected by glass walkways. When erected in 1973 these were the largest M.I.T. complex built since 1916.

They were the gift of Sherman M. Fairchild, only son of a founder of IBM Corporation, inventor of the famed Fairchild aerial cameras and many innovations in airplanes, who had died two years earlier. The Research Laboratory of Electronics was created in 1946 to succeed, and take over, the invaluable equipment of the World War II Rad Lab, the incubator of microwave radar.

The two Fairchild units were linked in 1983 by the EG & G Education Center, with its three-story atrium on the Vassar Street side and with a five-story building, erected in a former courtyard, which has a 325-seat auditorium, large conference room, and labs and classrooms for teaching electronics and computer science. The initials EG & G stand for three M.I.T. College-mates in electrical engineering, named on the plaque outside the auditorium, who formed a lasting friendship and, in 1947, EG & G Inc., known for its electronic creations. Of "Doc" Edgerton, whose activities we saw in "Strobe Alley," his wife at the 1983 dedication in the atrium said she soon learned after her marriage that "Doc had another love—M.I.T." She added, however, that it has been "a happy triangle."

Before leaving the Center, look near the elevator bank in Fairchild's east lobby for a most unusual bust of Sherman M. Fairchild, in electroplated steel. It is like a partial sketch in fragments of metal, yet there he is, smiling!

On going back to the Bush Building we have on our left, along with the two-story one (Building 12) just to its south—two structures started early in World War II with government funds, to serve the fast-growing Rad Lab. They now have mixed use, though mainly for labs, offices, and classrooms. The one-story structure we are passing is the Laboratory for Nuclear Sciences, mainly for pure research in nuclear physics.

In the big lobby of the five-story 1965 Bush Building, Center for Materials Science and Engineering, is a fine likeness of Vannevar Bush, a clergyman's son, Tufts '13 and Harvard–M.I.T. '16 doctorate, happily at work while smoking his pipe. A colleague describes him in one of the original two-story labs, now part of the Bush Room that we saw earlier, working on a pioneer computer, his 100-ton differential analyzer. Seeming strange in this era of portable computers there was a big crane to pick up the analyzer's heavy machinery. Bush was also a successful businessman; together with his Tufts roommate in 1922, he set up the highly successful Raytheon Company.

Bush had become an M.I.T. associate professor in 1919 and went on to be dean of M.I.T. Engineering (1932–38) before leaving to head Carnegie Institution. In 1957 he became chairman of the M.I.T. Corporation and served the University for years, coming in regularly from his home in Belmont, until his death in 1974 at eighty-four. Bush has been most honored for having mobilized the scientific resources of the nation in the World War II crisis and, still more, for organizing production of the atomic bomb that promptly ended that war.

We go up the steps to the right of Bush's picture, past the Alumni Center, to the Maclaurin lobby.

EAST CAMPUS: EASTMAN TO EASTGATE

Resuming our walk eastward along the "Main Drag" we come to a long corridor that goes, on our left, to Buildings 12 and 24, which we passed, and on our right all the way to the Ellen Swallow lobby. We turn right along it and shortly, a couple of doors down on the left, we come to Room 4-133, a welding lab, but one of the most famous sites in the original 1916 building complex.

Here began M.I.T.'s Radiation Lab, on Armistice Day in 1940, as recounted by President Julius Stratton, who headed its successor, the Research Lab of Electronics, mainly occupying the big Fairchild Building that we just saw. A lot of two-story labs for big machinery, boilers, and dynamos used to be in these old wings, but they were floored over for classrooms in the 1970s. Students researching here, in quarters that led to modern radar and microwaves, enjoy inheriting the Rad Labs balcony (they call it "mezzanine" for storage) and "lots of power," a 480-volt bus bar carrying heavy current to electric circuits. From one room, the Rad Lab spread into acres of space in World War II for thousands of scientists, researchers, and trainees, based on Building 20, which we will presently see.

We return to the "Main Drag," turn right into the Eastman Laboratories, go along a corridor that extends all the way to the Math wing on the riverside wing, where we saw Norbert Wiener's office. Built in 1933, Eastman Labs are the center of the multibuilding School of Science that embraces seven departments, with labs—mainly physics and some chemistry—classrooms, and the school dean's and other offices in Eastman. About a third of the way along the corridor we enter an ornate lobby where, on the west wall outside the big, tiered lecture hall, is a bronze memorial to George Eastman (1854–1932), the "Friend of M.I.T." for whom the building was named.

After President Maclaurin got some funds to purchase the M.I.T. site he had next to acquire still more to erect buildings. In that crisis, Eastman, the inventor who revolutionized photography with his Kodak camera, was indeed M.I.T.'s friend, though for years anonymously. George Eastman, who believed, he said, that "the progress of the world depends almost entirely upon education," had quit school himself at fourteen to help his widowed mother support the family. He started as a $3-a-week office boy, later worked in a bank. At twenty-three he took up photography as a hobby, used the kitchen of his mother's boarding house as a lab, came up with an idea to replace the heavy, bulky photographic plates of that era. In 1888, only eight years later, he brought out his first camera.

By the turn of the century Eastman was devoting his fortune to helping education. He was not in Rochester when Maclaurin, on a tour of cities seeking donors, spoke there in 1912, but Eastman's plant manager, an M.I.T. graduate, wrote Maclaurin that Eastman "was inclined to help." They met in a New York City hotel and Maclaurin outlined his plans for the Institute. How much would that cost, asked Eastman. Two and a half million dollars, replied Maclaurin, whereupon, as Dean of Science Prescott reports in his *Boston Tech* that Mrs. Maclaurin had told him, Eastman quickly responded, "I'll send you a draft." There was one firm condition: Eastman must be known only as Mr. Smith.

That condition held for eight years. Meantime, when building firm foundations on filled land (for sensitive scientific instruments) boosted costs, Eastman sent along another $500,000. Eventually his gifts to M.I.T. would exceed $19,000,000. To finance M.I.T.'s post–World War I expansion, Maclaurin was busy again raising money. Eastman this time gave $4,000,000 in stock, which meant his name would have to be disclosed. Maclaurin got consent and wrote a speech for an alumni gathering in January 1920, to announce the drive's success but was unable, at the last minute, to attend. Coleman Du Pont, president of the alumni and a $1,000,000 donor to this drive, read Maclaurin's disclosure of the name. Ailing Maclaurin, only forty-nine years old, died of pneumonia a few days later. Eastman, who would give to education all his estate, said he considered M.I.T. "the greatest institution of its kind in the world."

The names of great scientists on the lobby's walls seem an appropriate setting in which to record that physicist William Shockley, M.I.T. '36, was the first graduate to share, in 1956, in a Nobel Prize for inventing the transistor, a device controlling the flow of electricity. In the three decades following Shockley's achievement M.I.T. graduates or faculty members brought the total to fifteen; of these, seven were in physics and two in chemistry.

Continuing south along the corridor we come, on our left, to an entry that students have decorated with lighthearted murals depicting elephants amid technology in a lush jungle. The glassed linkage leads to the Institute's central library, Hayden Memorial, dedicated in 1950, honoring alumni president and extensive benefactor Charles Hayden, M.I.T. 1890, a Boston financier who started as a ticker-tape (stock-market) boy and at twenty-one was a founder of Hayden, Stone & Company, which grew to be a Wall Street financial giant. On entering Hayden we have on our right the former Hayden Art Gallery, which was opened in 1950 through the efforts of President Killian in order to include art—an early desire of founder Rogers—among M.I.T.'s disciplines. The gallery was moved to much larger quarters, as we will see, when the resplendent new Arts and Media Building honoring another staunch patron of the humanities, President Jerome Wiesner, was opened in 1984.

Walking past the inner courtyard, with its bronze sculptures by Jacques Lipchitz, we have in the south, riverside wing, the Science Library occupying the main floor and the Humanities Library the upper floor. Notice the big portrait of Killian, on the left on entering the Science Library, which is handy to the numerous nearby scientific departmental buildings into which M.I.T. has expanded. The Humanities Library serves these disciplines located, in large part, in the upper floors of the north wing. Rows of drawers in the Humanities Library contain the Institute catalogue for all M.I.T. library books. Beyond it, near a window, is a bronze head of Iris created by Auguste Rodin and, through an entry to the east wing, the quite modern Women's Studies Program.

Going now along the first floor North Corridor, beside the inner courtyard, we come to another section of M.I.T. Archives that, beyond documents of M.I.T. history, particularly handles special collections and manuscript works of M.I.T. alumni, students, and faculty. Farther along this corridor, on our right, is the comfortable music library. Coming out the exit of the music lobby, we get a close-up view of the campus, dominated by I. M. Pei's twenty-one-story 1964 Earth Sciences Building. On our right is another creation of Lipchitz, *Birth of the Muses.* Before visiting Walker Memorial, we take the path beside Hayden to the river to see the sailing pavilion across from Hayden. Be cautious of traffic moving along Memorial Drive.

The sailing pavilion, built in 1937, is a monument to M.I.T.'s using sailing as a recreation. While the pavilion was being built, M.I.T. was assured the nation's largest collegiate yachting activity, with three dozen 12½-foot Tech dinghies that can be handled as sloops or catboats, a creation mainly of Professor George Owen, M.I.T. 1894, whose plans we saw in Hart Nautical Museum. The dinghies were built for M.I.T. at the famous Herreshoff yards. Illustrious yachtsman Walter C. "Jack" Wood, M.I.T. '17, came back to M.I.T. in 1936 to be director of sailing, a role he filled until he retired, at seventy, in 1964. He was also Master of nearby Senior House. Nowadays, six types of craft are widely used, and in 1976 the pavilion was renamed in honor of M.I.T.'s first, ever-popular sailing master, "Jack" Wood.

Walker Memorial, with its dignified Doric Portico, was built in 1917 by the alumni as a memorial gift to one of M.I.T.'s greatest presidents, its third, Francis A. Walker, who had been chosen as a successor by President Rogers. Walker, like Rogers, died suddenly in 1897 after serving for sixteen years, and the bereaved alumni began fund raising right after the funeral. Construction was delayed by plans to move to Cambridge. Walker, son of a college professor, a Civil War volunteer at twenty-one, was severely wounded at the Battle of Chancellorsville, and came out of the war as a brevet brigadier general at twenty-five. He held many important federal positions, won renown as an economist, and had been a professor at Yale for seven years before coming to Old Tech in Boston in 1881.

Under Walker's guidance, with his establishing Electrical Engineering in 1882 and Chemical Engineering in 1888, the Boston Tech went on to be a national institution, with its student body quadrupled to 1,200 and the faculty tripled. Early years of his presidency were difficult financially, and he had to devote much anxious time to fund raising. Largest gift of his presidency and, up to that time for M.I.T., was the $750,000 bequeathed in 1896 by Henry L. Pierce, twice mayor of Boston, member of the M.I.T. Corporation, who developed the well-known Walter Baker chocolate mills in Dorchester. Walker, stricken by apoplexy when only fifty-six, died before seeing the urgently needed construction that Pierce's will financed. Building 1, the riverside southwest wing of Maclaurin complex, was named in 1917, in Pierce's memory, the Pierce Engineering Laboratory. In the Museum we saw, along with Walker's medals and uniform, the bust by Daniel Chester French that the alumni commissioned right after Walker died.

Walker Memorial reflects earlier times, when the East Campus was intended for dormitories and student activities. Walker Memorial was to have been a student center with "Walker Gym" on the third, top floor. The main floor still provides a dining room, now second largest to the present Student Center. The top floor is set up for basketball courts, but often is pressed into use as a classroom. The big mural on the dining room's north wall was presented by Edwin H. Blashfield, M.I.T. 1869, depicting homage to alma mater in glory immediately above M.I.T.'s complex by the Charles.

On leaving Walker memorial by the north exit we enter McDermott Court, with its gigantic 40-foot-high black metal stabile of Alexander Calder's *Big Sail*, a gift in 1966 of Eugene McDermott, a founder and head of Texas Instruments, life member of M.I.T. Corporation, who, with his wife, established in 1960 M.I.T.'s largest endowed scholarship fund. On the east side of the court, but with their entries facing eastward toward a similar 1924 block of dorms built by architect Bosworth, is a 1931 row of dorms called East Campus Alumni Houses, though used for undergraduate housing. They all have lounges, kitchens for those who wish to do their own cooking, and laundries.

The central Earth Sciences Building is flanked on two sides by modern laboratory buildings constructed after the Earth Sciences Building, two of them also by I. M. Pei. On the west side the five-story Dreyfus Building, designed by Pei, was dedicated in 1970 by M.I.T. President Johnson, who commented on how the chemistry department has grown remarkably since it started in old Boston Tech with a faculty of two. This is the department that enrolled the first woman student, Ellen Swallow, and in which she became the first woman instructor. Camille Édouard Dreyfus headed Celanese Corporation of America, which grew from his development of cellulose textiles and plastics. The building's exterior corridors make interesting walks. Nobel laureate Har G. Khorana, professor of biology and chemistry, has had his office-lab on the northeast corner of Dreyfus fifth floor since he came to M.I.T. when the building was new.

To the north of the Earth Sciences Building is the 1965 Whitaker Building that, with the Dorrance Building joined to it on its west end, comprises the eight-story Center for Life Sciences, with labs and classrooms devoted chiefly to biology. Uncas A. Whitaker, M.I.T. '23, international manufacturer of electrical components, with his wife Helen, both life members of the M.I.T. Corporation, have been among the Institute's foremost benefactors, in medicine also, as we will presently see. Nobel laureate Salvador E. Luria, who directed M.I.T.'s Center for Cancer Research, now emeritus, has his office-lab diagonally across the areaway from Khorana on the fourth floor of the Whitaker Building. Dorrance Building, dedicated in 1953, was a gift from John T. Dorrance, M.I.T. 1895, who developed the revolutionary idea of condensed soup, began as a chemist in his uncle's canning factory and went on to build one of the world's largest canning firms, Campbell Soup Company, of which he was president. The Department of Nutrition and Food Science is quartered in Dorrance.

Just to the east of Whitaker is the 1976 Landau Chemical Engineering Building, designed by I. M. Pei and named for prominent scientist Ralph Landau, M.I.T. '41, who, in 1946, founded his own high-technology and process-development company. The University's first course in chemical engineering (1888) was the humble origin of the five floors of extensive labs, classrooms, and offices devoted here to teaching and research. A lecture hall is on the first floor and a lounge on the floor above. Landau, triangular in shape, is the eastern end of M.I.T.'s linkage system that makes available covered passageways and corridors all the way from Ames Street westward to the grand lobby of the Rogers Building, the exit on Massachusetts Avenue.

Paramount in all the midcampus, of course, is the Earth Sciences

Building, named for another member of the famed M.I.T. class of 1923, Cecil H. Green, distinguished for his use all over the globe of geology and geophysics to locate oil, a founder of Texas Instruments, and for his wife, Ida, donor of Green Hall, which we saw on West Campus. A 300-seat lecture hall on the first floor was named for Eugene McDermott, close friend and colleague of Green in Texas Instruments.

McDermott not only gave the giant Calder but had the site beautified as the approach to the Green Building. Although the building appears to be apart from M.I.T.'s linkage system, actually it is not, for it is connected by underground, basementlike corridors or tunnels to its neighbors, Dreyfus, Whitaker, and, via Dreyfus, to Hayden Library. Only Walker Memorial, in this part of the campus, has no linkage.

The directory, beside the elevators in the east entry, tells succinctly about the large number of disciplines gathered in the labs and offices of the Green Building—among them, earth, atmospheric, and planetary science, along with meteorology and oceanography. A library serving all these fields is on the second floor. The elevator bank indicates eighteen floors, but two floors above these accommodate mechanical equipment, and on the twenty-first, the roof, are two spheres or radomes of the meteorology department. One is the big, white sphere we have easily seen from the ground, actually a protective plastic cover for an 18-foot radar dish, and the other sphere, near the roof's southeast corner and far less conspicuous, shelters an 8-foot weather dish from wind and storm.

Leaving Green Building from its north exit, we go diagonally left to the Whitaker lobby, opposite the north end of Dreyfus. We continue from the lobby to Compton Court on the north side of Whitaker.

On our right is the three-story tan brick structure of the Alumni Swimming Pool, a 1940 gift from the alumni. It was located here, originally with a clear view to the Charles River, before development of athletics, like dorms, was shifted to the West Campus. It has its trophies, but the large pool (there is also an adjoining small pool) is old 75-foot Olympic size, though very attractive. Eight squash courts were added in 1943 and it has locker rooms, showers, and other facilities.

Straight ahead, the three-story, sprawling wooden building with many wings—neighbors of the resplendent labs to which they paved the way—comprised the famous old Rad Lab of World War II, which we will visit shortly. And on our left, the main structure on Compton Court, is the five-story Compton Laboratories (1957), named in memory of M.I.T. President Karl Taylor Compton, and, until his death in 1954, chairman of the M.I.T. Corporation. President Killian, his successor, tells how these labs, too, were "made possible" by M.I.T.'s munificent benefactor Alfred P. Sloan, Jr., M.I.T. 1895.

Like nearby Fairchild Building, Compton Labs have components of the Research Laboratory of Electronics (RLE), but are mainly labs, offices, and classrooms for physics research. Compton, member of a renowned educational family, had headed Princeton's department of physics and was developing the new field of electronics when he came to M.I.T. as president in 1930. His distinguished leadership has been credited with M.I.T.'s speedy growth into a university. He arranged its disciplines into M.I.T.'s present five schools, and among his great appointments was choosing Professor Vannevar Bush as M.I.T.'s first vice-president and dean of engineering. When President Franklin Roosevelt picked Bush to mobilize America's scientific resources in the World War II era, Compton, Bush's former chief, enthusiastically joined Bush, along with other top United States scientists, who would beat the Nazis to the atomic bomb. To Compton principally was given the task of developing radar, a peak accomplishment of his that has been credited officially with shortening World War II.

The windowless, low, brick structure, a sort of wing on the northeast side of Compton Laboratories, was fashioned as an innovative, theatrelike lecture hall with 418 seats. The chairs are arranged so that they can be entered or left without disturbing fellow students. Every conceivable aid to teaching was made available, from audio to visual, a film projection room, a large television projector, a 48-foot-wide blackboard, along with three 16-foot blackboards, and a huge movie screen that can be raised and lowered. It even had a monorail to bring in heavy apparatus. Across from the auditorium is a lounge, named also for Compton.

Four wings of the old Rad Lab, now called Building 20, extend, from the main structure and corridor along Vassar Street, toward Compton Court and the Alumni Pool. Rad Lab, which would occupy more than a dozen acres of space, spread rapidly from the present welding lab, Room 4-133, which we saw off the "Main Drag." These three-story wooden military barracks buildings started going up in 1943 as temporary quarters to relieve the spread of Rad Lab in just about every scattered available space on and off campus. Fully 4,000 scientists, engineers, and technicians did research work or gave instruction during Rad Lab's five-year existence, and some 8,000 military personnel, officers and men, were trained in the use of microwave radar.

President Julius Stratton, recounting these exciting war years, said that the activity of the Rad Lab was matched only by the Manhattan Project, which produced the atomic bomb. Perfecting microwave radar stemmed from the Magnetron that we saw in the M.I.T. Museum, a device for generating microwaves that the British, on a secret mission, brought over in fall 1940. Besides perfecting microwave radar for use in the struggle in the air and at sea, Rad Lab also developed a novel radio signal system, LORAN, to guide navigation of ships and planes. Rad Lab became sort of a seedbed for the M.I.T. presidency. Future president James Killian, then executive assistant to Compton, helped administer Rad Lab while Compton was away on vital missions for our national defense. And after Rad Lab, at war's end, was renamed Research Laboratory of Electronics (RLE), and given all its precious equipment, it was directed in succession by two future M.I.T. presidents, Julius Stratton and Jerome Wiesner.

A walk along the still barrackslike corridor of the western wing, Wing A, discloses no indication that it was here Rad Lab expanded when Building 20 first became available. An M.I.T. Quarter Century Club is now there. Wing E's first and second floors are quarters for the Reserve Officers Training Corps (R.O.T.C.), which has been continuous at M.I.T. since it began. The top floor here, and the next wing, Wing D, serve the Linguistic and Philosophy Department of Humanities. The celebrated linguist Professor Noam Chomsky, who has taught at M.I.T. since 1955, has his office on the second floor. Use of the offices and labs over the years has changed quite often to meet the Institute's needs, and also the University has many maintenance workshops. We use the far-from-elaborate main lobby at 18 Vassar Street, and head right to Main Street.

Please notice M.I.T.'s East Garage, on our right, because we will return this way after a brief visit to see Technology Square and the world-famous Charles Stark Draper Laboratories, concentrating nowadays on sensationally novel space-age technology. We go left, on crossing Main Street, and just beyond the railroad tracks that border the east side of Technology Square. The expansive square was an urban redevelopment project of the early 1960s, in which M.I.T. joined with the city, clearing away old factories, tenement houses, and a batch of small streets. The University rents eight floors of the nine-story 1963 buildings at 545 Technology Square, the nearest one to the square's southeast corner. The curvaceous, high building, next one to the north, is the main Draper Lab, at 555 Technology Square.

To get a quick look at the square, we enter and go through the lobby of number 545, a building M.I.T. uses mainly as its Laboratory for Computer Science. One floor, the sixth, is rented by Polaroid, which is no surprise, for as we go out the west exit of number 545 to the plaza, every other building we see, the entire small one and the two tall ones at 565 and 575, save for physics labs on one M.I.T. floor in 575, are occupied by Polaroid. We go right to the Draper Lab. The work at Draper is classified, so that a visit to the lobby takes in little more than the fine picture of Draper and the shovel he used at the 1974 ground breaking.

Charles Stark Draper is certainly in the forefront of M.I.T.'s scientific geniuses. Draper, who continued at M.I.T. after his 1926 graduation, has told how he created the famous Instrumentation Laboratory around 1930, came to head it, and later the Aeronautics (to which he added Astronautics) Department for nearly four decades. Here, with application of gyroscopic guides, he provided incredible accuracy for missiles to bring down dive bombers or Kamikazes and to perfect navigation for ships and planes. A year after his device landed the Apollo mission on the moon, a fantastic journey that Draper, though sixty-seven, wanted to make, the Instrumentation Lab, then spread, like the Rad Lab, to more than a dozen locations on and off the campus, was renamed Draper Laboratories in his honor.

Three years later M.I.T. divested itself of the lab, and by 1976 it was all brought together in the new number 555 Technology Square structure that we see here.

The divestiture was the result of M.I.T.'s announcing that it would no longer accept classified research on campus, a policy spurred by campus protest marches, often laced with violence and clashes with the police that were headline features of American campus life, especially in the 1960s and the early 1970s war years. The policy has not applied to the inestimable space-age projects undertaken at M.I.T.'s Lincoln Laboratory, created in 1951 at Hanscom Field, Lexington, which has produced the computer-radar Distant Early Warning (DEW) line to protect the United States from the intercontinental missiles. Draper Lab has been a recurrent target of nuclear protesters. Draper, in his mid-eighties, still comes in regularly from his Newton home to work in his lab here. "It's his life," said a security guard, who went on to say that Draper is a "very considerate man—although we all know him well, he always has his security badge in sight so that checking in is easy."

Draper Lab, in this age of spaceships, space walks, and manned flights to the moon and possibly to other planets, continues to grow. Ahead of us, as we continue our walk between Draper Lab and the garage on our left, we see the tower and red brick buildings along Hampshire Street, once those of a large Cambridgeport manufacturer, Boston Woven Hose and Rubber Company, founded in the 1880s. The garage we have been passing was the site of Cambridgeport's largest soap manufacturer, Lever Brothers, its odor of soap filling the air hereabouts for pedestrians and passing motorists. Two buildings of Boston Woven Hose were demolished to provide for the new 1984 Hill Building, at 1 Hampshire Street, an addition to Draper Lab, with the third-floor skybridge joining them.

Although work here, too, is classified, a visitor may look at the displays in the lobby of the building, which was named for physicist Professor Albert G. Hill, former director of the Research Lab of Electronics, a fellow Missourian and M.I.T. colleague of Draper since the 1930s, who kept Draper Lab strong during the troublesome divestiture. Hill too, also emeritus, is here regularly working in his lab. The displays are fascinating, for they exhibit some of Draper's famed devices, his "Shoe-box" gunsight that led to the celebrated Mark 14 gunsight of World War II, his slimming down the 25-pound gyro navigator to less than 1½ pounds for the Apollo mission, and many others. Recently renovated, a dozen buildings of the once-flourishing Boston Woven Hose remain in this block and along Cardinal Medeiros Avenue, the former Portland Street, a relic of earlier manufacturing in Cambridgeport that we will again see.

We return now to the right of the East Garage. The six-story Whitehead Institute, on the opposite corner of Main Street, which came here in 1984, is an independent, nonprofit research institute, its staff all members of the M.I.T. faculty. Nobel laureate David Baltimore, M.I.T. '61, who for several years had his lab in M.I.T.'s nearby Center for Cancer Research, has headed the Institute since it was created and financed in 1982 by Edwin C. "Jack" Whitehead, a founder of Technicon Corporation, for basic biomedical research. Labs and lounge areas are arranged to maximize discussion and interaction among M.I.T.'s graduate students who study or research here.

We go past the odd-shaped Office of Naval Research (ONR) structure, built in 1941 to house a landmark Van de Graaff Generator, used for nuclear research. Long obsolete, like the former cyclotron on Vassar Street, the generator was moved to the Museum of Science, on Charles River Dam, and the ONR structure is used by the M.I.T. Physics Department. We turn left, with the campus view to the eastward across Ames Street emphasizing why architect I. M. Pei made his Landau Building triangular and placed the gatewaylike tall pillar and crosspiece atop the steps beside the 1984 Wiesner Building, also by Pei, as a distinctive approach to the rapidly redeveloping easternmost part of the campus.

The six- and seven-story brick buildings on the east side of Ames Street, toward Main Street, were Daggett candy factories, built in the 1920s and acquired by M.I.T. in 1961, used mainly for administrative and College services offices. The nearest, the six-story at 40 Ames Street, a 1932 factory of Brigham's ice cream and candy, became a M.I.T. Center for Cancer Research in 1975, and it was here that Nobel laureates Luria, director of the Center, and Baltimore had their research labs and taught.

It also includes cell-culture and arteriosclerosis centers, and was named for a West Coast professor of radiation therapy, Dr. Seeley G. Mudd, who willed a large fortune to aid further research.

On the far east side of the big courtyard the glassed, five-story atrium has pictures and a plaque honoring Uncas and Helen Whitaker, who just seventeen years after these two lifetime M.I.T. Corporation members gave the big Whitaker Life Sciences Building we saw, helped, in 1982, to construct six-story Whitaker College, which the atrium joins, on its north side, to the five-story Health Services Center and Infirmary (1982) on its east side. The College has laboratories, library, lecture rooms, and a joint Harvard–M.I.T. program in health sciences and technology. We have fascinating campus views—even of the Great Dome—from the top atrium crosswalk.

The Wiesner Arts and Media Building is resplendent with contemporary atrium, large theatre, and labs so well equipped with the latest high-technology equipment that its cost about matched that of the building itself. Hayden Gallery, just off the lobby, enjoys far larger space than it had in Hayden Library, and is now part of the galleries of the Visual Arts Center, named for M.I.T. benefactors Vera and Albert List of New York, a center long the goal of the M.I.T. Council for the Arts, founded by President Wiesner in 1971. The second floor, and those above, have Media Labs, researching new communications technologies in print, film, video, publishing, and other fields.

Most interesting is that here two recent ex–M.I.T. presidents have northwest-corner offices, one above the other. Jerome B. Wiesner, for whom the building was named, has his office on the second floor, just off Media Lab headquarters. Though Wiesner was School of Science dean and White House science adviser to Presidents John Kennedy and Lyndon Johnson, it was Wiesner who not only founded but headed M.I.T.'s Council for the Arts. He now holds seminars for graduate students. On the fourth floor is the office of former President Howard W. Johnson, celebrated economist and former director of the Sloan School of Management, which we will presently visit, who still holds weekly seminars on management here.

Continuing along Ames Street riverward, we have on our left, at the north corner of Amherst Street a former (1913) three-story commercial building that M.I.T. renovated and has used since 1963 for its Department of Psychology. On crossing Amherst we have on our left architect Bosworth's original (1916) Senior House dorms that flank, on its north and east sides, the two-story villa (1917) with penthouse that Bosworth also designed, built as President Maclaurin's official residence. It is currently the dwelling of M.I.T.'s fourteenth president, Paul E. Gray, M.I.T. '54, an M.I.T. electrical engineering professor before becoming chancellor and succeeding Wiesner in 1980.

Senior House for some years has been undergraduate dorms. Those facing the river also have an excellent view of official receptions within the brick walls separating them from the formal presidential garden with its pavilion. Lively, smiling students say they sometimes use the stone bench or open fireplace to scale the brick wall and join the receptions. All college presidents find fund raising a top duty. President Gray has emphasized that M.I.T. needs more funds for building and updating endowments. With the University's 125th anniversary in 1986, a new fund drive is expected, and the goal may well exceed the $250,000,000 raised under President Wiesner in the 1975 five-year M.I.T. Leadership Campaign.

Going downriver next, we see the big 1950 apartment complex (on M.I.T. land) at 100 Memorial Drive, with entries on Amherst Street so that all possible residents have river views from their apartments. It was intended mainly as a convenience for the faculty, to spare them from commuting. It has been home to a number of prominent M.I.T. personnel, including former Presidents Compton, Killian, Johnson, and "Doc" Edgerton, who enjoys strolls from here to his lab.

The three-story 1945 building at the west corner of Wadsworth Street, formerly leased to Electronics Corporation of America, was renovated by M.I.T. in 1980 as classrooms and offices for the neighboring original Sloan School of Management, with which it is linked by skybridge on the third floor. On the second floor is also the office of the dean of the School of Humanities and Social Science. Internationally famous Sloan School is at the east corner of Wadsworth Street, a 1938 Lever Brothers corporate headquarters that was purchased and occupied by M.I.T. in 1952 through the generosity of Alfred P. Sloan, Jr., whose gifts to the University exceed $64,000,000 in the records of M.I.T.'s treasurer.

On coming to the two-floor-high lobby of Sloan School we see, at the gallery level overhead, a portrait of "generous and far-seeing benefactor" Sloan. Back in 1938, President Killian said, Sloan sponsored the innovative M.I.T. fellowship program for midcareer executives to study advances in management. Sloan's perfecting the staff principle of management at General Motors led in 1952 to his creating this school of management (named for him in 1965) for its teaching and research. On that occasion Sloan told how he got the idea for the management school at an evening get-together at the 50th reunion of his 1895 class, at which classmates talked about their careers since they had left College.

The murals in the lobby, by Francis Scott Bradford, were done for the original owners, Lever Brothers, and depict mainly Boston and Charles River scenes, from skating in the Public Garden to Anderson Bridge as it appears from Soldiers Field riverside. Sloan Fellows, like the students, have a lounge, but best of all is the M.I.T. Faculty Club, with its grand river views from the top of the building, lounge, portraits, and plenty of table service (membership only). "They have everything here," said a smiling, approving waiter. The faculty includes many outstanding economists. Nobel laureate Franco Modigliani, teaching and writing, has his office riverside on the third floor, and just above him Nobel laureate Paul A. Samuelson, now retired, still comes regularly from his home in Belmont to his office.

A third-floor skybridge leads to neighboring 1965 Hermann Building, mainly the gift of Grover M. Hermann, industrialist, long head of the giant Martin Marietta Corporation, a friend and partner of Sloan in financing this four-story building to meet growth of the Sloan School. The Dewey Library for management and social services, which started small in the Sloan School, now occupies the first two floors of the Hermann Building. A portrait of President Howard Johnson, former director of the school, is on the library stairway to the second floor. Upper floors provide more classrooms for Sloan School and the Political Science Department.

On coming out across the plaza to Wadsworth Street, notice the tall Picasso creation amid trees and shrubs to the right of the steps.

Farther to our right is Eastgate, and on the north corner of Amherst Street, just across Wadsworth Street, is a former 1930 printing plant, renovated by M.I.T. in 1969 for energy research and other labs. Eastgate, twenty-nine-story sentinel at the east end of the campus, was built in 1957 for married students and faculty. Besides an outdoor park and playground for the youngsters it has a day-care center with kindergarten on the first floor—and, for families, on the top floor, besides a laundry, a lounge has panoramic river and city views.

One of M.I.T.'s most celebrated professors, Jay Forrester, M.I.T. '45, director of the Sloan School's system dynamics group, comes regularly from his Concord home to his second-floor office, in the Energy Building at 1 Amherst Street, where he has a lab and gives lectures and seminars. Forrester is among the scientists who ushered mankind into the high-technology age by bringing his huge Whirlwind I digital computer on line in 1953. He did so nearly a decade and a number of labs later, after Forrester, then an M.I.T. junior, began his Whirlwind research in 1944 in the World War II Servo-Mechanism Laboratory.

Forrester has recalled to friends that when he attained Whirlwind's sensational success in 1953, his lab was in the present Graphic Arts Building at 211 Massachusetts Avenue, the former two-story laundry we saw at the corner of Windsor Street shortly after our visit to the M.I.T. Museum. After Whirlwind, Forrester in 1956 changed careers and joined the faculty of the Sloan School.

KENDALL SQUARE TO EAST CAMBRIDGE

Kendall Square, which we enter at the north end of Wadsworth Street, developed as the junction of turnpikes that terminated at Main Street after the causeway-with-roadway route from Pelham Island was built along riverside marshes and mud flats to the landmark 1793 West Boston Bridge.

Early in 1805, encouraged by increasing traffic flowing to the West Boston Bridge, the proprietors of the Concord Turnpike got a charter to bring their toll road along the road that is now Broadway and, diagonally on our left, joins Main Street in Kendall Square. In that same period Middlesex Turnpike proprietors were also chartered to extend along present Hampshire Street and join Broadway in the square where we saw the new Hill Building of Draper Lab.

On our right we see, in midhighway, the subway bed slanting upward for the rapid-transit "T" trains to cross the Charles River on the Longfellow Bridge of 1906, a successor to the 1793 bridge that led to much creation and development in the formerly almost unpopulated Cambridgeport. When erected, the present structure was named Cambridge Bridge, its four ornate turrets and style copied, said civic leader Richard Henry Dana III, from "a celebrated bridge in Prague." Through efforts by the Cambridge Historical Society its name was changed in 1927 to Longfellow, whose poem that began "I stood on the bridge at midnight . . ." told of exciting views from the original bridge.

That original bridge, low over the river, was 40 feet wide, nearly 3,500 feet long, with a causeway more than 3,300 feet in length. It had a mile-and-a-quarter row of oil lamps on either side of the roadway, and narrow walks for pedestrians on the outer side of the lights. The bridge was opened with much ceremony on Thanksgiving Day. Enthusiasm for its construction had been so intense that Judge Francis Dana and his associates were able to sell all shares within three hours of offering them to the public. The bridge was renewed in 1854 and four years later became toll-free, like most of the other bridges then crossing the Charles to Cambridge.

Longfellow was not alone in his delight with the old bridge. Young Thomas Wentworth Higginson talks of joyful walks to Boston with future poet James Lowell, then a law student but feeling he should instead be a poet. They would go to antislavery meetings to hear Garrison and Phillips, and on Sunday to hear Theodore Parker and James Freeman. Those were days when "far more vessels" were on the river. Higginson told how over the years the dim oil lamps "gave place to kerosene, then came gas, then electricity." Dean Howells loved to see the State House dome above the Beacon Hill rooftops, not so distinctive or easy in this age of tall buildings. To Howells, the river views and far hills were always "dreamy."

The most exciting Cambridge event of 1805, one that had spurred the turnpike builders, was when the federal government, on January 11, 1805, made Cambridge a "port of delivery." Some developers had already been urging this step, for they felt that the traffic in produce and wares that had brought major highways, inns, taverns, and stores should be shipped from a port right here: namely, Cambridgeport. Royal Makepeace, in particular, now that his partner Vose had died, joined with Boston merchant Rufus Davenport and built canals linked to the Charles River to provide wharves for vessels.

A network of canals—long gone save for one we will see—was then hopefully dug in this Kendall Square area. Broad Canal, the chief one, was 80 feet wide from the Charles River and half a block north and parallel to Main Street, just ahead of us. This canal was extended, parallel to Broadway and, with drawbridge, even beyond the present Cardinal Medeiros Avenue that we saw. Other canals, including a South Canal, south of Broadway, whose site we will presently see, where as eagerly dug. But alas for the promoters, who would end up bankrupt, the 1807–1809 Jefferson Embargo and the War of 1812 wrecked any prospects of competing with Boston's handy port and market facilities.

Kendall Square, at first, was even called Dock Square. Industry, though at first small, did develop. In this area we have walked between Ames and Wadsworth streets were wharves mainly for wood and coal merchants. Among them was a boiler factory owned by kindly Edward Kendall, for whom the square was named. Kendall, deacon during Civil War times for the Second Evangelical Congregational Church near Central Square, served the city as alderman and state representative in the 1870s. The

Square has seen public transportation change from one-horse hacks and four-horse omnibuses, horsecars, and horsecars on rails to electric cars in 1889. After the Civil War larger industry, drawing on immigrant laborers, developed in Cambridgeport and nearby filled river marshland.

On our left, at 238 Main Street, the Kendall Building, with its three-story clock tower, built in the World War I period, has been a Kendall Square landmark. The wall directory inside quickly confirms that its earlier usage has shifted to high-tech research and related services. It reflects, though close to a college campus, modern scenes on the Route 128 Electronic Gulch, Michigan's Automation Alley, and California's Silicon Valley. At the junction of Main and Broadway, across the street, the 1908 generating plant that long furnished power for the "T" 's transit system has been replaced by a 1984 computerized substation that may be built over to accommodate hotel expansion of the new Marriott, Cambridge Center's centerpiece, a twenty-six-story tower that started going up in 1985.

As we have observed, former factories are being rehabilitated for modern uses, and Cambridgeport too has for some years been undergoing industrial change. Cambridge Center, on our right, is a modern complex covering twenty-four acres from Kendall Square to the Whitehead Institute, which we saw at 9 Cambridge Center. A modernized Kendall subway station was being installed as the Marriott tower rose directly across from the Marriott Plaza entry.

Walking toward the 1898 fire station, on our left, just beyond Dock Street, a name that goes back to its once being close to South Dock, Cambridge Center seems to confirm that little building of the past will long remain here near Kendall Square. The University has acquired several of these older buildings, including, in 1974, the corner Old Suffolk Building at 292 Main Street, where we see the M.I.T. Press bookstore, and in 1961 the seven-story former candy factory beyond, at the corner of Ames Street. The F. & T. Diner, between the two, has been a Kendall Square fixture since its leaner post–World War I days.

Current plans include terminating the old 1898 fire station and building a larger new one in 1987, four blocks north on Binney Street. To get a delightful view of the area, go now across Main Street to the west side of Marriott's Plaza and past 3 Cambridge Center to the garage door ahead marked "Elevators to Parking and Roof Garden." Views from the large, lovely landscaped garden on the sixth-floor roof are truly unusual. The west side of this garden is above the site of the old South Dock. This dock was connected with the Charles River by a creek and canal across Main Street, west of Dock Street, under the "Little Bridge." South Canal ran from the garage site here parallel to Broadway and through sites where we can see Draper Lab and the big garage that was once Lever Brothers soap site. Do not miss interesting sights in Marriott's Plaza and the attractive lobby.

On emerging from the hotel lobby we see across Broadway a thirteen-story building, surrounded by five much lower structures, built in the 1960s, after urban renewal cleared the area, for electronic research by the National Aeronautics and Space Administration. When NASA, under President Lyndon Johnson, was moved to Texas, this complex was taken over by the National Transportation Department, mainly for research. We continue east on Broadway to Third Street. This street, formerly known as Court Street, because it led to the courts in the center of East Cambridge, still leads to the courts, now in the twenty-two-story building to our north with the band of red five floors from the top. We will head toward it presently.

First, though, we walk toward Longfellow Bridge to see what remains of the Broad Canal. On either side of the midhighway strip of park and of the rapid transit to the bridge, a high-rise building boom in the 1980s has absorbed land formerly little used, or with small or old structures and even wasteland. On our right, on the M.I.T. side of the bridge, One Memorial Drive, a twenty-story complex of offices, residences, and garage got under way in early 1985. It replaces an eight-story Filene's warehouse, built in the early 1920s but occupied in the past three decades by the Electronics Corporation of America, an occupancy made known by its huge, blue neon sign.

The eighteen-story Cambridge Gateway, at the east corner of Third Street and Main, was built in 1969 for a design and building engineering subsidiary of Raytheon called Badger Company. A second tower, projected for the parking lot, which we pass next, was on the original plans. The four-story red brick row, 145–137 Main Street, occupied for a quarter century chiefly for pharmaceutical research by Moleculon BioTech, goes back to the years right after the Civil War when it was built at the top of a pier for storing grain. Before we turn left to see Broad Canal, notice ahead of us that the remainder of the land to First Street is called Riverfront Office Park. In it are two high-rises, the nineteen-story Saddlebrook Building (1983), named for its biggest tenant, a software firm, at 101 Main Street; and, at the corner of First Street, the thirteen-story Com/Energy Building, to be completed in 1987. The latter is also named for its prime tenant, the Cambridge utility and part owner, Commonwealth Energy System of Cambridge.

We go past the entrance of the Saddlebrook Building garage, which occupies the first three floors of this building, to the Broad Canal. The "River Walk" along the canal to First Street, with its bollards, benches, gazebo, and landscaping are compliments of the owners of Riverfront Office Park. Land on both sides of the canal became the property of Cambridge Electric, whose generating plant, with successively larger and more modern buildings to the present 1949 one on the east side of the canal, began in 1889. Broad Canal used to go to the Boston Woven Hose and Rubber Company and, under a drawbridge on the present Cardinal Medeiros Avenue, to West Dock, now the site of the 1985 Italian Culture and Social Center, named for the poet Dante. Schooners under sail, ships, and barges have used the canal, supplementing the railroad in bringing supplies to and products from Boston Woven Hose and other factories. A 60-foot-wide North Canal once ran from Broad Canal, near Boston Woven Hose, to Miller's River via a creek across Gore Street, completing encirclement of East Cambridge by water and, in effect, making it an island for several decades until the 1880s.

We enter East Cambridge by the First Street drawbridge. Coal and later oil delivered via canal to the Cambridge Electric Light plant by lighters has, since 1984, come by oil trucks, and operation of the drawbridge was suspended then. The old six-story Carter's Ink Building at 245 First

Street (1909) was, like ECA with its huge neon sign, a landmark for decades. The big Carter's rooftop sign and clock were highly visible to everyone, especially "T" passengers, using the Charles River bridges hereabouts. The building was renamed Riverview I when recycled in 1984, and by 1985 was connected by a six-story glassed atrium in back to Riverview II, a 1985 skyscraper with nineteenth-floor penthouse, lower floors for garaging, and most upper ones for high-tech tenants.

When the next building, the five-story Athenaeum Building, with its goddess Athena on its pediment at 215 First Street, was completed to supply printing for Ginn & Company in 1895, the people of Cambridge rejoiced. On the 50th anniversary of Cambridge in the following year, it was hailed in Arthur Gilman's anniversary book as "one of the noblest monuments of industry in Cambridge." The mud flats from Old Court Street to the river were among the last to be filled, blocked by Broad Canal. But progress began when First Street was extended in 1874, some embankment wall built in the 1880s, and the First Street drawbridge was finally built. Erection of this building, then the largest in the area, confirmed that progress had really been achieved. Interesting old presses are on view in the lobby of the Athenaeum House, a building beautifully redone for its mostly high-tech occupants. Above all, the sadly decayed terra cotta statue of Athena, long missing, has been replaced on its pediment by the new owners with an identical bronzelike replica.

To accommodate modern growth, Commercial Avenue, running northeast to another currently inactivated drawbridge, is to be expanded to two three-lane highways. Auto traffic along the present Cambridge Parkway is to be eliminated and, as the foresighted Cambridge Park Commission of 1892 sought when it preserved a strip of embankment for the public, there will be a riverside mall and park with benches for all.

Building along Cambridge Parkway goes back to post–World War II days. Those, mostly offices and small warehouses, have about all been replaced in recent years. Opposite Athenaeum House, at 100 Cambridge Parkway, are the new quarters of the nonprofit research organization that the distinguished scientist Edwin H. Land has directed since his 1982 retirement as Polaroid chairman, Rowland Institute. Land, in his mid-seventies, comes regularly to his second-floor, riverside lab probing vision and color perception. We can see farther along this row of buildings, before we return to Athenaeum House, Orion Research at number 75, the 1985 nine-story Riverside Place headquarters of Lotus Development Corporation, one of the nation's top software firms, at number 55, and just beyond, the 1984 twelve-story wing that doubled the Royal Sonesta's 1961 hotel to 400 rooms. During this riverfront construction there disappeared two labs, at numbers 35 and 37, where Doctor Charles Stark Draper had part of his famous Instrumentation Lab from 1964 to 1976.

From Athenaeum House we go past another Lotus plant at 161 First Street, a former valve manufactory, and turn left at Rogers, go a block and turn right on Second Street toward the East Cambridge high-rise Courthouse that we could see from farther up Second Street, four blocks away. We have been walking, till we have reached Spring Street and the beginning of slowly rising land, through former marsh and tideland. A bit farther up Second Street we will see presently where the Redcoats made their landing that, within a few hours, touched off the Revolution. All Middlesex County Courts, save probate, are now in this 1974 skyscraper. The red band we have been seeing is enamel paneling on the inside of a narrow exterior balcony all around the sixteenth floor. To warn low-flying planes of this tallest of East Cambridge structures the balcony holds red high-intensity lights that flash at night.

To see the site of the first residence in Cambridge, we go left (west) along Spring Street. Just beyond the former district courthouse (1932), now used by the state for storage, on "the northerly side . . . between Third and Fourth Streets" until demolished around 1820 there stood, according to historian Lucius Page, the dwelling of Thomas Graves of Gravesend, England. Much-traveled Graves was a man of many talents, especially engineering, and the Puritans were so eager for his help that they agreed, if he would stay three years, to pay him a big salary, £50 a year, give him a hundred acres, and build a house for him, his wife, five children, and two servants. On arrival in Salem in June 1629, Graves was sent right away with about a third of Governor John Endicott's Puritans to plan and build the town of Charlestown and protect the Puritans' charter claim to Massachusetts Bay Colony.

The link between Graves's house, on the upland by the tidewater, and Richard Lechmere is quite direct. Graves, about whom little is known, loved the site—"I never came into a more goodly country in my life," he wrote to a friend in England. He apparently considered it part of Charlestown, but by 1632, when the bounds were drawn, it was placed in Newe Towne. Graves by then had 130 acres. In 1635 it all belonged to wealthy Atherton Hough, former mayor of old Boston borough in England, who came over in 1633 with Reverend John Cotton. Hough, who had a fine house in Boston, was a representative for seven years and a member of the Governor's Council. By the time the estate here was bought in 1706 by future Lieutenant Governor Spencer Phips it included 326 acres. On Phips's death it was divided among his heirs in 1759 but Lechmere, who had married Phips's daughter Mary in 1753, bought out all the others.

Wealthy Lechmere, whose mother was a granddaughter of Governor John Winthrop, was son of the king's surveyor-general and nephew of Lord Lechmere, had a former mansion, which we have seen on Tory Row, and one in Boston. He rejected joining General Gage's Mandamus Council but fled with the Redcoats to Halifax and died in England in 1814 at eighty-seven. Reverend Abiel Holmes relates how, in 1793 when West Boston Bridge was built, the only property in all East Cambridge was Lechmere's farmhouse and barn, confiscated in 1778, on the present Spring Street. All of East Cambridge, because of Lechmere's lengthy ownership, was long called Lechmere's Point.

We return to Third Street, and go left (north), to Thorndike Street. Before turning left, notice diagonally across Third Street the successor to Charles Bulfinch's 1814 courthouse that we will shortly visit. On the northwest corner of Thorndike is East Cambridge's oldest extant church, minus cupola atop its tower, erected in 1827 for the Third Congregational Society, Unitarian. Cambridge's first mayor, Reverend James D. Green, whose house we will see nearby, was its minister until 1840. Denominational changes that we observe in East Cambridge churches reflect successive waves of immigration, especially in the later 1800s, which brought workers to East Cambridge's rapidly growing industries. From 1875 the church was Episcopal, added stained glass in memory of Reverend Phillips Brooks, and in 1942 became the Holy Cross Polish National Catholic Church.

On our right, as we go along Thorndike Street, number 73, part of the first double residence with graceful, fluted columns, was the birthplace in 1857 of the well-known Cambridge philanthropist Frederick H. Rindge. Rindge's grandfather, member of an old Massachusetts Bay family, was attracted here by the great New England Glass works. Two years after Frederick's birth, his father, highly successful in Boston's banking world, moved to 334 Harvard Street, now gone. On our left, in the next mid-block, the 1826 brick house at 96 Thorndike, now a two-family dwelling, was the residence of Mayor Green. Green, after resigning from the ministry in 1840, became a selectman in 1845, served in the Legislature, was chosen mayor in spring 1846, and reelected to four more terms by 1861.

We continue downhill to Sixth Street and turn right. On the west side of the street are Sacred Heart Rectory, across from the branch library, and Sacred Heart Church, now the oldest Catholic Church in East Cambridge. When St. John's parish, whose earlier 1843 church site we will see, found its church had become too small for its membership, enlarged by escapees from Ireland's famine and later immigrants, it began building this large Gothic edifice in 1874 and completed it in 1883. The spire was once 180 feet high, but the church was ravaged by fire; parishioners restored it, though, and the high, beautifully carved marble altar, made abroad in 1882, can still be seen.

Before we turn right (east) on Otis Street we record the location, two blocks ahead of us and across Gore street, where, beside the vanished (it was filled) Miller's River, was the extensive plant of East Cambridge's once largest employer, John P. Squire & Company, a pork-packing firm he started in 1855, which grew to cover many acres here. It had great smokestacks, and, as old-timers will tell you, "The smell was more than pigs." In the 1960s the old buildings, long past their heyday, were swept by fire. Now there is just a huge skating rink and open recreation area the old-timers call Squire's Park. About two blocks farther west on Gore

Street a small wooden bridge over Miller's River and causeway across the marshes that long ago led to Lechmere's farmhouse played a role, as we will see, on the first day of the Revolution.

Continuing uphill on Otis Street we come, on our left in midblock beyond Fifth Street, to another church reflecting changes brought by immigration. St. Hedwig's Polish Catholic Church was built a year after the 1938 hurricane that blew down and ruined the 1865 church that the Universalists had built here and sold in 1907 to the Polish Catholics. Diagonally across the street on the corner, and on East Cambridge's highest ground, is one of its most historic spots—once the center of General Washington's Fort Putnam, which provided crucial help in forcing the Redcoats to flee Boston.

The three-story red brick building at 86 Otis, now called Putnam Apartments, providing housing for the elderly, was built in 1848 to replace an 1825 Putnam School here that the local population had outgrown. East Cambridge's first schoolhouse, a small one, had been built on Third near Gore Street. This former Putnam School was succeeded, in 1971, by the new, extensive school complex three blocks southwest of here that was named for President Kennedy's brother Robert, assassinated three years earlier.

Fort Putnam's fortifications covered about four present city blocks on the hilltop. General Putnam and four hundred men, on Washington's orders, began throwing up redoubts in mid-December 1775, and continued the work, despite heavy British fire from ships and floating batteries once the work, delayed by frozen ground, reached the hilltop. The 13-inch brass cannon that Putnam christened "Congress" helped, until it burst, but it was heavy cannon and mortars that Colonel Knox fetched from Ticonderoga that packed lethal power into the cannonade of Boston, which Washington ordered March 2, 1776. Covering his seizure of Dorchester Heights, the shelling was a death knell to the British supply line from the sea should they try to cling to Boston. They were soon heading for Halifax.

Where we see the playground on the northeast corner was the site on which East Cambridge's first Catholic church, St. John's, was built in 1842.

Eight years earlier the parishioners had taken over the former Universalist Academy around the corner of the north side of Cambridge Street. As the parish grew, Sacred Heart Church was built and St. John's served as a school until demolished in the 1930s. By the fiftieth anniversary of Cambridge's cityhood, several other Catholic parishes that we have seen grew from this one, which had originally served all Cambridge. On the northeast corner of Cambridge Street, a block north of us, is a former 1837 Baptist Church, now St. Francis of Assisi Catholic Church, with masses in English and Italian. A little chapel is just inside the main door, and the campanile, built in 1932 by the Franciscans, who have living quarters here, is, on the crest of the hill, a Cambridge landmark.

Thorndike and Otis Streets, which we have been walking, especially high on the hill, became favorite places for businessmen and professionals serving the courts to reside. In later years their once-spacious lots were utilized for more compact housing, and currently many are undergoing "gentrification," which disperses many old residents of "the Point." At Third Street we turn right to enter the oldest building in the present Bulfinch Square, the 1814 original courthouse, beneath the recently renovated cupola with gilded scales of justice and a clock.

Andrew Craigie, whose famed house we saw on Tory Row, acquired, like Phips and Lechmere before him, about all the 300-odd acres in East Cambridge. He set about the task secretly for nearly a decade, through relatives and friends, and disclosed no ownership until 1803. Once the bridge he planned would be built, as it was in 1809, all the land he had bought for some $20,000 could be worth far more. To boost sales, depressed by the embargo and the War of 1812, he and his associates gave this city block for a $24,000 courthouse that they would construct, thus shifting the Middlesex County government and courts here from Harvard Square. Craigie was reimbursed for a cost overrun on the courthouse of some $4,000. The associates also gave the west half of the adjoining block, where the high-rise courthouse now stands, for a jail.

Craigie had ample political influence with the county, and on Beacon Hill, for his maneuvering. Streets we have been walking, shown on his 1811 street plans, still bear some names of his associates: Christopher

Gore, governor in 1809; Harrison Gray Otis, speaker and senate president, 1803–1806, and future United States senator and Boston mayor; and Israel Thorndike, a top China-trade merchant in Boston and a major figure for thirteen terms in the state legislature.

Already-famous architect Charles Bulfinch built the center portion of the building in 1814. Growth of county business and necessity of repair led architect Ammi Young, who would win renown for the original Boston Custom House, not only to add two wings in 1848 but to practically redo Bulfinch's work. Save for some wood in midbuilding, little by Bulfinch remains. Earlier county plans on the 1974 high-rise courthouse called for demolishing all four county buildings in this block and replacing them with a garage. Preservationists were strongly opposed, and instead a big, five-floor city garage, a block away at Thorndike and First Street, is to be completed in 1986. Eminent modern architect Graham Gund and his associates won a competition to restore and improve this complex of buildings, a widely applauded effort begun in 1980 and still under way. Gund is the son of George Gund, Cleveland banker who gave Harvard its 1972 Graduate School of Design, the Gund Hall we saw near Memorial Hall.

To see one of the most attractive areas in Cambridge, we go through the old Bulfinch Building, with its former courtroom now new offices, mostly used by Gund Associates, to the beautifully landscaped pedestrian mall. Gund did demolish one 1889 building that, in connecting old Bulfinch with two buildings on the east side of the mall, mostly covered the beautiful—as we can see—east façade and portico. On our right the pavilion is a 1985 addition to the red brick ambience of the courtyard. The bronze eagle with wings outspread, from Gund's art collection, once topped off the now-vanished main Boston Post Office in old Post Office Square. And on our left, to which we now walk, Gund plans to extend the mall on Otis Street between Second and Third and add a fountain sculpture and colonnade. Enter the 1889 Clerk of Court building, on our right, to see the magnificently restored Hall of Records, now used by the prime tenant, Cambridge Multicultural Arts Center, a ballroom and theatre.

At the southwest corner of Second Street and Otis the stone marker, behind the iron railings, recalls that it was along here, with the shoreline slanting from the high-rise courthouse northeast to the present Lechmere Square, 700 to 800 Redcoats waded ashore, ankle to knee deep in tidewater, around midnight. They had come in boats, past guns of their war vessels, from the south side of Boston's Common. Not until 2 A.M. on April 19th did Lieutenant Colonel Francis Smith give orders to march along the cartway of Lechmere's farm; the time was consumed in ferrying over munitions, rations, and officers' horses. On reaching the small wooden bridge we mentioned on Gore Street, Smith, worried that tramping on planks would compromise secrecy, ordered his men to wade across. The tide was in and the men, on a chilly night with forty miles of marching ahead, as one recorded, were in water "up to our middles." Unknown to Smith, Paul Revere had already galloped to Lexington with his alarm, by midnight, and Dawes got there shortly after him.

Before heading along Second Street to Cambridge Street, notice the eight connected four-story block of brick buildings on the south side of Otis Street between Second and First Streets. Recycling for office and retail space of these former plants got under way in 1985. Built from 1869 to 1910, they housed the well-known wood-carving firm of Irving & Casson and the furniture factory whose name is still remembered in fine sofas called davenports.

East Cambridge's earliest large employer, New England Glass Company, where Frederick H. Rindge's father worked, was once ahead of us where Second Street led to the shore of Miller's River. Taking over in 1818 some small furnaces of the first works begun in 1814, and a successor glassworks that had failed, New England Glass grew to be the largest glass firm in the world. Its biggest smokestack, built in 1851, among its many shops and sheds on the shore, rose 235 feet, higher than Bunker Hill Monument. In 1888 New England Glass moved to Ohio to be closer to supplies of raw material and became the Libbey Glass Company. Nothing now remains here, just railroad tracks over filled land.

We go presently to the site of Craigie's bridge, which spurred development in East Cambridge as the West Boston Bridge did in Cambridgeport. First we go left along Cambridge Street to see the helpful illustrated posters of the Cambridge Historical Commission, on the west side of the impressive main-portico entrance to the 1900 Registry of Deeds and Probate Court. Elevators are handy to give us, from the fourth-floor balconies, a view of the atriumlike lobby. The parking space across from the Registry on the southwest corner of Third and Cambridge Streets is where East Cambridge had its first church, a Methodist church, in 1825. Its successor, built in 1872, had future President Teddy Roosevelt as a Sunday school teacher in 1880 during his senior year at Harvard.

En route now along Cambridge Street to the bridge site, we see an entire row of factories, from 134 Cambridge to number 100, the factory outlet, terminating the late-nineteenth-century, four-story brick portion, which turns out an old-time Cambridge manufacture, candy. Deran Confectionery is now a part of Borden, Incorporated.

Cambridge Street, which, at the present Lechmere Square, joined the former Bridge Street (now Monsignor O'Brien Highway), approach to Craigie's 1809 bridge, was built in the same year by Craigie and his associates from the Concord Turnpike (Broadway), just east of the Common. Craigie's hope was to attract traffic from the Concord as well as the Middlesex Turnpike to use his bridge. After a struggle, Craigie overcame the opposition of Justice Dana's West Boston Bridge associates, who owned an interfering 750-foot stretch of woodland and blueberry bushes midway, where Elm Street crosses Cambridge Street. Just as, along Main Street after the 1793 bridge was completed, inns, stables, and blacksmith shops appeared along the bridge approach here to serve farmers, drovers, and draymen.

The Lechmere Canal area is again in transition. Lechmere Canal, unlike the other canals, was not dug. On its Bridge Street side wharves had appeared early, chiefly for lumber and coal merchants, and their water access continued when, at the turn of the century, the Commercial Avenue–Parkway area was filled. An original, roughly four-block extension of Lechmere Canal paralleling First Street was filled in recent years to provide parking and commercial space. For an overall view of how the canal area has been renewed, we take the first street on our right to the drawbridge that, as part of the widening of Commercial Avenue, will be rebuilt. The city started the canal park in 1983 by forming the circular basin, which we see at the far end, and putting stone edging in place. A fountain was planned for the pool, with a public pavilion for concerts, and a marina and other park attractions. The first of the office, retail, and residential buildings to go up on this sixteen-acre park area was the six-story Edgewater Place on our left, started in 1984.

We head now to where Craigie built his bridge, where, in midriver, the boundary runs between Boston and Cambridge, we see the Museum of Science on the 1910 dam, now called Science Park. We have written about the Museum in a companion book, *Historic Walks in Old Boston.* The new entry is part of a 1984 enlargement of the Museum's east wing, named for the parents of the principal donor, Museum trustee David Mugar, Marian and the late Stephen, business leader.

Using the bridge site for the dam was a major saving, because the bridge had long needed replacement. The dam itself, at last maintaining the water level, put an end to the stench from mud flats and sewage (at its worst in summer) that had long required facing buildings away from the river. It is fascinating to reflect that the Museum of Science and M.I.T., whose first buildings shared only one city block in the newly filled Boston Back Bay, currently enjoy expansive sites facing the beautiful Charles River Basin.

Transportation by the "T" is close, either to the center of Boston or along the two-mile Cambridge Street route that Craigie built to Harvard Square, where we began our walks.

BIBLIOGRAPHY

Many individuals have been helpful in my preparation of this book, and it is a pleasure to thank them all, especially Rodney Armstrong and his staff at the Boston Athenaeum; Harvard Archivist Harley Holden and his staff; staff at M.I.T. archives, particularly Michael Yeates and Heidi Saraceno; Widener Library; Schlesinger and Hilles Libraries; Cambridge Public Library; Hayden Memorial Library; Baker Library, especially Florence Bartoshesky; and staff in the *Boston Globe* library, especially Dave Jennings. A lifetime association with Cambridge and reading books about it have made the community's history and personages more fascinating. Among the books, besides those mentioned in the text, I would particularly include some old, some recent:

Amory, Thomas C. *Old Cambridge and New.* Boston: James R. Osgood & Co. 1871.

Batchelder, Samuel F. *Bits of Cambridge History.* Cambridge: Harvard University Press, 1930.

Bentinck-Smith, William (ed.). *The Harvard Book.* Cambridge: Harvard University Press, 1953, 1982.

Blair, Clay, Jr., and Joan Blair. *The Search for JFK.* New York: Berkley Publishing Corporation, 1976.

Bush, Vannevar. *Pieces of the Action.* New York: Morrow, 1970.

Cambridge Historical Commission, *Survey of Architectural History in Cambridge,* five volumes, from Report One: Cambridge, 1965, to Report Five: Northwest Cambridge, 1977. Cambridge: MIT Press.

Cambridge Historical Society Publications, Vol. 1, 1906, to Vol. 43, 1978.

Carr, William H.A. *The Du Ponts of Delaware.* New York: Dodd, Mead, 1964.

Colonial Society of Massachusetts Publications.

Conant, James B. *My Several Lives.* New York: Harper & Row, 1970.

Copeland, Melvin T. *And Mark an Era: The Story of the Harvard Business School.* Boston: Little, Brown, 1958.

Crimson Key Guide Book. Cambridge: Crimson Key Society, 1981.

Dana, Richard Henry. *Journal,* edited by Robert F. Lucid, 3 vols., Cambridge: Harvard University Press, 1968.

D.A.R. *Historic Guide to Cambridge.* Cambridge: Hannah Winthrop Chapter, D.A.R., 1907.

Davis, John H. *The Guggenheims.* New York: William Morrow, 1978.

Davis, Walter G. *Cambridge: Fifty Years a City, 1846–1896.* Cambridge: Riverside Press, 1897.

Day, Gardner M. *History of Christ Church.* Cambridge: Riverside Press, 1951.

Donham, Wallace B. "The Graduate School of Business Administration," in *The Development of Harvard*, edited by Samuel Eliot Morison. Cambridge: Harvard University Press, 1930.

Drake, Samuel Adams. *Historic Mansions and Highways Around Boston.* Boston: Little, Brown, 1899.

Education, Bricks and Mortar. Cambridge: Harvard University, 1949.

Eliot, Charles W. *Harvard Memories.* Cambridge: Harvard University Press, 1923.

Eliot, Samuel A. *A Sketch of History of Harvard College.* Boston: Charles C. Little and James Brown, 1848.

Eliot, Thomas H. *Two Schools in Cambridge: Browne & Nichols and Buckingham.* Cambridge: Windflower Press, 1982.

Freese, John W. *Historic Houses and Spots in Cambridge.* Boston: Ginn, 1897.

Friedman, Norman. *e.e. cummings.* Baltimore: The Johns Hopkins University Press, 1960.

Gardiner, John H. *Harvard.* New York: Oxford University Press, 1914.

Gilman, Arthur (ed.). *The Cambridge of 1896.* Cambridge: Riverside Press, 1896.

Hamilton, Ian. *Robert Lowell.* New York: Random House, 1982.

Harris, William T. *Epitaphs from the Old Burying-Ground in Cambridge.* Cambridge: John Owen, 1845.

Hastings, Lewis M. *The Streets of Cambridge.* Cambridge: Cambridge City Council, 1921.

Higginson, Henry Lee. *Two Addresses.* Boston: Merrymount Press, 1902.

Higginson, Thomas W. *Cheerful Yesterdays.* Boston: Houghton Mifflin, 1898.
——. *Old Cambridge.* Cambridge: Riverside Press, 1899.

Holmes, Reverend Abiel. *History of Cambridge.* Boston: Samuel Hall, 1801.

Howells, Dorothy E. *A Century to Celebrate: Radcliffe College, 1879–1979.* Cambridge: Radcliffe College, 1978.

Howells, William Dean. *Suburban Sketches.* Cambridge: Riverside Press, 1871.

James, Henry. *Charles W. Eliot,* 2 volumes. Boston: Houghton Mifflin, 1930.

Kaplan, Martin H. *Harvard Lampoon Centennial Celebration: 1876–1973.* Boston: Little, Brown, 1973.

Lant, Jeffrey L. (ed.). *Our Harvard: Reflections on College Life by Twenty-two Distinguished Graduates.* New York: Taplinger Publishing Company, 1982.

Lawrence, Bishop William. *Memories of a Happy Life.* Boston: Houghton Mifflin, 1926.

Longfellow, Ernest. *Random Memories.* Boston: Houghton Mifflin, 1922.

Lorant, Stefan. *The Life and Times of Teddy Roosevelt.* New York: Doubleday, 1959.

Lowell, James Russell. *Cambridge Worthies—Thirty Years Ago.* Boston: Ticknor and Fields, 1861.

Massachusetts Historical Society Proceedings.

Matthiessen, Francis O. *The James Family.* New York: Knopf, 1948.

McCord, David T. *Notes on the Harvard Tercentenary.* Cambridge: Harvard University Press, 1936.

————. *An Acre for Education.* Cambridge: Harvard University Press, 1938.

Morison, Samuel Eliot. *The Founding of Harvard College.* Cambridge: Harvard University Press, 1935.

————. *Three Centuries of Harvard.* Harvard University Press, 1936.

Paige, Lucius R. *History of Cambridge, Massachusetts, 1630–1877.* Cambridge: Riverside Press, 1877, with index by Mary Isabella Gozzaldi, Cambridge Historical Society, 1930.

Payne, Edward F. *Dickens Days in Boston.* Boston: Houghton Mifflin, 1927.

Peabody, Reverend Andrew Preston. *Harvard Reminiscences.* Boston: Ticknor and Company, 1888.

———— *Harvard Graduates Whom I Have Known.* Boston: Houghton Mifflin, 1890.

Prescott, Samuel C. *When M.I.T was "Boston Tech."* Cambridge: Technology Press, 1954.

Quincy, Josiah (1772–1864). *History of Harvard University,* 2 volumes. Cambridge: John Owen, 1840.

Quincy, Josiah (1802–82). *Figures of the Past.* Boston: Roberts Brothers, 1883.

Rettig, Robert Bell. *Guide to Cambridge Architecture: Ten Walking Tours.* Cambridge: MIT Press, 1969.

Robinson, Edwin Arlington. *Selected Letters.* New York: Macmillan, 1940.

Rusk, Ralph L. *Ralph Waldo Emerson.* New York: Columbia University Press, 1949.

Santayana, George. *Persons and Places.* New York: Scribner, 1963.

Simpson, Eileen B. *Poets in Their Youth.* New York: Random House, 1982.

Sloan, Alfred P., Jr. *My Years with General Motors.* New York: Doubleday, 1963.

Stark, James H. *Loyalists of Massachusetts.* Boston: James H. Stark, 1910.

Vaille, F. O., and H. A. Clark (eds.). *The Harvard Book,* 2 volumes. Cambridge: Welch, Bigelow and Company, University Press, 1875.

Warren, Charles. *History of the Harvard Law School,* 3 volumes. New York: Lewis Publishing Company, 1908.

Wildes, Karl L., and Nilo A. Lindgren. *A Century of Electrical Engineering and Computer Science at M.I.T., 1882–1982.* Cambridge: MIT Press, 1985.

Wylie, Francis E. *M.I.T. in Perspective.* Boston: Little, Brown, 1976.

Yeomans, Edward. *The Shady Hill School.* Cambridge: Windflower Press, 1979.

Yeomans, Henry A. *Abbot Lawrence Lowell.* Cambridge: Harvard University Press, 1948.

INDEX

Aalto, Alvar, 319, 321
Abbot, Edwin H., 10–11, 247, 248
Abbot, Henry, 249
Abbot Building, 247
Abbot castle, 247
Aberdeen Avenue, 224
Abraham Hill house, 29
Acacia Street, 205
Academy of Arts and Sciences, 281
A.D. Club, 139–40
Adams, Abigail, 98, 100, 182
Adams, Henry, 55, 84, 119–20, 221
Adams, John, 6, 14, 38, 39, 98, 100, 123, 138, 182, 216, 221, 299
Adams, John Quincy, 48–49, 62, 82, 123, 221, 299
Adams, Samuel, 6, 23, 39, 43
Adams House, 134, 136–38, 141
Addams, Jane, 197
Advocate, 127
Aeronautics and Astronautics Research, M.I.T., 333
Agassiz, Alexander, 40–41, 156, 247, 273
Agassiz, Elizabeth Cary, 4, 122, 193, 194, 195, 197, 227, 241
Agassiz, Louis, 41, 119, 122, 193, 255, 268, 273, 287
Agassiz Hall, 40
Agassiz House, 196, 197
Aiken, Conrad, 105
Albany Street, 313–14
Aldrich, Nelson W., 169
Aldrich Hall, 168, 169
Aldrin, Edwin E., Jr., 316
Alewife Brook, 19
Alger, Horatio, 57, 278
Allen, Ethan, 27–28
Allston, Martha, 302, 303, 304
Allston, Washington, 236, 244, 290, 302, 303–4
Almshouse Lot, 304
Almshouse at Riverside, 304
Almy, Charles, Jr., 230
Alpha Delta Phi, 140, 312
Alsop, Joe, 111
Alumni Center, M.I.T., 331, 336
Alumni Hall, 284
Alumni Pool, M.I.T., 345
Alumni Swimming Pool, M.I.T., 343
Ambassador Hotel, 286
American Revolution, 6, 17, 25–26, 29–30, 31, 33, 43–44, 47, 97–98, 115, 178, 185, 205, 207–8, 219, 225, 236, 237–38, 239, 243, 256, 261, 263, 265, 298, 300–301, 302, 304, 313–14, 359, 360, 362, 364–65

American Repertory Theatre, 192
Ames Street, 348–50
Amherst Alley, 319
Amherst Street, 350, 352
Amory, Cleveland, 139
Anderson, Larz, 131, 159
Anderson Bridge, 10, 152, 157, 159, 170, 173, 174
Andover Hall, 280–81
Andover Theological Seminary, 280–81
Annex House. *See* Fay House
Apley Court, 123–24
Appian Way, 188–91
Appleton, Frances ("Fanny"), 209–10
Appleton Chapel, Memorial Church, 52, 64, 80–81, 82, 88, 270
Apthorp, East, 135–36, 238–39
Apthorp House, 98, 134, 135–37, 238, 239, 295
Argonauts, the, 121
Arnold, Benedict, 208, 220
Arrow Street, 141–42
Arsenal Square, 248
Arthur M. Sackler Museum, 286–87
Arts and Media Building, M.I.T., 339
Asa Gray House, 255
Ash Street, 181, 200–201, 230
Ashdown, Dr. Avery A., 322
Ashdown House, 321–22
Athenaeum Building, 301, 358, 359
Athletic Center, M.I.T., 318–19
Atkinson, Brooks, 154
Auburn School, 184–85
Auburn Street, 302
Austin, Edwin, 261, 269–70
Austin family, 304
Austin Hall, 269–70
Avon Hill, 261

Back Bench Pub (sculpture), 271
Bacon, Robert, 141
Baez, Joan, 146
Baker, Everett M., 319
Baker, George F., 165, 166, 167, 168, 169
Baker, George F., Jr., 169
Baker, George Pierce, 40, 110, 170, 180, 191–92, 197, 223, 283, 296
Baker Hall, 170
Baker House, 319, 320, 321
Baker Library, 114, 164–65, 166, 167–68
Ballou, Hosea, 227, 305
Baltimore, David, 348
Baptist Church, 296, 363
Bardeen, John, 156
Barry, J. Fred ("Jack"), 266

Barry's Corner, 266
Barrymore, John, 50
Bartlett, John, 122, 218
Bath Lane, 201
Battle Road, 262–63
Bechtel Room, Emerson Hall, 85
Beck, Charles, 289, 295
Beck Hall, 295–96
Beck House, 289
Beck's Park, 295
Beebe, Lucius, 121
Beech Street, 263
Belcher, Andrew, 100
Belcher, Andrew, Jr., 100
Belcher, Jonathan, 100, 205, 236
Belfer, Robert Alexander, 175–76
Belfer Center for Public Management, 174, 175–76
Bell, Alexander Graham, 176, 307
Benchley, Robert, 50, 133
Benet, Stephen, 50
Benjamin, Asher, 304
Benton, Thomas Hart, 332
Bergman, Ingrid, 180
Berkeley Street, 245–46, 249, 260
Bernard, Francis, 42, 43, 48, 51, 239
Berryman, John, 189
Bertram Hall, 252, 253
Bexley Hall, 317
Bigelow, Dr. Jacob, 226, 227–28
Bishop Richard Allen Drive, 304
Bishop's Palace, 206
Bitter, Francis, 313
Blacksmith House, 185–86
Blaschkas, 273–74
Blashfield, Edwin H., 341
Blodgett, John W., Jr., 161
Blodgett Pool, 161
Blue Anchor Tavern, 97, 100, 103, 117, 122, 258
Bogart, Humphrey, 180
Bok, Derek, 189, 192, 199, 222, 259
Bond, George, 251
Bond, William Cranch, 251, 290–91
Bond Street, 251–52
Bordman, Andrew, IV, 306
Bordman, William, 13, 115
Boston Symphony Orchestra, 18
Boston Tea Party, 17, 43, 104
Boston Woven Hose and Rubber Company, 347, 348
Bosworth, Welles, 323, 327, 329, 341, 350
Botanical Garden, 236, 254
Boulanger, Nadia, 247
Bow Street, 134, 136, 137, 140–41, 145

Bowditch, Nathaniel, 107
Bowdoin, James, 14, 38
Boylston Hall, 90–91, 274
Bradford, Francis Scott, 351
Bradford, Robert F., 228
Bradford, William, 214, 228, 229
Bradish, Ebenezer, 97
Bradish, Sister, 117–18
Bradish's, 97–98
Bradstreet, Anne, 3, 11, 96, 141
Bradstreet, Simon, 11, 107
Braintree Company, 95, 97
Brandeis, Louis D., 59–60, 271
Brattle, Thomas, 178–79, 180, 181, 201, 256, 259
Brattle, William, 140, 181, 205, 228, 238
Brattle Building, 19
Brattle Hall. See Brattle Theatre
Brattle House, 179, 181–83, 259, 329
Brattle Square, 133, 176, 178, 179
Brattle Station, 176
Brattle Street, 3, 6, 10, 11, 19, 60, 103, 116, 132, 133, 173, 178, 179, 180–86, 191–93, 198–99, 202, 204, 207, 215–19, 223–24, 277, 329
Brattle Theatre, 180
Brattle's Mall, 178–79
Brewster, William, 184, 215, 226
Bridge, John, 31, 107, 238
Bridge, Samuel, 61
Bridge Street, 366
Briggs, Frank H., 317–18
Briggs, LeBaron R., 161, 191, 193, 198, 199, 253
Briggs Athletic Center, 161
Briggs Hall, 253
Briggs' Athletic Field, 315, 317
Bright Hockey Center, 163
Brighton Street, 159
Brimmer, George W., 226
Broad Canal, 354, 356, 357, 358
Broadway, 7, 297, 305
Brooks, Phillips, 52–53, 56, 63, 81, 131, 206, 284, 361
Brown, John Mason, 111
Browne, George H. ("Daddy"), 190
Browne and Nichols School. See Buckingham Browne and Nichols School
Bryan Hall, 154
Bryant Street, 280
Buckingham, Harriet, 192
Buckingham Browne and Nichols School, 190–91, 214, 228, 229–30, 246, 249–50
Buckingham House, 192, 193
Buckingham Place, 249–50

Building 20, 332, 344, 345. *See also* Rad Lab
Bulfinch, Charles, 55, 61, 136, 360, 364
Bulfinch Building, 363–64
Bulfinch Square, 363–64
Bundy, McGeorge, 156
Bunker Hill, Battle of, 25, 26, 27, 31, 45, 219, 220, 228, 267, 269, 275
Bunker Hill Monument, 365
Bunting, Mary I., 195, 248, 253
Bunting Institute, 193, 248, 273
Burden, William A. M., 170
Burden Auditorium, 169–70
Burgoyne, John ("Gentleman Johnny"), 6, 33, 98, 136, 216, 239
Burnham Hall, 203
Burr, Francis H., 289
Burton, Alfred E., 320
Burton Hall, 320
Burton House, 320
Busch, Adolphus, 277
Busch–Reisinger Museum, 277, 296
Bush, Vannevar, 288, 310, 330, 335–36, 344
Bush Builidng, 335
Byerly, William E., 195
Byerly Hall, 114, 195–96, 241

Cabot, Godfrey Lowell, 268
Cabot, Dr. R. C., 253
Cabot, Mr. and Mrs. Thomas Dudley, 274
Cabot Hall, 253
Cabot House, 253
Cabot Science Complex, 274
Cage, Carey, 163
Calder, Alexander, 333, 341, 343
Caldwell, Sarah, 247
Cambridge Armory, 314
Cambridge Boat Club, 201, 230
Cambridge Bridge. *See* Longfellow Bridge
Cambridge Cemetery, 230, 289, 305
Cambridge Center, 355–56
Cambridge Center for Adult Education, 181, 185
Cambridge Common, 5, 23–33
Cambridge Dramatic Club, 191
Cambridge Forum, 24
Cambridge Gas Works, 201
Cambridge Gateway, 356–57
Cambridge Grammar School, 237
Cambridge Historical Commission, 301, 365–66
Cambridge Historical Society, 183, 217, 329, 353
Cambridge Hospital, 232
Cambridge Latin School, 190, 297
Cambridge Manual Training School, 297
Cambridge Multicultural Arts Center, 364

Cambridge I fire station, 177
Cambridge Parkway, 358–59
Cambridge police station and jail house, 19
Cambridge Public Library, 219
Cambridge Rindge and Latin School, 297–98
Cambridge School for Girls, 193, 196, 243, 248
Cambridge Social Dramatic Club, 248
Cambridge Social Union, 180, 181, 183, 191
Cambridge Street, 7, 267, 286, 366
Cambridge Tavern, 12
Cambridge Taylor Club band, 305
Cambridge Tire, 314
Cambridge Water Company, 69
Cambridgeport, 3, 7, 299–308, 353–57
Canaday Hall, 81–82, 287
Canada, Ward Murphy, 81–82
Canal Bridge. *See* Craigie's Bridge
Captain's Island, 301–2
Cardullo, Frank, 96
Carpenter Center for Visual Arts, 287–88
Carr, Jasper B., 319
Carret House, 188, 189, 191, 194, 255
Carter's Ink Building, 357–58
Casino, the, 201
Celanese Corporation of America, 342
Center for Advanced Engineering, M.I.T., 333, 334
Center for Cancer Research, M.I.T., 348, 349
Center for Life Sciences, M.I.T., 342
Center for Materials Science and Engineering, M.I.T., 335
Center for Space Research, M.I.T., 334
Central Avenue, 227
Central Square, 136, 295, 301, 302, 303
Chamberlain, Samuel E., 30
Channing, Edward, 85
Charles Hotel, 177
Charles River, 5, 6, 29, 41, 64, 79, 80, 83, 90, 96, 97, 101, 106, 141, 157, 173, 229, 263, 273, 289
Charles River Dam, 7, 114, 133, 311, 348
Charles River Embankment Company, 311
Charles Stark Draper Laboratories, 346
Charlestown ferry, 44
Charlestown–Watertown King's Highway, 25, 29
Charlestown–Watertown Path, 29, 97, 202
Chase, Salmon B., 166
Chauncy, Charles, 236
Cheeshahteaumuch, Caleb, 72
Cherry Street, 306
Chesholme, Thomas, 108, 117
Chester, John, 239
Child, Francis J. ("Stubby"), 46, 63, 190, 283
Child, Paul, 282

Chomsky, Noam, 156, 345
Christ Church, 25, 27, 30, 135, 185, 235, 237, 238–40
Church, Dr. Benjamin, 38–39, 206
Church of Jesus Christ of Latter-day Saints, 211
Church of the New Jerusalem, 285–86
Church Row. *See* Brattle Street
Church Street, 16, 19, 183
Churchill, Winston, 77–78, 285, 287, 291, 318
City Hall, 295, 299–300, 301
Civil War, 23, 30–31, 32, 63, 83, 160, 232, 249, 252, 284, 304, 310, 340, 354
Civil War Monument, 27, 29
Clark, Henry A., 56
Class Day Tree, 53, 54
Class of 1880 Gate, 141
Claverly Hall, 134, 135
Clerk of the Court Building, 364
Cleveland, Grover, 71, 79
Clinton, Sir Henry, 262
Clough, Arthur Hugh, 191
Club of 1862, 32
Club 47, 146
College Hall, 43–44, 46
College House #1, 16, 33, 134
College House #2, 16–17, 45
Colonial Club, 289
Com/Energy Building, 357
Commander, the, 245
Commercial Avenue, 358
Compton, Karl Taylor, 318, 344, 345, 350
Compton Court, 343, 345
Compton Laboratories, 344
Comstock, Ada Louise, 199, 200, 253
Conant, James B., 39, 77, 78, 79, 86, 90–91, 110, 111, 135, 139, 169, 189, 213, 271, 274, 279–80, 285, 287, 288, 291
Conant Hall, 273
Concord Avenue, 7, 186, 248, 272–73
Concord–Cambridge turnpike of 1807, 29
Concord Turnpike, 353
Congregational Church, 204
Conner, Arthur J., 320
Conner Hall, 320
Continental Congress, 208, 239, 299
Continental Hotel, 247–48
Converse Lab, 274
Cooke, Joseph, 129
Cooke, Josiah, 63, 90
Coolidge, Calvin, 322
Coolidge, Charles A., 148
Coolidge, Josiah, 228, 229
Coolidge Avenue, 228–30
Coolidge Hall, 191, 286
Coolidge Hill, 213, 229, 290

Coolidge Hill Road, 228–29
Cooper, John, 260
Cooper, Samuel, 260
Cooper family, 260–61
Cooper Tavern, 262–63
Copeland, Charles Townsend ("Copey"), 49, 50, 57, 82–83, 243
Copley, John Singleton, 39
Corlet, Elijah, 108, 124, 237
Cornerstone Baptist Church, 264
Cornerstone Park, 264
Cotting Hall, 166
Cotton, John, 109, 360
Court House, Harvard Square, 17
Courthouse, East Cambrdige, 359
Cowperthwaite Street, 149
Cox, Archibald, 259
Craigie, Dr. Andrew, 133, 178, 208–9, 210, 223, 231, 242, 251, 263–64, 267, 366
Craigie, Elizabeth, 209, 210, 212
Craigie Bridge, 7, 133, 208, 262, 365, 366, 367
Craigie House, 3, 212
Craigie Street, 213, 249
Crane, Charles, 167
Creek Lane, 96
Crimeds, 132, 139
Cronkhite, Bernice Brown, 200
Cronkhite Graduate Center, 200, 201
Cronyn, Hume, 180
Crooked Lane, 124, 177. *See also* Holyoke Street
Cummings, E. E., 59, 83, 105, 282
Currier House, 253, 254

Daggett candy factories, 348
Dana, Edmund Trowbridge, 301
Dana, Elizabeth, 191
Dana, Ernest, 210–11
Dana, Francis, 44, 125, 133, 178, 223, 236, 282, 295, 298, 299, 302, 307, 310–11, 353, 366
Dana, Richard H., Sr., 219
Dana, Richard Henry, III ("Dick"), 4, 49, 66, 102, 122, 183, 184, 191, 199, 210, 211–12, 215, 217, 230, 231, 236, 245, 246, 249, 250, 290, 299, 303–4, 353
Dana, Sarah, 304
Dana family, 125, 210, 240, 295, 302, 313
Dana Hill, 297, 299, 300
Dana House, 245–46, 251, 299, 302
Dana Library, 301
Dana–Palmer House, 288, 290–91
Dana Square, 302
Dana Street, 295, 298–99

Dana tomb, 236
Dane, Nathan, 15, 17
Dane Hall, 15, 17, 20, 23, 24, 69
Danforth, Thomas, 100, 276
Darwin, Charles, 254, 255
Daughters of the American Revolution, 26
Davenport, Charles, 307, 308, 311
Davenport, Rufus, 308, 354
Davenport Tavern, 262
David, Donald K., 168-69
Dawes, William, 6, 7, 25-26, 104, 159, 256, 257
Daye, Matthew, 13, 87
Daye, Stephen, 12-13, 87, 124, 237
De Voto, Bernard, 121
Deane, Charles, 214, 215
Dean's House, Harvard, 164-65, 169
Delphic Club, 135
Delta, 267-68, 286
Delta Upsilon, 110
Dever, Paul, 250-51
Dewey Library, 351
DeWolfe Street, 145-46, 148-49
Dexter Gate, 140
Dickens, Charles ("Boz"), 3, 18, 88, 209-10, 221, 247, 303
Dickinson, Emily, 250
Diehl, Leo, 266
Dillon, Clarence, 161
Dillon Field House, 161-62
Divinity Avenue, 90, 276, 277-79
Divinity Hall, 88, 277, 278-79, 281
Dock Steet, 355
Dock Square. See Kendall Square
Dole, Elizabeth, 259
Donham, Wallace B., 164-65, 166, 168, 169
Dorrance, John T., 342
Dorrance Building, M.I.T., 342
Dos Passos, John, 50, 59
Draper, Charles Stark ("Doc"), 333, 346-48, 359
Draper, William F., 175
Draper Lab, 333, 346-48, 353, 356
Dreyfus, Camille Edouard, 342
Dreyfus Building, 341
Drowne, Shem, 241
D. U. Club, 108, 110
Du Bois, W.E.B., 282-83
Du Pont, David Flett, 314
Du Pont, Lamont, 314
Du Pont, T. Coleman, 311, 319, 324, 325, 338
Du Pont Athletic Center and Rockwell Cage, 314-15, 317, 318-19
Du Pont Court, 324
Dudley, Samuel, 111

Dudley, Simon, 96
Dudley, Thomas, 5, 11, 95, 102, 106, 107, 108, 111, 129, 140-41, 200, 204, 307
Dudley Gate, 141
Dudley House, 108, 110-11, 123-24, 260
Dunlop, John T., 269
Dunster, Henry, 13, 37-38, 72, 73, 102, 117-18, 124, 150, 179, 235-36
Dunster Hall, 110
Dunster House, 110, 129, 149, 150-51, 170
Dunster Street, 5, 12-13, 106-11
Duveneck, Frank, 85
Dyke Street, 152

Earth Sciences Building, M.I.T., 309, 339, 341-42, 343
East Asian Research Institute, 286
East Cambridge, 7, 357-67
East Campus Alumni Houses, 341
Eastgate, M.I.T., 309, 352
Eastman, George, 337-38
Eastman Laboratories, 337
Eaton, Nathaniel, 72, 73, 116-17
Edgerton, Harold E. ("Doc"), 310, 332, 335, 350
Edgewater Place, 367
Edward Pickman Concert Hall, 247
EG & G Education Center, 334-35
Egyptian Gateway, 226, 228
Ehrlich, David P., 121
Eisenhower, Dwight D., 316, 331
Election Oak, 31, 37
Electrical Engineering and Computer Science Department, M.I.T., 334
Eliot, Abigail, 280
Eliot, Charles, 214, 230
Eliot, Charles W., 4, 9, 10, 24-25, 49, 52, 57-58, 59, 61, 63, 64, 69, 78-79, 81, 83, 84, 90, 113, 114, 119-20, 131, 147, 155, 160, 162, 164, 183, 188, 192-93, 194, 195, 214, 222, 223-24, 230, 247, 253, 254, 268, 270, 273, 277, 278-79, 280, 282, 283, 284, 288, 297, 306
Eliot, John, 108, 142
Eliot, T. S., 50, 105, 115, 123, 151, 156-57, 180, 201, 285
Eliot Bridge, 229, 230
Eliot Gate, 288
Eliot Hall, Radcliffe, 253
Eliot House, 112, 154-57, 170, 173
Eliot Square, 176
Eliot Street, 6, 10, 104, 173, 176, 177
Ellen Swallow lobby, 337
Ellery, William, 299
Ellery Street, 298

Elm Street, 305
Elmwood (estate), 221, 223, 231, 276
Elmwood Avenue, 220, 223
Emerson, Ralph Waldo, 3, 18, 24, 30, 46, 49, 63, 82, 85, 102, 119, 145, 160, 217, 242, 278, 279, 329
Emerson, William, 30, 217
Emerson Hall, 85–86, 288
Emmanuel College, 97
Endicott, John, 359
Endicott Street, 319
Energy Building, M.I.T., 352
Episcopal Divinity School (E.D.S.), 202–4, 206, 218, 246
Everett, Edward, 24, 46, 56, 78, 119, 195, 209
Everett Street, 272

Fairbank, John F., 127–28, 286
Fairchild, Sherman M., 334, 335
Fairchild Building, 337, 344
Faneuil Hall, 241
Farrar Street, 283
Farwell, Levi, 11–12, 185
Farwell Place, 11, 184–85, 191
Farwell's Corner, 11, 12, 13
Fay, Maria, 58, 188, 194
Fay, Samuel, 195
Fay House, 58, 188, 190, 194–95, 241, 243, 299
Fayerweather, Hannah, 219
Fayerweather, Thomas, 219
Fayerweather House, 219
Feldstein, Martin S., 269
Felix M. Warburg Hall, 287
Fellow's Orchard, 13, 87
Felton, Cornelius, 3, 276
Felton Hall, 190
Fermi, Enrico, 288
Fields, James T., 210, 246, 260
Filene, A. Lincoln, 189
First Baptist Church, 302
First Cambridge Universalist Church, 301, 305
First Church (Congregational), 27, 29, 181, 241–42
First Church of Christ, Scientist, 258
First Parish Meeting House, 140
First Unitarian Church, 188, 235, 242
Fisher, George, 306
Fiske, John, 202, 246, 249, 260
Fitchburg Railroad, 260–61, 266
Flagg Street, 149, 150, 157
Flagstaff Park, 25
Fly Club, 131, 139, 154
Flynt, Henry, 238
Fogg Art Museum, 69, 82, 145, 229, 281, 287

Follen, Charles, 283–84, 289
Follen Street, 10
Football Club, 52
Forbes, Edward W., 114, 145, 147, 217, 229, 281, 287
Forbes Arcade, 125
Forbes Plaza, 114–15
Forrester, Jay W., 310, 352
Fort #1, 297, 298
Fort #2, 296–97, 298
Fort Putnam, 362
Fort Washington, 313–14
47 Workshop, 40, 197, 283, 296
Forum, the, 175
Fox Club, 100
Foxcroft House, 276
Francis Avenue, 279–80
Frankfurter, Felix, 83, 223
Franklin, Benjamin, 42, 64, 100, 208
Freedom Square, 131, 133
Freeman, James, 354
French, Daniel Chester, 4, 32, 61, 130, 184, 202, 211, 215, 267, 274, 309, 341
Fresh Pond, 41, 100, 184, 186, 213, 215, 219, 220, 223, 224–26, 236, 243, 244
Fresh Pond Inn, 225
Fresh Pond Lane, 224
Fresh Pond Parkway, 223
Freshman Union, 289–90
Frick, Henry Clay, 167
Friends Center, 211
Front Street, 309, 310–11, 312
Frost, Gideon, 261
Frost, Neptune, 238
Frost, Robert, 4–5, 59, 83, 111, 138, 213, 261, 285
Fuller, Alvan T., 214, 317
Fuller, Buckminster, 146, 162, 187
Fuller, Margaret, 8, 146, 182–83, 187, 298, 299, 301, 306
Fuller, Thomas, 299
Fuller, Timothy, 182–83
Fusion Center, M.I.T., 313

Gage, Thomas, 14, 17, 18, 206, 216, 217, 220, 243, 263, 360
Galbraith, John Kenneth, 269, 280
Gallatin, Albert, 166
Gallatin Hall, 169
Gallows Hill, 261
Gannett, Caleb, 256, 259
Gannett House, 31, 256–57
Garden Street, 25, 26–27, 185, 196, 235, 236–41, 245, 246–48, 252, 299
Gardner, Isaac, 265

Garrison, William Lloyd, 23, 303, 305, 354
Gas House, 126
Gates, Horatio, 182
Gay, Edwin F., 64–65
General Court, 38, 42, 43, 51, 61–62, 107, 108, 109
Gentleman's Society, the. *See* Porcellian Club
George III, King, 43, 220
Germanic Museum, 286
Gerry, Elbridge, 221, 224, 228, 231
Gerry's Landing, 102, 213, 220, 223, 228, 229, 231, 246
Gilman, Arthur, 192–93, 194, 195, 196, 197, 227, 243, 248, 249, 358
Gilman, Samuel, 195
Gilman Gate, 198, 199
Gingold, Hermione, 180
Glass, Carter, 166
Glover, John, 208
Glover, Jose, 102, 117
Goddard, Robert H., 333
God's Acre, 7, 25, 26, 30, 202, 221, 235–38, 261, 299
Goffe, Edward, 117
Goffe's College, 117
Gold Coast, 101, 106, 110, 114, 123, 131, 133, 135, 147, 295
Gomes, Peter J., 276
Gookin, Daniel, 142, 238
Gordon Indoor Track and Tennis Facility, 163
Gordon McKay Engineering Research Laboratory, 274–75
Gore, Christopher, 87, 125, 152, 363–64
Gore Courtyard, 153
Gore Hall, 53, 87–88, 90, 106, 152–53
Gore Library, 13, 58
Gould, Thomas, 31–32
Grace Methodist Church, 302
Grand Junction railroad, 311
Graphic Arts Building, M.I.T., 352
Graves, Thomas, 359–60
Gray, Asa, 227, 254–55
Gray, Francis Calley, 69
Gray, Horace, 224
Gray, Paul E., 326, 350
Gray, William ("Billy"), 69, 224
Gray's Hall, 69–70, 224
Great Bridge, 96, 104, 159, 173, 263
Great Court, 323, 324–25, 326, 330. *See also* Killian Court
Great Dome, 309, 313, 332, 349
Great Hall, 132
Great House, 108
Great Rebellion of 1834, 32
Greek Orthodox Church, 302

Greeley, Horace, 298
Green, Cecil H., 321, 343
Green, Ida, 321, 343
Green, James D., 305, 360, 361
Green, Samuel, 72, 108
Green Building, M.I.T., 343
Green Hall, 321, 343
Greenhouse Courtyard, 268
Greenleaf, James, 199
Greenleaf, Simon, 199, 201
Greenleaf House, 180, 199, 200
Greenough, James B., 191, 192
Grendel's Den, 101–102, 108, 177
Griffin Gate, 153–54, 156, 157
Grolier Book Shop, 139
Gropius, Walter, 271, 286, 288
Grozier, Edwin A., 218
Guggenheim, Daniel, 333
Guggenheim Building, 333
Guglielmo, Joseph Austin de, 179
Gund, George, 364
Gund, Graham, 364
Gund Hall, 84, 275, 285, 286, 364
Gutman, Monroe C., 188
Gutman Library, 185, 188

Hadzi, Dmitri, 20
Halcyon Lake, 228
Hall, Ebenezer, 47
Hall, Samuel, 47
Hamilton, Alexander, 166, 170
Hamilton Hall, 170
Hancock, John, 6, 14, 38, 43, 44–45, 49, 100, 206, 216
Hancock Tower, 313
Hardwick, H. R. ("Tack"), 161
Harkness, Edward S., 40, 129–30, 148, 155, 271
Harkness Commons, 271–72
Harris, Richard, 102
Harrison, Peter, 238–39
Hart, Albert Bushnell, 85, 183, 191, 249
Hart Nautical Museum, 327, 328–29, 340
Harte, Bret, 210
Harvard, John, 4, 5, 32, 37, 42, 53, 61–62, 72, 73, 86, 87, 109–10, 116–17, 124, 267, 290
Harvard (sloop), 107, 152
Harvard Advocate, 104–105, 150–51
Harvard Alumni Bulletin, 111
Harvard Annex, 188. *See also* Fay House
Harvard Athletic Department, 103
Harvard Athletics ticket office, 46
Harvard Band, 137, 158, 163
Harvard Boat Club, 157, 160
Harvard Book Store, 139, 140

Harvard Bridge, 311–12, 324
Harvard Business Review, 166–67
Harvard Cadets, 32
Harvard Center for Asian Research, 127
Harvard Center for International Affairs, 286
Harvard Charter, 107
Harvard College, 11, 12–14, 16, 23, 24, 30, 32–33, 72–73, 96, 103, 116, 117, 125. *See also* Harvard Yard
Harvard Cooperative Society, 15, 17, 18, 19, 166
Harvard Crimson, 55, 56, 132–33, 137, 138–39, 142, 290
Harvard Divinity School, 260, 276, 280–81
Harvard Dramatic Club, 197
Harvard Faculty Club, 288
Harvard Glee Club, 18, 52, 115
Harvard Graduate School of Business Administration, 64–65, 82
Harvard Graduate School of Design, 82, 113
Harvard Grammar School, 301
Harvard Hall, 5, 37, 39, 41, 42–47, 48, 51, 55, 58, 61, 73, 78, 86, 113, 116, 239
Harvard Information Center, 114
Harvard Lampoon, 49, 60, 70, 71, 101, 105, 125, 126, 131–34, 150, 260
Harvard Law School, 15–17, 23, 31, 45, 60, 138, 159, 167, 222, 252, 257, 258–59, 269, 270, 271, 272, 278–79, 287
Harvard magazine, 296
Harvard Medical School, 51–52, 236, 243, 247
Harvard Motor House, 177
Harvard Museum, 215
Harvard Observatory, 207, 251, 268, 291
Harvard Poetry Society, 59
Harvard–Radcliffe Catholic Student Center, 142
Harvard–Radclife Dramatic Club, 192
Harvard–Radcliffe Fund, 120
Harvard–Radcliffe Graduate School of Education, 188, 189, 241
Harvard–Radcliffe Hillel B'nai B'rith, 126
Harvard–Radcliffe Science Center, 195–96, 267, 268, 270, 275, 276
Harvard School of Architecture and Landscape Architecture, 84, 286
Harvard Square, 3–20, 25, 26, 68, 201, 262, 300
Harvard Stadium, 6
Harvard Street, 295, 296
Harvard Subway Station, 179
Harvard Union, 289
Harvard University. *See entries beginning with* Harvard
Harvard University police station, 248
Harvard University Press, 277

Harvard Varsity Club, 163, 289
Harvard Way, 164, 166, 167, 169
Harvard–Yale football game, 162–63, 173
Harvard Yard, 12, 16, 23, 25, 32, 37–73, 201
Harvard-Yenching Institute, 90, 277–78
Hastings, "Yankee John," Sr., 257
Hastings family, 258, 269
Hastings Hall, 257–58
Hasty Pudding Club, 41, 49, 55–56, 69–70, 99, 122–23, 126, 127, 145, 146, 195
Haughton, Percy D., 162
Hawthorn Street, 205
Hayden, Charles, 339
Hayden Art Gallery, 339, 349
Hayden Library, 343, 349
Hayden Memorial, 339, 340
Hayes, Rutherford B., 15, 78–79, 126–27, 221, 271
Haymarket Square. *See* Central Square
Haynes, John, 102
HCKP Club, 146
Health Services Center and Infirmary, M.I.T., 330, 349
Hearst, William Randolph, 60, 70–71, 132
Heath, William, 98, 136, 263
Hebrew Room, 46
Heizer, Michael, 325
Hemenway, Augustus, 196, 257
Hemenway Gymnasium, 196–97, 257, 268, 286
Hemingway, Ernest, 50
Henderson, Lawrence J., 156
Henderson, Robert, 264
Henderson Carriage Building, 263–64
Henry, Prince of Prussia, 277, 286
Henry Vassall House. *See* Vassall House
Hermann, Grove M., 351
Hermann Building, 351
Herreshoff, Nathaniel G., 328
Herreshoff yards, 340
Hicks, John, 104, 107, 265
Hicks House, 104, 126, 154
Higginson, Henry Lee, 83, 131, 160–61, 194, 247, 289–90
Higginson, Thomas Wentworth, 18, 63, 99, 162, 164, 183, 219–20, 235, 250, 275, 353–54
Highland Street, 213–14
Highway to Menotomy, the, 256
Hill, Albert G., 347
Hilles Library, 198, 252
Hilliard, William, 186
Hilliard Street, 4, 186–87, 188
Hillyer, Robert, 59, 121
Hither Pyne Swampe, 259

Hocking, Agnes, 290
Hocking, William E., 290
Holden, Jane, 51
Holden Chapel, 44, 51, 129
Holden Quadrangle, 51–54, 55
Hollis, Thomas, 48, 239
Hollis family, 118
Hollis Hall, 16, 23, 42, 44, 45, 47, 48–51, 55, 56, 57, 59
Holmes, Abiel, 24, 124–25, 140, 242, 256, 295, 302, 360
Holmes, John, 12, 102, 189
Holmes, Oliver Wendell, 8, 12, 24, 56, 78, 102, 124–25, 131, 189, 225, 235, 240, 242, 256, 261, 269, 270, 284, 299, 301
Holmes Field, 138–39, 159, 163, 270–71, 284
Homes House, 268, 269, 270, 275
Holmes Place, 256, 268, 269
Holworthy, Sir Matthew, 57
Holworthy Gate, 267
Holworthy Hall, 56, 57–58, 67
Holy Cross Armenian Catholic Church, 101–2
Holy Cross Polish National Catholic Church, 361
Holy Trinity Armenian Church, 215
Holyoke, Edward, 42, 46, 113, 119, 129, 236, 242
Holyoke Center, 111, 113–14, 124, 126, 142, 149, 281
Holyoke House, 114–15
Holyoke Place, 129–31
Holyoke Street, 56, 108, 114, 122–25, 126–28, 129, 177
Homberg, Richard M., 330
Homberg Building, 329–30, 334
Homer, Winslow, 4, 32, 225, 241, 292–99
Hong Kong Restaurant, 140
Hooker, Thomas, 29, 95, 97, 102, 109, 116, 118, 213
Hooker–Shepard House, 117
Hopkinson, Charles, 259
Horner, Matina, 199
Horsford, Eben, 213
Horsford, Lillian, 213
Houdon, Jean Antoine, 245
Hough, Atherton, 360
Houghton, Henry O., 298
Houghton Library, 48, 86
House Plan, 40, 80, 101, 104, 106, 110, 129, 131, 134, 135, 139, 141, 145, 146, 147–48, 150, 155, 173, 229, 253
Howard–Epworth Methodist Church, 258
Howe, Elias, Jr., 306
Howe, Estes, 255, 276
Howe, Lois, 255

Howells, William Dean, 8, 179, 210, 225, 246, 248–49, 259–60, 273, 354
Howes family, 240
Hubbard, Gardiner G., 201
Humanities Library, M.I.T., 339
Hunt Hall, 82
Huntington Hall, M.I.T., 331–32
Hurley, Charles F., 224
Huron Avenue, 224
Hutchinson, Anne, 31, 43, 109, 110, 118
Hutchinson, Thomas, 14, 43, 51, 136, 216, 220, 238, 241–42

Idler Club, 195, 197
Indian College, 72, 108
Indoor Athletic Building, Harvard, 104, 106, 107, 126
Inman, Ralph, 300
Inman House, 136, 295, 302, 310
Inman Street, 300, 301
Institute Chapel, 317
Institute of Geographical Exploration, 277–78
Institute of 1770, 123
Institute of Politics, J.F.K. School of Government, 175
Instrumentation Lab, M.I.T., 333, 346
Inventors' Hall of Fame, 310
Ireland, Abraham, 25
Iroquois clubhouse, 126
Irving and Casson, 365
Irving Street, 245, 280, 281–82
Italian Culture and Social Center, 357

Jackson, Andrew, 62, 183
Jackson, Dr. James, 52
James, Alice, 296
James, Henry, Jr., 289
James, Henry, Sr., 288–89
James, William, 4, 15, 57, 60, 83, 85, 111, 191, 225, 245, 250, 278, 282–83, 289, 296
James House, 288–89
James Street, 198–99
Jared Sparks House, 275
Jarvis, Leonard, 299, 300, 310–11
Jarvis Field, 52, 159, 162, 259, 272, 284
Jarvis Street, 258, 259
Jefferson, Thomas, 194, 224, 244, 275, 323, 354
Jefferson Lab, 270
Jenner, Dr. Edward, 244
J.F.K. Memorial Park, 173, 174
J.F.K. Presidential Library, 174
John F. Kennedy Institute, 147
John F. Kennedy School of Government, 153, 170, 173–76, 268

John P. Squire and Company, 361
Johnson, Howard W., 349, 350, 351
Johnson, Lyndon, 341, 349, 356
Johnson, Philip, 286
Johnston Gate, 37, 53, 267
Johnston, Samuel, 37
Jones, Howard Mumford, 280
Jones's Hill, 261
Josef Louis Sert Gallery, 287

Keller, Helen, 200, 229, 248, 249
Kendall, Edward, 354
Kendall, Goody, 261
Kendall Building, 355
Kendall Square, 353–57
Kennedy, Caroline, 174
Kennedy, Frank A., 217–18
Kennedy, John F., 69, 79, 96, 123, 125, 137, 139, 152–53, 174, 175, 179, 264, 349
Kennedy, Joseph, Jr., 69
Kennedy, Robert, 125, 152–53, 362
Kennedy Road, 217–18
Kennedy Street, 10–12, 95–99, 100, 103, 104, 159, 170
Kent, Amos, 258
Kepes, Gyorgy, 271
Keynes, John Maynard, 223
Khorana, Har G., 342
Kilby Street, 307
Killian, James R., Jr., 316, 325, 330–31, 333, 339, 344, 345, 350, 351
Killian Court, 330, 332
Kimball, Mrs. David Pulsifer, 253
King, Martin Luther, Jr., 297
King's Highway, 5, 207, 220, 242, 275
Kingsley Park, 225
Kiosk, Harvard Square, 19–20
Kirkland, John T., 61, 62, 99, 107, 119, 154, 227, 254, 278, 280
Kirkland House, 104, 106, 107, 154
Kirkland Street, 267, 275, 280, 283
Kissinger, Henry, 286
Kittredge, George Lyman, 46–47, 105, 187
Knox, Henry, 27–28, 208
Kresge, Sebastian S., 169, 317
Kresge Auditorium, 315, 317
Kresge Hall, 168, 169
Kress, Claude W., 168
Kress Library of Business and Economics, 168

La Farge, John, 284
Laboratory for Computer Science, M.I.T., 346
Laboratory for Nuclear Science, M.I.T., 335
Lafayette, Marquis de, 14, 44
Lamont, Thomas W., 86, 139, 290

Lamont Library, 86, 118, 140–41, 290
Lampoon. See Harvard Lampoon
Land, Edwin, H., 176, 218, 307–8, 358–59
Landau, Ralph, 342
Landau Chemical Engineering Building, 342, 348
Landis, James M., 280
Lane, Katherine, 279
Langdell Hall, 270–71, 272
Langdell, C. C., 15, 131, 269, 279, 287
Langdon, Samuel, 31, 115, 269
"Larches, The," 224
Larsen, Roy Edward, 189
Larsen Hall, 189, 203
Laud, Archbishop William, 97
Law, Bernard Francis, 136–37
Lawn Avenue, 227
Lawrence, Abbott, 268
Lawrence, Amos A., 203
Lawrence, Bishop William, 54, 81, 165, 183–84, 196, 206–7
Lawrence Hall, 203, 204, 207
Lawrence Scientific School, 268, 274, 278
Le Corbusier, 288
Le Gallienne, Eva, 180
Leavitt and Peirce smoke shop, 121
Lechmere, Richard, 215, 360, 362, 363
Lechmere Canal area, 366–67
Lechmere farm, 365
Lechmere House, 215
Lechmere Point, 267, 360
Lechmere-Sewall House, 237
Lechmere Square, 365, 366
Lee, Charles, 182
Lee, "English Thomas," 237
Lee, Joseph, 217
Lee, Robert E., 249
Lehman Hall, 5, 13, 15–16, 110–11, 124
Lesley, Edith, 272
Lesley College, 248, 272, 273, 275
Lesley School for Children, 248
Lever Brothers, 347
Leverett, George, 267
Leverett, John, 38, 41, 61, 103, 118, 148, 236
Leverett House, 148–49
Lexington Green, 6
Liberty Tree, 51
Lincoln, Abraham, 3, 23, 30, 46, 195, 260, 304, 305
Lincoln Laboratory, M.I.T., 347
Lincoln's Inn Society, 258
Lindbergh, Charles, 333
Linden Street, 135–36
Linnaean Street, 25, 254, 260–61
Lionel Hall, 53

Lipchitz, Jacques, 339, 340
Lippmann, Walter, 50, 83, 279
List, Albert, 349
List, Vera, 349
Littauer, Lucius N., 174
Littauer Center of Public Administration, 174–75, 257, 261, 267, 268–69
Littauer Foundation, 176
Little, Arthur D., 316
Little Cambridge, 97, 159
Little Common, 10, 257
Little Neck Way, 296
Little's Block, 115
Lobby Shop, 317
Lobdell, Harold E., 316
Lodge, Henry Cabot, 240
Lodge family, 122
Loeb, John Langeloth, 192
Loeb Drama Center, 191, 203, 286
Longfellow, Alice, 183, 190, 193, 195, 211, 213
Longfellow, Edith, 211, 245
Longfellow, Ernest, 12, 201, 211
Longfellow, Henry, 3, 8, 18, 23, 63, 82, 88, 160, 162, 163, 179, 185, 186, 188–89, 190, 199, 202, 209–11, 212, 221, 225, 227, 235, 245, 246, 247, 249, 250, 276
Longfellow Bridge, 7, 133, 353–54, 356
Longfellow Hall, 188, 190–91
Longfellow House, 133, 207–12
Longfellow Park, 160, 204, 206, 210–11
Longworth, Nicholas, 122
Longy, Georges, 247
Longy School of Music, 247
Lotus Development Corporation, 359
L'Ouverture, Toussaint, 23
Love Lane. See Linnaean Street
Lowell, A. Lawrence, 8, 16, 40, 42, 53, 63–64, 80, 81, 88, 101, 104, 106, 111, 112, 118, 119, 129–30, 131, 135, 139, 141, 145, 146–48, 154, 155, 164, 165, 166, 167, 173, 191, 218, 222, 223, 229, 231, 249, 268, 274, 288, 275, 296, 324, 325, 329
Lowell, Amy, 59, 130, 197
Lowell, Anna, 155
Lowell, Augustus, 324–25
Lowell, Charles, 221
Lowell, James Russell, 19, 24, 56, 63, 66, 99, 130, 131, 155, 160, 219, 221, 235, 276, 308, 353–54
Lowell, Percival, 130
Lowell, Robert, 107, 130, 151, 298
Lowell Court, 324–25
Lowell House, 108, 114, 129–31, 146, 150
Lowell Institute School, 329

Lowell Lecture Hall, 275
Lowell Memorial Park, 223
Luria, Salvador E., 342
Luxford, James, 124
Luxford House, 124
Lyceum Hall, 18, 23
Lyons, Louis M., 280

McCarthy, Joseph, 87
McCollum Center, 170
McCord, David, 50, 111, 120
McCormack, Katherine Dexter, 321, 326
McCormick, Cyrus, 321
McCormick Hall, 321, 326
McCulloch Hall, 169
McCusker Center, 301
McDermott, Eugene, 341, 343
McDermott Court, 341
Macdonald, Torbert H. ("Torby"), 69
MacGregor, Frank S., 320
MacGregor House, 320
McKay, Gordon, 274–75
McKean, Joseph, 55, 118, 121, 194, 212
McKean Gate, 118, 121
McKenna, Margaret A., 273
McKinlock Hall, 147–48, 152
McNamara, Robert S., 147
Maclaurin, Richard C., 217, 227, 311, 312, 323–24, 327, 337, 338, 350
Maclaurin Building, 323, 330, 336
MacLeish, Archibald, 11, 50, 280
Madison, James, 221
Magazine Street, 301, 302–3
Magenta, 52, 56. *See also Harvard Crimson*
Mailer, Norman, 105, 150–51
Main Drag, 337, 345
Main Street, 7, 307
Malkin, Peter L., 126
Mallinckrodt, Edward, 274
Mallinckrodt Laboratory, 91, 274
Manhattan Project, 288
Manley, John, 182
Manter Hall School, 125
Margaret Hutchinson Compton Gallery, 331
Marjorie Pierce House of Women's Independent Living Group (WILG), 312
Mark (slave), 261
Marketplace, the, 20
Markham, Jeanette, 250
Markham Building, Buckingham School, 250
Marquand, John P., 3–4, 133, 135, 187
Marrett, Amos, 219
Marriott Plaza, 355, 356
Marsh, the, 231
Marsh Lane, 104

Marshall, George, 77
Marshall, John, 186, 271
Marti-Mercurian Band, 45, 46
Martin Street, 260
Martineau, Harriet, 23
Mary Baker Eddy memorial, 228
Mason Building, 270
Mason Street, 27
Massachusetts Avenue, 6, 11, 16, 31, 72, 117, 121, 133, 141, 178, 256–59, 260, 261–64, 265, 266, 295–96, 297, 298, 299–300, 301, 309–22
Massachusetts Hall, 37–41, 42, 44, 70, 78
Massachusetts Institute of Technology. See M.I.T.
Mather Hall, 148
Mather House, 149
Mather, Cotton, 48, 96, 118, 149, 237
Mather, Increase, 47, 103, 149
Mather family, 38, 46, 81
Matisse, Henri, 59
Matthews, Nathan, 69
Matthews Hall, 69, 70–72
Maugham, Somerset, 150–51
Mayhew, Jonathan, 239
Media Lab, M.I.T., 349
Mellen, John, 259
Mellen Street, 259
Mellon, Andrew, 166
Memorial Church, 77, 78, 80–82
Memorial Drive, 149, 150, 152, 173, 174, 230, 311, 319–22
Memorial Hall, 3, 50, 61, 69, 267, 283
Memorial Stone, M.I.T., 334
Mercantile Library, 310
Merriman, Robert B. ("Frisky"), 85, 275
Metropolitan Storage Warehouse, 313, 314
Microsystems Technology Lab, 334
Mid-Harvard, 77–91
Middlesex Court, 18
Middlesex Turnpike, 262, 281–82, 353
Mifflin, Thomas, 181–82
Milk Row, 263
Mill Street, 146–47
Miller's River, 362
Milmore, Martin, 227
Minutemen, 6, 14, 25, 27, 29–30, 97, 219, 220, 228, 242, 256
Miro, Joan, 271
Miss Lesley's School, 272
M.I.T., 4, 20, 217, 226, 268, 273, 275, 286, 307
M.I.T. Council for the Arts, 349
M.I.T. East Campus, 323–36, 337–52
M.I.T. Faculty Club, 351

M.I.T. Museum, 309–10
M.I.T. Press, 301, 355
M.I.T. School of Architecture and Planning, 326, 329
M.I.T. School of Engineering, 332
M.I.T. School of Science, 337
M.I.T. West Campus, 309–22
Modigliani, Franco, 351
Monis, Judah, 103
Monroe, James, 62
Moor Tavern, 258
Moore, Abel, 258
Moore, Henry, 325
Moore, Josiah, 242
Moore's Tavern, 121
Moors Hall, 253
Morgan, Dr. John, 182
Morgan, J. Pierpont, Jr., 126, 166
Morgan, Mary, 182
Morgan Hall, 164–66
Morison, Samuel Eliot, 37, 85, 89, 111, 121
Morris, Robert, 165
Morris Hall, 165
Mostel, Zero, 180
Mount Auburn Cemetery, 53, 223, 226–28, 305
Mount Auburn Hill, 227–28
Mount Auburn Hospital, 113, 214, 231–32, 252
Mount Auburn Street, 7, 16, 24, 97, 100–101, 110, 112, 113, 125–26, 129, 130–31, 133, 140, 145, 146, 177–78, 229, 231–32
Mount Auburn woods, 186
Mower Hall, 53
Mowlson, Anne Radcliffe, 194. See also Radcliffe, Anne
Mrs. Mooney's, 135
Mugar, David, 367
Munsterberg, Hugo, 85, 296
Murray Research Center, 196–97
Murray Street, 176–77
Museum of Science, 348, 367

National Magnet Lab, M.I.T., 313
Natural History Society, 40–41
Neck, the, 295
Nelson Robinson, Jr. Hall, 84
Neptune (slave), 261
New England Confectionery Co. (NECCO), 312
New England Glass Company, 361, 365
New Harvard Hall, 129
New Lecture Hall. See Lowell Lecture Hall
New West Campus Houses, 320
New York Harvard Club, 160

Newe Towne, 5, 37. *See also* Old Cambridge
Newe Towne cemetery, 202
Newe Towne Court public housing, 307
Newe Towne Marketplace, 10
Newell, Marshall, 160
Newell Boathouse, 159–60, 163
Newton, Isaac, 330
Newton tree, 330
Nichols, Edgar H., 190
Nichols House, 185, 191
Nieman, Agnes, 279–80
Nieman Foundation Center, 279
Nitze, Paul, 175
Noble and Greenough Preparatory School, 191
Nolen, William, 115, 125
Norfolk Street, 304
North Avenue Congregational Church, 261
North Harvard Street, 164, 170
North House, 254
North Street. *See* Massachussetts Avenue
Norton, Andrews, 282
Norton, Charles Eliot, 51, 71, 190, 241, 281, 282, 283, 287
Norton's Woods, 278, 280, 282, 283, 290
Nuclear Reactor Lab, M.I.T., 313

Oakes, Urian, 140
Observatory Hill, 212
Oklahoma redbud tree, 330
Old Cambridge, 95–142
Old Meeting House, 23
Old Parsonage, 140
Old Stoughton Hall, 42, 44, 47
Old Suffolk Building, 355
Old Yard. *See* Harvard Yard
Oliver, Dr. James, 238
Oliver, Thomas, 17–18, 207, 220
Olmstead, Frederick Law, 230
Onassis, Jackie, 140
Oneida Club, 157
O'Neill, Eugene, 40, 296
O'Neill, Pat, 265
O'Neill, Thomas P., Jr. ("Tip"), 3, 264, 265–66
Opposition House, 300
O'Reilly, John Boyle, 290
Osborn Street, 307–8
Ossoli, Marchese, 182
Otis, Harrison Gray, 125, 364
Otis, James ("Jemmy"), 38, 43, 56, 285
Otis Street, 361–62
Owen, George, 328, 340
Owens, Elisabeth A., 259
Owl Club, 129

Ox Marsh, 104, 173
Oxford Street, 91, 260, 273, 275

Paige, Lucius R., 258, 305–6, 359
Paine, John Howard, 270
Paine Hall, 270
Palfrey, James G., 260, 273
Palfrey, William, 239
Palmer, Alice Freeman, 85, 291
Palmer, George Herbert, 85, 86, 291
Palmer Street, 19
Pangloss bookstore, 140
Papanti, Lorenzo, 18–19
Park, Maud Wood, 198
Parker, Isaac, 17, 45
Parker, John, 219
Parker, Theodore, 278, 354
Parkman, Francis, 41
Parkman, George, 246–47
Parkman, Henry, 278
Parsons, Emily, 232, 252
Parsons, Theophilus, 125, 232, 252, 279
Parsons Building, Cambridge Hospital, 231–32
Peabody, Andrew P., 17, 33, 295
Peabody, Francis G., 81, 149, 276
Peabody Museum, 278
Peabody Street, 267
Peabody Terrace, 149–50, 170
Pearl Street, 303
Peary, Robert E., 320
Peck, William D., 254
Pei, I. M., 286, 339, 341, 342, 348
Peke, Robert, 271
Pelham, Herbert, 11, 107, 307
Pelham Island, 107, 295, 299, 307, 353
Percy, Lord, 6, 7, 26, 256, 261, 263, 265
Perkins Hall, 273
Peyntree, William, 116
Peyntree House, 116
Phi Beta Kappa, 46, 121, 127, 139, 197, 285
Phillips, John, 231, 281–82
Phillips, Wendell, 57, 354
Phillips Brooks House, 32, 52–53, 267
Phillis (slave), 261
Phips, Henry, 205
Phips, Penelope, 205–6
Phips, Rebecca, 217
Phips, Spencer, 142, 205, 207, 215, 217, 306, 360, 363
Phips, Sir William, 142
Phoenix–SK Club, 126
Pi Eta Club, 101, 145–46
Pierce, Harold W., 320
Pierce, Henry L., 341

Pierce Boathouse, 320–21
Pierce Engineering Lab, M.I.T., 341
Pierce Hall, 270
Pierian Sodality (band), 18
Pig Club, the. *See* Porcellian Club
Pike's stables, 184
Pilgrim Congregational Church, 302
Plympton Street, 135, 136, 139
Polaroid Corporation, 307–8, 309, 346
Poonsters, 132–33. *See also Harvard Lampoon*
Porcellian Club, 55, 99, 118, 121–22, 127, 139, 140, 141–42, 195, 258
Porter, Israel, 98
Porter, Kingsley, 221
Porter, Zachariah, 262
Porter Square, 8, 262
Porter Square Station, 262
Porter's (hotel), 98–99, 262
Porter's Tavern, 53, 66
Pound, Roscoe, 258–59
Pound Hall, 258–59
Pratt, Charles H., 327
Pratt, Dexter, 185, 186, 238
Pratt Building, 326, 327
Prescott, Samuel C., 328, 338
Prescott, William H., 31, 45, 49, 122
President's House, 288
Professors' Row, 275, 278, 280, 282
Prospect Hill, 297
Pub, the, 169
Pusey, Nathan M., 67–68, 87, 113, 146, 148, 149, 154, 156, 189–90, 195, 200, 267, 277, 288
Pusey Library, 86–87, 89
Putnam, Israel ("Old Put"), 30, 104, 136, 220, 296, 300–301, 362
Putnam Apartments, 362
Putnam Avenue, 296
Putnam House, 192, 254
Putnam School, 362

Quarter Century Club, M.I.T., 345
Quincy, Josiah ("Old Quin"), 17, 24, 32, 33, 49, 54, 62, 67, 146, 186
Quincy Hall, 141, 147
Quincy House, 146, 147, 148, 149
Quincy Street, 80, 86, 141, 285, 287, 295

Rad (Radiation) Lab, M.I.T., 331, 332, 334, 335, 337, 344–45
Radcliffe, Anne, 73. *See also* Mowlson, Anne Radcliffe
Radcliffe Choral Society, 52
Radcliffe College, 3, 4, 39, 73, 77, 79, 87, 101, 105, 114, 138, 146, 166, 180, 188, 241,

243, 248, 272. *See also* Radcliffe Yard; *and entries beginning with* Harvard–Radcliffe
Radcliffe Dance Center, 197
Radcliffe Quadrangle, 252–55
Radcliffe Recreational Center, 252
Radcliffe Yard, 4, 5, 6, 15, 16, 27, 180, 188, 192, 241
Ramsay's Pharmacy, 19
Randall Hall, 277
Randolph Hall, 16, 134, 135, 136, 137
Random Hall, 312
Read House, 185, 191
Rebellion Tree, 51, 67
Red Lion Inn, 258
Reed, Benjamin Tyler, 203
Reed, John, 50, 133
Reed Hall, 203
Reischauer, Edwin O., 286
Remington, Jonathan, 236
Remington Street, 296
Research Laboratory of Electronics, M.I.T., 334, 337, 345
Reservoir Hill, 213, 225
Reservoir Street, 213–14
Revere, Paul, 6, 25
Revolutionary War. *See* American Revolution
Rice, Dr. A. Hamilton, 88, 277–78
Richards, Robert H. ("Uncle Bobby"), 326, 331
Richardson, Henry H., 83, 202, 269–70
Richardson, James P., 304
Richardson, Moses, 257, 265, 304
Ridgely Hall, 134, 140
Rieber, Winifred, 85–86
Riedesel Avenue, 215
Riesman Center, 126
Rindge, Frederick H., 219, 258, 297–98, 299–300, 361, 365
Rindge Avenue, 265–66
Rindge library, 297
Rindge Tech, 297
River Street, 302
River Walk, 357
Riverbank Court Hotel, 322
Riverfront Office Park, 357
Riverside Press, 298
Riverview Avenue, 152–53
Riverview I, 358
Riverview II, 358
Rivlin, Alice, 175
Robeson, Paul, 180
Robinson, Edwin Arlington, 3, 105
Robinson Hall, 287
Rockefeller, John D., Jr., 168–69, 281
Rockefeller Hall, 281

Rockwell, Dr. John A., 318
Rodgers, John, 235
Rodin, Auguste, 339
Rogers, Emma, 332
Rogers, Robert E. ("Tubby"), 316
Rogers, William Barton, 227, 310, 315, 327–28, 329
Rogers Building, 286, 310, 315, 326, 327–28, 330, 332, 342
Roosevelt, Alice, 122, 127, 269
Roosevelt, Eleanor, 197
Roosevelt, Franklin Delano, 69, 77, 79, 111, 122, 123, 131, 137, 146, 223, 285, 290, 307, 324, 344
Roosevelt, Theodore, 58–59, 69, 111, 122, 123, 126, 127, 129, 131, 137, 141–42, 162, 174, 184, 206–7, 212, 225, 240, 269, 271, 285, 366
Root, Elihu, 271
Rowland Institute, 359
Royal Makepeace, 308, 354
Royall, Isaac, 205, 271
Royce, Josiah, 85, 86, 282
Rudolph, Paul, 286
Ruggles, George, 219
Runkle, John D., 268, 328
Russell, Richard M., 297
Russell, William E., 219, 297, 300
Russell Hall, 137
Russell Street, 264

Saarinen, Eero, 317
Sacco–Vanzetti trial, 223
Sachs, Paul J., 281, 282, 287
Sackler, Arthur M., 287
Sacramento Street, 259–60
Sacred Heart Church, 361, 363
Saddlebrook Building, 357
Sailing pavilion, M.I.T., 340
St. Francis of Assisi Catholic Church, 363
St. Gaudens, Augustus, 31
St. Hedwig's Polish Catholic Church, 362
St. James' Episcopal Church, 262
St. John's Catholic Church, 362–63
St. John's Memorial Chapel, 202–3
St. John's Road, 203
St. Mary's of the Annunciation, 304
St. Mary's Orthodox Church, 301
St. Paul's Catholic Church, 141, 142, 145, 146
St. Peter's Church, 185, 243
St. Peter's Parochial School, 250
Salisbury, F. O., 130
Saltonstall, Leverett, 80
Saltonstall, Sir Richard, 80, 102–3, 122, 127, 230–31

Saltonstall, William, 80
Samuelson, Paul A., 351
Sanders, Charles, 284
Sanders Theatre, 77, 78, 83, 84, 200, 284–85, 318
Santayana, George, 49–50, 57, 60, 83, 85, 111, 115, 133, 282, 289
Sargent, John Singer, 89, 155
Save the Sycamores campaign, 174
Schiff, Jacob Henry, 278
Schlesinger, Arthur, Jr., 127, 156
Schlesinger, Arthur M., Sr., 85, 198
Schlesinger, Elizabeth, 198
Schlesinger Library, 196, 197–98, 248
Schoenhof's Foreign Books, 126, 140
School Court. See Farwell Place
Schwartz, Delmore, 189, 298
Science Center. See Harvard–Radcliffe Science Center
Science Library, M.I.T., 339
Science Park, 367
Scott Street, 283
S.D.S. (Students for a Democratic Society), 67–68
Second Evangelical Congregational Church, 354
Seidman, Gay, 138
Semitic Museum, 278
Senior House, M.I.T., 350
Sennott Park, 230, 305
Sert, Dean, 126
Sert, Jose Luis, 113, 149
Sert, Louis, 281
Sever, James W., 83
Sever Hall, 78, 82–83
Sever Quadrangle, 78, 84–86, 284
Sewall, Ester, 216
Sewall, Jonathan, 215–16
Shady Hill mansion, 280, 283
Shady Hill School, 228–29, 230, 290
Shannon Hall, 103
Shaw, Robert Gould, 87, 284
Shepard, Thomas, 96, 97, 109, 116, 118, 129, 237
Shepard Memorial Church College, 125
Shepard Street, 252
Sheridan Square, 265–66
Sherman, John, 166
Sherman Hall, 170
Sherrill, Henry Knox, 203
Sherrill Hall, 203–204
Sherrill Library, 204, 218
Sherwood, Arthur, 70
Sherwood, Robert, 133
Sherwood, Samuel, 70
Shockley, William, 338

Sibley, John L., 245
Sigma Chi, 319–20
Signet Club, 69, 111, 140
Simon's Hill, 231
Sir Richard's Landing, 230–31
"Sister Polly," 210
Skinner, B. F., 156, 277
Skinner, Otis, 301
Sloan, Alfred P., Jr., 332–33, 344, 351
Sloan Laboratories, 334
Sloan School of Management, 349, 350–51, 352
Smibert, John, 39
Smith, Francis, 263, 365
Smith Hall, 106, 154
Society of Fellows, 111–12, 113, 155, 156
Soden, Thomas, 302
Soden Farm, 302
Soden Street, 302
Soldiers' Field, 83, 114, 131, 160–63, 164, 257
Soldiers' Monument, 30
Sons of Liberty, 6, 38, 43, 205, 217, 220, 239, 259, 263, 265, 299
Sophocles, Evangelinus Apostolides, 57–58
South Canal, 356
South Street, 103–5
Spanish–American War, 290
Sparks, Jared, 84, 196, 209, 246
Sparks House, 27, 285
Sparks Street, 213–15
Speakers Club, 145
Spee Club, 124, 125–26
Sphinx Memorial, 227
Spring Street, 133, 178
Squire's Park, 361
Squire's Wharf, 142
Stadium Bridge, 159
Standard Oil Company, 332
Standish, Myles, 154
Standish Hall, 106, 152, 153, 154, 157
Starr, Harry, 176
Starvation Hollow, 65
Stearns, Asahel, 17
Stedman, Cato, 238
Stein, Gertrude, 4, 59, 197, 250
Steinbrenner, George, 319
Steinbrenner, Henry G., 319
Steinbrenner track, 319
Stillman Infirmary, 113
Stone, Samuel, 96–97, 102, 109
Stone, Simon, 226, 231
Stone's Woods, 226
Story, Joseph, 15, 17, 186, 199, 227
Story, William, 219
Stoughton, Mrs. Edwin Wallace, 202

Stoughton, William, 47, 57, 64
Stoughton Hall, 23, 51, 55, 56, 57, 59, 60, 61, 64
Stratton, Julius A., 315, 323, 333, 337, 345
Stratton Student Center, 315–17
Strauss Hall, 6, 91
Strobe Alley, 332, 335
Stuart, Gilbert, 39, 115
Students' Center, 272–73
Sullivan, Anne, 200, 229, 249
Sumner, Charles, 15, 18, 23–24, 32, 37, 210, 240, 278
Swallow, Ellen H., 326, 331, 342
Sweet Auburn. See Stone's Woods

Tandy, Jessica, 180
Tang, Ping Yuan, 320
Tang Residence Hall, 320
Taussig, Frank W., 82, 131, 164, 283
Taylor, Zachary, 305
Tech, The, 316
Tech Coop, 317
Tech Talk, 328
Technology Review, 331
Technology Square, 346
Teller, Edward, 175
Telltale, The, 56
Tercentenary Theatre, 73, 77–80, 84
Thackeray, 210, 221, 276
Thatcher, Samuel, 228, 242
Thayer, John, 59
Thayer, Nathaniel, 254, 255–56
Thayer, Nathaniel, Jr., 59
Thayer Commons, 257
Thayer Hall, 59–60, 254
Third Congregational Society, Unitarian, 360–61
Thoreau, Henry David, 40, 49
Thorndike, Israel, 364
Thorndike Street, 360–61
Titanic, 89, 91
Tory Row, 18, 26, 100, 135, 136, 142, 363. See also Brattle Street
Tower Courtyard, 149
Town Creek, 157, 173, 176, 177–78, 180
Town Pond, 114, 124
Town Spring, 178, 180
Towne, Peter, 103
Tree Spreads, 53
Trinity Church, 330
Trollope, Anthony, 7, 210
Trowbridge, Edmund, 125, 236
Truman, Harry, 318
Tuchman, Barbara, 253
Tuchman Hall, 253–54

Tudor, Frederick ("Ice King"), 225-26
"Tunnel, The," 272
Twain, Mark, 249
Twenty Chimneys (lounge), 316

Underground Railway, 289
Union Railway Company, 299
Union Square, 297. *See also* Porter Square
Unitarian Church, 24, 78, 235
University Book Store, 122
University Hall, 37, 51, 61-68, 69, 78, 164
University Museum, 273-74
University Press, 124, 179, 186
Updike, John, 121, 130, 133, 260
Usher, Hezekiah, 108

Van Buren, Martin, 62
Vane, Henry, 31, 37, 61, 256
Vassall, Elizabeth, 220
Vassall, Henry, 204, 238, 240
Vassall, John the elder, 231, 237
Vassall, John, Jr., 205, 207, 215, 219, 220
Vassall, William, 243
Vassall family, 251
Vassall House, 100, 204-7
Vassall Lane, 215
Vietnam War, 67-68, 147, 300
Visual Arts Center, M.I.T., 349
Visual Studies Center, M.I.T., 326-27
von Riedesel, Baron and Baroness, 98, 103, 205, 216-17
Vose, Robert, 308

Wadsworth, Benjamin, 115, 236
Wadsworth House, 4, 62, 72, 115-16, 118-20, 236
Walker, Francis A., 309-10, 328, 340-41
Walker Building, 330
Walker Memorial, 340-41, 343
Walnut Avenue, 227
Walter Baker chocolate mills, 341
War of 1812, 20
Ward, Artemas, 269
Ware, Henry, Sr., 276, 278, 280
Ware Hall, 296
Ware Street, 296
Warren, Dr. John Collins, 51, 52, 243
Warren, Dr. Joseph, 45
Warren, Henry C., 289
Warren, Herbert L., 286
Warren, James, 45, 100
Warren, Joseph, 25, 269
Warren, Mercy, 100
Warren House, 289
Washburn Hall, 203

Washington, George, 4, 6, 14, 26-28, 29-30, 38, 43-44, 55, 115-16, 118-19, 123, 182, 206, 207, 208, 209, 236, 237, 239, 241, 245, 269, 290, 296-97, 300, 302, 313, 362
Washington, Martha, 208, 239
Washington Corps, 32, 46
Washington Elm, 27, 188, 242
Washington Grammar School, 184, 202, 241
Washington Memorial Gateway, 26-27
Washington Street, 305-6
Watch Hill site, 13
Watch House Hill, 5
Water Street. *See* Dunster Street
Waterhouse, Dr. Benjamin, 51-52, 217, 243-44, 248, 254
Waterhouse Street, 25, 242-44
Watertown, 102, 223, 230-31
Watertown–Charlestown Path, 267, 275
Watson, Jacob, 265
Watson, Thomas A., 307
Watson's Corner, 104
Webber, Samuel, 236
Webster, Daniel, 78, 271
Webster, Dr. John W., 185, 246-47
Weeks, John W., 152
Weeks, Sinclair, 152
Weeks Bridge, 152
Weinberger, Caspar, 138, 259
Weld, George Walker, 157
Weld, Stephen Minot, 69
Weld Boathouse, 157-58, 159
Weld Hall, 69, 90, 153
Wells, William, 219-20
Wells's School, 220
Wendell, Madame, 259
Wendell Street, 259
West Boston Bridge, 7, 8, 25, 133, 136, 141, 178, 236, 242, 262, 282, 295, 297, 300, 302, 307, 353, 360, 365
West Cambridge, 256
West Dock, 357
Westengard House, 191
Westgate, 202
Westgate Tower, 320
Westmorly Court, 137-38, 141, 290
Weston Jesuit Community, 211
Weston School of Theology, 204
Wheelwright, Edward M., 131-32
Wheelwright, John, 109
Whitaker, Helen, 342, 349
Whitaker, Uncas A., 342, 349
Whitaker Life Sciences Building, M.I.T., 342, 349
White, Theodore H., 127, 286
White, Trenwell M., 272

White Hall, 272
Whitefield, George, 242
Whitefield elm, 242
Whitehead, Alfred North, 85, 156
Whitehead, Edwin C. ("Jack"), 348
Whitehead Institute, 348, 355
Whitney, Anne, 23-24
Whittier, John Greenleaf, 199
Whittier, Mary, 199
Widener, Eleanor Elkins, 277
Widener, Harry Elkins, 89, 90
Widener, Mrs. George D., 88
Widener Library, 13, 78, 79, 80, 86-90, 127-28, 153, 277, 278, 288
Widow Nolen's, 115, 125
Wiener, Norbert, 325-26, 337
Wiesner, Jerome, 319, 331, 339, 345, 349, 350
Wiesner Arts and Media Building, M.I.T., 348, 349
Wigglesworth, Edward, 118
Wigglesworth Hall, 118, 140
Wilbur, Richard, 156
Wilder, Thornton, 89-90, 151
Willard, Joseph, 44-45, 236
Willard's Hotel, 12
William James Hall, 277
Williams, Gluyas, 131, 133
Wilson, E. O., 156
Wilson, John, 31
Wilson, Woodrow, 60, 131
Windmill Hill, 173, 201
Windmill Lane. See Ash Street
Windsor Street, 306, 309
Winslow, Charles, 241
Winsor, Justin, 86, 214, 250
Winthrop, Hannah, 100
Winthrop, John, 11, 31, 37, 42, 43, 64, 72, 78, 100, 102, 106, 109, 115, 116, 124, 142,

154, 200, 219, 231, 256, 261, 304, 360
Winthrop, Mrs. John, 26, 98
Winthrop, William, 142
Winthrop Hall, 203
Winthrop House, 106, 152-54, 173
Winthrop Square, 100-103, 117, 179
Winthrop Street, 103, 107, 127, 177
Winthrop Triangle, 106
Wister, Owen, 122, 123, 133, 139
Wiswall, Daniel, 16
Wiswall's Den, 16, 33
Wolbach Hall, 253
Wolfe, Tom, 40, 89
Women's Archives. See Schlesinger Library
Women's Laboratory, M.I.T., 326
Wood, Walter C. ("Jack"), 340
Wood, William, 95
Woodbine Lane, 186
Woollcott, Alexander, 50
Worcester, Joseph Emerson, 212
Worcester's Pond, 212
World Religions Center, 281
Wright, Frank Lloyd, 288
Wright Brothers Wind Tunnel, 334
Wursthaus, 96, 179, 266
Wyeth, Jacob, 225
Wyeth, Nathaniel Jarvis ("Nat"), 225-26
Wyeth family, 223-24
Wyman, Dr. Jeffries, 90
Wyman, Dr. Morrill, 183-84, 214-15, 232, 240
Wyzanski, Charles, 259

Yale, 40. See also Harvard-Yale football game
Yard, the. See Harvard Yard
Yenching Chinese Cuisine, 122, 140
Young, Ammi, 364

Zeta Psi, 312

ABOUT THE AUTHOR

A true son of New England, John Harris was born in Boston in 1908. He is a graduate of the nation's two oldest schools, Boston Public Latin School and Harvard University. Mr. Harris has applied his lifelong interest in American and especially Boston history to numerous books, including *America Rebels* (1976) and Globe Pequot's *Historic Walks in Old Boston* (1982) and *A Century of New England in News Photos* (1983). Mr. Harris was the political editor, the Washington correspondent, Sunday editor, and associate editor of the *Boston Globe* during his fifty-six-year tenure with that newspaper.